Legal Regulations, Implications, and Issues Surrounding Digital Data

Margaret Jackson
RMIT University, Australia

Marita Shelly
RMIT University, Australia

A volume in the Advances in Information Security,
Privacy, and Ethics (AISPE) Book Series

Published in the United States of America by
    IGI Global
    Information Science Reference (an imprint of IGI Global)
    701 E. Chocolate Avenue
    Hershey PA, USA 17033
    Tel: 717-533-8845
    Fax: 717-533-8661
    E-mail: cust@igi-global.com
    Web site: http://www.igi-global.com

Library of Congress Cataloging-in-Publication Data

Names: Jackson, Margaret, 1953- editor. | Shelly, Marita, editor.
Title: Legal regulations, implications, and issues surrounding digital data
  / [edited by] Margaret Jackson, Marita Shelly.
Description: Hershey : Information Science Reference, 2020. | Includes
  bibliographical references and index. | Summary: ""This book examines
  the legal issues and regulations surrounding digital data and how the
  law applies to online issues such as defamation, cyberbullying, scams,
  and data protection and privacy. It also explores the legal implications
  of technologies such as artificial intelligence and
  blockchain"--Provided by publisher"-- Provided by publisher.
Identifiers: LCCN 2019048545 (print) | LCCN 2019048546 (ebook) | ISBN
  9781799831303 (hardcover) | ISBN 9781799831310 (paperback) | ISBN
  9781799831327 (ebook)
Subjects: LCSH: Computer crimes--Law and legislation. | Information
  technology--Law and legislation--Criminal provisions. |
  Cyberbullying--Law and legislation. | Data protection--Law and
  legislation. | Information technology--Security measures. | Blockchains
  (Databases)--Law and legislation. | Privacy, Right of.
Classification: LCC K5215.5 .L44 2020 (print) | LCC K5215.5 (ebook) | DDC
  345/.0268--dc23
LC record available at https://lccn.loc.gov/2019048545
LC ebook record available at https://lccn.loc.gov/2019048546

This book is published in the IGI Global book series Advances in Information Security, Privacy, and Ethics (AISPE) (ISSN: 1948-9730; eISSN: 1948-9749)

British Cataloguing in Publication Data
A Cataloguing in Publication record for this book is available from the British Library.

For electronic access to this publication, please contact: eresources@igi-global.com.

Advances in Information Security, Privacy, and Ethics (AISPE) Book Series

Manish Gupta
State University of New York, USA

ISSN:1948-9730
EISSN:1948-9749

MISSION

As digital technologies become more pervasive in everyday life and the Internet is utilized in ever increasing ways by both private and public entities, concern over digital threats becomes more prevalent.

The **Advances in Information Security, Privacy, & Ethics (AISPE) Book Series** provides cutting-edge research on the protection and misuse of information and technology across various industries and settings. Comprised of scholarly research on topics such as identity management, cryptography, system security, authentication, and data protection, this book series is ideal for reference by IT professionals, academicians, and upper-level students.

COVERAGE

- Privacy-Enhancing Technologies
- Global Privacy Concerns
- Security Information Management
- Information Security Standards
- Telecommunications Regulations
- Network Security Services
- Electronic Mail Security
- Tracking Cookies
- Computer ethics
- CIA Triad of Information Security

IGI Global is currently accepting manuscripts for publication within this series. To submit a proposal for a volume in this series, please contact our Acquisition Editors at Acquisitions@igi-global.com or visit: http://www.igi-global.com/publish/.

Titles in this Series

For a list of additional titles in this series, please visit:
http://www.igi-global.com/book-series/advances-information-security-privacy-ethics/37157

Privacy Concerns Surrounding Personal Information Sharing on Health and Fitness Mobile Apps
Devjani Sen (Independent Researcher, Canada) and Rukhsana Ahmed (University at Albany, SUNY, USA)
Information Science Reference • © 2020 • 300pp • H/C (ISBN: 9781799834878) • US $215.00

Safety and Security Issues in Technical Infrastructures
David Rehak (VSB – Technical University of Ostrava, Czech Republic) Ales Bernatik (VSB – Technical University of Ostrava, Czech Republic) Zdenek Dvorak (University of Zilina, Slovakia) and Martin Hromada (Tomas Bata University in Zlin, Czech Republic)
Information Science Reference • © 2020 • 499pp • H/C (ISBN: 9781799830597) • US $195.00

Cybersecurity Incident Planning and Preparation for Organizations
Akashdeep Bhardwaj (University of Petroleum and Energy Studies, Dehradun, India) and Varun Sapra (University of Petroleum and Energy Studies, India)
Information Science Reference • © 2020 • 300pp • H/C (ISBN: 9781799834915) • US $215.00

Blockchain Applications in IoT Security
Harshita Patel (KLEF, Vaddeswaram, Guntur, Andhra Pradesh, India) and Ghanshyam Singh Thakur (MANIT, Bhopal, Madhya Pradesh, India)
Information Science Reference • © 2020 • 300pp • H/C (ISBN: 9781799824145) • US $215.00

Modern Theories and Practices for Cyber Ethics and Security Compliance
Winfred Yaokumah (University of Ghana, Ghana) Muttukrishnan Rajarajan (City University of London, UK) Jamal-Deen Abdulai (University of Ghana, Ghana) Isaac Wiafe (University of Ghana, Ghana) and Ferdinand Apietu Katsriku (University of Ghana, Ghana)
Information Science Reference • © 2020 • 302pp • H/C (ISBN: 9781799831495) • US $200.00

Handbook of Research on Multimedia Cyber Security
Brij B. Gupta (National Institute of Technology, Kurukshetra, India) and Deepak Gupta (LoginRadius Inc., Canada)
Information Science Reference • © 2020 • 372pp • H/C (ISBN: 9781799827016) • US $265.00

Security and Privacy Applications for Smart City Development
Sharvari C. Tamane (MGM's Jawaharlal Nehru Engineering College, India)
Information Science Reference • © 2020 • 300pp • H/C (ISBN: 9781799824985) • US $215.00

701 East Chocolate Avenue, Hershey, PA 17033, USA
Tel: 717-533-8845 x100 • Fax: 717-533-8661
E-Mail: cust@igi-global.com • www.igi-global.com

Table of Contents

Preface.. xi

Chapter 1
Enforceability of Contract Terms Displayed on Social Media 1
    Gordon Hughes, Davies Collison Cave Law, Australia

Chapter 2
Digital Death: What Happens to Digital Property Upon an Individual's Death................................. 23
    Marita Shelly, RMIT University, Australia

Chapter 3
A Framework for Ameliorating Risk in Australian University Crowdfunding....................................... 41
    Jonathan O'Donnell, RMIT University, Australia

Chapter 4
Reforming Australia's Safe Harbour for Internet Intermediaries: A Comparison of Horizontal
Immunity – Australia and the USA.. 68
    Sam Alexander, Swinburne Law School, Australia

Chapter 5
Use of Big Data Analytics by Tax Authorities 86
    Brendan Walker-Munro, Swinburne University, Australia

Chapter 6
The Regulation of Blockchain in Africa: Challenges and Opportunities 111
    Michael Casparus Laubscher, Faculty of Law, North-West University, South Africa
    Muhammed Siraaj Khan, Faculty of Law, North-West University, South Africa

Chapter 7
Smart Contracts: An Overview 127
    Michael Laubscher, Faculty of Law, North-West University, South Africa
    Muhammed Siraaj Khan, Faculty of Law, North-West University, South Africa

Chapter 8
Robots: Regulation, Rights, and Remedies.. 136
    Migle Laukyte, Faculty of Law, Pompeau Fabra University, Spain

Chapter 9
Regulating AI.. 159
    Margaret A. Jackson, RMIT University, Australia

Chapter 10
A Matter of Perspective: Discrimination, Bias, and Inequality in AI.............................. 182
    Katie Miller, Deakin University, Australia

Compilation of References 203

About the Contributors 237

Index.. 239

Detailed Table of Contents

Preface.. xi

Chapter 1
Enforceability of Contract Terms Displayed on Social Media 1
    Gordon Hughes, Davies Collison Cave Law, Australia

It is a prerequisite for the use of virtually any social media that the user enter into a contract with the provider. Typically, the user is required to click "OK" or "I accept" at the foot of a lengthy set of online terms and conditions. Sometimes contracts of this nature are described as "clickwrap" or "browsewrap" agreements. Given that a majority of users will typically not read the terms and conditions or, if they do, will feel they have no option but to accept them, and given further that service providers are aware that this is the case, the question arises as to whether and to what extent such terms and conditions are, or should be, in fact, legally enforceable. This chapter explores relevant Australian and overseas case law and commentary dealing with this modern social media legal phenomenon.

Chapter 2
Digital Death: What Happens to Digital Property Upon an Individual's Death................................. 23
    Marita Shelly, RMIT University, Australia

An increasing use of social media platforms and other mobile applications (apps) has led to the creation, purchase, storage, and use of online information and data including personal or financial information, email communications, photographs, or videos. The purposes of this chapter are to discuss digital property and to determine whether under estate planning and administration law digital property can be inherited like other real and personal property. This chapter will examine relevant legislation in Australia, United States (US), and other jurisdictions including Canada, as well as legal cases that have discussed the issue of accessing or transferring digital property held by service providers such as Facebook. It will also discuss examples of service providers' terms of use and whether these terms allow for digital property to be accessed by a third party. It will conclude with recommendations about how an individual can manage their digital property as part of their will or estate.

Chapter 3
A Framework for Ameliorating Risk in Australian University Crowdfunding.................................... 41
    Jonathan O'Donnell, RMIT University, Australia

Crowdfunding is a balance of risk versus reward. Crowdfunders take a public risk that they will fail to raise funds. Donors take the risk that the campaign will not be funded or that they will not see a return for their support. In an ideal world, both sides are rewarded through the development of something new. If the campaign is being run by a staff member at a large organisation, the organisation should consider a number of risks. These include legal risks such as corruption and misrepresentation, as well as reputational risks and risks relating to exploitation of staff. There is also the risk of funding foregone due to excessive caution regarding crowdfunding. This chapter uses universities in Australia as a case study to illustrate some of these risks. It analyses them through a framework for managing risk in business centric crowdfunding platforms. It contributes a new framework for ameliorating risk before, during, and after crowdfunding campaigns.

Chapter 4
Reforming Australia's Safe Harbour for Internet Intermediaries: A Comparison of Horizontal
Immunity – Australia and the USA... 68
    Sam Alexander, Swinburne Law School, Australia

The internet safe harbour created by section 230 of the Communications Decency Act has been described as one of the laws that built Silicon Valley. Australia does not have an equivalent law. The closest available is clause 91(1) of schedule 5 of the Broadcasting Services Act 1992 (Cth) (BSA Immunity), a law described by the NSW Department of Justice as of limited 'utility'. The purpose of this chapter is to conduct a comparative analysis of section 230 and the BSA Immunity. On the one hand, the chapter seeks to outline how section 230 has helped develop some of the world's most successful platforms while, on the other hand, the chapter argues that the BSA Immunity's lack of utility has had a 'chilling effect' on internet businesses in Australia. Following this comparison, the chapter discusses potential reforms to the BSA Immunity, which could assist in the development of future Australian start-ups.

Chapter 5
Use of Big Data Analytics by Tax Authorities 86
    Brendan Walker-Munro, Swinburne University, Australia

This chapter provides a thematic analysis for the Australian context of the legality and challenges to the use of big data analytics to identify risk, conduct compliance action, and make decisions within the tax administration space. Recent federal court jurisprudence and research is discussed to identify common themes (i.e., privacy/opacity, inaccuracy/bias, and fairness/due process) currently influencing the legal treatment of big data analytics within the tax administration and compliance environment in Australia.

Chapter 6
The Regulation of Blockchain in Africa: Challenges and Opportunities 111
    Michael Casparus Laubscher, Faculty of Law, North-West University, South Africa
    Muhammed Siraaj Khan, Faculty of Law, North-West University, South Africa

Blockchain and blockchain technology have captured the imagination of the world. It is being used increasingly more in business and has found its way into the legal profession as well. Blockchain as such has immense potential and can certainly be extremely beneficial. However, since it is such a dynamic, innovative, and recent development, there is a need for regulation of this phenomenon. Regulation will bring more clarity, protection, and assurance. One of the main objectives of a blockchain, however, is to move away from centralised control, so the issue of regulation is a sensitive and complex one. Regulators and policymakers find it difficult to maintain the balance between effective regulation and allowing blockchain to fulfil its potential.

Chapter 7

Smart Contracts: An Overview 127

Michael Laubscher, Faculty of Law, North-West University, South Africa
Muhammed Siraaj Khan, Faculty of Law, North-West University, South Africa

When Nick Szabo pioneered the idea of a smart contract in the 1990s, the economic and communications infrastructure available at that time could not and did not support the protocols needed to execute and apply smart contracts. While smart contracts may be viewed as an example of the use of blockchain and blockchain technology which offers great opportunities to the field of law; others are more sceptical. The use of smart contracts in law is anything but straightforward, but this should not deter jurists from investigating the opportunities this instrument offers. This chapter aims to provide an overview of smart contacts, explaining how they work, the ways they differ from written contracts, their legal status, and the advantages and disadvantages associated with using them. Finally, it identifies the main challenges facing businesses and the legal profession with regard to the expanding use of smart contacts.

Chapter 8

Robots: Regulation, Rights, and Remedies 136

Migle Laukyte, Faculty of Law, Pompeau Fabra University, Spain

More and more often legal scholars notice that developments in robotics are becoming increasingly relevant from a legal point of view. This chapter critically assesses the current debate in the regulation of artificial intelligence (AI)-based robotics, whose scope should be seen as part of a wider debate that concerns AI. Indeed, what interests legal scholars are those robots that are able to act autonomously and intelligently, that is, robots embedded with AI. The chapter looks at such robots from the twofold perspective: on the one hand, robot as a product (and therefore the chapter refers to consumer protection) and, on the other hand, robot as entity (and therefore it addresses robot rights). The chapter also includes a brief overview of some of the initiatives to regulate AI and robotics interpreting the nuances so as to extract some ideas on national priorities in this regard.

Chapter 9

Regulating AI 159

Margaret A. Jackson, RMIT University, Australia

Artificial intelligence (AI) is already being used in many different sectors and industries globally. These areas include government (help desks, sending demand letters), health (predicative diagnosis), law (predicative policing and sentencing), education (facial recognition), finance (for share trading), advertising (social media), retail (recommendations), transport (drones), smart services (like electricity meters), and so on. At this stage, the AI in use or being proposed is 'narrow' AI and not 'general' AI, which means that it has been designed for a specific purpose, say, to advise on sentencing levels or to select potential candidates for interview, rather than being designed to learn and do new things, like a human. The question we need to explore is not whether regulation of AI is needed but how such regulation can be achieved. This chapter examines which existing regulations can apply to AI, which will need to be amended, and which areas might need new regulation to be introduced. Both national and international regulation will be discussed; Australia is the main focus.

Chapter 10
A Matter of Perspective: Discrimination, Bias, and Inequality in AI.. 182
  Katie Miller, Deakin University, Australia

The challenge presented is an age when some decisions are made by humans, some are made by AI, and some are made by a combination of AI and humans. For the person refused housing, a phone service, or employment, the experience is the same, but the ability to understand what has happened and obtain a remedy may be very different if the discrimination is attributable to or contributed by an AI system. If we are to preserve the policy intentions of our discrimination, equal opportunity, and human rights laws, we need to understand how discrimination arises in AI systems; how design in AI systems can mitigate such discrimination; and whether our existing laws are adequate to address discrimination in AI. This chapter endeavours to provide this understanding. In doing so, it focuses on narrow but advanced forms of artificial intelligence, such as natural language processing, facial recognition, and cognitive neural networks.

Compilation of References 203

About the Contributors 237

Index 239

Preface

The increased use of the internet over the past two decades and, specifically, the use of social media, has resulted in an enormous amount of digital data including personal information being available online. Individuals, governments and corporations are all involved in collecting, storing, using, disclosing and transferring information online. It is individuals, though, who contribute significant amounts of personal data online.

Every year, there are advances in the way we deal with information, as individuals, governments and organisations. We live and work predominantly online, and there are developments in how that information is used. The themes of this publication explore the role of digital data today and in the future.

The chapters in this book examine the legal issues around digital data and how the law applies to online issues such as ownership of personal data, crowdfunding activities and 'big data' analysis. It also discusses the legal implications of newer technologies such as artificial intelligence and blockchain. It aims to assist readers to understand the current technology they are using, how digital data is being used by governments and organisations, and the current legal issues around these areas which set out challenges in everyday life. It attempts to explore whether this environment can be regulated, who should be doing it and what are the future issues to be addressed.

When we think about digital data, we think of the internet. The internet was originally established in the early 1960s by the American military to serve as a way to link computer networks. Later, it was used by scientists, researchers and academics around the globe. The World Wide Web (WWW), developed in 1989 by Tim Berners-Lee, allowed users of the internet to locate and share information. The WWW was designed so that it would not be controlled by one government or one authority but would be available to everyone. Berners-Lee made the source code freely available. Over the next three decades, the 'free' online environment enabled by the WWW became controlled by large digital companies, media organisations and, to a lesser extent, governments. Part of the reason for this global control was the fact that social media technologies offered individuals the ability to post information and photographs to be shared by friends and the world, to communicate with family and friends, and often the world, and to create blogs and online businesses easily. To use the platforms, all users had to sign user agreements. These agreements allowed the technology providers to access and use an individual's personal data. The vast amount of personal data willingly provided by users under the user agreements was then used to raise advertising and marketing revenue. Because so much of this personal data is publicly accessible, many other organizations and governments also accessed this personal data for a variety of reasons, not all of it for the benefit of the individual.

Regulation of the internet and the WWW did not exist when either was first developed but today, much of the online activity on the internet and WWW is governed by private contract law as set out in user agreements. Any other form of regulation is challenging because of the international nature of the internet and WWW. In many instances, censoring data online and monitoring the online activities of citizens is only possible for some governments that can control the internet at a national level and restrict access to social media services, like China, Iran, Saudi Arabia, and North Korea (Freedom House, 2019). In more democratic countries, some national regulation has been introduced such as privacy legislation, defamation laws and money laundering laws, which can apply to the internet and WWW. However, governments are frustrated by the growth in areas such as terrorism, cyberbullying, fraudulent ('fake') news reporting and child pornography, and the lack of control they have over restraining or preventing it.

It is the content or digital data that governments most want to control in some way. Much of the existing laws that apply to the internet deal with the content but, in a way, this is merely the surface layer of the internet. It is the underlying software that enables online social interaction to occur that sets the parameters and rules for how users can load and share digital content and what is and is not allowed.

The global companies that control the social media sites on the internet have been reluctant to attempt any controls over the use of those sites, apart from setting requirements for users such as having to register and agree to abide by the user agreements. Users of many sites are able to defame, harass, ridicule and threaten other people without restraint or even having to provide a real name and contact details. Fake news is spread without any checks and videos with horrific content can be streamed live. Companies like Facebook and Twitter have claimed that they are not the publishers of the digital data placed on their sites and so they cannot be responsible for the content. But filtering of data content is increasingly being expected of platforms, some of whom are responding.

Governments are critical of the responses of the global technology companies to date and are exploring ways to obtain some mechanisms to force them to address concerns about terrorism, data protection abuses, tax avoidance, and the lack of controls over offensive and horrific behaviours online. The European Union has introduced a stronger data protection regulation and is actively pursuing the technology companies for antitrust breaches. Even the United States (US) has concerns. One of the key protections for the big platforms like Google and Facebook has been the protection granted to them by section 230 of the US *Communications Decency Act,* which states that these companies are not publishers of the material accessible on their sites. In a recent talk titled *Nurturing Innovation or Fostering Unaccountability?* the US Attorney General queried whether it was still required (Department of Justice, 2020).

There are exciting new developments in the area of digital data that are also explored in this book. Interestingly, they all raise issues of control to some extent. One such development is blockchain technology. This is technology that supports and enables wide-spread recorded information wherein the parties to the blockchain can then share this information (Rajput, Singh, Khurana, Bansal, & Shreshtha, 2019). Once the data is captured, it can never be erased or removed and the blockchain then has "an explicit and clear record of each and every exchange whenever created" (Rajput et al., 2019, p. 909). The challenge with blockchain technology is that it is decentralised and can operate outside channels and financial platforms, making it hard for regulators to control. Smart contracts are one example of the use of block chin technology. Smart contracts are computer programmes that automate certain actions based on set codes and parameters and agreements between parties to the agreement. They may have legal status but are often prepared by technologists rather than lawyers.

The final area of new development relating to data is that of artificial intelligence (AI). AI involves the use of computers or software programs designed to perform tasks generally performed by humans. Rather than writing software to prepare a certain task, the architectural design of AI software is different, as it involves the selection of appropriate data and tuning and training of a neural network, rather than coding in a programming language. How the algorithm then develops may be in ways not intended or expected from the original intent (Otega, Maini & DeepMind Safety Team, 2018). AIs are intended to learn, develop and improve, and we may not always know why they took certain actions and reached certain decisions. This leads to questions how 'explainability' and 'foreseeability', with issues about 'bias' and 'discrimination' needing to be considered. It also raises the question of liability should an AI's actions lead to injury or damage, and to issues around the future legal status of AIs.

The book covers three broad themes:

1. People-oriented use of digital data (digital death, crowd funding, and online contracts);
2. Business and government use of digital data (internet intermediaries, big data analysis, block chain, and smart contracts), and
3. Artificial intelligence regulation and issues (AI regulation, robots, and bias and discrimination)

PEOPLE-ORIENTED USE OF DIGITAL DATA (DIGITAL DEATH, CROWD FUNDING, AND ONLINE CONTRACTS)

Contract law governs the use of the internet to a certain extent. As discussed in Chapter One, user agreements containing terms of use are required to be agreed to by every person wanting to visit, use or join a web site. The jurisdiction by which the agreement is governed will vary but generally, the agreements are fairly consistent in what they cover. Information about how personal information is to be handled may be included in the agreement or be in a standalone document. The first three chapters examine some of the ways that individuals use digital data, from examining the user agreements they sign to access social media and other online sites, to what happens to their personal data when an individual dies, and to one specific use of online interaction, that of crowdfunding.

Chapter 1: Enforceability of Contract Terms Displayed on Social Media

It is a prerequisite for the use of virtually any social media that the user enters into a contract with the provider. Typically, the user is required to click 'OK' or 'I accept' at the end of a lengthy set of online terms and conditions. Sometimes contracts of this nature are described as 'clickwrap' or 'browsewrap' agreements. Given that a majority of users will typically not read the terms and conditions or, if they do, will feel they have no option but to accept them, and given further that service providers are aware that this is the case, the question arises as to whether and to what extent such terms and conditions are, or should be, in fact legally enforceable.

Chapter 1 explores relevant Australian and overseas case law and commentary dealing with this modern social media legal phenomenon.

Chapter 2: Digital Death – What Happens to Digital Property Upon an Individual's Death

With evolving technologies and increased use of the internet over the last two decades, the use of social media platforms and other mobile applications (apps) has led to the creation, purchase, storage and use of online information and data. This type of information and data can include personal or financial information, email communications, photographs or videos. (Mackinnon, 2011; Lamm, Kunz, Riehl, & Rademacher, 2014). Digital property can be created or purchased and stored on computers, the 'cloud', smart phones, websites and other electronic devices such as e-readers.

Chapter 2 discusses digital property, and seeks to determine whether, under estate planning and administration law, digital property can be inherited like other real and personal property. This chapter examines relevant legislation in Australia, United States (US) and other jurisdictions including Canada, as well as legal cases that have discussed the issue of accessing or transferring digital property held by service providers such as Facebook or Google. It also discusses examples of service providers' terms of use and whether these terms allow for digital property to be accessed by a third party. It concludes with recommendations about how an individual can manage their digital property as part of their will or estate.

Chapter 3: A Framework for Ameliorating Risk in Australian University Crowdfunding

Crowdfunding—raising funds from a group for a project—is an example of the way in which individuals use social media. It also provides a new method for funding research at universities. This chapter focuses on the crowdfunding activities of academics at Australian universities in the scope of their institutional research commitments. Drawing on 23 interviews with Australian university staff and archival research, it identifies fifteen types of legal, institutional and personal risks: fraud; theft of intellectual property; misrepresentation; non-performance of service; failure by success; corruption; breach of terms and conditions; false pledges by supporters; missing payments from supporters; risks related to university policies; conflict of interest; risk of missed opportunities; risks to reputation; risks related to social norms; stalking and harassment; and risks related to personal morality.

Chapter 3 provides a new framework for ameliorating these risks, providing academics, administrators and supporters with an understanding of the risks and suggestions for reducing the effect of those risks. The framework is capable of being used outside of the university sector.

BUSINESS AND GOVERNMENT USE OF DIGITAL DATA (INTERNET INTERMEDIARIES, BIG DATA ANALYSIS, BLOCK CHAIN, AND SMART CONTRACTS)

Businesses and governments use digital data in a variety of ways. Governments have actually taken a proactive role in encouraging the growth of online service provider and some governments have legislated to provide protections to assist the industry. There is a growing concern that there has been too much growth, particularly in the case of the US technology companies. Section 230 of the US *Communications Decency Act*, which states that these companies are not publishers of the material accessible on their sites, has been a key legal initiative providing support for US companies and it is interesting to see the approach taken by other countries such as Australia.

'Big Data' has offered opportunities to governments to provide better services to citizens but analysis of this data has proved challenging. New technology is offering improved capacity to analyse data but there are a number of legal issues associated with its use. As well, new technology such as blockchain technology appears to offer opportunities for business but uncertainty exists about whether it should be regulated and how that regulation should operate.

Chapter 4: Reforming Australia's Safe Harbour for Internet Intermediaries – A Comparison of Horizontal Immunity: Australia and the USA

The internet safe harbour created by section 230 of the *Communications Decency Act* has been described as one of the laws that built Silicon Valley. Australia does not have an equivalent law. The closet available is clause 91(1) of schedule 5 of the *Broadcasting Services Act 1992* (Cth) (BSA Immunity), a law described by the NSW Department of Justice as of limited 'utility'.

Chapter 4 undertakes a comparative analysis of section 230 and the BSA Immunity. On the one hand, the chapter seeks to outline how section 230 has helped develop some of the world's most successful platforms; while, on the other hand, the chapter argues that the BSA Immunity's lack of utility has had a 'chilling effect' on internet businesses in Australia. Following this comparison, the chapter discusses potential reforms to the BSA Immunity, which could assist in the development of future Australian start-ups.

Chapter 5: Use of Big Data Analytics by Tax Authorities

Computers and smart devices continue to play an increasingly significant role in our daily lives. The seamless integration of computers, smartphones, tablets and Internet-enabled devices into our society has facilitated the rise of 'big data', the notion that near-infinite storage and computer processing has permitted the mass collection and storage of information regarding all aspects of our lives. Yet having access to enormous amounts of data is one thing; the ability to derive useful connections and observations from such data is what has fuelled significant growth in another field, 'big analysis'.

Chapter 5 provides a thematic analysis for the Australian context of the legality and challenges to the use of big data analytics to identify risk, conduct compliance action and make decisions within the tax administration space. Recent Federal Court jurisprudence and research is discussed to identify common themes (i.e., privacy/opacity, inaccuracy/bias, and fairness/due process) currently influencing the legal treatment of big data analytics within the tax administration and compliance environment in Australia.

Chapter 6: The Regulation of Blockchain in Africa – Challenges and Opportunities

Blockchain and blockchain technology has captured the imagination of the world. It is being used increasingly more in business and has found its way into the legal contracts as well. Blockchain as such has immense potential and can certainly be extremely beneficial. However, since it is such a dynamic, innovative and recent development, there is a need for regulation of this phenomenon. Regulation will bring more clarity, protection and assurance. One of the main objectives of a blockchain, however, is to move away from centralised control, so the issue of regulation is a sensitive and complex one. Regulators and policy makers find it difficult to maintain the balance between effective regulation and allowing blockchain to fulfil its potential.

There is a definite lack of effective regulation worldwide with regard to blockchain and in Africa there seems to be none whatsoever. A country like South Africa, seems to realise there is a need to address the issue of regulation, but very little has been done at this stage. It might be beneficial for Africa, and South Africa in particular, to consider the example of Malta, one of the first countries to introduce blockchain regulation, when it comes to local regulation.

Chapter 7: Smart Contracts – An Overview

Smart contracts find their roots in blockchain and blockchain technology and offer potentially endless possibilities and opportunities in various fields including law. They originated in the 1990s and basically involve the execution of the provisions of a contract via the use of computer protocols. Smart contracts and traditional contracts overlap in various aspects and both types of contracts have the fundamental objective of putting into effect an agreement between parties which is legally binding. The question is whether there is sufficient infrastructure and applicable regulation to facilitate the use of smart contracts and ensure that they are legally binding. The advantages of smart contracts are many, such as savings in costs and time, and using technology in a meaningful manner, however, there are significant challenges in their use thereof, including consent, contractual capacity, jurisdiction and complying with relevant law. This chapter offers an overview of some of these issues, using South Africa as a focus.

ARTIFICIAL INTELLIGENCE REGULATION AND ISSUES (AI REGULATION, ROBOTS, AND BIAS AND DISCRIMINATION)

The growth of AI should have a positive impact for individuals, governments and corporations as it has the potential to improve health care, social services, financial services, taxation services, and so on. But there are areas, too, in which AI could disadvantage individuals, if discrimination and bias arises, or if AIs injure individuals in some way. An AI regulatory framework, which include ethical principles, standards and laws, is slowly emerging but many issues about the nature of AIs are yet to be addressed.

Chapter 8: Robots – Regulation, Rights, and Remedies

More and more often, legal scholars notice that developments in robotics are becoming increasingly relevant from a legal point of view. Chapter Eight critically assesses the current debate in the regulation of AI based robotics, whose scope should be seen as part of a wider debate that concerns AI. Indeed, what interests legal scholars are those robots that are able to act autonomously and intelligently, that is, robots embedded with AI.

Chapter 8 looks at such robots from the twofold perspective: on the one hand, the robot as a product, so the chapter discusses consumer protection, whereas on the other hand, the focus is on the robot as entity and therefore it addresses robot rights. The chapter also includes a brief overview of some of the initiatives to regulate AI and robotics so as to extract some ideas on national priorities in this regard.

Chapter 9: Regulating AI

AI is already being used in many different sectors and industries globally. These areas include government (help desks, sending demand letters); health (predicative diagnosis), law (predicative policing and sentencing), education (facial recognition), finance (for share trading), advertising (social media), retail (recommendations), transport (drones), smart services (like electricity meters) and so on. At this stage, the AI in use or being proposed is 'narrow' AI and not 'general' AI which means that it has been designed for a specific purpose, say, to advise on sentencing levels or to select potential candidates for interview, rather than being designed to learn and do new things, like a human. The question we need to explore is not whether regulation of AI is needed but how such regulation can be achieved.

Chapter 9 examines which existing Australian regulation can apply to AI, which will need to be amended and which areas might need new regulation to be introduced. While both national and international regulation will be discussed, Australia is the main focus of the chapter.

Chapter 10: A Matter of Perspective – Discrimination, Bias, and Inequality in AI

We live in an age when some decisions that affect us are made by humans, some are made by AI and others are made by a combination of AI and humans. For the person refused housing, a phone service or employment, the experience is the same – but the ability to understand what has happened and obtain a remedy may be very different if the discrimination is attributable to or contributed by an AI system. If we are to preserve the policy intentions of our discrimination, equal opportunity and human rights laws, we need to understand how discrimination arises in AI systems; how design in AI systems can mitigate such discrimination; and whether our existing laws are adequate to address discrimination in AI.

Chapter 10 endeavours to provide this understanding. In doing so, it focuses on 'narrow', but advanced, forms of artificial intelligence, such as natural language processing, facial recognition and cognitive neural networks.

CONCLUSION

This book has provided an in-depth examination of many of the issues and challenges around digital data. In particular, it has attempted to analyse what regulation will need to be introduced in response to these issues and challenges. Many of the new developments raised by the authors, such as crowdfunding, AI, and block chain technology offer the prospect of great benefits for individuals in particular, but also for businesses and governments. It is clear, though, that an international approach to regulation of the new developments discussed here will be needed, rather than only relying on national level approaches.

Marita Shelly
RMIT University, Australia

Emeritus Margaret Jackson
RMIT University, Australia

REFERENCES

Barr, W. (2020). *Nurturing innovation or fostering unaccountability?* Retrieved from https://www.justice.gov/opa/speech/attorney-general-william-p-barr-delivers-opening-remarks-doj-workshop-section-230

Broadcasting Services Act 1992 (Cth).

Communications Decency Act 47 U.S.C. § 230 (1996).

Freedom House. (2019). *Freedom in the world 2019.* Retrieved from https://freedomhouse.org/report/freedom-world/freedom-world-2019/democracy-in-retreat

Lamm, J. P., Kunz, C. L., Riehl, D. A., & Rademacher, P. J. (2014). The digital death conundrum: How Federal and State laws prevent fiduciaries from managing digital property. *University of Miami Law Review*, *68*, 385–420.

McKinnon, L. (2011). Planning for the succession of digital assets. *Computer Law & Security Review*, *27*(4), 362–367. doi:10.1016/j.clsr.2011.03.002

Otega, P.A., Maini, V., & DeepMind Safety Team. (2018, Sept. 27). *Building safe artificial intelligence: specification, robustness, and assurance.* Retrieved from https://medium.com/@deepmindsafetyresearch/building-safe-artificial-intelligence-52f5f75058f1

Rajput, S., Singh, A., Khurana, S., Bansal, T., & Shreshtha, S. (2019). *Blockchain technology and cryptocurrenices.* Paper presented at the 2019 Amity International Conference on Artificial Intelligence (AICAI), Dubai, UAE. 10.1109/AICAI.2019.8701371

Chapter 1
Enforceability of Contract Terms Displayed on Social Media

Gordon Hughes
Davies Collison Cave Law, Australia

ABSTRACT

It is a prerequisite for the use of virtually any social media that the user enter into a contract with the provider. Typically, the user is required to click "OK" or "I accept" at the foot of a lengthy set of online terms and conditions. Sometimes contracts of this nature are described as "clickwrap" or "browsewrap" agreements. Given that a majority of users will typically not read the terms and conditions or, if they do, will feel they have no option but to accept them, and given further that service providers are aware that this is the case, the question arises as to whether and to what extent such terms and conditions are, or should be, in fact, legally enforceable. This chapter explores relevant Australian and overseas case law and commentary dealing with this modern social media legal phenomenon.

INTRODUCTION

It is a prerequisite for the use of virtually any social media that the user enters into a contract with the provider. Typically, the user is required to click 'OK' or 'I accept' at the end of a lengthy set of online terms and conditions. Sometimes contracts of this nature are described as 'clickwrap' or 'browsewrap' agreements.

Given that a majority of users will typically not read the terms and conditions or, if they do, will feel they have no option but to accept them, and given further that service providers are aware that this is the case, the question arises as to whether and to what extent such terms and conditions are, or should be, in fact legally enforceable.

Australian case law is sparse in relation to the enforceability of online agreements, but the underlying principles are well established – essentially, if a customer signifies their acceptance of terms to which they are given adequate prior access, they will be deemed to have read and understood them. But is this nothing more than a legal fiction, in an era when it is accepted that the average user will not have read (or, almost certainly, not understood) the terms?

DOI: 10.4018/978-1-7998-3130-3.ch001

This scenario has direct privacy consequences. Australian privacy legislation – particularly the *Privacy Act 1988* (Cth) (the Privacy Act) - is underpinned by the notion of consent. Express or implied consent generally enables a data recipient to act in a manner which would otherwise be contrary to restrictions imposed by the Australian Privacy Principles. If 'consent' forms part of online contractual terms applicable to social media usage, there is a need to query whether meaningful consent has been obtained at all.

This chapter explores relevant Australian and overseas case law and commentary dealing with this modern social media legal phenomenon.

The Issue

Thousands of people in Australia sign up to new social media terms and conditions every day.

There is a standard process which involves clicking 'I consent', or something similar, with each new download. Sometimes, by way of alternative, the terms may include a statement to the effect that 'if you use this service, you will be deemed to have accepted these terms and conditions'.

Either way, few users, if any, read these terms and conditions. To borrow from the words of former United States (US) Secretary of Defence, Donald Rumsfeld, it is a "known known" that virtually nobody reads the terms and conditions (United States Department of Defence, 2002, Response to the Could I Follow Up … Question section); and the content of these terms and conditions is for the most part a 'known unknown' – that is, most people are aware that they are acquiring a service subject to online terms and conditions, but have no idea what those terms and conditions are.

Some users – perhaps a majority – are aware that by accepting the terms and conditions, they are entering into a contract of some sort. They are possibly not aware – but could nevertheless assume – that well-established contractual principles dictate that by clicking 'I accept', they are deemed to have read and agreed to the terms and conditions.

Most users are aware that by accepting the terms and conditions, they may be potentially compromising their privacy. This is a risk that many are prepared to take, but often there is a degree of ignorance about what constitutes 'privacy', and therefore what rights are being compromised.

The commercial success of most popular social media services is dependent upon the consent of the user as a means of circumventing privacy and spam constraints in order to attract advertising revenue.

The issue, however, is that the entire process is built upon a legal fiction. The 'fiction' is that the user has had an opportunity to read the terms and conditions, has consciously elected not to do so, and is therefore assumed to have agreed to them. This principle is founded upon traditional hard copy contract signatures – it is not reflective of the reality of the online age.

Users do not read the terms and conditions because they do not have time to do so, and probably would not understand much of what is written in any event. It is impractical to expect a lay person to analyse terms which, if attached to a conventional commercial contract, would warrant a visit to a lawyer's office. This is not how the world works – yet our courts perpetuate the myth that the user has exercised an appropriate degree of judgement in agreeing to enter the contract.

A practical barrier to even attempting to read the full terms and conditions accompanying a social media product or service is that often the terms contain links to additional terms, such as privacy terms or "supplemental terms" specific to a particular activity. For example, the YouTube Terms of service comprise multiple links (YouTube, 2019, Applicable Terms section, para. 1):

Your use of the Service is subject to these terms, the YouTube Community Guidelines and the Policy, Safety and Copyright Policies which may be updated from time to time (together, this 'Agreement'). Your Agreement with us will also include the Advertising on YouTube Policies if you provide advertising or sponsorships to the Service or incorporate paid promotions in your content.

The time and effort required to undertake this process would generally be disproportionate to the value of the product. The question thus becomes – do we need to re-evaluate traditional contract law principles in order to put an end to the myth of contractual consent?

TYPICAL SOCIAL MEDIA TERMS

Whilst it is inappropriate to generalise, terms to the following effect can be expected to accompany a majority of social media applications. Facebook's terms of service (2019, para. 2; The Permissions You Give Us section) state:

By using our Products, you agree that we can show you ads that we think will be relevant to you and your interests…

You give us permission to use your name and profile picture and information … next to or in connection with ads, offers and other sponsored content that we display across our Products, without any compensation to you.

The Google Terms of Service (2019, Your Content in Our Services section, para. 2; Liability for our Services section, para. 2) state:

When you upload, submit, store, send or receive content to or through our Services, you give [us] (and those we work with) a worldwide license to use, host, store, reproduce, modify, create derivative works (such as those resulting from translations, adaptations or other changes we make so that your content works better with our Services), communicate, publish, publicly perform, publicly display and distribute such content…

To the extent permitted by law, [our] total liability … for any claims under these terms, including for any implied warranties, is limited to the amount you paid us to use the Services (or, if we choose, to supplying you the Services again).

While the WhatsApp Terms of Service (2016, Privacy Policy and User Data section) state:

You agree to our data practices, including the collection, use, processing, and sharing of your information as described in our Privacy Policy, as well as the transfer and processing of your information to the United States and other countries globally where we have or use facilities, service providers, or partners, regardless of where you use our Services.

These common examples demonstrate that by using a service, a user may consent to receiving advertisements, consent to the widespread distribution of their personal information and consent to a cap on the service provider's liability. Often this will be an inherent part of the service, and something which the user will anticipate. In other instances, however, a user might unwittingly make similar concessions even though the proposed use of their information is not necessarily an inherent part of the service.

HOW CONSENT IS OBTAINED

Consent is generally obtained in one of three ways, each of which is commonly referred to in terminology ascribed by American courts.

First, a process whereby the user is required to click 'I accept' in response to terms which accompany the online product or service, and as a technical pre-condition to accessing the product or service, is known as a 'clickwrap' contract. Second, where the user is referred to terms located separately on the service provider's website, a 'browsewrap' contract may be involved. Third, where the process requires the user to register for a service, but no link or reference is made to terms and conditions, a 'sign-in wrap' contract may be involved.

The effectiveness of any of these methods of creating a contract is dependent upon the effectiveness of the consent process. To what extent was the user made aware, or provided with a meaningful opportunity to become aware, of the terms and conditions accompanying the service?

Australian Law Regarding the Effectiveness of Consent

A number of traditional, well-established principles underpin any consideration of the enforceability of online contracts in Australia.

Whilst it may be testament to the resilience of the common law, it is perhaps both ironic and significant that it is a 1906 decision of the High Court of Australia which underpins the enforceability of many social media terms and conditions.

In *Robertson v Balmain New Ferry Co* (1906), the High Court considered whether a sign posted next to turnstiles at the entrance to a wharf formed part of the conditions of entry. The sign advised commuters that there would be no refund once they purchased their tickets at the turnstiles. The court held that the notice formed part of the conditions of sale, relying upon the fact that the respondent would have been aware of their existence, and especially taking account of his prior experience in catching the ferry from that location.

This principle directly flows through to situations in which downloading or use of a service is subject to terms and conditions which can be bypassed – or overlooked – by the user (that is, there is no mandatory 'click' requirement preceding the ability to download or use). The terms will not be enforceable unless it can be demonstrated that the user had prior knowledge, or at least the opportunity for prior knowledge.

Of equal significance is the High Court's affirmation in *Toll (FGCT) v Alphapharm Pty Ltd* (2004), that a person who signs a contract is deemed to have read it. Importantly, nevertheless, the court added certain caveats, particularly in the case of unsigned contracts – "a person who signs a contractual document without reading it is bound by its terms only if the other party has done what is reasonably sufficient to give notice of those terms" (*Toll (FGCT) v Alphapharm Pty Ltd,* 2004, para. 53); in the case of an unsigned contract, however, proof of assent to the terms will be required.

While *Toll (FGCT) v Alphapharm Pty Ltd* (2004) did not involve the use of social media, it can be extrapolated that a person who 'clicks' or 'signs'[1] online terms will be deemed to have read them. However, where that link is absent, the onus will be on the service provider such as Facebook or Google to establish that the user had, or should have had, adequate awareness of the existence of the terms.

As a corollary, it is well established that terms brought to the attention of a customer subsequent to the commencement of the contract will be ineffective (see *Thornton v Shoe Lane Parking Ltd*, 1971, for instance) – unless, of course, the customer has, incautiously or otherwise, agreed under the original terms that it would be bound by any subsequent changes to those terms regardless of notification.

A typical clause permitting post-commencement modification of contract terms is (YouTube Terms of Service, 2019, Modifying This Agreement section):

We may modify this Agreement ... to reflect changes to our Service or for legal, regulatory, or security reasons. [We] will provide reasonable advance notice of any material modifications to this Agreement and the opportunity to review them except that, where legally permitted, modifications addressing newly available features of the Service or modifications made for legal reasons may be effective immediately without notice. Modifications to this Agreement will only apply going forward. If you do not agree to the modified terms, you should remove any Content you have uploaded and discontinue your use of the Service.

There is nothing inappropriate or impractical about the above approach. The real question is whether the implications are fully appreciated by any user who chooses to read the terms in the first place.

Traditional Australian Contractual Principles in an Online Age

There has been limited judicial consideration in Australia regarding the application of traditional contract law principles in a social media context.

In relation to clickwrap terms, the issues were first addressed in an Australian context, at least indirectly, by the Federal Court in *eBay International AG v Creative Festival Entertainment Pty Ltd* (2006). This case involved a consideration of what contractual terms applied to persons who acquired tickets via the respondent's website in circumstances where the terms had changed subsequent to the time that purchasers conducted the transaction online. The purchaser placed an order for the tickets by clicking on a box next to the words "I have read and agree to the following terms and conditions" (*eBay International AG v Creative Festival Entertainment Pty Ltd*, 2006, para. 23). A pop-up dialog box then appeared with the message "Please agree to the terms and conditions before you proceed" and the option "OK" appeared in that box. The purchaser would next have to click the word "OK" and the pop-up box then disappeared from the web page (*eBay International AG v Creative Festival Entertainment Pty Ltd*, 2006, para. 23). The purchaser then clicked on to the box next to the words "I have read and agree to the following terms and conditions" and a tick appeared in the box (*eBay International AG v Creative Festival Entertainment Pty Ltd*, 2006, para. 23). The purchaser then clicked on the words "Place an order" (*eBay International AG v Creative Festival Entertainment Pty Ltd*, 2006, para. 23). Rares J accepted the applicant's contention that a contract in writing was made on the terms displayed on the website.

Clickwrap terms were also considered by the Supreme Court of the Northern Territory in *Centrebet Pty Ltd v Baasland* (2013). Hiley J found that a contract was entered into when the customer opened an account by completing an online registration form in 2004, a process which included a requirement to tick a box acknowledging that he had read and understood the relevant terms and conditions. It was held that the online contract was enforceable and that the contract was subject to the law and jurisdiction of the Northern Territory in accordance with its terms.

In both instances, the court appeared to proceed on the assumption that the tick-box process was legally effective, and little further consideration was given to that aspect. Similarly, in *Smythe v Thomas* (2007), Rein AJ in the Supreme Court of New South Wales considered a disputed eBay purchase and focused in his judgment solely upon an interpretation of the terms, not on the issue of whether the contracting process was legally effective in the first place. In each case, the assumption made by the court was consistent with traditional Australian common law principles.

In a browsewrap context (that is, where the user is referred to terms located separately on the service provider's website), the process was found to be legally effective by the Supreme Court of New South Wales in *Gonzalez v Agoda Company Pte Ltd* (2017).[2]

The plaintiff completed a transaction on the defendant's travel booking website without ticking any box acknowledging the terms. The website required the plaintiff to click on a button marked "Book Now". The words "I agree with the booking conditions and general terms by booking this room ..." appeared above that button (*Gonzalez v Agoda Company Pte Ltd*, 2017, para. 13). Button J found that a contract had been 'signed' for the purposes of the *Electronic Transactions Act 1999* (Cth), and that the link to the printed terms was sufficiently proximate to incorporate those terms into the contract thus formed (*Gonzalez v Agoda Company Pte Ltd*, 2017).

It can thus be concluded that, notwithstanding the absence of close judicial analysis, social media terms (and hence any consent which forms part of those terms) will be legally effective in Australia if presented by way of a clickwrap format, requiring the user to click 'I accept' before proceeding. Where the 'click' process can be bypassed, or is non-existent, it becomes a question of whether the user had adequate knowledge of the existence of the terms. None of this gives rise to a requirement that the user actually read and comprehend the terms – the assumption remains that if a user clicks acceptance of the terms, or can otherwise be proved to have had an opportunity to read them, those terms will be binding no matter how complex or convoluted.

International Approach

Clickwraps

Clickwrap contracts have received greater judicial attention in Canada and the US, and have consistently been found to be enforceable. The key requirements of enforceability have been that the terms must be clearly identified, the user must have had an opportunity to read the terms, and the click function must unambiguously connote acceptance of the terms. Because clickwrap contracts are equated with signed contracts, it is not relevant whether the user actually reads the terms in such circumstances.

Convoluted or lengthy text has not proved to be an obstacle to enforceability.

The US District Court for the Central District of Illinois reiterated in *DeJohn v. TV Corp International* (2003), that a party does not need to have actually read the terms of a clickwrap agreement in order to be bound by it. The terms were made available through a hyperlink located directly above the box, which the user was required to click. The Court considered that this provided the plaintiff with an adequate opportunity to review the terms. According to Manning J, "the fact that DeJohn claims that he did not read the contract is irrelevant because absent of fraud (not alleged here), failure to read a contract is not a get out of jail free card" (*DeJohn v. TV Corp International,* 2003, p. 919).

Complexity of the clickwrap terms has not proved to be an issue.

In the Canadian decision of *Rudder v Microsoft Corp* (1999), Winkler J was not persuaded that a failure to contain the entire terms and conditions on a single screen was a fatal flaw. A scroll box was considered adequate, being no different from a multi-page written document which required a party to turn the pages.

Likewise, the US District of Columbia Court of Appeals resolved in *Forrest v Verizon Communications Inc.* (2002), that a clickwrap agreement comprising a scroll box with 13 pages of terms and conditions was enforceable and not "inimical to the provision of adequate notice" (*Forrest v Verizon Communications Inc.*, 2002, p. 1011).

The fact that terms are accessible only via hyperlink does not render them too remote to be enforceable.

A hyperlink was deemed to constitute acceptable notification in *DeJohn v. TV Corp International* (2003), referred to above, whilst in *Whitt v Prosper Funding* (2015), the US District Court for the Southern District of New York held that by clicking an acceptance box connected to hyperlinked terms, the user had at least constructive knowledge of the terms. The Court in *Whitt v Prosper Funding* (2015) rejected as 'frivolous' an alternative argument by the plaintiff that he had been unable to access the terms via the link when he tried.

Whilst clicking a box is generally accepted by North American courts as being an effective means of indicating assent to terms associated with that box, the process must nevertheless be unambiguous as to what the click represents.

In *Sgouros v TransUnion Corporation* (2016), a clickwrap contract was held by the US Court of Appeals for the Seventh Circuit, to be unenforceable because it was not made clear to the user that there were contract terms associated with the process of clicking. The user was told that it was mandatory to click their acceptance in order to receive the service, but no indication was given that clicking would be deemed to constitute acceptance of the service provider's terms and conditions. The court did not consider that a reasonable person would have known this without being told of it specifically.

For similar reasons, the acceptance process must be uncomplicated. In *Williams v America OnLine Inc.* (2001), the Massachusetts Superior Court expressed reservations (without it being necessary to make a final determination) about the complicated process by which the users were given the option of selecting "I agree" or "read now", the default between the two choices being set to "I agree". Even if a user selected "read now", it was then necessary to make a second choice between "Okay, I agree" and "read now" (*Williams v America OnLine Inc.*, 2001, p. 3). Only by overriding both of these defaults would the user be presented with the text of the agreement. Justice Hinkle expressed concern about a process in which "the actual language of the TOS [terms of service] agreement is not presented on the computer screen unless the customer specifically requests it by twice overriding the default" (*Williams v America OnLine Inc.*, 2001, p. 3).

As indicated above, it is common for online terms to procure the consent of the user to future contract changes which may be made unilaterally by the service provider. This has been considered and accepted as valid by the US District Court for the eastern District of New York in the context of the Amazon. com terms of service.

In *Nicosia v Amazon.com, Inc.* (2015), the conditions of use to which the plaintiff agreed included a term stating "We reserve the right to make changes to our site, policies and these conditions of use at any time" (*Nicosia v Amazon.com, Inc.*, 2015, p. 3). The Court held that this was sufficient to place the plaintiff on notice each time he accessed the website on subsequent occasions. Townes J considered, inter alia, that (*Nicosia v Amazon.com, Inc.*, 2015, p. 15):

the fact that [the user] expressly agreed, when signing-up for an Amazon.com account, to be bound by the terms of the Conditions of Use (including a provision notifying him that the Conditions are subject to change), this Court concludes that Plaintiff assented, each time he made a purchase on Amazon.com, to be bound by the terms of the then-current Conditions of Use.

On the basis of the above cross-section of cases, it can be concluded that North American courts will generally uphold the validity of a clickwrap contract[3] (including future unilateral changes by the service provider) regardless of whether the terms are complex or lengthy, and even if only accessible by hyperlink. There should, however, be no ambiguity as to what the acceptance process relates, and the process itself should not be unnecessarily complicated.

One can further conclude that despite jurisprudential differences between the US, Canada and Australia, Australian courts applying traditional Australian contract law principles would most likely reach a similar conclusion.

Browsewraps

Different considerations are involved in determining the validity of a browsewrap agreement. Again it is appropriate to look at US law for guidance.

Browsewrap agreements do not involve a manifestation of assent through a check-box process. As such, it becomes a question of proof as to whether the user's attention had been adequately brought to the existence of the terms, and whether it is reasonable to infer that the user would have made a conscious decision to proceed in the knowledge that the terms existed regardless of whether the terms were actually read (Hughes & Sharpe, 2012).

A browsewrap agreement will be enforced by a US court if there is evidence that the user was, or should have been, aware of the existence of the separate terms and conditions.

In *Register.com Inc. v Verio Inc.* (2004), the defendant argued that there was no enforceable contract because it had not agreed to be bound by the plaintiff's terms. In rejecting the defendant's argument, the US Court of Appeals for the Second Circuit stressed that an "I Accept" box was not a mandatory pre-condition for enforceability, and other evidence that a user was aware of the terms may suffice. In this regard, the Court observed that "while new commerce on the internet has exposed courts to many new situations, it has not fundamentally changed the principles of contract" (*Register.com Inc. v Verio Inc.*, 2004, p. 17). In this instance the terms were clearly displayed and, in any event, the defendant was a frequent and experienced internet user.

By way of contrast, the US District Court for the Southern District of New York determined in *Specht v Netscape Communications Corp.* (2001), that the existence of terms of use on the service provider's website was too remote and disconnected from the user's act of downloading the program to form part of the contract between the two parties. The court considered that the terms and conditions were not binding because they were not set out on the website page containing the download function. The reference and link to the terms and conditions could only be seen if the user scrolled down to the next page, past the download icon, and it was not necessary for the user to visit that page as part of the downloading process. There was in the circumstances no evidence that the user had seen or consented to the terms and conditions. It was significant that the user was not required to take any positive action in order to indicate consent prior to downloading. A mere request for users to read and agree to the terms and conditions was not conclusive that the user had in fact done so or that the user had, as a consequence, provided informed consent.

Consistent with the *Specht v Netscape Communications Corp.*(2001) case, the US District Court for the Northern District of Illinois (Eastern Division) emphasised in *Van Tassell v United Marketing Group* (2011), that the absence of a warning or reference to terms existing at a separate location did not make a browsewrap contract unenforceable per se, but that each case had to be considered on its facts.[4]

For completeness, it flows from the above line of decisions that a browsewrap agreement will not be unenforceable solely by virtue of the fact that the terms are hyperlinked – the essential issue is whether the user's attention has been adequately brought to the attention of the hyperlink. A number of US decisions have considered this issue, with decisions for and against enforceability based on the extent to which, and manner in which, the user was made aware that the transaction was subject to terms and conditions, together with the relative ease and convenience with which those conditions could be accessed. Decisions for enforceability include, for example, *Hubbert v Dell Corporation* (2005) and *Major v McAllister, Kalupto Creations, LLC and ServiceMagic* (2009). A decision against enforceability is *Affinity Internet Inc. v Consolidated Credit Counselling Services* (2006).

Sign-in Wraps

There is little conceptual or practical difference between a 'browsewrap' and a 'sign-in wrap' contract, as those terms are used by US courts. The term was first used by Judge Jack Weinstein of the US District Court for the Eastern District of New York in *Berkson v Gogo* (2015), as a means of describing certain online agreements falling between a clickwrap and a browsewrap. Prior to that decision, the concept had been considered District Court for the Southern District of New York in a more generic sense (that is, without being ascribed the name "sign-in wrap") in *Fteja v Facebook, Inc.* (2012), and subsequently adopted by Judge Woodlock of the US District Court of Massachusetts in *Cullinane v Uber Technologies* (2016).

In *Cullinane v Uber Technologies* (2016), it was emphasised that in a sign-up wrap contract, a user is presented with a button or link to view terms of use. It is usually not necessary to view the terms of use in order to use the service, and the agreements did not have an 'I accept' box typical of clickwrap agreements. Instead, they usually contained language to the effect that, by registering for an account, or signing into an account, the user agrees to the terms of service to which he or she could navigate from the sign-in screen.

As with browsewraps, enforceability is dependent upon whether the user was, or should have been, aware of the existence of the terms when a conscious decision to proceed was made.

One relevant consideration is the familiarity of the user with the process – in *Fteja v Facebook, Inc.* (2012), Holwell J rejected the plaintiff's contention that he had not agreed to Facebook's terms of service, based on the plaintiff's extensive experience as a social networker.

Again as with browsewraps, the enforceability of sign-in wrap terms is ultimately dependent upon the extent to which the existence of the terms is made unambiguously clear to the user. In *Berkson v Gogo* (2015), Judge Weinstein was not satisfied with an access process that utilised a notice which stated: "By clicking 'Sign In' I agree to the terms and conditions and privacy policy" (*Berkson v Gogo*, 2015, p. 374) with a hyperlink to the terms and conditions and privacy policy respectively. The court was concerned that the existence of the terms and conditions had not been sufficiently obvious to the plaintiff, particularly as "the hyperlink to the 'terms of use' was not in large font, all caps, or in bold" (*Berkson v Gogo*, 2015, p. 404).

The court was particularly critical of the fact that "the importance of the 'terms of use' was obscured by the physical manifestation of assent, in this case clicking the 'SIGN IN' button" (*Berkson v Gogo*, 2015, p. 404).

These browsewrap and sign-in wrap cases clearly demonstrate that in the US, the onus is on the service provider to demonstrate that the user had been made aware, or that reasonable steps had been taken to make the user aware, of terms and conditions governing the use of the service, whether hyperlinked or not. It is likely that the same result in any of these cases would have been reached if the process had been governed by Australian law.

It remains the case, however, that it is irrelevant, from an enforceability perspective, whether the user actually reads and understands the terms.

The Problem Exposed, Then Buried, in the US

Courts have been reluctant to address the user's 'known unknown' – that is, the fact that the typical social media user does not read the terms and conditions which can directly impact their legal rights and their privacy.

There have nevertheless been some judicial murmurings, at least in the US.

In August 2017, the US Court of Appeals for the Second Circuit in *Meyer v Kalanick* (2017), overturned a trial judge's decision that Uber's terms of use failed to adequately procure the consent of users to waive a jury trial in favour of arbitration. Despite being overturned, however, the trial judge's decision continues to resonate. The initial decision was delivered by Judge Jed Rakoff in the United States District Court for the Southern District of New York (*Meyer v Kalanick*, 2016).

The trial judge's decision turned primarily on the means of notification, as opposed to the content of the terms, with the judge expressing particular concern about the multiple stage registration process, the use of small and un-highlighted font and the fact that it was possible for a user to click on the "register" button without clicking on the hyperlink to the terms and conditions.

His honour did, however, make comment on the terms themselves which comprised "nine pages of highly legalistic language that no ordinary consumer could be expected to understand" (*Meyer v Kalanick*, 2016, p. 5). He specifically took issue with the premise that consumers voluntarily surrender their rights "in response to endless, turgid, often impenetrable sets of terms and conditions, to which, by pressing a button, they have indicated their agreement" (*Meyer v Kalanick*, 2016, p. 411).

In the event, Judge Rakoff failed to ignite a reappraisal of traditional legal assumptions governing online terms.

In overturning Judge Rakoff's decision, the appeals court focused solely the adequacy of the registration process. It refused to take the bait on the content of the terms and conditions, making a simple passing observation that "while it may be the case that many users will not bother reading the additional terms, that is the choice the user makes; the user is still on inquiry notice" (*Meyer v Kalanick*, 2017, p. 16).

In this context, Rakoff's reference to turgidity raises other issues. Are complicated and detailed terms and conditions the product of increasing caution by lawyers in an increasingly litigious world or, as Zuboff postulates, an exercise in cynical exploitation (2019, p. 49):

[Digital terms] can be expanded, distributed, reproduced and archived at no additional cost. Once firms understood that courts were disposed to validate their click-wrap and browse-wrap agreements, there was nothing to stop them expanding the reach of these degraded contracts [to extract from consumers additional benefits unrelated to the transaction].

Privacy and Spam Implications

Privacy

Whilst a majority of the decided cases have focused on the enforceability of contractual rights, the concept of consent plays a critical, independent role in the area of privacy protection. A manifestation of consent by clicking a button may, in addition to creating a binding contractual commitment, authorise the use of personal data in a way which would not otherwise be permissible.

Consent plays a pivotal role in Australia's privacy framework. Service providers will for the most part be subject to the Privacy Act. It is important to note that businesses with an annual turnover of $3 million or less are, with some exceptions, are totally exempt from the Act (s. 6C). The key rights and obligations are set out in the Australian Privacy Principles (APP) which are contained in sch. 1 of the Act.

Under the APP, consent is required for the collection of sensitive personal information (APP 3.3(a)), and constraints on the use or disclosure of personal information (APP 6.1(a)), hard-copy direct marketing (APP 7.3(b)(i)) and cross-border transfers (APP 8.2(b)) can be negated by the consent of the data subject.

The Privacy Act provides little guidance as to the meaning of "consent", other than to stipulate in s. 6(1) that it may be "express" or "implied". Some guidance is provided, however, in the Privacy Commissioner's Australian Privacy Principles Guidelines (APP Guidelines) (OAIC, 2019).

The Guidelines state that "implied consent" arises where consent may reasonably be inferred in the circumstances. It should not be assumed that implied consent exists just because the collection appears to be advantageous to the individual, nor where an individual's intent is ambiguous, or where an individual has failed to "opt-out" (although an opt-out mechanism may be appropriate "in limited circumstances") (OAIC, 2019, para. B.37–B.40).

The Guidelines emphasise that consent must be provided voluntarily, that the individual must be adequately informed as to what they are consenting to, and that any consent must be current and specific (OAIC, 2019, para. B.43–B.44, B.47).

Consent will, according to the APP Guidelines, only be regarded as 'voluntary' if the individual has had a genuine opportunity to provide or withhold it and, in this regard, it is relevant to consider what alternatives may have been open to the individual if they chose not to consent. Consent will only be 'informed' if the individual is aware of the implications of providing or withholding consent.

Importantly in the current context, "bundled consent" tends, according to the Privacy Commissioner, to undermine the voluntary nature of consent (OAIC, 2019, para. B.46). Bundled consent refers to the practice of "bundling" together multiple requests for an individual's consent to a wide range of collections, uses and disclosures of personal information, without giving the individual the opportunity to choose which collections, uses and disclosures they agree to and which they do not (OAIC, 2019, para. B.45).

An individual must have the capacity to consent, meaning that factors such as age, disability and language skills may have to be considered. There is no minimum age for providing consent under the Act and, according to the Guidelines, a young person's capacity to consent needs to be assessed on a case-by-case basis – in broad terms, a young person will be deemed to have capacity to consent when they have "sufficient understanding and maturity to understand what is being proposed" (OAIC, 2019, para. B.52–B.58).

It is clear that the Privacy Commissioner is sensitive to the question of whether consent is valid, particularly when procured in circumstances where the individual feels powerless to object or lacks the capacity to make an informed decision. These considerations are relevant to consent procured from users seeking to access social media, but the Commissioner's caveats will struggle to withstand a carefully drafted access process if courts continue to uphold the enforceability of clickwrap terms.

Spam

Mention should also be made at this point of the *Spam Act 2003* (Cth) (the Spam Act). The Spam Act regulates the sending of "unsolicited commercial electronic messages" (s. 3) – in other words, email or text advertising.

Under the Spam Act, there are three basic rules for commercial electronic messages with an Australian link. Unsolicited commercial electronic messages must not be sent unless the recipient consents (s. 16); all such messages must include accurate sender information (s. 17), and all messages must contain a functional unsubscribe facility (s. 18).

Again, the concept of 'consent' is pivotal, and the Spam Act is perhaps more generous towards service providers than the Privacy Act, or at least the Privacy Commissioner's APP Guidelines

Schedule 2 of the Spam Act elaborates on the meaning of 'consent', noting that it can be "given expressly or … [it] can be reasonably inferred from the conduct, business and other relationships of the recipient of the message" (*Spam Act 2003* (Cth), sch. 2, s.2).

Guidelines issued by the Australian Communications and Media Authority (ACMA) specifically state that express consent may be procured through 'ticking a box' (ACMA, n.d.).

Again it is the case that, as with privacy, the legislation is clear but so too is the mechanism for circumventing it. This in turn is dependent upon users not reading linked terms and conditions, or at least not being concerned about the consequences.

Cambridge Analytica

The relevance and significance of consent in the context of personal data usage was highlighted in 2018 by the Facebook-Data Analytica political scandal, when it was revealed that Cambridge Analytica, a British political consulting firm, had harvested millions of Facebook profiles without consent for political advertising purposes (Davies, 2015).

The issue centred upon the misuse of a research application (app). The app incorporated an informed consent process which was ostensibly limited to academic research. However, Facebook's design enabled the collection of data relating not only to the consenting respondents but also to people in the Facebook social networks of those respondents. This enabled Cambridge Analytica to acquire data from millions of Facebook users without their consent (Davies, 2015).

The data thus collected by Cambridge Analytica was used in connection with the Ted Cruz 2016 presidential campaign, accompanied by allegations that targeted marketing was designed to intentionally sway voters (Davies, 2015).

In one sense the incident is not relevant to the matters under discussion in this chapter. Misuse of data can occur regardless of any contractual protections and regardless of the existence of informed consent.

The events do highlight, however, the relevance of informed consent and the potential consequences of personal data being used in a manner to which an individual has not consented.

Consumer Rights

Regardless of any waiver of contractual rights, there are certain consumer protections which will benefit most Australian social media users. These take the form of the "unfair contract terms" and "consumer guarantee" provisions contained in the *Australian Consumer Law* (ACL), set out in Schedule 2 to the *Competition and Consumer Act 2010* (Cth).

Unfair Contract Terms

Part 2-3 of the ACL contains provisions which avoid unfair terms in standard form "consumer contracts" (s. 23(3))[5] and "small business contracts" (s. 23(4)).[6]

It can be assumed that any online terms and conditions, once validly accepted by the user, will constitute a "standard form contract" (ACL, s. 27).[7]

Section 24(1) of the ACL stipulates three elements which need to be satisfied in order for a term to be considered "unfair", namely, the term represents a significant imbalance in the parties' rights and obligations, it is excessive to the supplier's legitimate commercial needs, and it would be potentially detrimental to the consumer if enforced.

Section 25(1) provides a list of 14 examples of the kind of contract terms that may be unfair, including:

1. A term that permits, or has the effect of permitting, one party (but not another party) to avoid or limit performance of the contract.
2. A term that permits, or has the effect of permitting, one party (but not another party) to terminate the contract.
3. A term that penalises, or has the effect of penalising, one party (but not another party) for a breach or termination of the contract.
4. A term that permits, or has the effect of permitting, one party (but not another party) to vary the terms of the contract.
5. A term that permits, or has the effect of permitting, one party (but not another party) to renew or not renew the contract.

There are numerous examples of social media terms and conditions which potentially meet some of these criteria. Where this is the case, the term may be void regardless of any consent or waiver by the user.

Consumer Guarantees

Part 3-2 of the ACL contains a series of "consumer guarantees" which are effectively a form of implied term.

The consumer guarantees apply to contracts for the supply of goods (ss. 51-59), and contracts for the supply of services (ss. 60-63), and include fundamental guarantees to the effect that goods will be of acceptable quality (s. 54), and that services will be provided with due care and skill (s. 60).

Consumer guarantees cannot be excluded, restricted or modified (s. 64), although a contract for the supply of goods or services (other than of a kind ordinarily acquired for personal, domestic or household use or consumption) will not be void under s 64 merely because it limits a person's liability for failure to comply with a guarantee in a prescribed manner (s. 64A).

The consumer guarantees certainly provide a level of default protection for a user who receives a defective product or service under a contract which they have failed to read and/or in respect of a contract under which they have waived a cross-section of rights and remedies which would otherwise be available to them.

Consumer guarantees are not, however, the ultimate panacea. Whist they provide non-excludable protection against defective goods or services, the protection is of a fundamental nature and, more significantly, will generally not provide a remedy in respect of the exploitation of personal data to which an individual user has provided enforceable consent.

THE ACCC SPEAKS OUT

In July 2019, the Australian Competition and Consumer Commission (ACCC) released *Digital Platforms Inquiry: Final Report* relating to the impact of online search engines, social media and digital content aggregators on competition in the media and advertising services markets, with a particular emphasis on the substantial market power of Google and Facebook.

A number of the issues addressed in the report related to the concerns addressed in this chapter.

The report emphasized that the ubiquity of digital platforms in the daily lives of consumers meant that many are obliged to join or use these platforms and accept their non-negotiable terms of use in order to receive communications and remain involved in commonplace communications. Consumers, according to the ACCC, required a greater awareness of what personal information is being collected, together with an ability to "exercise real choice and meaningful control" (ACCC, 2019, p. 22)

The report comprised wide-ranging recommendations relevant to social media, not all of which were confined to privacy and consumer protection. Nevertheless, the projected changes to Australia's privacy and consumer protection regimes were potentially significant to the issues and problems arising out of the interaction between social media users and heir service providers.[8]

Privacy

The report recommended a number of changes to the Privacy Act. The recommendations of most relevance to social media usage related to consent, collection, the introduction of a European-style 'right to be forgotten' and the proposed introduction of a data protection Code of Practice to regulate the activities of just Facebook and Google.

With respect to consent, the report emphasized the need for consents required under the Privacy Act to be freely given, specific, unambiguous and informed in the context of both collection and disclosure of personal information.

In relation to the interaction between consent and data collection, the consent of an individual is presently only required APP 3 where 'sensitive information' is involved. The report recommended that this requirement be extended to any circumstances in which personal information (sensitive or otherwise) is collected, subject to certain public interest exceptions.

In relation to the interaction between consent and disclosure, the report noted that consent is not required under APP 6 where the use of personal information is consistent with the "primary purpose of collection". It expressed concern that "primary purpose" is not defined and could be broadly construed by the data collector, and accordingly "stronger consent requirements are critical to ensuring that consumers have adequate control over how and why their personal information is used and disclosed to third parties" (ACCC, 2019, p. 464).

Generally with regard to consent, the report recommended an express requirement that consent involve "a clear affirmative act that is freely given, specific, unambiguous and informed (including about the consequences of providing or withholding consent)" (ACCC, 2019, p. 466).

With respect to data collection, the report advocated in Recommendation 16(b) the strengthening of notification requirements under the Privacy Act to ensure that the collection of consumers' personal information directly, or by a third party, is accompanied by a more meaningful collection notice than is currently mandated under the Act.

In this regard, the report acknowledged that APP 5 requires entities to "take such steps (if any) as are reasonable in the circumstances" to notify the individual of such matters regarding the data collection "as are reasonable in the circumstances" (ACCC, 2019, p. 461). It considered this requirement to be too imprecise, however, and it recommended a more specific obligation to ensure that collection notices are concise, transparent, intelligible and easily accessible, written in clear and plain language (particularly if addressed to a child), and provided free of charge (ACCC, 2019, p. 461).

With respect to the 'right to be forgotten', the report recommended in Recommendation 16(d) the introduction of a requirement for entities to erase a consumer's personal information without undue delay upon receiving a request for erasure, except in certain circumstances (ACCC, 2019).

This issue attracted considerable attention in 2014 following the finding by the European Court of Justice in *Google Spain v Gonzalez,* (2014) that such a right existed under the *1995 EU Data Protection Directive* (the forerunner to the General Data Protection Regulation, or GDPR). The "right to erasure" is now enshrined in art. 17 of the GDPR. The introduction of such a right would, in the ACCC's opinion, bring Australian law into closer alignment with the GDPR, a sentiment clearly evident across all its privacy recommendation.

Relevant to the ACCC's proposal for a 'right to erasure', or 'right to be forgotten', the Australian Law Reform Commission had previously recommended in 2014 the introduction of a new Australian Privacy Principle dealing with the right of individuals generally to request the destruction or de-identification of their personal information, a recommendation which was ultimately rejected. The ACCC has adopted a different approach. Noting that a broad mandatory deletion obligation could create a significant regulatory burden, the ACCC considered it more appropriate for this obligation to be confined only to digital platforms collecting, using and sharing a large volume of personal information, rather than to all entities (ACCC, 2019). Accordingly, it recommended that the obligation should be set out in a proposed Data Protection Privacy Code, discussed below.

With respect to the Code recommended by the ACCC, Part IIIB of the Privacy Act provides for the creation of privacy codes which, once registered, are deemed under section 26B of the Act to be legislative instruments. This option is seen as an effective mechanism for addressing unique privacy issues confronting certain industries, but to date there have been a limited number of initiatives in this regard.

The ACCC (2019) noted that several aspects of digital platforms' notification and consent processes raised unique or pronounced privacy concerns, particularly notification and consent requirements, opt-out control, the handling of children's data, information security, retention of data and complaints handling.

Recommendation 18 of the report recommended that these data protection issues be addressed in part via an enforceable Privacy Code of Practice applicable to digital platforms, to be known in generic terms as the 'DP Privacy Code' (ACCC, 2019).

The DP Privacy Code should, according to the report, contain provisions targeting particular issues arising from data practices of digital platforms, such as (ACCC, 2019, p. 36):

1. **Information**: Requirements to provide and maintain multi-layered notices regarding key areas of concern and interest for consumers.
2. **Consent**: Requirements to provide consumers with specific, opt-in controls for any data collection for a purpose other than the purpose of supplying the core consumer-facing service and, where consents relate to the collection of children's personal information, additional requirements to verify that consent is given or authorized by the child's guardian.
3. **Opt-out Controls**: Requirements to give consumers the ability to select global opt-outs or opt-ins, such as collecting personal information for online profiling purposes or sharing of personal information with third parties for targeted advertising purposes.
4. **Children's Data**: Additional restrictions on the collection, use or disclosure of children's personal information for targeted advertising or online profiling purposes and requirements to minimize the collection, use and disclosure of children's personal information.
5. **Information Security**: Requirements to maintain adequate information security management systems in accordance with accepted international standards.
6. **Retention**: Requirements to establish a finite time period for the retention of any personal information collected or obtained that is not required for providing the core consumer-facing service.

The ACCC (2019) thus made a bold attempt to confront the privacy issues presented by social media, including the propensity of users to unwittingly, and in some instances recklessly, waive their privacy rights. The tightening of APPs 3 and 6, the clarification of what constitutes 'consent' and the introduction of a Code of Conduct for the major social media platforms which, amongst other things, would facilitate an opt-out process, are all worthwhile proposals. Still, the problem remains that service providers, supported by the courts, will continue to extract consent from a largely indifferent or ignorant user base.

Consumer Protection

The ACCC (2019) identified conduct by service providers relevant to social media usage which it considered detrimental to consumers and which was not effectively addressed or did not neatly fit under the existing ACL.

In particular, the report referred to terms observed in contracts which it considered demonstrated a significant imbalance in the rights of consumers and digital platforms but which, if held to be an unfair contract term, would not be subject to penalties. While individual terms that are 'unfair' for the purposes of the ACL can be declared 'void' by a court, the ACCC (2019) considered that this remedy was not of much benefit to a consumer and did not effectively deter businesses from using such terms.

Accordingly the report urged the introduction or tightening of provisions in the ACL dealing with unfair contract terms and unfair business practices (ACCC, 2019).

With respect to unfair contract terms, the report recommended at Recommendation 20 the introduction of civil pecuniary penalties in order to more effectively deter businesses, including digital platforms, from leveraging their bargaining power to include unfair contract terms in their terms of use or privacy policies (ACCC, 2019).

With respect to unfair business practices, the report observed a range of practices that could be significantly detrimental for consumers but which did not neatly fit under existing consumer laws (ACCC, 2019). These practices were driven in part by the significant increase in the amount of consumer data now collected and the increased sophistication in data analysis and consumer targeting.

These practices included (ACCC, 2019, p. 26):

1.   Changing terms on which products and services are provided without reasonable notice or the ability to consider the new terms, including in relation to products with subscriptions or contracts that automatically renew.
2.   Adopting business practices to dissuade a consumer from exercising their contractual or other legal rights, including requiring the provision of unnecessary information in order to access benefits.
3.   Inducing consent or agreement in very long contracts, or providing insufficient time to consider terms, or offering a service via all-or-nothing "click wrap" consents.

The ACCC (2019) recommended in Recommendation 21 that the ACL be amended to include a prohibition on certain unfair trading practices, noting that such prohibitions have been used to address similar practices overseas.

As with its privacy reform recommendations, the ACCC's approach to consumer protection law reform within the social media environment is positive. The introduction of civil pecuniary penalties for unfair contract terms should act as a deterrent to extreme disclaimers or data exploitation, and the introduction of a prohibition on unfair business practices might likewise afford consumers an added degree of comfort.

Yet, apart from a deterrent value, any amendments to the ACL can at best only provide a remedy for past infringements. These amendments are not capable of saving users from their own indifference. So long as a consumer's 'consent' conforms with any legislative definition of the term, data exploitation can continue.

The Government Responds

In December 2019, the Australian Government released its response to the ACCC's *Digital Platforms Inquiry* final report (Prime Minister of Australia, 2019). In addition to foreshadowing a commitment to address bargaining power concerns and a staged process to reform media regulation, the response reiterated an earlier commitment to increase penalties for privacy breaches and to strengthen Privacy Act protections. Most significantly, the government agreed with the ACCC's recommendation that the OAIC should develop a binding privacy code to apply to social media platforms and other online platforms that trade in personal information (Australian Government, 2019; Prime Minister of Australia, 2019).

The government foreshadowed legislation to "require these entities to be more transparent about data sharing; to meet best practice consent requirements when collecting, using and disclosing personal information; to stop using or disclosing personal information upon request; and include specific rules to protect personal information of children and vulnerable groups" (Australian Government, 2019, p. 5).

In relation to consumer protection, the government foreshadowed (Australian Government, 2019, pp. 6-7):

amending the definition of personal information' in the Privacy Act to capture technical data and other online identifiers; strengthening existing notice and consent requirements to ensure entities meet best practice standards; and introducing a direct right of action for individuals to bring actions in court to seek compensation for an interference with their privacy under the Privacy Act.

The Government's response, albeit short on detail and timing, was encouraging to the extent that it reinforced the ACCC's recommendations for reform. The shortcomings of the status quo nevertheless remain.

FURTHER RESEARCH DIRECTIONS

The reliance on the assumption that individuals read, understand and consent to the terms and conditions in online contracts means that, even though this assumption is false, little if any thought is being given to how to better protect the rights of individuals. One area of further research is to explore how individuals can retain control over their personal data using blockchain and other technology. Another area is to identify current national approaches to protect online personal data and evaluate which approach might be most effective.

CONCLUSION

There is a problem which needs to be addressed. It is partly legal, partly social. It might be described as the 'in elephant in the room'.[9]

There is a realisation that social media users, among other consumers of online goods and services, require greater protection – from social media platforms, and from themselves. This has prompted (limited) judicial comment, lengthy dissertation from commentators, a formal government inquiry, and a government press release promising reform. All of this is positive.

The problem, however, is that there are no initiatives afoot to confront the legal myth which underpins the vulnerability of social media users – that is, the assumption that a person who signs or in some other way accepts online terms and conditions is deemed to have read and understood them. Everyone knows that this assumption, whilst correct from a traditional legal perspective, is a manifestation of a false premise. No one reads the terms and conditions.

Courts have gone to some lengths to ensure that service providers bring the existence of their terms and conditions to the attention of the user. They have, however, thus far avoided a confrontation with established legal principle which has evolved over centuries – they continue to accept without challenge that a user has a realistic option to read terms and conditions in order to make an informed choice as to whether or not to proceed with a purchase.

There may be scope for some judicial activism here. One line of thinking which has not been seriously explored is that "the length of the documents which contain the terms can have a negative effect on the adequacy of notice" (O'Sullivan, 2014, p. 20).

Perhaps the approach of the courts is forgivable, certainly understandable. Maybe the answer can only lie in legislation. But this then begs the question – how can legislation solve the problem?

Perhaps the answer is that the onus needs to be reversed and enhanced. The onus should be on the service provider to demonstrate not only that terms were brought to the attention of the consumer, but that a realistic attempt was made to ensure the user understood them.

Perhaps this could be achieved by a series of check-boxes, rather than a simple, single, 'I accept' box. Perhaps a user should be asked to acknowledge an understanding and acceptance of specific aspects of the terms, such as the fact that their contact details or profile may be sold for advertising purposes, their data may be stored overseas, and that their right to recover damages is limited. A user could be required to tick 'Yes' or 'No' to each proposition, and in the event of a 'No', the transaction would not proceed.

An approach of this nature would make the transaction process more convoluted, but perhaps that is not a bad thing. Perhaps users should be willing to sacrifice the speed of a download in exchange for greater awareness.

This would not be the perfect solution. Lip service can, and no doubt would, still be paid by the average user to the questions. As the 12th century proverb says, 'you can lead a horse to water but you can't make it drink'.[10] But it is nevertheless a responsibility of law makers to address the problem – it is somewhat absurd that we continue to ignore the 'elephant in the room'.

REFERENCES

Affinity Internet Inc. v Consolidated Credit Counselling Services, No 4D05-1193 (Fla Dist. Ct App 4th Dist. 2006).

Australian Communications and Media Authority (ACMA). (2019). *Avoid sending spam.* Retrieved from https://www.acma.gov.au/avoid-sending-spam#get-permission

Australian Competition and Consumer Commission. (2019). *Digital platforms inquiry: Final report.* Retrieved from https://www.accc.gov.au/publications/digital-platforms-inquiry-final-report

Australian Government. (2019). *Government response and implementation roadmap for the digital platforms inquiry.* Retrieved from https://treasury.gov.au/publication/p2019-41708

Berkson v Gogo, 97 F.Supp.3d 359 (E.D.N.Y. 2015).

Centrebet Pty Ltd v Baasland [2013] NTSC 59.

Competition and Consumer Act 2010 (Cth), (Australia Consumer Law), sch. 2.

Cullinane v Uber Technologies (2016) 4-14750-DPW.

Davies, H. (2015, 12 December). Ted Cruz using firm that harvested data on millions of unwitting Facebook users. *The Guardian.* Retrieved from https://www.theguardian.com/us-news/2015/dec/11/senator-ted-cruz-president-campaign-facebook-user-data

DeJohn v. TV Corp International, 245 F Supp 2d 913 (ND Ill 2003). eBay International AG v Creative Festival Entertainment Pty Ltd (2006) 170 FCR 450; [2006] FCA 1768.

Electronic Transactions Act 1999 (Cth).

European Commission. (1995). *Directive 95/46/EC of the European Parliament and of the council of 24 October 1995 on the protection of individuals with regard to the processing of personal data and on the free movement of such data.* Retrieved from https://eur-lex.europa.eu/legal-content/en/TXT/?uri=CELEX%3A31995L0046

European Commission. (2016). *Regulation (EU) 2016/679 of the European Parliament and of the council of 27 April 2016 on the protection of natural persons with regard to the processing of personal data and on the free movement of such data, and repealing directive 95/46/EC (General Data Protection Regulation).* Retrieved from https://eur-lex.europa.eu/eli/reg/2016/679/oj

Facebook. (2019). *Terms of service.* Retrieved from https://www.facebook.com/terms.php

Forrest v Verizon Communications Inc., 805 A2d 1007 (DC 2002).

Fteja v Facebook Inc., 841 F. Supp. 2d 829 (S.D.N.Y. 2012).

Gonzalez v Agoda Company Pte Ltd, [2017] NSWSC 1133.

Google. (2019). *Terms of service.* Retrieved from https://policies.google.com/terms?hl=en-US

Google Spain v Gonzalez, c-131/12 (2014).

Hubbert v Dell Corporation, 835 NE 2d 113 (Ill App Ct 2005).

Hughes, G., & Sharpe, A. (2012). *Computer contracts: Principles and precedents.* Sydney: Thomson Reuters.

Major v McAllister, Kalupto Creations, LLC and ServiceMagic, 02 S.W.3d 227 (Mo. Ct. App. 2009).

Meyer v Kalanick, 185 F. Supp. 3d 448 (S.D.N.Y. 2016).

Meyer v Kalanick, No 16-2750 (2d Cir. 2017).

Nicosia v Amazon.com, Inc., Case 1:14-cv-04513-SLT-MDG (EDNY 2015).

O'Sullivan, T. (2014). Online shopping terms and conditions in practice: Validity of incorporation and unfairness. *Canterbury Law Review, 20*, 1.

Office of the Australian Information Commissioner (OAIC). (2019). *Australian privacy principles guidelines: Privacy Act 1988 (Cth).* Retrieved from https://www.oaic.gov.au/privacy/australian-privacy-principles-guidelines/

Prime Minister of Australia. (n.d.). Response to digital platforms inquiry. *Media Release.* Retrieved from https://www.pm.gov.au/media/response-digital-platforms-inquiry

Privacy Act 1988 (Cth).

Register.com Inc. v Verio Inc. (2004) 356 F 3D 393.

Robertson v Balmain New Ferry Co. (1906) 4 CLR 37.

Rudder v Microsoft Corp [1999] OJ No 3778 (Sup Ct J).

Smythe v Thomas (2007) 71 NSWLR 537; [2007] NSWSC 844.

Spam Act 2003 (Cth).

Specht v Netscape Communications Corp. (2001) 150 F Supp 2d 585.

Thornton v Shoe Lane Parking Ltd (1971) 1 All ER 686.

Toll (FGCT) v Alphapharm Pty Ltd (2004) 219 CLR 165.

United States Department of Defence. (2002, 12 February). *News transcript Department of Defence news briefing Secretary Rumsfeld and General Myer.* Retrieved from https://archive.defense.gov/Transcripts/Transcript.aspx?TranscriptID=2636

Van Tassell v United Marketing Group (2011) 795 F Supp 2d 770.

WhatsApp. (2016). *Terms of service.* Retrieved from https://www.whatsapp.com/legal/#terms-of-service

Whitt v Prosper Funding LLC, 1:15-cv-GHW (SDNY, 2015).

Williams v America OnLine Inc. (2001) unreported, Massachusetts, Superior Court, 00-0962, YouTube. (2019). *Terms of service.* Retrieved from https://www.youtube.com/static?template=terms&gl=AU

Zuboff, S. (2019). *The age of surveillance capitalism: The fight for the future at the new frontier of power.* London: Profile Books Ltd.

KEY TERMS AND DEFINITIONS

Browsewrap Agreement: Where a user is referred to terms located separately on the service provider's website where the user is referred to terms located separately on the service provider's website.

Clickwrap Agreement: A process whereby a user is required to click 'I accept' in response to terms which accompany an online product or service, and as a technical pre-condition to accessing the product or service.

Sign-In Wrap Agreement: A process which requires a user to register for a service, but no link or reference is made to terms and conditions.

ENDNOTES

1   Under the *Electronic Transactions Act 1999* (Cth), s 10 (and equivalent provisions in State and Territory legislation), the click process will be adequate to constitute a 'signature'.

2   See also Surfstone Pty Ltd v Morgan Consulting Engineers Pty Ltd [2016] 2 Qd R 194.

3   There are numerous other US decisions not included in this section. See *Via Viente Taiwan LP v United Parcel Service Inc* 2009 WL 398729; *Moore v Microsoft Corp* (2002) 741 NYS 2d 91; *Wholesale Telecom Corp v ITC Deltacom Communications Inc.* No 05-13404 (11th Cir. 2006).

4   For decisions similar to *Specht* and *Van Tassell*, see, e.g., *Pollstar v Gigmania Ltd* 170 F Supp 2d 974 (ED Cal 2000); *In Re Zapos.com, Inc* 3:12-cv-00325-RCJ-VPC (2012); *Vitacost.com, Inc v James McCants* (No. 4D16-3384, 2017).

5   A 'consumer contract' is a contract for: (a) a supply of goods or services; or (b) a sale or grant of an interest in land; to an individual whose acquisition of the goods, services or interest is wholly or predominantly for personal, domestic or household use or consumption: *Australian Consumer Law*, s 23(3).

6   A 'small business contract' is a contract in which the upfront price payable under the contract does not exceed $300,000 (for contracts lasting up to 1 year), or does not exceed $1,000,000 (for contracts lasting more than 1 year); and in respect of which, at the time the contract is made, one (or more) of the parties is a business that employs fewer than 20 persons: *Australian Consumer Law* s 23(4).

7   The term 'standard form' is not defined in the *Australian Consumer Law* but it will unquestionably meet the indicative criteria referred to in s 27 of the *Australian Consumer Law.*

8   The commentary on the ACCC report is based in part on commentary previously published by the author. See Hughes, G. (2019). *ACCC report to impact privacy and consumer protection laws.* Retrieved from https://dcc.com/services/commercialisation/commercialisation-and-licensing/accc-report-to-impact-privacy-consumer-protection-laws/.

9   The 'elephant in the room' is a phrase attributed to Russian author Ivan Andreyevich Krylov (1769 – 1844), to describe something obvious and incongruous.

10 The 'you can lead a horse to water, but you can't make it drink' phrase is attributed to John Heywood's proverb collection of 1546.

Chapter 2
Digital Death:
What Happens to Digital Property Upon an Individual's Death

Marita Shelly
RMIT University, Australia

ABSTRACT

An increasing use of social media platforms and other mobile applications (apps) has led to the creation, purchase, storage, and use of online information and data including personal or financial information, email communications, photographs, or videos. The purposes of this chapter are to discuss digital property and to determine whether under estate planning and administration law digital property can be inherited like other real and personal property. This chapter will examine relevant legislation in Australia, United States (US), and other jurisdictions including Canada, as well as legal cases that have discussed the issue of accessing or transferring digital property held by service providers such as Facebook. It will also discuss examples of service providers' terms of use and whether these terms allow for digital property to be accessed by a third party. It will conclude with recommendations about how an individual can manage their digital property as part of their will or estate.

INTRODUCTION

With evolving technologies and increased use of the internet over the last two decades, the use of social media platforms and other mobile applications (apps) has led to the creation, purchase, storage and use of online information and data. This type of information and data can include personal or financial information, email communications, photographs or videos (Mackinnon, 2011; Lamm, Kunz, Riehl, & Rademacher, 2014). Digital property can be created or purchased and stored on computers, the 'cloud', smart phones, websites and other electronic devices such as e-readers.

Five years ago, it was estimated that the average internet user had 90 online accounts including social media, email and bank accounts, and that by 2020 this number would increase to over 200 (Le

DOI: 10.4018/978-1-7998-3130-3.ch002

Bras, 2015). With each online account, an individual is creating information and data, some of which an individual may wish to transfer to a third party, specifically upon the individual's death.

Regardless of whether the number of individual online accounts has increased beyond 90, attempting to keep track of all the online accounts one creates is difficult enough for an individual. It could be near impossible for family and friends of the deceased person or the executor of an estate, unless there is some planning.

The purpose of this chapter is to discuss digital property, and to determine whether under estate planning and administration law, digital property can be inherited like other real and personal property. This chapter will examine relevant legislation in Australia, United States (US) and other jurisdictions including Canada, as well as legal cases that have discussed the issue of accessing or transferring digital property held by service providers such as Facebook. It will also discuss examples of service providers' terms of use and whether these terms allow for digital property to be accessed by a third party. It will conclude with recommendations about how an individual can manage their digital property as part of their will or estate.

BACKGROUND

A 2017 Australian survey (Steen et al., 2017) found that 82 percent of respondents had some type of digital property, predominately in the form of a social media account, email account or bank account. However, most of the respondents (71 percent) had not considered what would happen to this property upon their death (Steen et al., 2017). A similar study conducted by the NSW Trustee and Guardian found that while 9 in 10 of Australians had a social media account and as a result has some form of digital property, only three percent who had a will had included instructions about their digital property in their will (Steen et al., 2017). Likewise, in the US, 72 percent of the public uses some form of social media (PEW Research Center, 2019) and as a result would have created some form of digital property such as photographs or videos. However, a recent survey found that only 37 percent of respondents had a will (US Legal Wills.com, 2016), which means that most Americans have not considered what will happen to their digital property upon their death. This is similar to Australians with only 55 percent of Australian adults having a will (NSW Trustee & Guardian, n.d.).

Traditionally as part of estate planning, an individual prepares a written will outlining their wishes in terms of what happens to their real and personal property upon their death. As with personal property, an individual may wish for some of their digital property such as photographs to be inherited. In Australia there is no formal legislation relating to the transfer of digital property as part of estate planning or administration (Society of Trust and Estate Practitioners, 2017). Likewise, in the United Kingdom (UK) and New Zealand (NZ), laws relating to the succession of property have struggled to keep up with the development of technology (Lynn, 2019; NZ Law, 2019). However, both the US and Canada have recently introduced legislation relating to digital property as part of estate planning and administration.

DEFINITION OF PROPERTY

Often the term 'property' refers to a thing that belongs to an individual or entity but as noted by the High Court of Australia (*Yanner v Eaton*, 1999, pp. 365-366):

'property' does not refer to a thing; it is a description of a legal relationship with a thing. It refers to a degree of power that is recognised in law as power permissibly exercised over the thing. The concept of 'property' may be elusive. Usually it is treated as a bundle of rights.

In Australia, the term property has been defined in legislation such as the *Interpretation Act 1987* (NSW) and the *Succession Act 2006* (NSW). In the *Interpretation Act 1987* (NSW) property is defined as "any legal or equitable estate or interest (whether present or future and whether vested or contingent) in real or personal property of any description, including money, and includes things in action" (s. 21). While under the *Succession Act 2006* (NSW), property "includes any valuable benefit" (s. 3(1)). A valuable benefit can have a financial and/or sentimental value. Other Australian states and territories have similar legislation such as the *Administration and Probate Act 1*958 (Vic), *Interpretation Act 1954* (QLD) and the *Succession Act 1981* (QLD) which all include similar definitions of property.

Similar to the definition in Australian legislation, the *Uniform Probate Code* (1969)[1] which has been enacted in full by at least 20 US States defines property as including "both real and personal property or any interest therein and means anything that may be the subject of ownership" (UPC §. 1-201(38)).

So, in relation to estate administration and planning, the term 'property' is generally defined by its dictionary definition and includes both real property such as a house or a land holding and personal property such as furniture, artwork or jewellery (Lamm, et al., 2014; Mann, 2018). However, it is not clear whether digital property falls under the legal definition of 'property' and, in regards to estate planning, whether an individual after their death has the right to transfer a specific digital property to another person (Edwards & Harbinja, 2013). It becomes more complex when you consider that some digital property such as electronic books are only accessed via a licence or subscription which expires on the death of the user (Woodman, 2017).

Digital Property

Unlike other jurisdictions such as the US and Canada, which have defined the term 'digital asset' in relevant legislation (see for example the *Revised Uniform Fiduciary Access to Digital Assets (RUFADA) Act* in the US and the *Uniform Access to Digital Assets by Fiduciaries Act 2016* in Canada), the term 'digital asset' or 'digital property' does not currently have a legal definition in Australia or the UK.

As technology is evolving faster than the law can adapt (Beyer, 2015), and until Australian and UK legislation includes a legal definition of 'digital property', some legal academics have suggested the following definition (Beyer, 2015, p. 28; Reid, 2017, p. 116):

text, images, multimedia information, or personal property stored in a digital format, whether stored on a server, computer, or other electronic device ... and regardless of the ownership of the physical device upon which the digital asset is stored. ... [It] includes, without limitation, any words, characters, codes, or contractual rights necessary to access the digital [property].

Potentially digital property could be classified into four categories: personal, business, financial and other. Examples of each category include:

- **Personal**: emails, photographs, e-book or music collections, social media profiles or videos.
- **Business**: customer details, a website or intellectual property rights such as copyright, trademarks, patents or domain names.
- **Financial**: online bank accounts, cryptocurrency or online share or investment accounts.
- **Other**: online gaming accounts or online gambling accounts.

TRANSFERRING DIGITAL PROPERTY

Traditionally, the transferring of property including personal possessions that may have both financial and sentimental value was part of estate planning and property law (Hopkins, 2013). Like personal property, digital property can have both financial and sentimental value. Financial value can be a monetary amount in an online bank account or gambling account, or a right that could generate an income such as intellectual property (IP) rights.

Emails, photographs and videos may have a sentimental value to a deceased's family and friends and allow them to reminisce. To allow family and friends to remember a loved one online, there is a growing trend of converting social media profiles into memorial pages following a death.

Developing a plan to handle digital property at death could help protect personal information and overcome problems relating to the loss of the paper trail as more documentation, including bank statements, are only available in electronic form.

However, while there are benefits for transferring digital property as part of an estate, in some instances, an individual may not want all of their digital information to be included in their estate. In many cases, it would be fair to say that when an individual writes an email or adds an entry into a personal diary, the individual is not contemplating the scenario that following their death, this personal data or information could be accessed by family members or friends.

Unless an individual considers how they wish to manage their digital property on death, an executor may have some difficulties obtaining access to digital property following a death. As noted in the introduction, given the average number of online accounts an internet user currently has is 90 and growing, an executor of an estate may not be aware of all the accounts that may need to be deleted or transferred. Also, access to digital property might be prevented by password protection, service providers' terms of use, and laws that restrict access and sharing of data, such as criminal laws relating to the unauthorised access or use of a computer, privacy laws or IP laws.

Digital property is often hosted by online service providers such as Amazon, Apple, Facebook or Google. In most cases, the terms and conditions of a service provider do not allow the transferring of digital property to a third party, including an immediate family member, upon death, as ownership of an account and its content expires upon death (Mackinnon, 2011; Woodman, 2017). For example, Amazon allows Kindle account holders to access "subscription content only as long as [they] remain an active member of the underlying membership or subscription program" (Amazon Australia Services, 2019, Use of Kindle section, para. 1).

Legal Cases

The access and transfer of digital property to a third party as part of an estate has not been widely litigated (Antoine, 2016). However, courts in the US, the UK and Europe, specifically Germany, have addressed this issue.

The first known legal case relating to the access and transfer of digital property was in the US in 2005. The request by a family for access to the deceased's digital property was against the service providers' terms and conditions and, at the time, there was no legislation relating to the access and transfer of digital property.

The *Re Estate of Ellsworth* (2005) case related to a family of a deceased Iraq solider requesting access to their son's email communications from the service provider, in this instance, Yahoo. The father was appointed the estate's representative and petitioned the Oakland County Probate Court in Michigan for access to his son's email communications including photographs. At the time that the solider created the email account, Yahoo's terms of service stated that (Yahoo, as cited in Cummings, 2014, pp. 899; Fox News, as cited in Cummings, 2014, p. 900):

You agree that your Yahoo account is non-transferable and any rights to your Yahoo ID or contents within your account terminate upon your death. Upon receipt of a copy of a death certificate, your account may be terminated, and all contents therein permanently deleted. Yahoo complied with the court order and provided copies of emails but stated it would continue to uphold [its] privacy commitment to [its] users.

Even if the *Revised Uniform Fiduciary Access to Digital Assets (RUFADA) Act* (RUFADA Act), which will be discussed in the US jurisdiction section below, had been enacted at the time of this case, access to the deceased's email communications and photographs may not have been granted to the father without a court decision. Under the RUFADA Act, an individual is required to provide express consent for access to their digital property in their estate planning documents such as a will. In this case, as there was no will, there was no express consent to provide access to their digital property upon their death. Also, without instructions within estate planning documentation, the terms and conditions of the service provider, in this case, Yahoo, would prevail. For example, the account is terminated, and all content is deleted (Yahoo, 2018, s. 28).

In the next case, following the introduction of the RUFADA Act, an executor of the Swezey estate (*Matter of Estate of Swezey*, 2019) contacted Apple and requested access to the deceased's photographs on their I-Tunes and I-Cloud accounts. As there were no instructions relating to the deceased's digital property in their will, Apple declined the request (Rottenstreich & Barkhorn, 2019). The New York County Surrogate Court in 2019, however, found that under "§. 13-A [of] the New York Estates, Powers and Trusts Law ("EPTL"), … there are different procedures" (Rottenstreich & Barkhorn, 2019, para. 1) for managing the disclosure of electronic communications compared to accessing other forms of digital property (Rottenstreich & Barkhorn, 2019). Disclosure of electronic communication requires consent from the user or a court order (*Matter of Estate of Swezey*, 2019). As the executor was seeking to access online photographs, which are not a form of electronic communication, the Court held that under §. 13-A of the Act, instructions relating to digital property were not required, "as digital [property] should be treated like other [property] which belonged to [the deceased] at death and are within the purview of the executor's general responsibility" (Rottenstreich & Barkhorn, 2019, para. 1). The Court ordered Apple to provide the photographs to the executor of the Swezey estate.

Another case relating to the issue of accessing a deceased individual's digital property involved a Facebook account (*In re Request for Order Requiring Facebook, Inc. to Produce Documents and Things*, 2012; McCallig, 2013). As part of a coroner's inquest into a death, the family was asked to provide information on the deceased's state of mind. The family submitted a request to Facebook for access to the deceased's account, as the family believed that there was evidence on the Facebook page showing the deceased's state of mind. The US District Court for the Northern District of California granted Facebook's motion to quash the request on the basis it would breach §. 2701 of the *Stored Communications Act, 18 U.S.C.* This section relates to the need for explicit authority to access a deceased's digital property, in this instance, the deceased's Facebook page. The Court noted that "to rule otherwise would run afoul of the "specific [privacy] interests that the [Stored Communications Act] seeks to protect" (*In re Request for Order Requiring Facebook, Inc. to Produce Documents and Things, 2012, para. 3*).

The Court also ruled that it lacked the jurisdiction to address whether the family may offer consent on behalf of the deceased so that Facebook may provide access to the Facebook page voluntarily (Antoine, 2016).

At the time of this case in 2012, there was no legislation relating to the access or transfer of digital property. It involved the complexity of different jurisdictions with both the Facebook account being created and the coroner's inquest being held in the UK and Facebook being located and this case being held in the US.

With both the Ellsworth and Swezey cases, without any relevant legislation relating to the access or transfer of digital property to a third party as part of an estate, other laws relating to privacy and contract take precedence.

In contrast to the *Re Estate of Ellsworth* (2005) and the *In re Request for Order Requiring Facebook, Inc. to Produce Documents and Things* (2012) cases, the Federal Court of Justice (BGH) in Germany held that "Facebook data, including messages, can be inherited in the same way as physical diaries or letters" (Humphries, 2018, para. 3). In the judgment it was stated that "it was common to hand over private diaries and correspondence to legal heirs after death, and there was no reason to treat digital data any differently" (BBC News, 2018, para. 11). If this ruling is not overturned, the interpretation of laws relating to the inheritance of digital property, particularly from social media platforms, may be changed in Europe under the General Data Protection Regulation (GDPR) and specifically in Germany (Humphries, 2018).

Laws

United States (US) Jurisdiction

In the US, the *Stored Communications Act* (part of the *Electronic Communications Privacy Act* of 1986) which online service providers such as Facebook and Google are subject to, does not allow individual's stored electronic communications (for example photographs and video) to be accessed by a third party (McKinnon, 2011). Under this statute, US courts have deemed emails, text messages and other personal electronic data located on a personal computer to be private unless the data has been shared publicly via a service provider (McKinnon, 2011).

Under the *Stored Communication Act*, specifically §. 2701, an executor or beneficiary could face criminal charges if they access the deceased's digital property without explicit authority (Antoine, 2016). Similarly, §. 2702 of the Act does not allow internet service providers (ISPs) to release the contents of online accounts without lawful consent (Antoine, 2016). In response to this, the US introduced the *Uniform Fiduciary Access to Digital Assets (UFADA) Act* (UFADA Act) in 2014. The purpose of the UFADA Act was to allow "fiduciaries with at least the authority to manage and distribute assets, copy or delete digital assets and access digital assets" (Uniform Law Commission, as cited in Antoine, 2016, p.17).

Delaware was the first US state to introduce the UFADA Act (Perzanowski & Schultz, 2016). Since 2013, at least 46 US states have introduced laws which allows access to a deceased individual's digital property with the majority of laws now based on the RUFADA Act (National Conference of State Legislatives, 2019).

An issue with the UFADA Act was that it failed to take into consideration the deceased's privacy, and it conflicted with many ISPs terms and conditions or terms of use (Antoine, 2016). US States have now started to introduce the RUFADA Act which addresses the privacy issue.

Section 2(10) of the RUFADA Act defines a digital asset as "an electronic record in which an individual has a right or interest". The RUFADA Act allows a fiduciary, such as an executor of an estate, to access the content of a deceased individual's digital property if the deceased has expressly consented to such access in their estate planning documents such as a will or what the RUFADA Act refers to as an 'online tool' (Walker, 2017). An example of an online tool is Facebook's legacy contact (Brown & Bruch, 2019). However, if the deceased has not provided instructions about their digital property, and it is stored with a service provider, the service provider's terms of use will apply (RUFADA Act, 2015, §. 4; Walker, 2017). The RUFADA Act (2015) does not cover family members or friends of a deceased individual who are not a fiduciary.

Australian Jurisdiction

In Australia, there is no specific legislation relating to the transferring of digital property, however, the News South Wales Law (NSW) Commission undertook a review of the laws relevant to the access to an individual's digital assets following their death or them becoming incapacitated (Department of Justice, 2019). It released a consultation paper, *Access to digital assets upon death or incapacity* (New South Wales Law Commission, 2018) seeking submissions on the issue. The final report into this review was submitted to the NSW Attorney General in December 2019 (Department of Communities and Justice, 2020).[2]

As part of the Australian Government's acceptance or acknowledgement of all of the suggestions from the Australian Competition and Consumer Commission (ACCC) digital platform inquiry, it was announced that the Government will conduct a review of the *Privacy Act 1988* (Cth) including the definition of personal information and potentially the introduction of a 'right to be forgotten' online (Briggs, 2019).

At present, when transferring digital property to a beneficiary as part of an estate, the following Australian Commonwealth or state / territory equivalent legislation would be relevant:

- *Probate and Administration Act.*
- *Succession Act.*
- *Wills Act.*

The probate and administration acts of Australian states such as the *Administration and Probate Act 1958* (Vic) and *Probate and Administration Act 1898* (NSW) do not address the question of access and transferal of digital property.

Under s. 4(1) of the *Succession Act 2006* (NSW), an individual can "dispose by [a] will of property to which the person is entitled at the time of the person's death". Property under the *Succession Act 2006* (NSW) "includes any valuable benefit" (s. 3(1)). Valuable benefit could include both financial and sentimental value.

Under this Act, digital property created and stored on a personal computer, such as photographs, could be transferred under a will. For content created and stored with a service provider, such as a video on YouTube, the terms and conditions of the service provider would need to be reviewed to determine if the property can be transferred to a third party following a death. Content accessed via a licence or subscription, such as an e-book or music collection via an Amazon Kindle or Apple I-Tunes, would not be allowed to be transferred to a third party, as access would be cancelled on the user's death. If an individual completes Google's inactive account manager settings or Facebook's legacy contact, but then provides contrasting instructions or wishes in their will, it is not clear which instructions will be implemented. Whether contract law (in relation to the service providers' terms of use) or estate laws (probate and administration acts or succession acts) takes precedence may not be resolved until Australia introduces legislation, or it is discussed as part of a court case.

Although Australian courts have not considered the accessing or transferring of digital property as part of estate planning or administration, they have considered and accepted informal wills. While an Australian will under a will's act such as the *Wills Act 1997* (Vic), should be in written form, signed and witnessed, Australian courts have accepted informal wills (*Alan Yazbek v Ghosn Yazbek & Anor*, 2012; *Equity Trustees v Levin*, 2004; *Estate of Masters, Hill v. Plummer*, 1994; *Estate of Sheron Jude Ladduhetti*, 2013; *Estate of Stewart*, 1996; *Marian Grace Burford In the will of Mark Edwin Tretheway*, 2002; *Re Application of Brown: Estate of Springfield*, 1991; *Re: Yu*, 2013). For example, s. 9 of the *Wills Act 1997* (Vic) states that:

a document which has not been executed in the manner in which a will is required to be executed by this Act may be admitted to probate if the Court is satisfied that that person intended the document to be his or her will.

Australian courts have accepted as informal wills, a file located on a computer that was titled 'will', an electronic Word document titled 'will', a document on an iPhone which started with the words 'This is the last will and testament …' and a webcam recording of the deceased (*Alan Yazbek v Ghosn Yazbek & Anor*, 2012; *Estate of Sheron Jude Ladduhetti*, 2013; *Re: Yu*, 2013).

Other Jurisdictions

Neither the UK or NZ currently have legislation that relates to the access and transferring of digital property as part of estate laws. However, with changes in society including an increasing use of digital technology, both countries' law commissions have announced reviews into wills or succession laws. The UK Law Reform Commission announced in 2017 a public consultation into the laws of wills. Due to other priorities, the timeline for the completion of this project is currently under review (Law Commission, n.d.). Similarly, in July 2019, the NZ Law Commission announced a review into succession laws with the scope and timeframe of the review still to be determined (New Zealand Law Commission, 2019).

Like the US, Canada introduced the *Uniform Access to Digital Assets by Fiduciaries (UADAF) Act* (UADAF Act) in 2016. However only one Canadian province, Alberta, has introduced legislation based on it relating to the access of digital property by fiduciaries (Woodman, 2017).

Under s. 1 of the UADAF Act 2016, the term 'digital asset' is defined as "a record that is created, recorded, transmitted or stored in digital or other intangible form by electronic, magnetic or optical means or by any other similar mean". In the comments relating to this definition it states that 'digital assets' refer "to any information stored on a computer and other digital devices, content uploaded onto websites, … and rights in digital property, such as domain names …" (Uniform Law Conference of Canada, 2016, p. 4).

Under ss. 3(1) and 5(1)(b) of the UADAF Act, a fiduciary such as an administrator of an estate has a default right to access the digital property of an account holder and "is deemed to have the consent of the account holder for the custodian to divulge the content of the digital asset … [and] is deemed to be an authorized user of the digital asset" (Uniform Law Conference of Canada, 2016, ss. 5(1)(b) and (c)). This right can only be modified by instructions from the account holder in a relevant instrument such as a will (Uniform Law Conference of Canada, 2016, s. 3(2)). If a service provider's terms of use prevent the access or transfer of the digital property of an account holder, these terms are void under the UADAF Act unless the account holder has provided instructions in a relevant instrument that meet the service provider's terms of use (Uniform Law Conference of Canada, 2016, s. 5(2)). The UADAF Act also provides a 'last-in-time' instruction within an instrument, where the last instructions about the individual's digital property provided takes "precedence over any earlier instrument, order or online instructions of an account holder" (Uniform Law Conference of Canada, 2016, p. 7).

In 2016, the European Union (EU) adopted the General Data Protection Regulation (GDPR), which includes the right to be forgotten. The 'right to be forgotten' has now been renamed a 'right to erasure' under art. 17 of the EU General Data Protection Regulation.

Article 17 gives data subjects the right to obtain from the controller the erasure of any personal data relating to them, including the right to obtain from third parties (to whom the data have been passed) the erasure of any links to, or copy or replication of that data. This is not an absolute right and there are exceptions for retaining data, for example, to the extent that the retention is necessary for exercising the right of freedom of expression (European Commission, 2013).

This means that an individual can submit a request to a search engine such as Google to remove a link to personal information. However, under art. 27 of the GDPR it states that "this regulation does not apply to the personal data of deceased persons. Member States [of the European Union] may provide for rules regarding the processing of personal data of deceased persons" (European Commission, 2016, art. 27).

While most service providers have terms and conditions that state digital property remains private, courts and governments have the view that privacy rights expire at the time of death. (McKinnon, 2011).

Service Providers' Terms of Use

Each time an individual signs up for an online account, whether it be a social media platform such as Instagram or an email account with Google, the individual must agree to the terms and conditions of the service provider. Anecdotal evidence would suggest that most individuals when registering an account do not read the full terms and conditions.

Some service providers' terms of use "may not provide for death … but contain provisions that provide for the deactivation of the account after a period of inactivity" (Walker, 2017, p. 205) or allow for the account holder to share their password or transfer the account to a third party (Walker, 2017).

Google and Facebook are two examples of service providers that have started to include within their terms of use instructions following the death of an account holder. Google's inactive account manager and Facebook's legacy contact both allow users to designate a digital heir to take over their account' (Perzanowski & Schultz, 2016, p. 95).

The inactive account manager setting allows Google users to "share parts of their account data or [for Google to notify a nominated contact if a user has] been inactive for a certain period of time" (Google 2019, para. 1).

A Google user can set up their account so that a nominated contact can receive an email from Google if the account has been inactive for a period of time. The subject line and content of the email are written by the user during the set-up phase. Google will also add a footer to the email "explaining that the [user has] instructed Google to send an email on [their] behalf after [they] stopped using their account" (Google, 2019, What will trusted contacts receive section). The user can also decide to share information and data that they have created via their Google account, such as email communications or video via YouTube. If the Google user is sharing digital property, the email that the contact receives will have a link to enable the downloading of the data (Google, 2019).

Facebook currently allows users to nominate to have their account deleted on their death or to have a legacy contact. A Facebook account is memorialised upon Facebook becoming aware that a user is deceased. Under the settings, a user can nominate a person to make decisions about their Facebook account once it is memorialised (Facebook, 2019a). The legacy contact can decide to delete a Facebook account, or to memorialise the account. If a legacy contact nominates to memorialise the account, they will be able to (Facebook, 2019b):

- Write a tribute post such as a final message or provide information about a memorial service.
- Change the profile picture.
- Accept friend requests and determine who can view and write tributes.
- If this feature is turned on, download information that the user has shared such as photographs and videos, wall posts, contact information and list of Facebook friends.

As a Facebook product, Instagram also allows accounts to be memorialised following a death. Under its terms, Instagram will memorialize an account once they are notified and receive "proof of death, such as a link to an obituary or news article" (Instagram, 2019a, Memorializing the account section, para. 3). Under its memorialize terms, Instagram will not allow "anyone to log into a memorialized account" (Instagram, 2019b, para. 1) or change the photographs on a memorialised page (Instagram, 2019b).

However, Instagram will delete an account following a request from an immediate family member of a deceased account holder. To delete an account of a deceased person, Instagram requires proof such as the deceased's birth or death certificate and that the person requesting the removal is an immediate family member or the representative of the estate (Instagram, 2019a).

Not all digital property can be purchased and owned as a permanent item. Rather some digital property, such as e-books and music, are accessed via a licence or a subscription. Users can subscribe to online services such as Spotify or Apple Music to access music while they maintain their subscription, however, upon cancelling the subscription, their access to music is stopped (Apple, 2019). Under Spotify's terms and conditions of use, the content "is not sold or transferred to [the user]" (Spotify, 2019, s. 5) and the user "will not redistribute or transfer ... the content" (Spotify, 2019, s. 5). Also, under the user guidelines for Spotify, a user must not share their password (Spotify, 2019).

Similarly, electronic book collections that a user reads via an e-reader, such as an Amazon Kindle, are not purchased as a permanent digital item, rather e-books are provided via a licence. While an individual could leave their e-reader to a beneficiary in their will, the beneficiary could access any of the downloaded items on the e-reader (while the e-reader still works and if the beneficiary can activate the e-reader) but they would not be allowed to maintain the user's account and purchase additional items. Under s 1 of the Kindle store terms of use, "Kindle content is licensed, not sold [to users]" (Amazon Australia Service, 2017). Amazon allows users to "view, use, and display ... Kindle content an unlimited number of times ... only as long as you remain an active member of the underlying membership or subscription program" (Amazon Australia Service, 2017, s. 1) and cannot transfer any content to a third party (Amazon Australia Service, 2017).

As service providers' terms of use may limit the access or transfer of digital property to a third party, it is important that an individual considers which digital property they own and how this property will be managed as part of their estate.

RECOMMENDATIONS FOR MANAGING DIGITAL PROPERTY

Any personal or real property regardless of whether it is in digital or physical form is part of an individual's estate and therefore it is important to provide instructions about what should happen to this property upon death (The Gazette, n.d.).

A first step to managing an individual's digital property is for the individual to keep a record of all online accounts that they have registered. An individual could use a cloud-based password management system such as SafeSecure[3] (McCallig, 2013) or a document or spreadsheet stored on a computer to record the information including the email address or username, but not the password as this could breach the service provider's terms of use. Whichever approach an individual uses to record their list of online accounts, a record needs to be included in their estate planning documentation.

For estate planning, a digital will, which is an online document, could be used to store the email address or username of the online accounts that an individual has registered. While this online document is different from an electronic will and is not a legal document, it could be used by the executor to retrieve any digital property that is to be included in the estate or to delete accounts, including customer accounts, from online stores or email accounts (Consumer New Zealand, n.d).

In additional to listing the details of online accounts and other digital property, an individual will also needs to consider "how and who is to manage" their digital property following their death (Lim & Wilson, 2016, p. 28). For example, an individual may want photographs from an Instagram or Flicker account, from a phone or a computer to be included in their estate and be distributed to beneficiaries, but communications from a personal email account to be deleted. This is where including a "digital asset management plan" as part of estate planning could be created and maintained (Lim & Wilson, 2016, p. 28).

Individuals could also use legacy policies such as those used by Facebook, Google and Twitter. It is recommended that as part of a will's letters of wishes or a memorandum of wishes, there is a note stating whether a legacy contact has been added to the account and if so, the name and contact details of the legacy contact.

Without amendments to current estate planning and administration laws, or the introduction of new legislation relating to managing digital assets or property, currently in Australia, UK and NZ, to enable an executor or a similar representative of an estate to access the digital property of a deceased individual, the individual may need to include passwords (in additional to email addresses or usernames) for some online accounts as part of their estate documentation. However, providing passwords to online accounts could be a breach of the service providers' terms and conditions or of laws that restrict access and sharing of data such as criminal laws relating to the unauthorised use of a computer or privacy laws.

It is anticipated that Australia, UK and NZ could implement laws like those in the US and Canada, that allow executors and other legal representatives to access and transfer an individual's digital property as part of an estate.

FUTURE RESEARCH DIRECTIONS

Future research could attempt to determine the current financial value of an individual's digital property, as it has been several years since the value of digital property has been calculated.[4] This financial value could then be used as part of raising awareness of the importance of an individual managing their digital property. Other research could examine how Australian courts could handle the issue of accessing and transferring digital property to a third party as part of an estate under current laws. Depending on the recommendations and outcomes of the NSW Law Reform Commission review relating to laws for accessing an individual's digital property (Department of Justice, 2019) as well as the outcomes and recommendations of the UK and NZ law commissions' reviews into succession laws, any recommended legislation could be analyzed to determine how they could operate in conjunction with other laws including contract, privacy and IP laws in an online environment with changing technology.

CONCLUSION

As the amount of digital information and data created and used continues to increase, individuals are often creating and purchasing digital property without giving any thought to what happens to it once they are no longer using it or die. For digital property that an individual no longer wants to use or needs, executors should be able to delete it and cancel the account if the digital property is held by a service provider.

Some digital property may have financial or sentimental value and, along with other real or personal property, an individual may wish to include this type of property in their estate and have it inherited by a beneficiary. For this to occur, it is important that an individual has an up to date and valid will that provides instructions to the executor about how to manage all property and personal possessions.

REFERENCES

Administration and Probate Act 1958 (Vic).

Alan Yazbek v Ghosn Yazbek & Anor [2012] NSWSC 594.

Amazon Australia Services. (2017). *Kindle store terms of use*. Retrieved from https://www.amazon.com.au/gp/help/customer/display.html?nodeId=201014950

Antoine, H. (2016). Digital legacies: Who owns your online life after death? *The Computer & Internet Lawyer*, *33*(4), 15–20.

Apple. (2019). *Apple media services terms and conditions*. Retrieved from https://www.apple.com/legal/internet-services/itunes/au/terms.html#SERVICE

BBC News. (2018, 12 July). Facebook ruling: German court grants parents' rights to dead daughter's account. *BBC News*. Retrieved from https://www.bbc.com

Beyer, G. W. (2015). Web meets the will: Estate planning for digital assets. *Estate Planning*, *42*(3), 28–41.

Briggs, T. (2019, 12 December). Government to evaluate 'right to be forgotten' but privacy reforms still years away. *The Age*. Retrieved from http://theage.com.au

Brown, J. H., & Bruch, R. E. (2019). Online tools under RUFADAA: The next evolution in estate planning or a flash in the pan? *Probate and Property (Chicago, Ill.)*, *13*(2), 60–63.

Consumer New Zealand. (n.d.) *Digital wills*. Retrieved from https://www.consumer.org.nz/articles/digital-wills

Cummings, R. G. (2014). The case against access to decedents' e-mail: Password protection as an exercise of the right to destroy. *Minnesota Journal of Law, Science & Technology*, *15*(2), 898–947.

Department of Communities and Justice. (2020). *Access to digital assets upon death or incapacity*. Retrieved from https://www.lawreform.justice.nsw.gov.au/Pages/lrc/lrc_current_projects/Digital%20assets/Project-update.aspx

Department of Justice. (2019). *Access to digital assets upon death or incapacity*. Retrieved from https://www.lawreform.justice.nsw.gov.au/Pages/lrc/lrc_current_projects/Digital%20assets/Project-update.aspx

Edwards, L., & Harbinja, E. (2013). What happens to my Facebook profile when I die? Legal issues around transmission of digital assets on death. In C. Maciel & V. C. Periera (Eds.), *Digital legacy and interaction: Post-mortem issues* (pp. 115–144). Cham, Switzerland: Springer International Publishing. doi:10.1007/978-3-319-01631-3_7

Equity Trustees v Levin [2004] VSC 203.

Estate of Masters, Hill v Plummer (1994) 33 NSWLR 446.

Estate of Sheron Jude Ladduhetti (2013) unreported, Supreme Court of Victoria.

Estate of Stewart (1996) unreported, Supreme Court of NSW.

European Commission. (2013). *LIBE committee vote backs new EU data protection rules* (Press release). Retrieved from https://europa.eu/rapid/press-release_MEMO-13-923_en.htm

European Commission. (2016). *Regulation (EU) 2016/679 of the European Parliament and of the council of 27 April 2016 on the protection of natural persons with regard to the processing of personal data and on the free movement of such data, and repealing Directive 95/46/EC (General Data Protection Regulation)*. Retrieved from https://publications.europa.eu/en/publication-detail/-/publication/3e485e15-11bd-11e6-ba9a-01aa75ed71a1/language-en

Facebook. (2019a). *What will happen to my Facebook account if I pass away?* Retrieved from https://www.facebook.com/help/103897939701143?helpref=related

Facebook. (2019b). *What is a legacy contact and what can they do with my Facebook account?* Retrieved from https://www.facebook.com/help/1568013990080948?helpref=faq_content

Google. (2019). *About inactive account manager*. Retrieved from https://support.google.com/accounts/answer/3036546

Hopkins, J. (2013). Afterlife in the cloud: Managing a digital estate. *Hastings Science and Technology Law Journal*, *5*(2), 209–243.

Humphries, M. (2018, 16 July). German court rules Facebook data can be inherited. *PC Mag Australia*. Retrieved from https://au.pcmag.com/

In re Request for Order Requiring Facebook, Inc. to Produce Documents and Things, Case No: C 12-80171 LHK (PSG), 9/20/201.

Instagram. (2019a). *How do I report a deceased person's account on Instagram?* Retrieved from https://help.instagram.com/264154560391256/

Instagram. (2019b). *What happens when a deceased person's account is memorialized?* Retrieved from https://help.instagram.com/231764660354188

Interpretation Act. (1954). QLD.

Interpretation Act. (1987). NSW.

Lamm, J. P., Kunz, C. L., Riehl, D. A., & Rademacher, P. J. (2014). The digital death conundrum: How Federal and State laws prevent fiduciaries from managing digital property. *University of Miami Law Review*, *68*, 385–420.

Law, N. Z. (2019). *Protecting your digital assets*. Retrieved from https://nzlaw.co.nz/news/protecting-your-digital-assets/

Law Commission. (n.d.). *Wills*. Retrieved from https://www.lawcom.gov.uk/project/wills/#related

Le Bras, T. (2015). O*nline overload – it's worse than you thought*. Retrieved from https://blog.dashlane.com/infographic-online-overload-its-worse-than-you-thought/

Lim, L., & Wilson, K. (2016). Clearing the cloud. *Law Institute Journal*, *90*(1/2), 28.

Lynn, A. (2019). *What happens to your digital assets when you die?* Retrieved from https://www.lexology.com/library/detail.aspx?g=288d7480-0d61-43cb-b5ff-e59b211c7bc5

Mann, T. (2018). *Australian law dictionary* (3rd ed.). Oxford University Press. Retrieved from https://www-oxfordreference-com

Marian Grace Burford In the will of Mark Edwin Tretheway (2002) VSC 83.

Matter of Estate of Swezey, New York County Surrogate Court, Case Number: 2017-2976/A.

McCallig, D. (2013). Facebook after death: An evolving policy in a social network. *International Journal of Law and Information Technology*. doi:10.1093/ijlit/eat012

McKinnon, L. (2011). Planning for the succession of digital assets. *Computer Law & Security Review*, *27*(4), 362–367. doi:10.1016/j.clsr.2011.03.002

National Conference of State Legislatives. (2019). *Access to digital assets of decedents*. Retrieved from https://www.ncsl.org/research/telecommunications-and-information-technology/access-to-digital-assets-of-decedents.aspx

New South Wales Law Reform Commission. (2018). *Access to digital assets upon death or incapacity* (consultation paper 20). Retrieved from https://www.lawreform.justice.nsw.gov.au/Documents/Publications/Consultation-Papers/CP20.pdf

New Zealand Law Commission. (2019). *Review of succession law*. Retrieved from https://www.lawcom.govt.nz/our-projects/review-succession-law

NSW Trustee & Guardian. (n.d.) Wills frequently asked questions. Retrieved from https://www.tag.nsw.gov.au/wills-faqs.html

Perzanowski, A., & Schultz, J. (2016). *The end of ownership: Personal property in the digital economy*. Cambridge, MA: MIT Press. doi:10.7551/mitpress/9780262035019.001.0001

PEW Research Center. (2019). *Social media fact sheet*. Retrieved from https://www.pewinternet.org/fact-sheet/social-media/

Privacy Act 1988 (Cth).

Probate and Administration Act. (1898). NSW.

Re Application of Brown: Estate of Springfield (1991) 23 NSWLR 535.

Re Estate of Ellsworth. (2005). *No. 2005-296, 651-DE*. Mich.: Prob. Ct.

Re: Yu [2013] QSC 322.

Reid, B. (2017). Legal life after death: Publicity, physical and digital assets. *Southern Journal of Business and Ethics*, *9*, 108–122.

Revised Uniform Fiduciary Access to Digital Assets (RUFADA) Act 2015 (US).

Rottenstreich, S. J., & Barkhorn, K. (2019). *What happens to my digital assests on death or incapacity*. Retrived from https://trustbclp.com/what-happens-to-my-digital-assets-on-death-or-incapacity/

Society of Trust and Estate Practitioners. (2017). *Digital assets special interest group digital assets: Practitioner's guide Australia.* Retrieved from https://www.step.org/sites/default/files/Digital%20Assets%20Practitioner%20Guide%20-%20Australia.pdf

Spotify. (2019). *Terms and conditions of use.* Retrieved from https://www.spotify.com/au/legal/end-user-agreement/#s19

Steen, A., D'Alessandro, S., Graves, C., Perkins, M., Genders, R., Barbera, F., . . . Davis, N. (2017). *Estate planning in Australia.* Charles Sturt University. Retrieved from https://researchoutput.csu.edu.au/ws/portalfiles/portal/19332794/Estate_Planning_in_Australia_Final_Report_021017.pdf

18. Stored Communications Act §§. 2701-2702 (US).

Succession Act. (1981). QLD.

Succession Act. (2006). NSW.

The Gazette. (n.d.). *What happens to digital assets on death?* Retrieved from https://www.thegazette.co.uk/all-notices/content/101190

Uniform Access to Digital Assets by Fiduciaries Act. (2016). Canada.

Uniform Fiduciary Access to Digital Assets (UFADA) Act 2014.

Uniform Law Conference of Canada. (2016). *Uniform access to digital assets by fiduciaries act 2016.* Retrieved from http://www.ulcc.ca/images/stories/2016_pdf_en/2016ulcc0006.pdf

Uniform Probate Code (1969).

USLegalWills.com. (2016). *Are there even fewer Americans without wills?* Retrieved from https://www.uslegalwills.com/blog/americans-without-wills/

Walker, M. D. (2017). The new uniform digital assets law: Estate planning and administration in the information age. *Real Property. Trust and Estate Law Journal, 52*(1), 51–78.

Wills Act. (1997). Vic.

Woodman, F. L. (2017). Fiduciary access to digital assets: A review of the uniform law conference of Canada's proposed uniform act and comparable American model legislation. *Canadian Journal of Law and Technology, 15,* 193–227.

Yahoo. (2018). *Yahoo terms of service.* Retrieved from https://policies.yahoo.com/us/en/yahoo/terms/utos/index.htm

Yanner v Eaton (1999) 201 CLR 351.

ADDITIONAL READING

Carroll, E., & Romano, J. (2011). *Your digital afterlife when Facebook Flickr and Twitter are your estate what's your legacy*. Berkeley: New Riders.

Dissanayake, D. N. (2019). *The challenges of digital legacy management on the value of digital objects to older Australians*. (Masters thesis). Retrieved from https://ro.ecu.edu.au/theses/2218

Gibbs, M., Meese, J., Arnold, M., Nansen, B., & Carter, M. (2015). #Funeral and Instagram: Death, social media, and platform vernacular. *Information Communication and Society*, *18*(3), 255–268. doi: 10.1080/1369118X.2014.987152

Leaver, T. (2013). The social media contradiction: Data mining and digital death. *M/C Journal*, 16(2). Retrieved from http://journal.media-culture.org.au/index.php/mcjournal/article/viewArticle/625

Maciel, C., & Periera, V. C. (Eds.). (2013). *Digital legacy and interaction: Post-mortem issues*. Cham, Switzerland: Springer International Publishing. doi:10.1007/978-3-319-01631-3

Sager, L. (2018). *The digital estate*. London: Sweet and Maxwell.

Van der Nagel, E., Arnold, M., Nansen, B., Gibbs, M., Kohn, T., Bellamy, C., & Clark, N. (2017). *Death and the internet: Consumer issues for planning and managing digital legacies*. Retrieved from the Australian Communications Consumer Action Network website: https://accan.org.au/files/Grants/Death%20and%20the%20Internet_2017-web.pdf

KEY TERMS AND DEFINITIONS

Digital Asset: A type of digital property that has financial or sentimental value.

Digital Asset Management Plan: Is a document that lists an individual's online accounts and other digital property and provides instructions on how their digital property is to be managed as part of their estate.

Digital Property: An electronic version of information or data including images, text, multimedia information, or personal property stored on the internet, a computer or on another electronic device.

Digital Will: Is not a legal document, rather it a list of the online accounts (including email address or username) that an individual has registered.

Electronic or Informal Will: Traditionally wills are in written form, signed and witnessed. However, courts have started to accept documents or written words saved on computers or other devices that indicate the document or written words are an individual's will.

Legacy Policy: Instructions provided to a service provider from user about how their account is to be managed following an inactive period or the user's death.

ENDNOTES

[1]   Last revised in 2010. Refer to https://www.uniformlaws.org/committees/community-home?CommunityKey=a539920d-c477-44b8-84fe-b0d7b1a4cca8

[2]   As of March 2020, the NSW Attorney General had not released a response to the final report.

[3]   https://www.securesafe.com/en/

[4]   In 2012, McAfee, the anti-virus software company valued an individual's digital property at $55,000 (US). See Woodman, F. L. (2017). Fiduciary access to digital assets: A review of the uniform law conference of Canada's proposed uniform act and comparable American model legislation. *Canadian Journal of Law and Technology*, 15, 193-227.

Chapter 3
A Framework for Ameliorating Risk in Australian University Crowdfunding

Jonathan O'Donnell
RMIT University, Australia

ABSTRACT

Crowdfunding is a balance of risk versus reward. Crowdfunders take a public risk that they will fail to raise funds. Donors take the risk that the campaign will not be funded or that they will not see a return for their support. In an ideal world, both sides are rewarded through the development of something new. If the campaign is being run by a staff member at a large organisation, the organisation should consider a number of risks. These include legal risks such as corruption and misrepresentation, as well as reputational risks and risks relating to exploitation of staff. There is also the risk of funding foregone due to excessive caution regarding crowdfunding. This chapter uses universities in Australia as a case study to illustrate some of these risks. It analyses them through a framework for managing risk in business centric crowdfunding platforms. It contributes a new framework for ameliorating risk before, during, and after crowdfunding campaigns.

INTRODUCTION

Crowdfunding - raising funds from a group for a project, typically using the internet - provides a new method for funding research at universities. This chapter focuses on the crowdfunding activities of academics at Australian universities in the scope of their institutional research commitments. It examines the risks for the individuals, the universities and the public in crowdfunding campaigns in Australia, using an existing framework for managing risk in crowdfunding services (Stack et al., 2017). Finally, to assist universities to address these risks, it provides a framework for ameliorating risk before, during and after crowdfunding campaigns.

DOI: 10.4018/978-1-7998-3130-3.ch003

The chapter does not seek to provide advice to academics who are undertaking crowdfunding in a personal capacity, or to provide advice to students or others affiliated with Australian universities. It focuses on crowdfunding as delineated through the employer-employee relationship of universities and their academics.

Restricting the discussion to universities limits the scope of this chapter to donation-based crowdfunding and rewards-based crowdfunding. While there are examples of universities using crowdfunding to raise equity, they are rare. Risks related to equity crowdfunding have been extensively discussed elsewhere (Cui & Zeng, 2016; Hornuf & Schwienbacher, 2017). The author has also not examined loan-based crowdfunding undertaken by universities.

The chapter begins by providing an understanding of the funding of research in Australian universities, of crowdfunding in general and of crowdfunding in Australian universities. It examines the literature on academic crowdfunding, risks related to crowdfunding in general and frameworks for understanding those risks. It describes the research undertaken for this chapter, including interviews and archival research. It outlines the difference between crowdfunding campaigns inside and outside of universities. It identifies risks relating to crowdfunding at Australian universities, using Stack's framework of ill-intentioned and well-intentioned actors. It then provides a new framework for ameliorating those risks.

BACKGROUND

Understanding Research and Crowdfunding

To understand how crowdfunding might fund research activities at Australian universities, it is first necessary to understand the research landscape at Australian universities. Research in Australian universities is defined as "creative and systematic work undertaken in order to increase the stock of knowledge – including knowledge of humankind, culture and society – and to devise new applications of available knowledge" (Department of Education and Training, 2017, p. 6).

This definition covers all research activities within the university sector. As most of the major art schools in Australia are attached to universities, it includes creative work such as visual art and creative writing when undertaken by university academics. For the purposes of this chapter, it includes activities associated with research, such as scholarly publication and research communication to the general public (also referred to as sci. comm.). It excludes activities related to teaching, except for research into education theory and practice.

Research at Australian universities is funded through a mix of competitive government grants, industry research contracts and philanthropic donations. Generally, an applicant for a grant responds to a call for applications, submits a written application which usually peer assessed, and undergoes a formal competitive selection process. Crowdfunding provides a new model for research funding in the university sector as it differs from other funding models in four ways.

First, it is not competitive. As crowdfunding campaigns are driven by personal networks, they are not necessarily competing against one another for contributions. Second, there is no written contract signed by all parties that specifies timelines, deliverables and outcomes. Third, aside from university policies, there are no rules specifying what work can and cannot be done, and what funds can and cannot be spent on. This means that crowdfunding can be used to fund work that can be difficult to fund otherwise:

- Extension or top-up funding for a grant or contract that does not provide quite enough funding.
- Pilot funding for exploring formative ideas or for background scholarship to develop ideas.
- Writing up and publication funds for completed work.
- Research communication and science communication, either through public awareness campaigns or research communication such as blogging or podcasting.
- Funding projects that have not been funding through a peer-review grant program.

Finally, there is no peer review process at the funding stage. In this, crowdfunding is more similar to industry research funding and a lot of philanthropic funding, which are often not peer reviewed.

Like any other form of research funding, crowdfunding contributions enable academics to do more than they would otherwise have been able to do without the funding.

Crowdfunding via the internet provides an innovative way for people and organizations to mobilize their networks to raise funds for equity, goods and services, loans or public benefit projects (Belleflamme et al., 2013; Cumming et al., 2015). A crowdfunding service provides a gateway or escrow service between those people who seek to raise funds (crowdfunders) and their contributors, who provide funds. The crowdfunding service provides a website (crowdfunding platform) which allows the crowdfunders to present their case to the public through a short narrative which presents the benefits of their work (Swords, 2018). Examples of crowdfunding services include Chuffed, FundScience, GetFunding, GoFundMe, Indiegogo, Kickstarter, Patreon, Pozible, Rockethub and Thinkable. While they all operate in slightly different ways, they all provide a way for contributors to provide funds to crowdfunders. Chuffed, Pozible and Thinkable are based in Australia. All the other crowdfunding services in this chapter are based in other countries but allow Australians to undertake crowdfunding. Australian crowdfunders (including academics) are not restricted to using Australian-based crowdfunding services. They can use any crowdfunding service that will transfer funds to an Australian bank account.

The work required for crowdfunding can be divided into three stages:

- **Before the Campaign**: Crowdfunders prepare a narrative that they will present to the public, describing what they want to do. They plan their communication strategy and identify the people and organizations that they will ask for funding. The crowdfunding service may undertake a brief review before the campaign is published, to ensure it meets their terms and conditions.
- **During the Campaign**: Crowdfunders publish their narrative on a crowdfunding platform, which signals the start of their crowdfunding campaign. They then implement their communication strategy to attract supporters. This generally involves reaching out to their personal networks through social media as well as presenting their narrative to broadcast media such as newspapers and talk-back radio. They may need to change strategy during the campaign, if they are not attracting enough contributions.
- **After the Campaign**: If the campaign has been successful, the crowdfunding service will transfer contributions to the nominated bank account. The crowdfunders should spend those contributions as described in the campaign and disperse any rewards, 'thank you' gifts and tax deductibility receipts. There is also a general expectation that crowdfunders will keep supporters informed of their progress.

In a university setting, there may be additional requirements to each of these three stages:

- **Before a Campaign**: If the university has a policy regarding crowdfunding, the crowdfunder may be required to submit the campaign for internal review. A communications or media team may also be able to advise on the communication plan.
- **During the Campaign**: Groups or units within the university may provide support. For example, the communications team may promote the campaign to the media and through social media. The alumni relations team may promote the campaign to alumni. The donor relations team may promote the campaign to potential donors. Parts of the university may also contribute funds to the campaign.
- **After the Campaign**: The funds must be transferred from a general university account to the crowdfunder's project account. The crowdfunder may be required to submit their research plan for ethics approval before beginning their research.

There are four main types of crowdfunding services. The first is donation crowdfunding where crowdfunders are raising funds for a cause or as a public good. The supporters are not seeking a material return for their funds, although they may receive some sort of 'thank you' gift (such as a coffee cup) or a tax deduction. Academic crowdfunders often fit into this category, as they are raising funds for research as a public good. The crowdfunding campaign funds a research project which does not seek to develop a specific product or service.

The second type is rewards crowdfunding in which crowdfunders are developing a new product or service. Their crowdfunding campaign is often designed to generate orders (pre-purchase) for their product or service. Supporters are funding this development in return for access to the product or service. Academics at Australian universities have raised funds to create art events (with tickets to the event as the reward) and fund publications (with the published book or magazine as the reward). Some independent research projects have used crowdfunding to raise funds for research-based product design, by generating orders for their final product.

The third type is equity crowdfunding in which crowdfunders are raising equity for a profit-making concern, and supporters are seeking a return on their investment. They gain an equity stake in the project. The fourth type is loan crowdfunding where crowdfunders are seeking a loan, and supporters expect them to pay back that loan, generally with interest.

As mentioned in the Introduction, the scope of this chapter is restricted to crowdfunding for donations and rewards, as universities rarely undertake crowdfunding for equity or loans.

Crowdfunding campaigns collect funds in three distinct ways:

- **All-or-nothing**: The crowdfunder sets a minimum target that must be reached over a set period of time. Supporters pledge payments during the campaign, which come due at the end of the campaign if the target has been reached. If the target is not reached, the crowdfunder gets nothing. All-or-nothing campaigns are suitable for projects where there are fixed costs, such as product development.
- **Flexible Funding**: The crowdfunder keeps all funds raised, no matter how small. Flexible funding campaigns are suitable for charitable projects, where every dollar can be used to help a cause. They are also known as 'keep-it-all' campaigns.
- **Crowd-patronage**: The crowdfunder collects regular funding contributions on an on-going basis. Crowd-patronage campaigns are suitable for supporting on-going episodic work, such as podcasts and YouTube channels.

These types of crowdfunding and ways of collection funds are combined in Table 1.

Table 1. Types of crowdfunding campaigns and funding, showing the scope of this chapter

	Donations	Rewards	Equity	Loans
All-or-nothing	e.g. Pozible	e.g. Kickstarter		
Flexible funding	e.g. Chuffed		Not considered in this chapter	
Crowd-patronage	e.g. Patreon			

Crowdfunding for donations and rewards is a very democratic process. Any individual or group can set up a crowdfunding campaign as long as they meet the terms and conditions of the crowdfunding service. They must meet an age limit (18 years or older to use Australian crowdfunding services) and must hold a bank account in a country that the crowdfunding service is authorized to operate in. Their campaign can be for any purpose that meets the terms and conditions of the crowdfunding service. As such, university academics may conduct campaigns in their personal or their professional capacity. If their campaign has no relation to their work, they might represent themselves as an individual, without any mention of their university affiliation. This would be appropriate if their campaign is related to a hobby or a charity that they support. Some will conduct a campaign as a public intellectual. If their campaign is related to their area of expertise, they might highlight their university affiliation and accreditation, but run the campaign outside of their university processes. In this instance, they are acting as a public intellectual, much as they would if they were speaking to the media. This might be appropriate if they were collaborating with academics from multiple universities, or if their university had no process or policy supporting crowdfunding. In this case, funds raised would not be transferred to their university. Finally, academics could undertake their campaign as an academic employed by their university, with funds being transferred to a university bank account. This will only work if their university has processes in place to enable is to happen.

So, an academic may undertake a crowdfunding campaign as an individual, or as the agent of their employer (the university). If they are acting as a public intellectual, it is unclear if they are acting as an employee or as an individual. They are relying on their association with their university, but the funds are not being transferred to a university bank account. This is an important distinction, as it will determine whether the employment contract between the academic and their university applies. It may also create a conflict of interest.

Academics at Australian universities began crowdfunding (in the modern sense of internet intermediated crowdfunding) in 2011. In that year, academics at Griffith University worked with others to raise funds for *56 Inch Circus* (McGuffin et al., 2011) and an academic at the University of New England was involved in a campaign to raise funds for *Subak with Art Festival* (Brooks et al., 2011). Since then, a small number of universities have encouraged staff to undertake crowdfunding as part of their academic role. The University of Western Australia, for example, clearly badges its crowdfunding campaigns with the university name (Personal communication, July 30, 2017). Deakin University has encouraged staff to undertake crowdfunding campaigns and provided a development program to assist them with their campaigns (D. Verhoeven, personal communication, March 4, 2016).

Universities occupy an interesting position in the crowdfunding space, as they have historically encouraged their academics to engage with the public as intellectuals as well as encouraging them to raise funds for their research. They are being encouraged by the government to demonstrate the public benefit or impact of their work (Brook, 2018; Chubb & Reed, 2018; Chubb & Watermeyer, 2016; Commonwealth of Australia, 2017; CSIRO, 2015; M. C. Evans & Cvitanovic, 2018; Jones et al., 2013; Penfield et al., 2014). Crowdfunding allows academics to undertake all these activities at the same time – they can present their ideas to the public in an attempt to raise funds for their work.

The public nature of crowdfunding makes it an excellent option for research activities that produce public good, which can used by others without exclusion or depletion, such as open source research (Mann & Blunden, 2010; Pomerantz & Peek, 2016). Conversely, it is not a suitable funding mechanism for all research. It is not suitable for research that is commercially sensitive or where a commercial advantage may be lost by revealing ideas to the public, research that involves confidential intellectual property, may lead to a theoretical breakthrough or where there is the possibility of being beaten to a discovery by rival researchers, or research that attracts the attention of well-organized opposition groups, such as animal liberationists or anti-vaxxers.

In undertaking a crowdfunding campaign, a series of contracts are formed between the parties, and several transactions take place. Figure 1 shows the relationships between the crowdfunders who are seeking funding, the crowdfunding service and the supporters who are contributing funds.

Figure 1. Simple model of crowdfunding

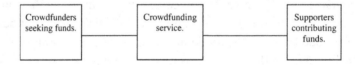

The crowdfunder and their supporters both form contracts with the crowdfunding service when they accept the terms and conditions of using the service. The significant moments in the relationships include:

- When the crowdfunding campaign is published.
- When a supporter makes a contribution.
- When the crowdfunding campaign closes.
- When the crowdfunding service releases funds to the crowdfunder.
- When the promised aim of the campaign is achieved, either by the creation of a public-good like research, or by the delivery of goods or services.

If the campaign is successful, a contract or trust is formed between the supporters and the crowdfunder. This contract comes to an end when the aim of the campaign is achieved.

In addition to this, all parties will have contracts with payment services, either to pay funds to the campaign (supporters), receive funds for the campaign and pay funds to the crowdfunder (crowdfunding service) and to receive funds from the crowdfunding service (crowdfunder).

The different parties are governed by a mixture of legislation, contract law, and/or common law.

The model shown in Figure 1 becomes more complicated when the crowdfunders are employees of an organization, such as a university. Figure 2 shows the way that the relationship changes when the crowdfunders are undertaking their crowdfunding activities as employees of an organization, such as a university.

Figure 2. Model of crowdfunding for organisational employees

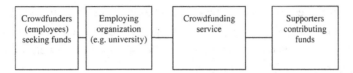

In Figure 2, additional contracts include the employment contract between the crowdfunding academic and their university. If the campaign succeeds, funds are transferred to the university. In this case, it is unclear whether the university has a contract with the crowdfunding service. On the one hand, the academic is acting as an employee of the university. On the other hand, the terms and conditions of crowdfunding services are generally designed with individuals, not organizations, in mind. In addition, it is unclear whether the supporters realize that they are forming a contract with the university when the funds are transferred.

As well, universities introduces a range of organizational policies that govern the behaviour of staff members.

RESEARCH METHODS

This chapter draws on several data sets. The first is data obtained from twenty-three interviews with crowdfunding academics (n = 9), university administrators (n = 13) and crowdfunding service personnel (n = 1) conducted in 2016 and 2017. The second is a literature review of publications relating to Australian crowdfunding. The third data set are changes in the terms and conditions governing use of Kickstarter between December 2010 and July 2019 (O'Donnell, 2019).

Interviews

As part of a PhD project to understand how universities were supporting crowdfunding, 23 interviews with academics and administrative staff at three universities and one crowdfunding service were conducted. While most interviews were one on one (20 interviews), a small number involved two interviewees (three interviews). The academics interviewed included those that had conducted both successful and unsuccessful campaigns. As preparation for these interviews, a review of the public material related to their campaigns was undertaken, both on the crowdfunding platform and on social media. Academic interviewees were asked to tell the story of their campaigns, with the campaign page open in front of them for reference. If they had conducted multiple campaigns, they were asked to focus on their most recent campaigns. Administrators who were interviewed included senior university staff who were responsible for setting policy, as well as bureaucrats from research administration, finance and advancement (donor relations) responsible for supporting the campaigns. Interviews with administrators all started with the seed question of 'please describe a problem associated with crowdfunding', to try to avoid discussions based on organizational narratives of success. In both cases, interviews were semi-structured and were designed to last an hour.

Interviews were analyzed both through close reading and thematically using NVivo (Guest et al., 2006; Rowley, 2002, 2012). For this chapter, interviews were coded for comments that discussed risk (including synonyms and antonyms), and legal or general issues that had been identified from the literature.

The main issues that emerged from the analysis of the interviews related to non-performance of service and breach of contract, concerns about intellectual property, false pledges and crowdfunding systems, missing payments and payment systems, university policies, university concerns about reputational risk, stalking and harassment by the public, and motivation.

Literature Review

The literature review encompassed research-related crowdfunding campaigns. Because crowdfunding for research is a relatively recent phenomena, this included both Australian and international campaigns. One example that illustrated the risks for universities was that of through the *Glowing Plants: Natural Lighting with no Electricity* campaign on Kickstarter (Callaway, 2013; A. Evans, n.d.; Franzen, 2013; Kickstarter, n.d.; Regalado, 2016). In 2013, independent synthetic biology researchers from the United States (US) raised US$484,013 from 8,433 supporters through the *Glowing Plants: Natural Lighting with no Electricity* campaign. Most supporters chose rewards that would provide them with seeds to grow glowing plants. The campaign attracted a great deal of controversy. People were concerned about the risk of bioluminescent plants spreading in the wild, and cross-pollinating with other species (Dzieza, 2013). After five years of work, the glowing plants researchers reported that, despite their best efforts, they had failed. Even so, many supporters were very vocal in their disappointment at not receiving seeds to grow their own glowing plants (Brewster, 2017; Regalado, 2016).

The author also undertook an archival search of articles and news items related to legal breaches and other risks related to Australian donation and reward-based crowdfunding campaigns. This was a snowball sample for content analysis (Krippendorff, 2018) starting with known issues (e.g. news items relating to footballer Israel Folau and medical fraud on GoFundMe), and working outward to track down other campaigns mentioned in news articles and blog posts.

It also drew on two independent web sites have been established to identify fraudulent crowdfunding campaigns, Kickscammed (https://kickscammed.com/) for Kickstarter and GoFraudMe (http://gofraudme.com/) for GoFundMe, which collect examples of questionable crowdfunding campaigns. Both of these sites were searched for Australian examples, as well as for examples that related to research activities.

Frameworks for Understanding Risk in Crowdfunding

While there are many frameworks that address crowdfunding, the author could only find three that specifically addressed risk in crowdfunding. In 2015, Arenas et. al. drew on Sherer and Alter's (2004) work system risk framework to examine risks related to three equity crowdfunding platforms. The work system risk framework is designed to categorize risks in information systems operations and projects. It provides for 33 types of risk factors, grouped into nine categories. These categories include risks related to: work practices; participants; information; technologies; products and services; customers; environment; infrastructure; and strategies. Risk factors range from 'technology performance is inadequate' in the 'technologies' category to 'inadequate managers and leaders' in the 'participants' category (Sherer & Alter, 2004). However, the work system risk framework is designed to help managers of information systems to understand and categories the large number of risks they face when they are managing, commissioning or developing information systems. Using this framework provides a techno-centric and managerial view of the risks involved. This has limited use when considering entrepreneurial activities related to financial transactions, such as crowdfunding.

In 2017, Schwienbacher published a model of entrepreneurial risk-taking in crowdfunding campaigns. It used micro-economic assumptions to model all-or-nothing rewards-based crowdfunding (pre-purchase) that might attract investors and that involved ideas could be replicated or stolen. Within this scope, it discussed the risk of not achieving a crowdfunding target, of achieving the target but not having enough funds to produce the reward, and the risk of having intellectual property stolen. It discussed varying the target amount for the campaign as a way of compensating for these risks, as well as varying the amount of effort involved, and attracting investment at the end of the campaign (Schwienbacher, 2017). The scope of this model was too specific to be useful for this paper.

In 2017, Stack et al published a useful framework for evaluating legal risk in crowdfunding. Stack et al. (2017, para. 10) posits "…that in any crowdfunding platform there are both well-intentioned and ill-intentioned fund seekers and investors…". Stack et al., (2017) used four examples of risks to illustrate the four different combinations of these four variables:

- **Fraud**: Ill-intentioned entrepreneurs stealing the funds of well-intentioned investors.
- Intellectual property theft: ill-intentioned investors stealing the intellectual property of well-intentioned entrepreneurs.
- **Money Laundering**: Ill-intentioned investors working with ill-intentioned entrepreneurs.
- **Failure by Success**: So many well-intentioned investors subscribing to the campaign of a well-intentioned entrepreneur that they cannot cope with the scale of the project

This was a useful framework as it combined the intention of the actor with their actions within the system. It provides a simple way to categorize most risks related to crowdfunding. The framework is designed for equity, lending and reward-based crowdfunding but it can also be applied to donation-based crowdfunding. However, it ignores the possibility of risks related to the crowdfunding service or other external factors.

Analysis and Synthesis

Each of the data sets were analyzed separately. This analysis was then combined through the application of Stack et. al's (2017) framework of ill-intentioned or well-intentioned actors. While this provided a useful understanding of the risks, it was found that some risks fell outside the framework. All risks (both those within the framework and those outside it) were grouped according to the coding used in analyzing the interviews.

Finally, the author has synthesized this discussion into a new framework for ameliorating risk in institutional crowdfunding. It provides suggestions on what organizations might consider doing before crowdfunding campaigns are developed, while crowdfunding campaigns are underway, and after crowdfunding campaigns are completed.

ACADEMIC CROWDFUNDING CAMPAIGNS

Research into academic crowdfunding has produced two distinct strands of literature; case studies of academics who have undertaking crowdfunding campaigns and detailed analysis of multiple campaigns. While crowdfunding generates much public data that lends itself to statistical analysis of large crowdfunding data sets, to date the author has not discovered any large-scale statistical analysis of research crowdfunding.

Personal case studies published through refereed articles and blog posts have provided valuable information on emerging activity. These publications emphasize the significant investment of time and effort required to attract funds, that the majority of funds come from friends, family and colleagues, and that campaigns with all-or-nothing targets often need large contributions to be successful (English, 2014; Gill, 2014; Teytelman, 2015a; Thomson, 2014). They explain the lack of other avenues of funding which had encouraged them to try crowdfunding, and how crowdfunding, while worthwhile, did not replace traditional sources of funding, particularly government funding (English, 2014; Moore, 2013; Teytelman, 2015b).

In 2015, Hui and Gerber interviewed 27 US academics who had undertaken crowdfunding campaigns. They found that academics were motivated through a desire to share their work and a need for funds, and that they needed to use more accessible language to attract an audience. Many crowdfunding campaigners are reluctant to ask their personal networks (often friends, family and colleagues) for funding. Academics have described it as 'hounding' or being a 'glorified begger' (Gerber & Hui, 2013; Hui & Gerber, 2015).

Byrnes (2012), Faulkes (2014) and Wheat et al (2013) analyzed 182 projects undertaken over a 33 to 45 day period of all-or-nothing research crowdfunding campaigns. Their main finding was that researchers need to engage a broad audience to meet their targets. They recommended that academics build their audience before they begin their crowdfunding campaigns. They were able to show that academics had to attract 100 views of their campaign webpage to gain one contribution. If they did not already have a large audience, it was difficult for them to build a support base while also trying to reach a target in 4 to 6 weeks (Byrnes, 2012; Faulkes, 2012, 2014; Wheat et al., 2013).

In 2018, Ikkatai, McKay and Yokoyama surveyed 950 members of the public and 30 Japanese academics who had conducted crowdfunding campaigns. They found that, while the public thought that peer review of crowdfunding was important, the great majority of their academic respondents did not think that peer review was desirable before academics could launch crowdfunding campaigns (Ikkatai et al., 2018).

Verhoeven and Palmer provided analysis of the first eight campaigns undertaken by an Australian university, and then subsequent analysis that included nineteen campaigns with all-or-nothing targets. They described crowdfunding as a "flipped funding model" where researchers proposed minimal targets which were fully funded, rather than aspirational grant application budgets that funding bodies often only partially fund (Verhoeven & Palmer, 2015, p. 6). They emphasized the value of research crowdfunding campaigns to develop the research communication and entrepreneurial skills of the participants, as well as providing their research with a visible presence in the community. They also touch on some of the organizational difficulties encountered when introducing a new funding model to a university (Verhoeven, Palmer, Seitzinger & Randall, n.d.). They discuss "...the collection and visualization of social media (Twitter) data related to the research crowdfunding projects..." (S. Palmer & Verhoeven, 2016, p. 291). Their analysis of the density and width of Twitter networks associated with eight research crowdfunding campaigns showed that research campaigns succeed more often when they move beyond tweets "by" researchers, to others tweeting "about" their campaigns. Success was achieved by "…not by sending lots of tweets per se, but by extending the sequence of retweets and other re-broadcasts about their project to new/unique potential pledgers" (S. Palmer & Verhoeven, 2016, p. 297).

LAW APPLICABLE TO CROWDFUNDING

The law that is relevant to the legal risks to universities in Australia when their academic staff engage in crowdfunding campaigns is quite complex as it depends on the nature of the crowdfunding campaign. However, in most cases, the funds provided through a crowdfunding campaign for academic research will be considered a donation.

For an Australian university to accept donations, it must be a registered charity, meeting the requirements set out in the *Australian Charities and Not-for-profits Commission Act 2012* (Cth), as well as any relevant State or Territory-based legislation governing charitable donations.

The Law Council of Australia in its document *Crowdfunding Guidance for Australian legal practitioners* (2019) points out that donation-based crowdfunding is treated as making a gift and generally a gift does not constitute an enforceable contract unless the crowdfunder makes specific promises regarding the use of the gift. This is rarely the case in crowdfunding. This means that there are very few enforceable remedies in contract law related to gifts if a supporter is not happy with the use of their funds.

The Australian Consumer Law (ACL) in the *Australian Competition and Consumer Act 2010* (Cth) does not apply to donation-based crowdfunding, as it applies to persons engaged in trade or commerce. The tort of deceit might apply to a misleading crowdfunding campaign if the academic made false representations knowing they were false, the funder relied on those representations and he or she suffered damage as a result (Law Council, 2019). Also, specific promises regarding the use of the gift may create a trust if the relevant agreement indicated that there was an intention to create such a trust.

With rewards-based crowdfunding that involves the promise of development or supply of products (either as the main purpose of the crowdfunding, or as small 'thank-you' rewards), s. 18 of the ACL may apply. It prohibits misleading and deceptive conduct in trade or commerce and offers protections against false or misleading representations about goods and services. This includes pre-purchase, as well as the provision of 'thank you' rewards in exchange for funds. As well, aggrieved supporters might also have remedies under contract law (Law Council of Australia, 2019; Matthew, 2019).

At this stage, crowdfunding does not fit well with the existing body of law. Vitale (2013, p. 310) argues that "the challenge regulators now face is to adapt the existing pre-crowdfunding framework to the post-crowdfunding world, so that the full benefits of the crowdfunding phenomenon may be enjoyed without compromising the overall regulatory outcome".

In Australia, the only legislation that specifically relates to crowdfunding pertains to equity-based crowdfunding, which is not discussed in this chapter. The two relevant acts are the *Corporations Amendment (Crowd-sourced Funding) Act 2017* (Cth) and the *Corporations Amendment (Crowd-sourced Funding for Proprietary Companies) Act 2018* (Cth).

However, contract law does play an important part in governing the relationships between the funders, the crowdfunding services and the supporters. To set up a campaign, the crowdfunder must agree to be bound by the terms and conditions of the service. As mentioned earlier, most of the crowdfunding services activities are covered by jurisdictions other than Australia. As events occur and problems arise, the crowdfunding services update their terms and conditions. To illustrate this, the author tracked every change of the text of Kickstarter's guidelines, rules, prohibited items and terms and conditions between December 2010 and July 2019 (when the data was collected). This dataset has been published as open data (O'Donnell, 2019).

Crowdfunding services can limit or encourage activity through their terms and conditions. After synthetic biology researchers raised US$484,013 through the *Glowing Plants: Natural Lighting with no Electricity* campaign, Kickstarter updated their prohibited items list to prohibit genetically modified organisms as rewards (Callaway, 2013; A. Evans, n.d.; Franzen, 2013; Kickstarter, n.d.; Regalado, 2016). This was a reversal of their Guidelines when they launched, which read "Kickstarter is full of imaginative applications of technology: ... open source DNA projects.... These projects are great!" (Kickstarter, 2010, para. 7).

In addressing the issue of whether rewards-based crowdfunding services are raising funds for research and development or are selling goods via pre-purchase. Kickstarter explicitly stated in 2012 that it was not a store (Strickler et al., 2012). That is, rewards-based crowdfunding campaigns are not a pre-purchase vehicle and are not engaged in the supply of goods to consumers. Others disagree, with (Ganatra, 2015, p. 1434) arguing that Kickstarter "functions as a platform for entrepreneurs that offer the very product in development as a "reward" either earlier than a formal release and/or at a discounted price".

However, Kickstarter's position was supported in 2018 by a judge in the Central District Court of Israel, who expressed a preliminary position that (Neuman, 2018, para. 17):

there is no promise on the part of the company to supply the finished product, but only a request for a financial donation that would help in its development – which sometimes succeeds, and sometimes does not.

In 2019, the US Federal Trade Commission seemed to also support Kickstarter's position when they commenced an action against Douglas Monahan, who ran multiple successful crowdfunding campaigns on Kickstarter and Indiegogo which raised US$800,000 to develop the iBackPack, a technological backpack (Federal Trade Commission, 2019; Monahan, 2016b, 2016a). The Federal Trade Commission believed that only a small proportion of the funds raised were used to develop the iBackPack. They stated that "if you raise money by crowdfunding, you don't have to guarantee that your idea will work... But you do have to use the money to work on your idea" (Federal Trade Commission, 2019, para. 3).

In 2017, a Kickstarter patron with the user name 'Encik Farhan' was making large pledges and then disputing the charges with their credit card company after the reward had shipped (Heberling, 2013a, 2013b). After it was discovered that the user had done this to multiple (possibly hundreds) of projects, Kickstarter changed their policies to protect creators from this sort of theft (Heberling, 2018).

Payment systems also place restrictions on what can be done through crowdfunding through their own terms and conditions. While it was still under development, Kickstarter's guidelines read "projects must meet Amazon payments' acceptable use policy" (Kickstarter, 2010a, para. 4).

Fraud, Misrepresentation and the Criminal Law Cases

There has been remarkably little research into legal risks related to donation or reward-based crowdfunding, aside from the examination of fraud in rewards-based crowdfunding. The research that has been done has mainly been focused on the US.

The wisdom of the crowd (Surowiecki, 2005) can sometimes help to detect fraudulent or misrepresentational claims in crowdfunding campaigns. However, this is not always the case. In 2016 Cumming et al identified 197 potentially fraudulent campaigns from Kickstarter, over the period from 2010 to 2015. They described a suspected fraudulent crowdfunding campaign as one where the rewards had been significantly delayed (by more than one year) and the campaign initiators cease communicating with their supporters for more than six months after an unmet delivery date. They also identified suspected fraud when the promised product or reward was never delivered and the supporters were not fully refunded. Of these 197 potentially fraudulent campaigns, 44 were detected and cancelled before the end of the campaign. The overwhelming majority (147 campaigns) were funded and only suspected of fraud when the promised product or reward was not delivered (Cumming et al., 2016).

There have been two prosecutions in Australia relating to donation-based crowdfunding to raise funds for cancer treatment costs. The first was in 2015 when Diakko Santaali raised A$10,550 via GoFundMe, to assist with treatment costs for pancreatic cancer. In 2016 he pleaded guilty to one count of dishonestly obtaining a sum of money in the Brisbane Magistrates Court (Brennan, 2016; GoFraudMe, 2016). In the second case in 2018, Lucy Wieland raised almost A$55,000 via GoFundMe, to assist with treatment related to ovarian cancer. She was charged with fraud in the Brisbane Magistrates Court in the same year. Shortly after she was charged, GoFundMe Australia introduced changes to its terms and conditions to protect supporters (Hinchliffe, 2018; Rafferty, 2018).

Both of these cases were exposed due to the public nature of crowdfunding. Other than that, as the Law Council of Australia notes, "there is little published case law that addresses crowdfunding and generally only in passing" (Law Council of Australia, 2019, p. 17).

For universities, though, the possibility of misrepresentation about what a crowdfunding campaign will do remains a potential risk to reputation.

DISCUSSION

Risks in University Crowdfunding in Australia

Fifteen risks have been identified through the interviews and the archival research. Table 2 lists the risks, the data that the risk was sourced from, and the types of crowdfunding campaigns that these risks pertain to.

These fifteen risks were categorized according to Stack et al's (2017) framework of crowdfunding risks.

Table 2. Summary of risks in university crowdfunding

Identified Risks	Source of Data	Type of Campaign	
Fraud	Stack et. al. and archives	Donations	Rewards
Theft of intellectual property	Stack et. al. and interviews	N/A	Rewards
Misrepresentation	Archives	N/A	Rewards
Breach of contract	Interviews	Donations	Rewards
Corruption	Stack et. al. and archives	Donations	Rewards
Breach of terms	Archives and Terms & Conditions	Donations	Rewards
False pledges	Interviews and archives	Donations	Rewards
Missing payments	Interviews	Donations	Rewards
University policies	Interviews and archives	Donations	Rewards
Conflict of interest	Archives	Donations	Rewards
Missed opportunity	Interviews	Donations	Rewards
Reputational risk	Interviews and archives	Donations	Rewards
Stalking & harassment	Interviews and archives	Donations	Rewards
Social norms	Interviews and archives	Donations	Rewards
Personal morality	Interviews	Donations	Rewards

Figure 3. Crowdfunding risks according to the actions of the actors
(Stack et al., 2017)

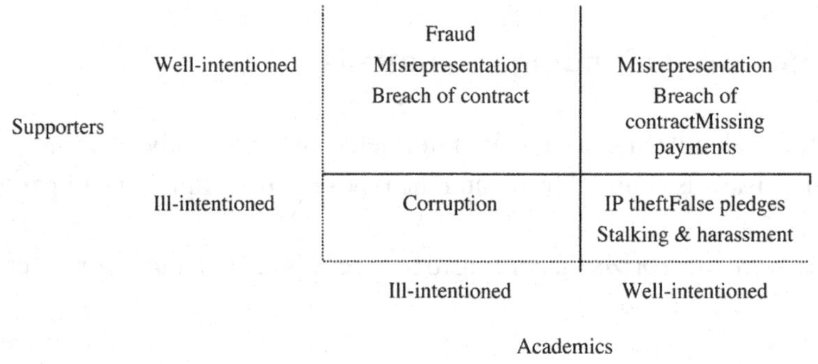

The framework accommodates seven of the identified risks:

1. **Fraud**: Ill-intentioned academics stealing the funds of well-intentioned supporters.
2. **Misrepresentation**: Ill-intentioned or well-intentioned academics leading well-intentioned supporters astray.
3. **Non-performance of Service (Breach of Contract):** Ill-intentioned or well-intentioned academics not fulfilling their contract with well-intentioned supporters.
4. **Corruption**: Ill-intentioned academics working with ill-intentioned supporters.

5. **Intellectual Property Theft**: Ill-intentioned supporters stealing the intellectual property of well-intentioned academics.
6. **Stalking and Harassment**: Ill-intentioned supporters targeting well-intentioned academics.
7. False pledges and missing payments.

Stack et al.'s (2017) framework fails to accommodate the remaining nine identified risks:

- Risks associated with the crowdfunding service who host the campaign or the payment services that facilitate the transactions.
  - **Breach of Terms and Conditions**: Ill-intentioned or well-intentioned academics not heeding the terms and conditions of the crowdfunding service or payment service.
- Risks associated with the wider society that the campaign sits within.
  - **Reputational Risk**: Well-intentioned academics being criticized by members of the public.
- Risks associated with the organization that the academic sits within.
  - **Missed Opportunity**: Organizations (or parts of organizations) forgoing the rewards of crowdfunding by banning crowdfunding by academics, or by not rewarding it.
- Risks related to university policies.
  - Well-intentioned academics finding that crowdfunding is difficult because of the implementation of existing policies by well-intentioned university administrators.
- Risks associated with conflict of interest
  - Ill-intentioned or well-intentioned academics conducting campaigns where it is unclear whether they are acting as private individuals or as employees of the university.
- Risks related to social norms
  - Well-intentioned academics finding that their expectations do not align with well-intentioned members of the public.
  - Well-intentioned supporters being surprised when they are contacted by well-intentioned administrators asking for further donations to the university.
- Risks related to personal morality
  - Academics who find that crowdfunding does not align with their own personal morality or beliefs.

These nine identified risks do not necessarily fit neatly within the framework because the framework sees crowdfunding as a two-sided market, with crowdfunders on one side and their supporters on the other. However, crowdfunding is more complex than that. Additional participants include the crowdfunding service, the payment service used for transactions and, in the case of academic crowdfunding, the university. They do represent important risks to be considered by a university if academics undertakes a crowdfunding campaign for academic research.

FRAMEWORK FOR MITIGATING AGAINST RISK

The following framework builds on Stack et.al.'s (2017) framework but includes the other risks identified from the interviews and literature review. Universities, like other organizations, can provide a great deal of assistance to their staff when they are undertaking crowdfunding campaigns. Part of that support includes assisting them to understand and ameliorate the risks associated with public campaigns for funding. In doing so, they will also reduce their own organizational risks.

These risks include legal risks related to fraud, misrepresentation, non-performance of service (breach of contract), as well as contractual issues relating to breach of terms and conditions. There are also issues that are best dealt with via organizational policies, such as corruption, reputational risks, public criticism and conflict of interest. There are also risks to staff such as public criticism, stalking and harassment.

Beyond that, there is the risk of missed opportunity, where universities discourage or do not allow their staff to undertake crowdfunding, and the risk that staff will be instructed to undertake crowdfunding against their better judgement or personal morality.

Organizations should consider how they might avoid, reduce or react to these risks before, during or after staff undertake crowdfunding campaigns.

Universities and other public organizations can mitigate most risks before crowdfunding campaigns are begun, and some risks after the campaign has ended. Since crowdfunding campaigns are relatively short (often four - six weeks), any mitigation strategies that take place during the campaign need to be clear and immediate. Table 3 provides a framework for dealing with the risks discussed in this chapter. It shows the mitigating actions that organizations such as universities can take before, during and after crowdfunding campaigns to ameliorate the risks discussed in this chapter of fraud; misrepresentation; non-performance of service (breach of contract); breach of terms and conditions; corruption; public criticism; conflict of interest; stalking and harassment; and missed opportunities due to 'no crowdfunding' rules and personal morality.

Table 3. Framework for ameliorating risk in organizational crowdfunding

	Mitigating Actions Before, During and After Campaigns		
Legal risks	Before	During	After
Fraud	Review of proposals	Cancel the campaign	Public statement
IP theft	Review of proposals		
Misrepresentation	Review of proposals	Cancel the campaign	Enforceable policies; public statement
Breach of contract	Review of proposals; education of staff	Cancel the campaign	Assistance to deliver Public statement
Corruption	Whistle-blower protection	Cancel the campaign	Enforceable policies
False pledges		Robust processes	Robust processes
Missing payments			Robust processes
Risks related to policies	Review of policies		Review of policies
Conflict of interest	Clear and enforceable policies on outside activity and conflict of interest		
Missed opportunity	Education of managers		Promotion of successful campaigns
Reputational risk	Education of staff	Support services	Public statement
Stalking & harassment	Education of staff	Support services	Support services
Social norms	Education of staff	Support services	Support services
Personal morality	Support services	Support services	Support services

Review of Proposals

A review process will help to protect against campaigns that are fraudulent, misleading or deceptive or in breach of the terms and conditions of the crowdfunding site or the payment facilities. A review will also help to identify campaigns that might have difficulty actually delivering what they promise. The review should happen before campaigns are launched, or as soon as the organization knows of a current campaign.

Both Deakin University and the University of Western Australia reviewed their projects (D. Verhoeven, personal communication, March, 4, 2016; Western Australian University, personal communication, July, 30, 2017) The primary purpose of the review process was to forestall projects or campaigners that may not be successful. However, the review process also provided an organizational perspective and an opportunity to block any proposal that the university felt was not bona fide.

Education of Staff

Because crowdfunding is a relatively new way of funding research, there is a reasonable amount of misunderstanding and confusion about it. Education and training will assist staff to understand the risks and responsibilities inherent in research crowdfunding campaigns.

In particular, crowdfunding campaigns open organizations up to the risk of public criticism, both at the individual and the institutional level. Criticism might take the form of critical comments towards campaigners or sustained campaigns by organized groups (e.g. anti-vaxxers; climate deniers; animal protectionists). Knowing the risks before they start can help staff to decide if they want to undertake crowdfunding campaigns.

Education can assist staff to understand the risks of harassment and stalking, as well as how to recognise it, what to do if they encounter it, and counselling and other remedies that are available if it happens.

Education could also be useful to help staff to understand what is expected of them in terms of successfully delivering what they have promised (non-performance of service).

Deakin University provided a peer-mentoring program, where staff that had already run successful crowdfunding campaigns were paired with staff that were undertaking campaigns for the first time (D. Verhoeven, personal communication, March, 4, 2016). While this was designed to assist staff to develop their campaigns, it also allowed experienced mentors to provide information about how to reduce risks and understand responsibilities.

Promotion of Successful Campaigns

One way to enthuse managers and staff regarding the possibilities of crowdfunding is to actively promote successful campaigns. This will help to demystify crowdfunding for those that are not familiar with it and encourage staff who may be interested in attempting a campaign. It will also send a clear signal that crowdfunding is an accepted practice at the university.

Enforceable Policies

Along with the education of staff, clear policies will help staff to understand their responsibilities, particularly around conflict of interest. Staff always have the option to run a campaign outside of their work. As public intellectuals, they can lend their support to campaigns being run by others. In this case, clear policies around outside activity and conflict of interest will assist staff to know when they should be acting as individuals, when they are acting as employees, and what the differences are between those two situations.

Clear policies can also help deal with misrepresentation, after the fact. Universities have procedures for dealing with issues related to research integrity. These policies and procedures can be used to deal with misrepresentation. Misconduct committees can determine whether staff were misguided or ill-intentioned when they misrepresented their research and recommend appropriate action.

These policies need to be enforceable. Where a staff member has egregiously breached university policies, they should be held accountable. There is an unfortunate tendency sometimes to take a lenient approach, backed by a non-disclosure clause, and allow offending staff to move institutions (or within an institution) with no discernible disadvantages (Oransky, 2018).

Review of Policies

Policies should be reviewed to ensure that they are fit for purpose. Policies that relate to issues such as stalking and harassment may have been developed in light of issues between students and staff. These may need to be revised to cope with stalking and harassment from members of the public. At regular intervals, policies can also be reviewed as new issues come to light. This is particularly important for a crowdfunding policy as it will be new and untested when first developed and may need to be reviewed and modified based on experience.

Robust Processes

Crowdfunding in universities requires robust processes to enact the policies. This is particularly true where accounting processes are concerned. Both academics and finance officers will need to understand what to do in the case of false pledges and missing payments. It should be clear who is responsible for following up on missing payments and what the processes are for doing so. Crowdfunding brings together a large number of relatively small contributions. Universities have robust processes for dealing with bad debtors, but may need to revise their processes to deal with a large number of relatively small missed payments.

Whistle-blower Protection

Some issues, such as corruption, are difficult to detect beforehand. Strong protective policies and procedures for whistle-blowers are probably the best way to encourage staff and students to come forward to report corrupt practices (Oransky, 2018).

Education of Managers

Because crowdfunding is an unconventional way to raise research funds, some managers may be opposed to it. This risks the university to losing the opportunity to gain the benefits (both monetary and intangible) that crowdfunding affords. Some discussion with, and education of, managers may be required before they will be willing to allow staff to undertake crowdfunding campaigns.

Support Services

In many instances, universities have programs in place to support staff for personal or professional reasons. Counselling services and legal advice should be available to staff if they are being publicly vilified, stalked or otherwise harassed. Staff should also feel supported if they choose not to undertake a campaign or undertake a campaign in a manner that fits within their personal ethical boundaries.

Assistance to Deliver

One of the simplest ways for an otherwise successful campaign to disappoint people is by failing to deliver what was promised. This may be despite the best efforts of the researchers, as was the case with the glowing plants campaign (Evans, n.d.). Disappointment might be as simple as an academic not sending out promised 'thank you' rewards, like coffee cups or tee-shirts. Often it may be because campaigners have not kept in communication with their supporters after the campaign has ended, even though the academic promised to do so.

In all cases, universities can assist crowdfunding academics to deliver on what they have promised. Just as with other grants and contracts, successful crowdfunding campaigns should go through a post-award service that identifies what the implied contract is with the supporters of the campaign, a timeline for deliverables and how funds should be disbursed. University post-award systems are effective at tracking research funds and associated activities, and they can provide academics with prompts that can help to keep a project on track.

For reward-based campaigns like the glowing plants campaign, this can come through helping the academics to communicate with their supporters, and to explain why research takes a long time and entails the risks that it does.

Where there is a significant requirement for fulfillment services, it might entail providing assistance and advice through the university mail service or other areas of the university that have expertise in fulfillment services.

For almost all campaigns, assistance from the communications or advancement department can help academics understand how to effectively keep in touch with their supporters over an extended period of time.

Cancel the Campaign

Review processes will not always be able to identify proposals that are fraudulent or at risk of misrepresentation. Most review processes will be undertaken by administrators or academics who are not experts in the domain of the campaign leader. As such, fraudulent or misrepresentation proposals may not be obvious until they are made public and can be scrutinised by domain experts. Campaigns that are designed to foster corrupt practices will be deliberately hidden from university administrators. The university should have the power to take down (withdraw) fraudulent and corrupt campaigns immediately. They should also have the power to cancel campaigns that are shown to be in breach of the terms and conditions of the crowdfunding service or the associated payment service.

Projects that are at risk of misrepresentation are more difficult to assess. All research entails risk, and academics need to be given a chance to try new approaches. Peer review processes often favour orthodox approaches at the expense of unorthodox ideas. One of the advantages of crowdfunding is that it creates new experimental spaces. As such, if there is significant criticism from experts, the crowdfunder should be given the opportunity to review that criticism and decide whether to take down the campaign.

Public Statement

In many cases, after a campaign is finished (either because it has been cancelled or run its course), a clear public statement by the campaigner and the university will often help to reduce public criticism or misunderstanding. Where a campaign has been cancelled due to fraud, misrepresentation or breech of terms and conditions, a message that plainly states what went wrong, what remedial action was taken, and what steps have been taken to prevent it happening again will help to restore confidence.

Where there has been significant public criticism and controversy over a project, a clear statement of principles and support of staff will help to make it clear where the university stands and help staff to understand that their organization supports them.

FURTHER RESEARCH DIRECTIONS

This chapter sits within a PhD project to examine whether crowdfunding can be a sustainable research funding mechanism for Australian universities. The main contribution of this chapter is the framework for ameliorating risks before, during and after crowdfunding campaigns. As such, the main avenue for further research would be testing the robustness of the framework and to refine it. It would also be worthwhile seeking to apply the framework to organizations other than universities.

In addition to this, further research could be undertaken to extend Stack et al.'s (2017) framework to include additional actors such as research services, payment services and the universities.

During the development of this chapter, the author undertook a close reading of the changes to the terms and conditions of the Kickstarter crowdfunding platform (O'Donnell, 2019). This data, while fascinating, has only been used to describe the change of rules relating to gene-modification. Further analysis would be useful to understand how crowdfunding services have responded to emerging risks and undesirable behavior by modifying their terms and conditions.

CONCLUSION

Based on a literature review interviews with university academics and administrators, archival research and a close examination of the terms and conditions of a crowdfunding platform, this chapter has identified fifteen risks that could result from academics undertaking crowdfunding at Australian universities.

These risks were categorized according to the Stack et al (2017) framework for evaluating risks in crowdfunding campaigns. A significant number of risks were found to fall outside of the framework, as the framework assumed crowdfunding was a two-sided market involving only the crowdfunder and their supporters. Risks that fell outside of the framework included risks related to other participants, such as the university, the crowdfunding service and the payment services that facilitate the crowdfunding transactions.

A new framework was developed to categorize the suggested ways of responding to these risks. This framework provides solutions that can be implemented before crowdfunding campaigns begin, during crowdfunding campaigns and after crowdfunding campaigns are concluded. These solutions will not eliminate the risks entirely. Nor will they provide a complete solution when the risks result in harm to an individual or an organization. They will, however, help to ameliorate the risks of crowdfunding in Australian universities.

This framework is provided so that academics, administrators, supporters, universities, crowdfunding services and regulators have a better understanding of both the risks involved and ways to reduce the effect of these risks. Academics undertaking crowdfunding campaigns can use the framework to improve the planning of their campaigns. While Australian universities that are providing support to researchers can use this framework as a checklist to improve their support for crowdfunding of academic research. Australian universities that are considering developing policies around crowdfunding can also use this framework to understand these risks and guard against them.

REFERENCES

Arenas, A., Goh, J. M., & Podar, M. (2015). A work-systems approach to classifying risks in crowdfunding platforms: An exploratory analysis. In *Twenty-First Americas Conference on Information Systems (AMCIS 2015) Proceedings*. Fajardo, Puerto Rico: US Association for Information Systems.

Australian Charities and Not-for-profits Commission Act (2012) (Cth).

Belleflamme, P., Lambert, T., & Schwienbacher, A. (2013). Crowdfunding: Tapping the right crowd. *Journal of Business Venturing, 29*(5), 585–609. doi:10.1016/j.jbusvent.2013.07.003

Brennan, R. (2016, June 13). Sick truth behind this bloke's GoFundMe appeal. *Courier-Mail*. Retrieved from https://www.couriermail.com.au/news/queensland/crime-and-justice/brisbane-man-diakko-santaali-guilty-of-fraud-after-gofundme-page-appeal/news-story/6fe077e6e3d6ec33b4f2b78442c57b0b

Brewster, S. (2017, April 19). Inside the glowing-plant startup that just gave up its quest. *Wired*. Retrieved from https://www.wired.com/story/inside-the-glowing-plant-startup-that-just-gave-up-its-quest/

Brook, L. (2018). Evidencing impact from art research: Analysis of impact case studies from the REF 2014. *The Journal of Arts Management, Law, and Society, 48*(1), 57–69. doi:10.1080/10632921.2017.1386148

Brooks, M., McMillan, C., & Surya Darma, I. G. M. (2011, December 13). Subak with art festival. *Pozible* [Crowdfunding platform]. Retrieved from https://pozible.com/project/4080

Byrnes, J. E. K. (2012, December 15). SciFund in 3 Rounds. *#SciFund Challenge*. Retrieved from https://scifundchallenge.org/2012/12/15/scifund-in-3-rounds/

Callaway, E. (2013). Glowing plants spark debate. *NATNews, 498*(7452), 15. doi:10.1038/498015a PMID:23739402

Chubb, J., & Reed, M. S. (2018). The politics of research impact: Academic perceptions of the implications for research funding, motivation and quality. *British Politics, 13*(3), 295–311. doi:10.105741293-018-0077-9

Chubb, J., & Watermeyer, R. (2016). Artifice or integrity in the marketization of research impact? Investigating the moral economy of (pathways to) impact statements within research funding proposals in the UK and Australia. *Studies in Higher Education*, *42*(12), 2360–2372. doi:10.1080/03075079.2016.1144182

Commonwealth of Australia. (2017). *Assessing the engagement and impact of university research*. National Innovation and Science Agenda. Retrieved from https://www.innovation.gov.au/page/measuring-impact-and-engagement-university-research

Corporations Amendment (Crowd-sourced Funding) Act (2017) (Cth).

Corporations Amendment (Crowd-sourced Funding for Proprietary Companies) Act (2018) (Cth).

CSIRO. (2015). *Impact evaluation guide*. Retrieved from https://www.csiro.au/impact

Cui, Y., & Zeng, C. (2016). *Regulation of Equity Crowdfunding in China. DEStech Transactions on Economics*. Business and Management. doi:10.12783/dtem/icem2016/4035

Cumming, D. J., Hornuf, L., Karami, M., & Schweizer, D. (2016). *Disentangling crowdfunding from fraud-funding*. Munich, Germany: Max Planck Institute for Innovation & Competition. doi:10.2139srn.2828919

Cumming, D. J., Leboeuf, G., & Schwienbacher, A. (2015). *Crowdfunding models: Keep-It-All vs. All-Or-Nothing*. Social Science Research Network. Retrieved from https://papers.ssrn.com/abstract=2447567

Department of Education and Training. (2017). *2018 Higher Education Research Data Collection: Specifications for the collection of 2017 data*. Retrieved from https://docs.education.gov.au/node/44986

Dzieza, J. (2013, August 18). *Plants that glow in the dark spark heated debate*. Retrieved from https://www.thedailybeast.com/articles/2013/08/18/plants-that-glow-in-the-dark-spark-heated-debate

English, R. (2014). Rent-a-crowd? Crowdfunding academic research. *First Monday*, *19*(1). doi:10.5210/fm.v19i1.4818

Evans, A. (n.d.). Glowing plants: Natural lighting with no electricity [Crowdfunding campaign]. *Kickstarter*. Retrieved from https://www.kickstarter.com/projects/antonyevans/glowing-plants-natural-lighting-with-no-electricity

Evans, M. C., & Cvitanovic, C. (2018). An introduction to achieving policy impact for early career researchers. *Palgrave Communications*, *4*(1), 88. doi:10.105741599-018-0144-2

Faulkes, Z. (2012, December 15). SciFund in 3 rounds, part 2: Box plot fever. *#SciFund Challenge*. Retrieved from https://scifundchallenge.org/2012/12/15/scifund-in-3-rounds-part-2-box-plot-fever/

Faulkes, Z. (2014, March 18). #SciFund round 4 analysis. *#SciFund Challenge*. Retrieved from https://scifundchallenge.org/2014/03/18/scifund-round-4-analysis/

Federal Trade Commission. (2019, May 6). *FTC charges operator of crowdfunding scheme*. Federal Trade Commission. Retrieved from https://www.ftc.gov/news-events/press-releases/2019/05/ftc-charges-operator-crowdfunding-scheme

Franzen, C. (2013, August 7). Kickstarter says it consulted scientists before banning genetically-modified organisms. *The Verge*. Retrieved from https://www.theverge.com/2013/8/7/4595876/kickstarter-founder-yancey-strickler-explains-ban-GMOs

Ganatra, J. H. (2015). When a Kickstarter stops: Exploring failures and regulatory frameworks for the rewards-based crowdfunding industry. *Rutgers University Law Review, 68*, 1425–1472.

Gerber, E. M., & Hui, J. (2013). Crowdfunding: Motivations and Deterrents for Participation. *ACM Transactions* on *Computer Human Interaction, 20*(6), 34:1–34:32. doi:10.1145/2530540

Gill, J. (2014, December 3). Crowd-funded science: Thoughts after 185 people gave us $10,733 for research. *The Contemplative Mammoth*. Retrieved from https://contemplativemammoth.com/2014/12/03/crowd-funded-science-thoughts-after-185-people-gave-us-10733-for-research/

GoFraudMe. (2016, June 13). Australian man pleads guilty to gofundme fraud, insists he really does have cancer. *GoFraudMe*. Retrieved from http://gofraudme.com/australian-man-pleads-guilty-gofundme-fraud-insists-really-cancer/

Guest, G., Bunce, A., & Johnson, L. (2006). How many interviews are enough?: An experiment with data saturation and variability. *Field Methods, 18*(1), 59–82. doi:10.1177/1525822X05279903

Harms, M. (2007). *What drives motivation to participate financially in a crowdfunding Community?* (Masters Thesis). Vrije Universitaet Amsterdam. Retrieved from https://www.ssrn.com/abstract=2269242

Heberling, A. (2013a, November 7). I feel like it's safe to discuss this publicly now. *Alexheberling*. Retrieved from https://alexheberling.tumblr.com/post/66288651102

Heberling, A. (2013b, November 8). Report: Kickstarter scammer 'Encik Farhan'—updated - the beat. *Alexheberling*. Retrieved from https://alexheberling.tumblr.com/post/66385162129

Heberling, A. (2018, May 19). We'll help resolve payment-card disputes. *Alexheberling*. Retrieved from https://alexheberling.tumblr.com/post/174069323037

Hinchliffe, J. (2018, October 25). GoFundMe changes policy to protect donors from sham causes. *ABC News*. Retrieved from https://www.abc.net.au/news/2018-10-25/gofundme-policy-changes-protect-donors-from-shams/10428180

Hornuf, L., & Schwienbacher, A. (2017). Should securities regulation promote equity crowdfunding? *Small Business Economics, 49*(3), 579–593. doi:10.100711187-017-9839-9

Hui, J. S., & Gerber, E. M. (2015). Crowdfunding science: Sharing Research with an extended audience. In *Proceedings of the 18th ACM Conference on Computer Supported Cooperative Work & Social Computing*. New York, NY: Association for Computing Machinery. 10.1145/2675133.2675188

Ikkatai, Y., McKay, E., & Yokoyama, H. M. (2018). Science created by crowds: A case study of science crowdfunding in Japan. *Journal of Science Communication, 17*(3), A06. doi:10.22323/2.17030206

Jones, M. M., Castle-Clarke, S., Manville, C., Gunashekar, S., & Grant, J. (2013). *Assessing research impact: An international review of the excellence in innovation for Australia trial* [Commissioned research]. Santa Monica, CA: RAND Corporation. doi:10.7249/RR278

Kappel, T. (2009). Ex ante crowdfunding and the recording industry: A model for the U.S. *Loyola of Los Angeles Entertainment Law Review, 29*(3), 375–385.

Kickstarter. (2010, December 3). *Community guidelines*. Retrieved from https://web.archive.org/web/20101203214618/http://www.kickstarter.com/help/guidelines

Kickstarter. (n.d.). Prohibited items. *Kickstarter*. Retrieved from https://www.kickstarter.com/rules/prohibited

Krippendorff, K. (2018). *Content analysis: An introduction to its methodology*. Thousand Oaks, CA: Sage Publications.

Law Council of Australia. (2019). *Crowdfunding: Guidance for Australian legal practitioners*. Retrieved from https://www.lawcouncil.asn.au/policy-agenda/regulation-of-the-profession-and-ethics/crowdfunding-guidance-for-australian-legal-practitioners

Mann, T., & Blunden, A. (Eds.). (2010). *Australian law dictionary* (1st ed.). Oxford, UK: Oxford University Press. doi:10.1093/acref/9780195557558.001.0001

Matthew, A. F. (2019). *The conceptual legitimacy of support for risk-taking, entrepreneurship and innovation in Australian corporate law: A theoretical examination* (PhD). Queensland University of Technology. doi:10.5204/thesis.eprints.132567

McGuffin, C., Wilks, N., Tomlinson, V., Anderson, B., & Griswold, E. (2011, October 11). 56 inch circus [Crowdfunding campaign]. *Pozible*. Retrieved from https://www.pozible.com/project/1141

Monahan, D. (2016a). Ibackpack 2.0—4g mifi, hitech batteries—smart cables [Crowdfunding campaign]. *Kickstarter*. Retrieved from https://www.kickstarter.com/projects/ibackpack/ibackpack-20-3g-4g-mi-fi-bulletproof-bluetooth-aud

Monahan, D. (2016b). Ibackpack—wifi, ultra-thin & powerful batteries [Crowdfunding campaign]. *Indiegogo*. Retrieved from https://www.indiegogo.com/projects/1395593

Moore, C. (2013, June 8). Was it really only 30 days? *Cryptocommonicon*. Retrieved from https://cryptocommonicon.wordpress.com/2013/06/08/was-it-really-only-30-days/

Neuman, E. (2018, September 20). First class action filed in the world of crowdfunding (The Marker). *Hamburger Evron & Co*. Retrieved from http://www.evronlaw.com/en/first-class-action-filed-world-crowdfunding-marker/

O'Donnell, J. (2019). *Kickstarter rule changes over time* [Data set]. Figshare. doi:10.6084/m9.figshare.8942738

Oransky, A. I. (2018, July 30). How institutions gaslight whistleblowers—And what can be done. *Retraction Watch*. Retrieved from https://retractionwatch.com/2018/07/30/how-institutions-gaslight-whistleblowers-and-what-can-be-done/

Palmer, S., & Verhoeven, D. (2016). Crowdfunding Academic Researchers: The Importance of Academic Social Media Profiles. In C. Bernadas & D. Minchella (Eds.), *ECSM2016-Proceedings of the 3rd European Conference on Social Media* (pp. 291–299). Sonning Common, UK: Academic Conferences and Publishing International Limited.

Penfield, T., Baker, M. J., Scoble, R., & Wykes, M. C. (2014). Assessment, evaluations, and definitions of research impact: A review. *Research Evaluation*, 23(1), 21–32. doi:10.1093/reseval/rvt021

Pomerantz, J., & Peek, R. (2016). Fifty shades of open. *First Monday*, 21(5). doi:10.5210/fm.v21i5.6360

Rafferty, S. (2018, October 18). Woman 'faked' ovarian cancer to collect $55k in donations, court told. *ABC News*. Retrieved from https://www.abc.net.au/news/2018-10-18/lu-wieland-accused-of-faking-stage-five-ovarian-cancer/10391034

Regalado, A. (2016, July 15). Why the promise of a plant that glows has left backers in the dark. *MIT Technology Review*. Retrieved from https://www.technologyreview.com/s/601884/why-kickstarters-glowing-plant-left-backers-in-the-dark/

Rowley, J. (2002). Using case studies in research. *Management Research News*, 25(1), 16–27. doi:10.1108/01409170210782990

Rowley, J. (2012). Conducting research interviews. *Management Research Review*, 35(3/4), 260–271. doi:10.1108/01409171211210154

Schwienbacher, A. (2017). Entrepreneurial risk-taking in crowdfunding campaigns. *Small Business Economics*, 51(4), 843–859. doi:10.100711187-017-9965-4

Sherer, S. A., & Alter, S. (2004). Information systems risks and risk factors: Are they mostly about information systems? *Communications of the Association for Information Systems*, 14(1). doi:10.17705/1CAIS.01402

Stack, P., Feller, J., O'Reilly, P., Gleasure, R., Li, S., & Cristoforo, J. (2017). Managing risk in business centric crowdfunding platforms. In *Proceedings of the 13th International Symposium on Open Collaboration*, Galway, Ireland: Association for Computing Machinery. 10.1145/3125433.3125460

Strickler, Y., Chen, P., & Adler, C. (2012, September 21). Kickstarter is not a store. *Kickstarter Blog*. Retrieved from https://www.kickstarter.com/blog/kickstarter-is-not-a-store

Surowiecki, J. (2005). *The wisdom of crowds: Why the many are smarter than the few* (reprint ed.). New York, NY: Anchor.

Swords, J. (2018). Interpenetration and intermediation of crowd-patronage platforms. *Information, Communication & Society*.

Teytelman, L. (2015a, March 24). Calibrating crowdfunding expectations. *Yes, Another Science Blog*. Retrieved from http://anothersb.blogspot.com.au/2015/03/calibrating-crowdfunding-expectations.html

Teytelman, L. (2015b, March 30). Biomedical funding is broken; crowdfunding is not the fix. *Yes, Another Science Blog*. Retrieved from http://anothersb.blogspot.com.au/2015/03/biomedical-funding-is-broken.html

Thomson, M. (2014, May 18). Unto the valley of death...of crowd funding science. *Dr Mel Thomson*. Retrieved from https://drmelthomson.wordpress.com/2014/05/18/unto-the-valley-of-death-of-crowd-funding-science/

Verhoeven, D., Palmer, S., Seitzinger, J., & Randall, M. (n.d.). *Research my world: Crowdfunding research pilot project evalutation*. Retrieved from https://www.deakin.edu.au/research/documents/research-my-world.pdf

Vitale, M. (2013). Crowdfunding: Recent international developments and its compatibility with Australia's existing regulatory framework. *Journal of Banking and Finance Law and Practice*, *24*(4), 300–310. doi:10.2139srn.2324573

Wheat, R. E., Wang, Y., Byrnes, J. E., & Ranganathan, J. (2013). Raising money for scientific research through crowdfunding. *Trends in Ecology & Evolution*, *28*(2), 71–72. doi:10.1016/j.tree.2012.11.001 PMID:23219380

ADDITIONAL READING

Budge, K., Lemon, N., & McPherson, M. (2016). Academics who tweet: "Messy" identities in academia. *Journal of Applied Research in Higher Education*, *8*(2), 210–221. doi:10.1108/JARHE-11-2014-0114

Byrnes, J. E. K., Ranganathan, J., Walker, B. L. E., & Faulkes, Z. (2014). To crowdfund research, scientists must build an audience for their work. *PLoS One*, *9*(12), e110329. doi:10.1371/journal.pone.0110329 PMID:25494306

Ferlie, E., Fitzgerald, L., Wood, M., & Hawkins, C. (2005). The Nonspread of innovations: The mediating role of professionals. *Academy of Management Journal*, *48*(1), 117–134. doi:10.5465/amj.2005.15993150

Kolenda, N. (2016). *The psychology of crowdfunding*. Retrieved from https://www.nickkolenda.com/pdf/crowdfunding-psychology.pdf

Lemon, N., McPherson, M., & Budge, K. (2015). Academics doing it differently: Wooing, hooking up and spinning stories. *Journal of Perspectives in Applied Academic Practice*, *3*(2). doi:10.14297/jpaap.v3i2.129

McPherson, M., Budge, K., & Lemon, N. (2015). New practices in doing academic development: Twitter as an informal learning space. *The International Journal for Academic Development*, *20*(2), 126–136. doi:10.1080/1360144X.2015.1029485

Munro-Smith, N., & Downs, J. (2011). Managing change in conservative institutions: Implementing and sustaining innovative educational design in university level courses. *International Journal of Learning*, *17*(11), 141–151. doi:10.18848/1447-9494/CGP/v17i11/47329

Palmer, A. (2014). *The art of asking: Or, how I learned to stop worrying and let people help*. Retrieved from https://amandapalmer.net/theartofasking/

Palmer, S., & Verhoeven, D. (2016). Crowdfunding academic researchers: The importance of academic social media profiles. In *ECSM2016-Proceedings of the 3rd European Conference on Social Media*. Caen, France: Academic Conferences and Publishing International Limited.

Verhoeven, D., & Palmer, S. (2015). Because it takes a village to fund the answers: Crowdfunding university research. In L. Bennett, B. Chin, & B. Jones (Eds.), *Crowdfunding the future - media industries, ethics, and digital society* (pp. 133–156). New York, NY: Peter Lang Publishing Inc.

KEY TERMS AND DEFINITIONS

Breach of Contract: Failure to perform a contract, either in whole or in part (Mann & Blunden, 2010).

Breach of Duty of Care: Failure to avoid or alleviate harm to others. The level of care required is measure by the standard of care (Mann & Blunden, 2010).

Crowdfunder: Person or group of people who conduct a crowdfunding campaign to raise funds.

Crowdfunding: Raising funds from a group of people for a project or cause, typically using the internet (Harms, 2007; Kappel, 2009).

Crowdfunding Campaign: The period when a crowdfunder is actively seeking funding.

Crowdfunding Service: Organisations that facilitate crowdfunding via the internet. Their websites are often referred to as Crowdfunding Platforms.

Fraud: Dishonestly gaining advantage (Mann & Blunden, 2010).

Misrepresentation: Falsehoods that induce someone to enter into a contract. Misrepresentation may be fraudulent when it is intentional, innocent when it is unintentional and negligent when it is unintentional but there is a duty of care (Mann & Blunden, 2010).

Morality: Prescriptions regarding right and wrong behaviour (Mann & Blunden, 2010).

Performance: Satisfactorily completing the terms of a contract. By inference, non-performance is not satisfactorily completing the terms (Mann & Blunden, 2010).

Public Good: Things that are available to all (nobody can be excluded) and cannot be used up (use by one does not reduce the use of another) (Mann & Blunden, 2010).

Risk: The measure of the chance of harm occurring (Mann & Blunden, 2010).

Social Norms: Cultural expectations governing the behaviour of people (Mann & Blunden, 2010).

Standard of Care: The benchmark for a person to avoid or alleviate the risk of harming others (Mann & Blunden, 2010).

Supporters: People who provide funds to a crowdfunding campaign. Also referred to as Backers. Supporters who receive a tax deduction for their contribution may be called Donors.

Chapter 4
Reforming Australia's Safe Harbour for Internet Intermediaries:
A Comparison of Horizontal Immunity – Australia and the USA

Sam Alexander

Swinburne Law School, Australia

ABSTRACT

The internet safe harbour created by section 230 of the Communications Decency Act has been described as one of the laws that built Silicon Valley. Australia does not have an equivalent law. The closest available is clause 91(1) of schedule 5 of the Broadcasting Services Act 1992 (Cth) (BSA Immunity), a law described by the NSW Department of Justice as of limited 'utility'. The purpose of this chapter is to conduct a comparative analysis of section 230 and the BSA Immunity. On the one hand, the chapter seeks to outline how section 230 has helped develop some of the world's most successful platforms while, on the other hand, the chapter argues that the BSA Immunity's lack of utility has had a 'chilling effect' on internet businesses in Australia. Following this comparison, the chapter discusses potential reforms to the BSA Immunity, which could assist in the development of future Australian start-ups.

INTRODUCTION

Generally, Google offers the same search engine services to customers in Australia and the United States. However, unfavourable results from Google's search engine have given rise to different outcomes under each countries' legal systems. For example, in *Trkulja v Google* (2018, [35]), the High Court of Australia unanimously held that Google's search engine results "had the capacity to convey one or more of the defamatory imputations alleged", while in similar circumstances, the United States Court of Appeals for the Tenth Circuit held that "Google [could not] be held liable for search results that yield content created

DOI: 10.4018/978-1-7998-3130-3.ch004

by a third party" (*Getachew v Google Inc.*, 2012, [8]). The reason for these different outcomes was that §. 230 of the *Communications Decency Act* (47 U.S.C. § 230 (1996)) (Section 230) protected Google from liability in the United States, while in Australia, Google was unable to rely on the 'safe harbour laws' in cl. 91, sch. 5 of the *Broadcasting Services Act 1992* (Cth) (BSA Immunity) due to its limitations.

Considering the above example, the purpose of this chapter is to compare and develop an understanding of the differences between the two abovementioned immunities — specifically, the different impacts Section 230 and the BSA Immunity have from a business and economic perspective. The chapter considers that Section 230 is one of the laws that built Silicon Valley (Chander, 2014) and, in turn, has been key to the financial success of the internet and internet businesses. On the other hand, the BSA Immunity has been of "limited utility" (NSW Department of Justice, 2018, p. 34) and due to its lack of practical use it has had a 'chilling effect' on internet businesses in Australia. The chapter also seeks to understand the potential reforms that could be adopted in Australia to address the BSA Immunity's flaws and where research in relation to this topic should focus going forward.

The chapter is broken into four parts. Part I considers the background to Section 230 and the BSA Immunity, including their history and technical features. Part II discusses the practical impact of Section 230 and the BSA Immunity from a business and economic perspective. Part III outlines reforms that could be made to the BSA Immunity to address its faults and for it to be of greater utility. Part IV outlines areas of further research and academic consideration.

BACKGROUND

To begin, this chapter will provide an overview of the background to Section 230 and the BSA Immunity. This includes a consideration of the text of each piece of legislation, its underlying purposes, history and relevant case law key to its interpretation.

The Rationale and History Behind Section 230

At a high level, Section 230 holds that websites and other online services are not liable for various actions that are caused by third-party content (Goldman, 2019a). However, despite its well-accepted application today, commentators are not entirely in agreement over the exact reasons and purposes behind Section 230. For example, Lukmire (2010) contends Section 230 was drafted with the sole intention of shielding children from objectionable content by encouraging online services to self-regulate. Although other commentators (Goldman, 2019a; Kosseff, 2019; Sheridan, 1997) agree that encouraging companies to develop their own moderation practices was a factor, they contend that another key factor was to inspire innovation and the development of the internet and internet businesses.

Under this latter understanding, Section 230 arose as a response to certain common law (and torts jurisprudence in particular) being deemed ill-suited to the internet age (Goldman, 2019a). Specifically, in passing Section 230 Congress sought to overrule the New York Supreme Court decision of *Stratton Oakmont Inc. v Prodigy Services Co.* (1995) (Stratton Oakmont) and its impact on online services (Ziniti, 2008). Broadly, under United States' common law, an entity's liability for third-party content is determined based on the level of control the entity can exercise over the content (Ehrlich, 2002). Different standards exist for 'publishers', 'distributors' and 'common carriers'.[1] In Stratton Oakmont, the Court held that Prodigy was a publisher and therefore was liable for the third-party content posted on its website, despite a lack of contribution to, or knowledge of, the posts (Ziniti, 2008). The Court reasoned that, as Prodigy held itself out as a "family-oriented computer network" and, in turn, as a "service exercising editorial control", it should bear heightened responsibility for third-party content (Lukmire, 2010, p. 378).

The Stratton Oakmont decision was considered problematic and unfair by some in Congress (Ziniti, 2008). In fact, one of Section 230's original drafters (Senator Ron Wyden) is quoted as saying he considered Stratton Oakmont "crazy" (Kosseff, 2019, p. 60). More specifically, there was concern Stratton Oakmont would give rise to what has been described as the "moderator's dilemma" (Goldman, 2019a, p. 3). Broadly, the 'moderator's dilemma' is where an internet intermediary has a choice between two approaches (Goldman, 2019a):

- actively moderate and remove potentially harmful content, which would risk accepting legal responsibility for it.

or

- take no action on the basis this may mean the intermediary does not have editorial control and so has a lower risk of legal liability.

As Senator Wyden explained some years after the passing of Section 230, the original drafters "were interested in allowing the platforms to take down some content that they believe should [not] be on their site without being held liable for all the content on the site, so that you could really encourage responsible behaviour" (Kosseff, 2019, p. 60).

However, as alluded to above, encouraging responsible behaviour was only one factor, another was supporting the development of the internet and internet businesses. Senator Wyden was quoted as saying that the drafters were also "interested in protecting the platforms from being held liable for the content posted on their sites and being sued out of existence" (Kosseff, 2019, p. 60). This intention is most clearly articulated in the words of Section 230 itself, which is laid out in a manner that includes the findings and policy underpinning the law. These policy intentions specifically state that Section 230 seeks "to promote the continued development of the Internet and other interactive computer services and other interactive media" (*Communications Decency Act* 47 U.S.C. §. 230(b)(1) (1996)) and "to preserve the vibrant and competitive free market that presently exists for the internet and other interactive computer services, unfettered by [f]ederal or [s]tate regulation" (*Communications Decency Act* 47 U.S.C. §. 230(b)(2) (1996)).

The Text and Interpretation of Section 230

After outlining the policy and findings, Section 230 then includes its two key operative provisions. The first provision, §. 230(c)(1), holds that "no provider or user of an interactive computer service shall be treated as the publisher or speaker of any information provided by another information content provider". Beginning with the seminal case of *Zeran v America Online Inc.* (1997), courts have interpreted this provision to have broad and expansive application (Goldman, 2017; Klonick, 2018). In fact, this provision has been interpreted by the courts as meaning that, with few exceptions,[2] websites and online service providers are not liable under various causes of action for user content, including comments, picture and videos (Kosseff, 2019). For example, the Supreme Court of California in *Barrett v Rosenthal* (2006, p.

34) noted that "[§] 230 has been interpreted literally. It does not permit [i]nternet service providers or users to be sued as 'distributors', nor does it expose 'active users' to liability".

There are three elements to §. 230(c)(1) (Goldman, 2019a; Burshtein, 2017) that must be satisfied:

1. The defendant must be a provider or user of an interactive computer service.
2. The action must treat the defendant as the publisher or speaker of the unlawful content.
3. The content, the subject of the dispute, must have been provided by another information content provider.

It is important to note that for each of these elements, courts have adopted a broad interpretation. In terms of the first element, courts have interpreted 'provider' and 'user' of an interactive computer service to cover almost all services on the internet and their customers (Ballon, 2017; Goldman, 2019a), while, in regards to the requirement of 'publisher or speaker', courts have extended the requirement to cover numerous causes of action, where the plaintiff seeks to hold the defendant responsible for third-party content, regardless of whether 'publisher or speaker' is an element of the originating claim (Ballon, 2017; Goldman, 2019a). For example, in *Zeran v America Online Inc.* (1997, p. 330) it was noted that Section 230 "creates a federal immunity to any cause of action that would make service providers liable for information originating with a third-party user of the service".

The second operative provision is §. 230(c)(2). At a high level, §. 230(c)(2) immunises activities related to online content filtering (Goldman, 2012). Specifically, §. 230(c)(2)(A) immunises 'good faith' filtering decisions, while §. 230(c)(2)(B) immunises the provision of the 'technical' means to filter to a third party. Due to the 'good faith' element required within § 230(c)(2), it is not relied on as commonly as §. 230(c)(1), which does not require this immunity hurdle (Ardia, 2010; Goldman, 2012). Accordingly, when a reference is made to Section 230 in this chapter, it generally means § 230(c)(1).

Importantly, it should be noted that there are statutory exceptions to Section 230. These are:

- criminal law
- intellectual property law
- the *Electronic Communications Privacy Act* (18 U.S.C. §§ 2510-2523 (1986))
- state laws to the extent that the laws are 'consistent' with Section 230
- amendments recently added by the *Allow States and Victims to Fight Online Sex Trafficking Act* (FOSTA) (47 U.S.C. § 230(e) (1996)).

BSA Immunity

Before delving into the BSA Immunity, it is important to note that the United States stands alone with Section 230. No other country has adopted a safe harbour that provides such broad protection for internet intermediaries (Goldman, 2019a). Whilst, it is possible Canada and Mexico may adopt similar safe harbours in the future, due to the operation of art.19.17 of the *United States-Mexico-Canada Agreement* (Office of the United States Trade Representatives, 2018), which requires treaty parties to adopt internet immunity laws similar to Section 230, at the time of writing this has not yet occurred. As such, at this point in time, other counties either have more limited immunity or impose liability on internet intermediaries. For example, Japan and the European Union do not have immunities as broad as Section 230 and South Korea can impose liability on intermediaries (Chander, 2014). There is a similar situation in

China and Hong Kong (Ong, 2013). The Australian approach discussed below is largely representative of a limited immunity approach and accordingly provides a stark contrast to the United States approach.

Broadly, cl. 91(1) of sch. 5 of the *Broadcasting Services Act 1992* (Cth) (BSA Immunity) provides "horizontal"[3] immunity for "internet content hosts" and "internet service providers" from liability under any rule of common law, equity or any state or territory statute where certain conditions are met (Turner, 2014, p. 56). Specifically, the BSA Immunity protects an entity from "liability (whether criminal or civil)" for carrying or hosting internet content where the entity is not "aware of the nature of the internet content" or the effect of the law is to require the entity to "to monitor, make inquiries about, or keep records of, internet content hosted by the host" or "carried by the provider" (*Broadcasting Services Act 1992* (Cth), cl. 91(1)).

Both internet content hosts (ICH) and internet service providers (ISP) are defined in the BSA Immunity. An ICH is "a person who hosts internet content in Australia, or who proposes to host internet content in Australia" and internet content is also defined as (BSA Immunity, sch. 5, cl. 3):

information that:
    (a) is kept on a data storage device; and
    (b) is accessed, or available for access, using an internet carriage service;
but does not include:
    (c) ordinary email; or
    (d) information that is transmitted in the form of a broadcasting service.

An ISP is a person who supplies, or proposes to supply, an internet carriage service (ICS) to the public (*Broadcasting Services Act 1992* (Cth), sch. 5, cl. 8). An ICS is also defined as a "carriage service that enables end-users to access the internet" (*Broadcasting Services Act 1992* (Cth), sch. 5, cl. 3). In other words, an ISP is an entity that provides internet access. As it will be outlined more substantially later in this chapter, who and what amounts to an ICH is more uncertain.

The initial history of the BSA Immunity has many similarities to the history of Section 230. The BSA Immunity was introduced into Australian law as part of a "controversial" reform package (Leonard, 2010, p. 254), namely, the *Broadcasting Services Amendment (Online Services) Act 1999* (Cth) (Online Services Act). Like the *Communications Decency Act* (47 U.S.C. § 223 (1996)), the Online Services Act sought to deal with "offensive and illegal content online" (Alston, 2000, p. 193) and like Section 230, the BSA Immunity was not at the heart of the dispute. In fact, in defending the Online Services Act, Minister Alston made only one reference to the BSA Immunity, namely that "ISPs and ICHs will not be liable for the content accessed through their service where they are not responsible for the creation of that content" (Alston, 2000, p. 196).

However, from this point forward Section 230 and the BSA Immunity go their separate ways. Initial predictions that the BSA Immunity may provide an unintended and potentially powerful defence (Eisenberg, 2000) have been found to be overstated. Instead, as this chapter will outline in greater detail, quirks in the drafting of the BSA Immunity has meant "that cl. 91 [of the BSA Immunity] is of limited utility" (NSW Department of Justice, 2018, p. 34).

ECONOMIC IMPLICATIONS OF SECTION 230 AND THE BSA IMMUNITY

In light of the background to each law, this part of the chapter will outline the practical economic and financial effects that each law has had on internet businesses in both the United States and Australia.

Implications of Section 230

In terms of Section 230, the practical effects of it on the development of US-based internet businesses can be summarised in one line by Professor David Post about §. 230(c)(1) when he said that "no other sentence in the U.S. Code, I would assert, has been responsible for the creation of more value than that one" (Post, 2015, para. 2). This view is not held by just one legal academic. For example, when looking into the development of internet intermediaries, the Organisation for Economic Co-operation and Development (OECD) (2011, p. 13) noted that Section 230 and similar legislation, "have been instrumental in the growth of internet service providers, e-commerce and emerging user-generated content (UGC) platforms". The financial importance of Section 230 was confirmed in a recent study, where it was found that the removal of Section 230 (and other safe harbours) would cost the United States economy $75 billion and 425,000 jobs (Dippon, 2017).

Internet intermediaries or platforms include some of the largest corporations in the world, such as Facebook, Google and Amazon. However, these companies may never have gotten off the ground if not for Section 230. As Chander (2014, pp. 653–654) outlines:

again and again [Section] 230 proved invaluable to shield web enterprises from lawsuits ... Perhaps every major internet enterprise has relied on the statute to defend itself over the years. [Section 230] insulated web enterprise from the reach of a variety of federal and state causes of action, both statutory and common law.

The list of companies that have successfully relied on Section 230 includes almost every major internet platform in the United States. For example, Google has been able to rely on the immunity for both search engine results (*Maughan v Google Inc.*, 2006) and for third-party advertisements (*Goddard v Google Inc.*, 2009). Facebook has relied on Section 230 for content posted on the platform (*Klayman v Zuckerberg and Facebook*, 2014) and for content-filtering decisions (*Fyk v Facebook Inc.*, 2019; *Sikhs for Justice 'SFJ'. v Facebook Inc.*, 2015). Likewise, Twitter has also successfully sought Section 230 protection for third party content (*Fields v Twitter Inc.*, 2016). As well, Amazon was held not liable for defamatory comments posted on its website by third parties (*Schneider v Amazon.com*, 2001). Businesses as varied as Microsoft and Yelp have also successfully relied on Section 230 defences (*Holomaxx Technologies v Microsoft Corporation Inc.*, 2011; *Westlake Legal Group v Yelp Inc.*, 2015).

However, Section 230 does not just defend online service providers from being held liable for damages and administrative penalties, it also protects the financial position of internet businesses in two other ways, namely, in terms of out of pocket defence expenses and advertising revenue. Firstly, it is important to note that the Section 230 immunity, "like other forms of immunity, is generally accorded effect at the first logical point in the litigation process" (*Nemet Chevrolet Ltd v Consumeraffairs.com Inc.*, 2009, p. 6). Accordingly, courts frequently grant motions to dismiss plaintiff cases based on §. 230(c)(1) defences (Goldman, 2019b). The opportunity to dismiss suits prior to discovery provides cost savings for defendants.

Secondly, Section 230 does not differentiate between commercial speech and other forms of speech (Goldman, 2019b). Instead, it can be relied on for commercial speech including online advertisements (*Goddard v Google Inc.*, 2009). Using the example of online advertising, Section 230 protects a revenue stream for online businesses worth approximately $112 billion in the United States. Only three other countries in the world have had online advertising revenue in excess of $10 billion (Statista, 2019). Even those in favour of reforming Section 230 note that it has been important to commercial speech. For example, Citron and Wittes (2017, p. 412) noted that "if ISPs and other 'communication conduits' were not protected by §. 230 immunity, they would likely remove valuable online content at the request of hecklers to avoid distributor liability".

It is important to note that the barriers to entry for an internet business are fundamentally lower than in other areas of economic life (Ziniti, 2008). New and small online companies also enjoy the protection of Section 230 and the financial benefits it provides (Lemley, 2007). If Section 230 was repealed these companies would suffer the most. This is on the basis that "Big Tech" companies such as Google and Facebook can afford the additional regulatory obligations, whereas smaller companies may not be able to (Goldman, 2019a). Accordingly, the removal of Section 230 would likely enhance Google and Facebook's 'marketplace dominance' and would impose barriers for new companies to enter the market.

Finally, Section 230 may also apply, at least partially, to so-called Web 3.0 enterprises (Lobel, 2016). Web 2.0 encompasses a number of enterprises traditionally covered by Section 230, for example, search engines and digital marketplaces (including Google and Amazon). Web 3.0, on the other hand, extends to the service economy by providing consumers with access to offline exchanges (for example Uber and Airbnb) (Lobel, 2016). While the initial decisions are mixed (see *Airbnb Inc. v City and County of San Francisco*, 2016), the financial and economic benefits that arise from Section 230 may continue to grow with the expansion of the 'shared or gig economy'.

Implications of the BSA Immunity

This chapter now turns to the practical implications of the BSA Immunity. Recently, Pappalardo and Suzor (2018, p. 469) noted that "online intermediary liability law in Australia is a mess … the legal bases on which intermediaries are liable for the actions of individuals online is confusing and, viewed as a whole, largely incoherent."

This incoherence is reflected in the case law, where despite the High Court first considering the interaction of the internet and defamation laws in 2002 (*Dow Jones & Co Inc. v Gutnick*, 2002), a New South Wales Supreme Court Judge in 2019 still described the law in this area as "emerging" (*Voller v Nationwide New Pty Ltd*, 2019, [91]). At the heart of this confusion and mess is the BSA Immunity, or rather the insignificance of the BSA Immunity.

The various deficiencies of the BSA Immunity have been discussed in detail (Leonard, 2010). However, three quirks in the drafting of the BSA Immunity have meant it "almost never has any work to do" (Pappalardo & Suzor, 2018, p. 493). Firstly, as alluded to earlier in this chapter, the BSA Immunity covers both ISPs and ICHs. What is an ICH and ISP is uncertain, especially for those seeking to rely on it as a defence. For example, in *Fairfax v Ibrahim* (2012, [87]), Basten JA noted, the terms, ISP and ICH are "jargon without any settled meaning".

Secondly, the BSA Immunity only applies to a "law of a state or territory, or a rule of common law or equity" (*Broadcasting Services Act 1992* (Cth), sch. 5, cl. 91(1)). In other words, the BSA Immunity does not apply to Commonwealth legislation. As Leonard (2010) notes, given the increasing areas governed by Commonwealth legislation, this means that a number of important areas of law fall outside its scope such as consumer protection law and vilification laws.

However, the main reason the BSA Immunity is rarely relied upon is the requirement for 'awareness'. Broadly, to be able to rely on the BSA Immunity, the ISP or ICH must not have been "aware of the nature of the internet content" (*Broadcasting Services Act 1992* (Cth), sch. 5, cl. 91(1)(a), cl. 91(1)(c)). For practical purposes, this means that the BSA Immunity cannot be relied upon once an entity has some form of 'knowledge' (Pappalardo & Suzor, 2018). In other words, in most circumstances once the ISP or ICH are advised of the infringement, the BSA Immunity does not apply. However, unlike 'knowledge', there is not a large body of case law involving the term "aware" (Leonard, 2010, p. 260). In particular, it is not clear what steps an ICH and ISP should take to determine whether content is infringing. This means it is not even certain when an ISP or ICH develops 'awareness'. It was for this primary reason that the New South Wales Department of Justice (2018, p. 34) noted that the BSA Immunity was of "limited utility".

This lack of utility of the BSA Immunity has had a damaging and 'chilling effect' on internet businesses, particularly start-ups in in Australia. Specifically, it places internet businesses in Australia in a perpetual state of 'moderator's dilemma'. As outlined by Goldman (2019c), in the context of the FOSTA amendments to Section 230, where 'knowledge' must be present, online services have three options: perfectly implement content moderation, turn off content moderation, or exit the industry. The lack of application of the BSA Immunity and the 'moderator's dilemma' it gives rise to has damaged Australian internet businesses in three key ways; namely, by potentially reducing revenue, by increasing financial costs, and through litigation risk.

In terms of reduced potential revenue, this can be seen in *Australian Competition and Consumer Commission v Allergy Pathway Pty Ltd (No 2)* (2011). To be clear, Allergy Pathway Pty Ltd (Allergy Pathway) was not a sympathetic respondent. It had previously been found to contravene the former *Trade Practices Act 1974* (Cth) and was ordered to embark on a series of undertakings as remedial action (*Australian Competition and Consumer Commission v Allergy Pathway Pty* Ltd, 2009). The Australian Competition and Consumer Commission (ACCC) alleged that Allergy Pathway had breached its undertakings. One of the allegations was that Allergy Pathway (and its sole director) was in contempt of court by allowing the publication of testimonials written and posted by clients on Allergy Pathway's Facebook and Twitter pages. These testimonials were of "benefit" or "added legitimacy" to Allergy Pathway due to their "praise" of Allergy Pathway's services (*Competition and Consumer Commission v Allergy Pathway Pty Ltd (No 2)*, 2011, [32]). Ultimately, in relation to this allegation Finkelstein J in *Competition and Consumer Commission v Allergy Pathway Pty Ltd (No 2)* (2011, p. 33), concluded:

while it cannot be said that Allergy Pathway was responsible for the initial publication of the testimonials … it is appropriate to conclude that Allergy Pathway accepted responsibility for the publications when it knew of the publications and decided not to remove them. Hence it became the publisher of the testimonials.

The BSA Immunity was not argued by the respondent as the immunity does not apply to Commonwealth legislation. However, even if it did apply to Commonwealth legislation, Allergy Pathway would have had to prove it was not 'aware'. In this matter it was "not disputed" that Allergy Pathway knew that persons had posted testimonies on its Facebook page (*Competition and Consumer Commission v Allergy Pathway Pty Ltd (No 2)*, 2011, p. 30).

This case leaves an awkward precedent for other and more sympathetic internet businesses. Do they leave positive testimonials and reviews online if the praise could be argued to be exaggerated? If the businesses leave the testimonials online, they face potential liable, but if they remove them, they could miss out on the financial benefits that might arise.

It also gives rise to an extreme version of the "heckler's veto" (Ziniti, 2008, p. 606). The 'heckler's veto' is derived from the language of Stevens J in his opinion to the court in *Reno v American Civil Liberties Union* (1997). Broadly, it holds that aggrieved individuals can have content removed they do not like, by making allegations to content hosts that the content is illegal or infringing (Goldman, 2019a). In Australia, following decisions such as *Competition and Consumer Commission v Allergy Pathway Pty Ltd (No 2)* (2011), competitors or others could allege that positive reviews are misleading and potentially scare the business into removing the content, to the business's financial detriment.

Following the decision of *Competition and Consumer Commission v Allergy Pathway Pty Ltd (No 2)* (2011) a subsequent decision demonstrated that the lack of application of the BSA Immunity is not just reducing entities' revenue, but also increasing its costs. In *Voller v Nationwide New Pty Ltd,* Rothman J was asked to consider whether a number of media organisations (of various sizes) were responsible for the publication of third party Facebook comments that were alleged to be defamatory. Ultimately, Rothman J found that the companies were 'publishers'. It is important to note that the BSA Immunity was again not argued, assumedly because the media organisations were 'aware' of the comments.

In finding that the media companies were 'publishers', Rothman J noted that the media companies could have delayed the publication and monitored comments (*Voller v Nationwide New Pty Ltd*, 2019). In relation to delaying publication, Rothman J contended that the media companies could have used tools within Facebook to "hide" all comments and only release those that were not defamatory (*Voller v Nationwide New Pty Ltd*, 2019, [227]). Rothman J also seemed to suggest that the media companies could have just hired more employees, where he noted the Australian News Channel would have needed an extra 2.5 employees to filter and monitor Facebook comments (*Voller v Nationwide New Pty Ltd,* 2019, [65]).

It is important to note relative to their international peers, Australian start-ups already have high labour and capital costs (Bloch & Bhattacharya, 2016). If the approach to monitoring Facebook comments proposed by Rothman J was adopted, the costs of internet businesses would rise even further. Specifically, businesses would be required to hire more employees and develop and deploy industrial grade content controls (Goldman, 2019d). This outcome would not occur in the United States, as Section 230 would likely protect companies from liability and, in turn, also protect them from being required to dedicate more resources to monitoring (Goldman, 2019a). Accordingly, this situation gives United States companies a financial cost advantage compared to their Australian competitors, as Australian companies are obligated (due to the ineffectiveness of the BSA Immunity) to spend more on compliance.

In addition to the loss of revenue and increased financial costs associated with the ineffectiveness of the BSA Immunity, the lack of safe harbour protection leaves Australian businesses facing litigation risks that their United States competitors do not have. Such litigation can be potentially destructive, especially in the context of start-ups in the high-tech industry (Karakashian, 2015). This is because litigation requires the reallocation of scare resources towards fighting the litigation rather than being allocated towards innovation and business development (Karakashian, 2015). The case of zGeeks.com suggests that the ineffectiveness of the BSA Immunity may force Australian internet businesses to face similar resource allocation issues.

zGeeks.com was described in pleading before the ACT Court of Appeal as a website "wherein members from across the world are able to post opinion and comment in discussion threads about the affairs of the day" (*Brisciani v Piscioneri (No 4)*, 2016, [6]). According to Twitter posts by the owner (Mr Brisciani), it was a "great community of 1.3 million Geeks" and was in operation from 2001 to 2015 (Brisciani, 2019). In 2005, Ms Piscioneri provided information that assisted in the quashing of the criminal conviction of two rapists. Mr Brisciani posted about these events on zGeeks.com under the heading of "Tool of the Week" and separately started a new forum called "Bitching and Rants" (*Brisciani v Piscioneri*, 2015, [23–24]). Various comments left by third parties to these posts were potentially defamatory to Ms Piscioneri. In December 2009, Ms Piscioneri wrote to Mr Brisciani requesting removal of the posts and a public apology. Without identifying Ms Piscioneri, Mr Brisciani posted about her legal request, which commenced another round of comments from third parties. In the light of these actions Ms Piscioneri brought a defamation matter before the Supreme Court of the Australian Capital Territory.

In finding for Ms Piscioneri, Burns J appeared to refer to the lack of application of the BSA Immunity due to awareness. He said (Brisciani v Piscioneri, 2015, [45]):

internet content hosts can, in some circumstances, be vicariously liable for matter published by others, by virtue of the failure to remove from public display defamatory material published by the third party. In order to be vicariously liable, the host must have failed to remove the material after being notified of its existence.

In the specific circumstances of this case, Burns J also noted (Brisciani v Piscioneri, 2015, [46]):

I am satisfied that the defendant cannot be said to be a mere passive facilitator of the zGeek posts, as his own post titled 'Tool of the Week' initiated the discussion of the plaintiff, he actively engaged in the ongoing discussion and he had the ability to remove the posts from zGeek at any time.

Ultimately, Burns J awarded Ms Piscioneri damages of $82,000. It is probable the dispute would have been a significant burden on Mr Brisciani's financial resources and time. This burden would likely not have been borne by Mr Brisciani's competitors in the United States. Kosseff (2019, p. 162) noted in discussing the decision that:

the Australian ruling against Brisciani — at least for the other users' posts — simply would not have been possible in the United States. Section 230 would have undoubtedly shielded him from being held legally responsible for any of the other users' posts.

Accordingly, in light of the comment of Kosseff, it is at least arguable the case demonstrates that due to the operation of the BSA Immunity, Australian internet businesses face legal risks that their United States counterparts do not.

SOLUTIONS AND RECOMMENDATIONS

So far, this chapter has sought to demonstrate the implications arising from two different approaches to intermediary liability. The first approach, in the form of Section 230, has assisted and fostered the development of some of the world's largest companies. The other approach, the BSA Immunity, has been found wanting. The BSA Immunity has left Australian internet businesses facing potentially lower revenues, higher costs, and increased litigation risks relative to their United States based competitors. Given these different outcomes between the United States and Australia, this chapter will discuss some potential reforms to strengthen the BSA Immunity.

Firstly, the requirement of 'awareness' must be removed. As discussed above, the key reason the BSA Immunity is rarely relied on is this requirement (Pappalardo & Suzor, 2018). However, as outlined by Pappalardo and Suzor (2018), knowledge of wrongdoing has limited connection to the question of whether an intermediary's technology, service or actions actually contributed to the alleged wrong. This disconnection gives rise to a number of issues discussed in this chapter, including the 'moderator's dilemma' and the 'heckler's veto'. Accordingly, the removal of the requirement of 'awareness' alone would fundamentally strengthen the BSA Immunity, making it more consistent with Section 230.

Secondly, consideration should be given to making it clearer who and what is covered by the BSA Immunity. As outlined earlier in this chapter, the existing definitions of ISP and ICH are highly uncertain. Accordingly, consideration should be given to replacing the existing definitions with either a definition consistent with Section 230 or with the concept relied upon in the *Manila Principles on Intermediary Liability* (the Manila Principles) (ManilaPrinciples.org, 2015b), the so-called "gold standard" (Keller, 2017, p. 6) of intermediary liability model laws, namely (ManilaPrinciples.org, 2015b, p. 6):

internet intermediaries bring together or facilitate transactions between third parties on the internet. They give access to, host, transmit and index content, products and services originated by third parties on the internet or provide Internet based services to third parties.

This definition has also been used by the OECD (2010) and the United Nations Educational, Scientific and Cultural Organisation (MacKinnon, Hickok, Bar, & Lim, 2014). As outlined in the background paper to the Manila Principles (ManilaPrinciples.org, 2015a), the definition is intended to cover ISPs through to social networks. However, to ensure there is no confusion as to which entities are covered, the relevant explanatory memorandum to the amending law should include sufficient examples to clarify that the law applies to a wide range of entities, including entities that use third party infrastructure, such as the media organisations in *Voller v Nationwide New Pty Ltd* (2019).

Thirdly, in the same manner as Section 230, the BSA Immunity should be amended to make it clear it covers a wide range of legal liabilities, with limited exceptions. In particular, the BSA Immunity should be extended to cover Commonwealth laws in addition to the laws currently covered.

Fourthly, like Section 230, there should be some consideration of exceptions to the law. Two potential areas are considered. The first exception should be where the intermediary has materially contributed to the infringing content. This exception is derived from the 9th Circuit Court's decision in *Fair Housing Council of San Fernando Valley v Roommates.Com LLC* (2008). In this case, it was held, that an exception to Section 230 existed where the intermediary "contribut[ed] materially to the alleged illegality of the conduct" (*Fair Housing Council of San Fernando Valley v Roommates.Com LLC*, 2008, p. 3462). The experience of the United States with this exception is that it has not abrogated Section 230 (Kosseff, 2017), but may provide a route for plaintiffs to bring intermediaries to account for contributing to appalling content, for example revenge porn (Franklin, 2014).

The second group of exceptions are areas of law where it would be difficult to obtain political support for the immunity and where, in turn, seeking to include the laws in the reform package could prevent wider reform. A possible example of a law in this category is copyright law.[4]

FURTHER RESEARCH DIRECTION

In light of the above discussion, this chapter notes that, while there is significant research in relation to the impact of Section 230 (Klonick, 2018; Kosseff, 2019), limited consideration has been given to the policy implications of the BSA Immunity. Previous examination of the BSA Immunity has focused on the text of the legislation and noted its lack of utility (Leonard, 2010; Turner, 2014). This chapter has sought to identify wider policy and economic implications arising from its ineffectiveness. However, there are further opportunities available to researchers to conduct more formal qualitative research into the implications of the BSA Immunity. As noted by Ritchie (2003, p. 27), qualitative research provides the researcher with the opportunity to "unpack" and display the phenomena as experienced by the study participants. Qualitative research into the impact of the limited utility of the BSA Immunity on the business decisions made by internet businesses, especially start-ups, could provide valuable insights for future legal reform. For example, identifying whether concerns about being sued (due to third-party content) discouraged start-ups from adopting particular business strategies could provide further evidence that the existing law is having a 'chilling effect' on innovation and growth.

CONCLUSION

This chapter has sought to compare and contrast two different approaches in Australia and the United States to regulating internet intermediaries. The United States, in the form of Section 230, has sought to limit intermediaries' liability, while the various deficiencies of Australia's BSA Immunity law has meant that it has had minimal practical use. This has resulted in two very different outcomes from a business and economic perspective. In the case of Section 230 it has been viewed by others as partially responsible for the creation of "a trillion or so dollars of value" (Post, 2015, Headline section). In the case of the BSA Immunity, however, this chapter has sought to outline how it has created an environment where internet businesses live in a perpetual state of 'moderator's dilemma' and have to deal with the economic, financial and policy consequences.

Going forward, this chapter has suggested that if Australian policymakers want to develop a strong start-up ecosystem, consideration should be given to amending the BSA Immunity to make it a more functional safe harbour. This is on the basis that safe harbours such as Section 230 have been "crucial to provide the space for innovation and experimentation with new technologies" (Suzor, 2019, p. 101).

What has been advocated in this chapter may be seen as contrarian in the current political atmosphere. The world is currently in the midst of a cyclone of proposals to regulate internet businesses, especially intermediaries. This includes Australia, which is actively seeking to impose liability on internet intermediaries for the actions of their users through regulations, such as the *Criminal Code Amendment (Sharing of Abhorrent Violent Material) Act 2019* (Cth). However, despite their good intentions, these proposals may have unintended consequences for economic growth, free speech and innovation. Instead, Australian policymakers should learn from the experience of the United States and reform the BSA Immunity to provide broad immunity and, in turn, the space for start-ups and internet businesses to innovate and grow.

REFERENCES

Airbnb Inc. v City and County of San Francisco, 217 F. Supp. 3d 1066 (ND Cal. 2016).

Allow States and Victims to Fight Online Sex Trafficking Act 47 U.S.C. § 230(e) (1996).

Alston, R. (2000). The government's regulatory framework for Internet content. *The University of New South Wales Law Journal*, *23*(1), 192–197.

Ardia, D. (2010). Free speech savior or shield for scoundrels: An empirical study of intermediary immunity under section 230 of the Communications Decency Act. *Loyola of Los Angeles Law Review*, *43*, 373–506.

Australian Competition and Consumer Commission v Allergy Pathway Pty Ltd [2009] FCA 960.

Australian Competition and Consumer Commission v Allergy Pathway Pty Ltd (No 2) [2011] FCA 74.

Ballon, I. (2017). *E-commerce & internet law*. New York: Thomson Reuters.

Barrett v Rosenthal, 146 P. 3d. 510 (Cal. 2006).

Bloch, H., & Bhattacharya, M. (2016). Promotion of Innovation and Job Growth in Small- and Medium-Sized Enterprises in Australia: Evidence and Policy Issues. *The Australian Economic Review*, *49*(2), 192–199. doi:10.1111/1467-8462.12164

Brisciani, A. [@zgeeks]. (2019). *ZGeek was a magical place full of turnips. From 2001 to 2015, a great community of 1.3 million Geeks. Laughs, fights and many shenanigans* [Tweet]. Retrieved from https://twitter.com/zgeek?lang=en

Brisciani v Piscioneri [2015] ACTSC 106.

Brisciani v Piscioneri (No 4) [2016] ACTCA 32.

Broadcasting Services Act 1992 (Cth).

Broadcasting Services Amendment (Online Services) Act 1999 (Cth).

Burshtein, S. (2017). The true story of fake news. *Intellectual Property Journal*, *29*, 397–446.

Chander, A. (2014). How law made Silicon Valley. *Emory Law Journal*, *63*, 639–694.

Citron, D., & Witts, B. (2017). The internet will not break: Denying bad samaritans § 230 immunity. *Fordham Law Review*, *86*(2), 401–423.

Communications Decency Act 47 U.S.C. § 230 (1996).

Criminal Code Amendment (Sharing of Abhorrent Violent Material) Act 2019 (Cth).

Dippon, C. (2017). *Economic value of internet intermediaries and the role of liability protections*. Retrieved from https://internetassociation.org/wp-content/uploads/2017/06/Economic-Value-of-Internet-Intermediaries-the-Role-of-Liability-Protections.pdf

Dow Jones & Co Inc. v Gutnick [2002] HCA 56.

Ehrlich, P. (2002). Communications Decency Act 230. *Berkeley Technology Law Journal, 17*(1), 402–419.

Eisenberg, J. (2000). Safety out of sight: The impact of the new online content legislation on defamation law. *The University of New South Wales Law Journal, 23*, 232–237.

Electronic Communications Privacy Act 18 U.S.C. §§ 2510-2523 (1986).

Fair Housing Council of San Fernando Valley v Roommates.Com LLC, 521 F. 3d. 1157 (9th Cir. 2008).

Fairfax v Ibrahim [2012] NSWCCA 125.

Fields v Twitter Inc., 217 F. Supp. 3d 1116 (ND Cal. 2016).

Franklin, Z. (2014). Justice for revenge porn victims: Legal theories to overcome claims of civil immunity by operators of revenge porn websites. *California Law Review, 102*(5), 1303–1336.

Fyk v Facebook Inc., No. C 18-05159 JSW (ND Cal. 2019).

Getachew v Google Inc., 491 F. App. 923 (10th Cir. 2012).

Goddard v Google Inc., 640 F. Supp. 2d 1193 (ND Cal. 2009).

Goldman, E. (2012). Online user account termination and 47 U.S.C. § 230(c)(2). UC *Irvine. Law Review, 2*, 659–673.

Goldman, E. (2017). The ten most important section 230 rulings. *Tulane Journal of Technology and Intellectual Property, 20*, 1–10.

Goldman, E. (2019a). An overview of the United States' section 230 internet immunity. In G. Frosio (Ed.), The Oxford handbook of intermediary liability online (pp. 1–15). Oxford, UK: Oxford University Press.

Goldman, E. (2019b). Why section 230 is better than the first amendment. *Notre Dame Law Review Online, 94*(4), 1–16. doi:10.2139srn.3351323

Goldman, E. (2019c). The complicated story of FOSTA and section 230. *First Amendment Law Review, 17*, 279–293.

Goldman, E. (2019d). Law and technology internet immunity and the freedom to code. *Communications of the ACM, 62*(9), 22–24. doi:10.1145/3349270

Holomaxx Technologies v. Microsoft Corporation Inc., 783 F. Supp. 2d 1097 (ND Cal. 2011).

Karakashian, S. (2015). A Software Patent War: The Effects of Patent Trolls on Startup Companies, Innovation, and Entrepreneurship. *Hastings Business Law Journal, 11*(1), 119–156.

Keller, D. (2017). *SESTA and the teachings of intermediary liability*. Retrieved from https://cyberlaw. stanford.edu/files/publication/files/SESTA-and-IL-Keller-11-2.pdf

Klayman v Zuckerberg and Facebook, 753 F. 3d. 1354 (DC Cir. 2014).

Klonick, K. (2018). The new governors: The people, rules, and processes governing online speech. *Harvard Law Review, 131*, 1598–1670.

Kosseff, J. (2017). The gradual erosion of the law that shaped the internet: Section 230's evolution over two decades. *The Columbia Science and Technology Law Review, 18*, 1–41.

Kosseff, J. (2019). *The twenty-six words that created the internet*. New York: Cornell University Press. doi:10.7591/9781501735783

Lemley, M. (2007). Rationalizing internet safe harbours. *Journal on Telecommunications & High Technology Law, 6*, 101–120.

Leonard, P. (2010). Safe harbours in choppy waters – building a sensible approach to liability of Internet intermediaries in Australia. *Journal of International Media & Entertainment Law, 3*(2), 221–262.

Lobel, O. (2016). The law of the platform. *Minnesota Law Review, 101*, 87–166.

Lukmire, D. (2010). Can the courts tame the Communications Decency Act? The reverberations of Zeran v America online. *NYU Annual Survey of American Law, 66*, 371–412.

MacKinnon, R., Hickok, E., Bar, A., & Lim, H. (2014). *Fostering freedom online: The role of Internet intermediaries*. Paris, France: UNESCO Publishing.

ManilaPrinciples.org. (2015a). *The Manila Principles on intermediary liability – background paper*. Retrieved from https://www.eff.org/files/2015/07/08/manila_principles_background_paper.pdf

ManilaPrinciples.org. (2015b). *The Manila Principles on intermediary liability*. Retrieved from https://www.manilaprinciples.org/principles

Maughan v Google Inc., 49 Cal. Rptr. 3d 861 (Cal. Ct. App. 2006).

Nemet Chevrolet Ltd v Consumeraffairs.com Inc., 591 F. 3d 250 (4th Cir. 2009).

NSW Department of Justice. (2018). *Statutory review – Defamation Act 2005*. Retrieved from https://www.justice.nsw.gov.au/justicepolicy/Documents/defamation-act-statutory-review-report.pdf

Office of the United States Trade Representatives. (2018). *United States-Mexico-Canada Agreement*. Retrieved from https://ustr.gov/trade-agreements/free-trade-agreements/united-states-mexico-canada-agreement/agreement-between

Ong, R. (2013). Internet intermediaries: The liability for defamatory postings in China and Hong Kong. *Computer Law & Security Review, 29*(3), 274–281. doi:10.1016/j.clsr.2013.03.006

Organisation for Economic Co-operation and Development (OECD). (2010). *The economic and social role of internet intermediaries*. Retrieved from https://www.oecd.org/internet/ieconomy/44949023.pdf

Organisation for Economic Co-operation and Development (OECD). (2011). *The role of internet intermediaries in advancing public policy objectives*. Retrieved from https://www.oecd.org/sti/ieconomy/theroleofinternetintermediariesinadvancingpublicpolicyobjectives.htm

Pappalardo, K., & Suzor, N. (2018). The liability of Australian online intermediaries. *The Sydney Law Review*, *40*, 469–498.

Post, D. (2015, August 27). A bill of internet history, or two members of Congress helped create a trillion or so dollars of value. *The Washington Po*st. Retrieved from https://www.washingtonpost.com/news/volokh-conspiracy/wp/2015/08/27/a-bit-of-internet-history-or-how-two-members-of-congress-helped-create-a-trillion-or-so-dollars-of-value/?utm_term=.9ffe926c6a84

Reno v American Civil Liberties Union, 521 U.S. 844 (1997).

Ritchie, J. (2003). The application of qualitative methods to social research. In J. Ritchie & J. Lewis (Eds.), *Qualitative research practice: a guide for social science students and researchers* (pp. 24–46). London: Sage Publications.

Schneider v Amazon.com, 31 P. 3d 37 (Wash Ct App. 2001).

Sheridan, D. (1997). Zeran v. AOL and the effect of section 230 of the Communications Decency Act upon liability for defamation on the Internet. *Albany Law Review*, *61*, 147–179.

Sikhs for Justice 'SFJ' v Facebook Inc., 144 F. Supp. 3d 1088 (ND Cal. 2015).

Statista. (2019). *Digital advertising*. Retrieved from https://www.statista.com/outlook/216/100/digital-advertising/worldwide#market-globalRevenue

Stratton Oakmont Inc. v Prodigy Services Co, WL 323710 (NY Sup Ct. 1995).

Suzor, N. (2019). *Lawless: The secret rules that govern our digital lives*. London: Cambridge University Press. doi:10.1017/9781108666428

Trade Practices Act 1974 (Cth).

Trkulja v. Google LLC [2018] HCA 25.

Turner, R. (2014). Internet defamation law and publication: A multi-jurisdictional analysis. *The University of New South Wales Law Journal*, *37*(1), 34–62.

Voller v Nationwide New Pty Ltd [2019] NSWSC 766.

Westlake Legal Group v Yelp Inc., 599 Fed. Appx. 481 (4th Cir. 2015).

Zeran v America Online Inc., 129 F.3d 327; 958 F. Supp. 1124 (ED Va. 1997).

Ziniti, C. (2008). Optimal liability system for online service providers: How Zeran v. America Online got it right and Web 2.0 proves it. *Berkley Technology Law Journal, 22*, 583–616.

ADDITIONAL READING

Barnes v Yahoo Inc., 570 F. 3d. 1096 (9th Cir. 2009).

Burrell, R., & Weatherall, K. (2008). Exporting controversy? Reactions to the copyright provisions of the U.S.–Australia Free Trade Agreement: Lessons for U.S. trade policy. *Journal of Law. Technology & Policy*, *2*, 259–319.

Doe v Internet Brands Inc., 824 F. 3d. 846 (9th Cir. 2016).

Federal Trade Commissioner v Accusearch Inc., 570 F. 3d. 1187 (10th Cir. 2010).

Nourse, V., & Schacter, J. (2002). The politics of legislative drafting: A Congressional case study. *New York University Law Review*, *77*(3), 575–624.

Omer, C. (2014). Intermediary liability for harmful speech: Lessons from abroad. *Harvard Journal of Law & Technology*, *28*(1), 289–324.

KEY TERMS AND DEFINITIONS

BSA Immunity: The immunity available from certain laws under clause 91(1) of schedule 5 of the Broadcasting Services Act 1992 (Cth).

Chilling Effect: The discouragement and abandonment of certain actions (including innovation) due to a threat of legal sanction.

Immunity: The legal status an entity experiences where it is not subject to a specific law or a type of law.

Intermediary Liability: The legal liability of intermediaries for the actions or content of third parties.

Internet Intermediaries: Entities that facilitate use of the internet.

Safe Harbour: A statutory exemption for certain entities from legal liability. A safe harbour may have various conditions that must be satisfied and application is limited to specific laws.

Section 230: The immunity available from certain laws under Communications Decency Act, 47 U.S.C. § 230 (1996).

ENDNOTES

[1]   Broadly, a publisher (e.g. of newspapers or books) has significant control over the content. A distributor merely distributes content and has liability upon showing knowledge or negligence (e.g. libraries and booksellers). A common carrier transfers information mechanically and has no opportunity for review (e.g. telephone companies).

[2]   There are two key exceptions. Firstly, as identified in *Fair Housing Council of San Fernando Valley v. Roommates.Com LLC* (2008), where the court held an entity will not be entitled to section 230 immunity "if it contribut[ed] materially to the alleged illegality of the conduct". In relation to this first category see also *Federal Trade Commissioner v. Accusearch Inc.* (2010). Secondly, the other type of exception is where the intermediaries are sued for activities other than publishing/speaking (see *Barnes v. Yahoo Inc.* (2009) and *Doe v. Internet Brands Inc.* (2016); see generally, Kosseff, 2017).

[3]   Horizontal immunity refers to immunity that covers liability, both civil and criminal, for most types of illegal activities initiated by third parties. See for example Omer (2014).

[4]   The political controversy of safe harbours and copyright in Australia is discussed in Burrell & Weatherall (2008).

Chapter 5
Use of Big Data Analytics by Tax Authorities

Brendan Walker-Munro
https://orcid.org/0000-0001-5484-1145
Swinburne University, Australia

ABSTRACT

This chapter provides a thematic analysis for the Australian context of the legality and challenges to the use of big data analytics to identify risk, conduct compliance action, and make decisions within the tax administration space. Recent federal court jurisprudence and research is discussed to identify common themes (i.e., privacy/opacity, inaccuracy/bias, and fairness/due process) currently influencing the legal treatment of big data analytics within the tax administration and compliance environment in Australia.

INTRODUCTION

Computers and smart devices continue to play an increasingly significant role in our daily lives. The seamless integration of computers, smartphones, tablets and internet-enabled devices into our society has facilitated the rise of 'big data', the notion that near-infinite storage and fast computer processing has permitted the mass collection and storage of information regarding all aspects of our lives. Yet having access to enormous amounts of data is one thing; the ability to derive useful connections and observations from such data is what has fueled significant growth in another field: 'big analysis'. Also known as analytics or data profiling, the growth of Big Analysis enables analysis of massive datasets and identification of trends, issues and risks invisible to human observation (Cohen, 2012). Fertik and Thompson (2015, p. 5) explains the difference between 'big data' and 'big analysis' as "knowing that you [a]re sitting on a gold mine [and] actually getting it out of the ground and turned into bullion".

Nowhere is this concept becoming more prevalent than in the labyrinthine, complex public administration and enforcement of tax statutes. Incorporation of technology into the tax process has always been somewhat of a *fait accompli*—technological innovations in the tax system foster improved connections between the tax authority and consumers, as well as reduce the opportunity for tax evasion (Maciejewski, 2016). In a world where computer programs can mine personal, social, economic or law enforcement

DOI: 10.4018/978-1-7998-3130-3.ch005

information and then use this data to make informed, evidence-based predictions on individuals' or classes of individuals' likely actions and risks (Pasquale, 2011), it is not surprising such programs are attractive to tax authorities.

The objective of this chapter is to examine the use of big data analytics by tax administrations as represented by the Australian Taxation Office (ATO) from the following thematic perspectives:

- Inaccuracy
- Privacy
- Opacity
- Due process
- Fairness/bias

These themes are considered important as they are distilled from the Administrative Review Council (ARC) 2004 report into technology-assisted decision making (TADM) (Attorney-General's Department, 2004), and synthesized with more recent observations emerging from both regulatory (OAIC, 2018b) and academic literature (Houser & Sander, 2016; Hogan-Doran, 2017; Veit, 2019). Thus, the pervasive use of information technology, data collection and storage provides substantial datasets of interest and utility to the tax authorities in protecting the public revenue. Yet these data sets are unwieldy and un-informative without powerful and speedy means by which the data can be analyzed, transformed and distilled into practical insights. The purpose of this chapter therefore is to scrutinize this tax use from the thematic perspectives of inaccuracy, privacy, opacity, due process, and fairness/bias and identify the challenges and opportunities for future use.

BACKGROUND

Since their invention, computers have been an invaluable tool for public service agencies (Savas, 1969). The ATO (like many other tax administrations) has certainly been using computers in its compliance activities since the 1970s. Though originally seen as a more powerful typewriter and then as a medium for entering and storing greater amounts of public information, growth in computing power has witnessed an increase in computer use for the purpose of decision-making, where there is a clear niche for computers to assist delegates in making the correct and preferable decision. The 2004 ARC report noted that numerous government departments of the time were already using TADM without a suitably strong oversight or review framework. To fill this void, the Department of Finance and Deregulation published a better practice guide to assist with TADM in 2007, which sought to ensure the ARC principles were implemented in a way that was practical and based on good sense (AGIMO, 2007).

But the ARC report and subsequent better practice guide highlight that TADM involves providing support and guidance to a delegate or decision-maker. Under Australian law, this follows an approach permitted by the principles set down in *Carltona Ltd v Commissioners of Works* (1943), where the English Court of Appeal determined a person in whom decision-making power is reposed has implied authority to authorize another to exercise that power on their behalf. This is especially so in government, where "ministers have so many functions and powers, administrative necessity dictates that they act through duly authorized officials" (*Carltona Ltd v Commissioners of Works*, 1943, p. 563). The computer algorithms and programs used under the auspices of TADM do not – of themselves – make decisions.

Going a step beyond TADM is where a computer program makes a decision on behalf of a human decision-maker, often without the input of a human being (what this author terms 'automated decision-making' or ADM). ADM emerged first in the marketing sector in the early 2000s in the guise of behavioral targeting – users are presented with advertisements for products or services that demonstrate linkages with a set of perceived interests based on their browser history (Brotherton, 2012). The correctness of these linkages is not checked, analyzed or validated by a human being. In 2012, the retail giant Target was criticized after its ADM programs sent coupons to women whose buying patterns suggested they might be pregnant (Hill, 2012). As business became more *au fait* with the use of big data and analytics, the financial services sector also used ADM programs to assess the creditworthiness of finance applicants. In the recent case of *ASIC v Westpac Banking Corporation* (2019), the Federal Court found that a decision made by a bank computer to either reject or accept home loan applicants based on an assessment of living expenses was not in breach of the *National Consumer Credit Protection Act 2009* (Cth).

The use of ADM in government is now commonplace. Under Australian Commonwealth law, there are 29 Acts which explicitly permit ADM. These Acts predominantly govern decisions made in relation to social security, but are also present in other Ministerial portfolios such as migration and citizenship, digital health records and customs, and biosecurity (Elvery, 2017). In these fields, specific statutory permissions often exist to allow computer programs to make delegated decisions, such as s. 6A of the *Social Security (Administration) Act 1999* (Cth):

6A Secretary may arrange for use of computer programs to make decisions

(1) The Secretary may arrange for the use, under the Secretary's control, of computer programs for any purposes for which the Secretary may make decisions under the social security law.

There are no similar provisions to s. 6A explicitly permitting ADM in any of Australia's taxation laws. This is despite the obvious benefits of using data analytics to protect the public revenue, where taxation data-matching has specific statutory and policy dynamic. Sections 6 and 7 of the *Data-matching Program (Assistance and Tax) Act 1990* (Cth) outline how the Education, Social Services, Veterans' Affairs and Human Services Departments may share information with the ATO for them to conduct data matching cycles and identify data that relates to particular individuals. At a policy level, the Australian Law Reform Commission (ALRC) noted that the former federal Privacy Commissioner described data matching as "the large-scale comparison of records or files ... collected or held for different purposes, with a view to identifying matters of interest" (ALRC, 1998, para 14.94). More recently this definition has been clarified by the Office of the Australian Information Commissioner's (OAIC) 2014 guidance that data matching comprises "the bringing together of at least two data sets that contain personal information, and that come from different sources, and the comparison of those data sets with the intention of producing a match" (OAIC, 2014, Key Terms section).

In 2008, the Australian National Audit Office (ANAO) published a report on the ATO's use of data-matching which had been in place since the 1970s (ANAO, 2008). The ANAO observed that the ATO used data to help service customers and identify compliance risks and "[i]n many cases it generates automatic correspondence to tax payers. It can also bring to notice discrepancies in the information provided by taxpayers in their tax returns and authoritative relevant third-party data" (ANAO, 2008, p. 46). According to the ATO this usage has continued to today (Australian Taxation Office, 2019, p. 1):

Data helps us get things right from the start—meaning we can address issues quickly, before they escalate. It also helps us to find taxpayers who are not doing the right thing. Data-matching is a powerful administrative and law enforcement tool.

It is important to observe that this data-matching by the ATO is not strictly ADM, as there is no specific decision being made. Because of Australia's self-assessment system for taxation, taxpayers carry the onus of proving the returns they lodge with the ATO comply with the relevant laws. Therefore, data analytics can assist the Commissioner and their staff in determining how and to what extent taxpayers comply with this onus (Veit, 2019).

Unfortunately for the ATO, the Full Federal Court recently ruled that in the absence of an enabling provision like s. 6A, the general tax jurisprudence does not support ADM. In *Pintarich v Deputy Commissioner of Taxation* (2018) (Pintarich case), a 2-1 majority held that the computerized issue of a "bulk template letter" (*Pintarich v Deputy Commissioner of Taxation*, 2018, para. 18) by the ATO did not involve a decision by a delegate of the Deputy Commissioner to remit general interest charges (GIC), and so granted the appeal.

So whilst ADM is not explicitly permitted in the taxation laws, there are grounds for it to be. Though in the minority judgment, His Honor Justice Kerr stated in Pintarich that technology is rapidly changing what it means to make a decision (*Pintarich v Deputy Commissioner of Taxation*, 2018, para. 47-49):

What was once inconceivable, that a complex decision might be made without any requirement of human mental processes is, for better or worse, rapidly becoming unexceptional. Automated systems are already routinely relied upon by a number of Australian government departments for bulk decision making... This trend is not restricted to government. Automated share trading is at the heart of international commerce. Machines make contracts with machines... The legal conception of what constitutes a decision cannot be static; it must comprehend that technology has altered how decisions are in fact made and that aspects of, or the entirety of, decision making can occur independently of human mental input.

More recently Veit (2019) claimed that the use of data analytics embeds and expands existing practices in tax administration, but now staff have the capacity to utilize more data to make their decisions in a more timely and accurate manner.

The next step in computerized decision-making is the integration of a simple business rules program into a machine learning or artificial intelligence (AI) program (that is, one that can learn from its previous mistakes and adapt itself to the need to make these decisions). Under these circumstances, AI may become so advanced that the capability for such a program to make reasoned, calculated decisions based on all relevant factors may match or even exceed the decision-making capability of human beings.

Though closely allied to the process of TADM, ADM and even AI, data analytics is not the same concept and faces a slightly more nuanced series of legal challenges. Data analytics (at least for the purposes of this chapter) is the mining, research or examination of large-scale datasets to yield evidence pertaining to past, present or future behavior (Maciejewski, 2016):

1. **Historical:** Datasets are mined to examine trends and fluctuations in certain behaviors or observable characteristics over time. For example, tax administrations may examine previously lodged returns for a given taxpayer to identify anomalies in reporting (e.g., increased or decreased income)

or the lodgement or claiming basis of a whole class of taxpayers (e.g., the number of particular occupations which claim certain work-related expense deductions).

2. **Real-time:** Data is examined either as it is submitted to the administration or after a short delay (which, in turn, is limited by the sophistication of the monitoring technology or process) to identify in real-time the types of behaviors or conduct of interest. For a tax administration, this can, for example, give detailed information on changes in asset ownership, share trading or preferential deals which may be relevant to declaring a particular tax position.

3. **Predictive:** Data is examined to identify and link observed characteristics to particular behaviors of interest, and make reasoned and evidence-based predictions of future behavior. In tax administrations, predictive analytics can be utilized to identify potential indicators of criminal behavior (e.g., money laundering, tax evasion, fraud or under-declaration of income), as well as allowing the deployment of proactive tools to prevent non-compliance (e.g., behavioral insight tools known as 'nudges').

Unsurprisingly, the use of computers in decision-making (including under the taxation laws) and particularly in arenas involving compliance and enforcement, has raised concerns among scholars and civil libertarians, especially given the scope of data analytics work enables tax administrations "to shift surveillance from 'targeting a specific suspect to categorical suspicion of everyone'" (Nunn, 2003, p. 457). Professor Roger Brownsword, a world-renowned expert in the field of technological regulation, explains that the concepts of choice, transparency and accountability can be undermined by the data analytics concept (Brownsword, 2004; Brownsword & Yeung, 2008; Brownsword & Harel, 2019). Therefore, data analytics can potentially be subject to the same corruption, bias, incorrectness and difficulty as many of our existing bureaucratic processes (Lepri, Staiano, Sangokoya, Letouze & Oliver, 2017).

CONCERNS ASSOCIATED WITH THE USE OF DATA ANALYTICS

Importantly, the focus of this chapter excludes certain challenges to data analytics which have been identified in the literature and appear to apply solely to the use of big data in the private sector. Some of these suggested challenges in relation to data analytics set out in academic and journalistic writings are ameliorated or even eliminated by the legal status of the tax administration as an organ of the State. For example, there is no tension in choosing between 'profit' and 'social need' as drivers for the use of 'big data' in an environment where tax administrations have no requirement to earn money for their shareholders. Because tax administrations are accountable to parliaments or congresses (and, thereby, the taxpayers themselves) and not shareholders, there is no conflict of interest between data collection and its ultimate use—the whole of society benefits when administrations reduce the number of tax cheats. Furthermore, the likely conflicts of competing interests involving fundamental human rights around privacy and interference with information are less likely to be 'ignored' by tax administrations' use of data analytics, not only because governments have a vested interest in maintaining legitimacy with their own privacy legislation, but also because the State has substantial interest in protecting the rights of those accused of crimes including those alleged to have engaged in tax evasion and fraud (Fellmeth, 2005). Instead, the five major domains of concern with big data analytics appear to come from:

- **Inaccuracy:** Analytics of large datasets is not always an indicator of future behavior.
- **Privacy:** Analytics moves tax surveillance from specific taxpayers to the systemic scrutiny of every taxpayer.
- **Opacity:** As the source code of data analytics programs is not publicly available, it is difficult to determine whether the program is operating correctly.
- **Fairness/Bias:** Corrupted, biased or incomplete data will likely produce corrupted, biased or incomplete decisions.
- **Due process:** It is difficult to challenge a tax decision where the steps in the decision (i.e., made by an analytical program) are not clear.

Inaccuracy

The first problem with big data analytics is the concept of inaccuracy. As a concept, inaccuracy has a number of definitions which are largely dependent on where the inaccuracy has arisen in the dataset to be analyzed, and whether the inaccuracy is inadvertent or deliberate. For example, the data may have been inaccurate when first recorded at its source. Government departments are not without error and tax administrations may count themselves included—it is a relatively simple mistake to add an 'e' to someone's surname where none exists, or to incorrectly record a birthdate of 1 February (1/2) as 2 January ('2/1'). Mistakes may also have been deliberately recorded at the source. Fraudulent actors in the taxation space may see great and obvious benefit in inaccurately recording their birthdate, address, income or other statistics, in turn helping to obfuscate or confuse the data-matching powers of the tax administration. Deliberate mistakes may also be engaged in by otherwise wholly law-abiding taxpayers for legitimate personal reasons. Consider the following:

- A taxpayer may post on their Facebook page a picture of a high-powered sports car with a caption implying they have just purchased it, which may be picked up by data analytics as evidence the taxpayer is living outside their means. However, the post was done only to impress their friends or perhaps as a joke.
- A taxpayer creates a webpage indicating they are operating a business and may, therefore, have undisclosed income not reported in their tax returns. However, the webpage could have been created in the name of artistic expression, satire, or could represent a moment of boredom with no real intent to follow through.
- A taxpayer changes their LinkedIn profile to state they work in a high-profile job at a law firm when, in fact, they are unemployed or drawing a pension or unemployment benefit. Whilst this may raise a red flag for a tax auditor, the taxpayer is simply trying to project a more socially acceptable digital identity.

These forms of deliberate misinformation being promulgated in open source or public websites/ blogs were found in a recent survey by the Australian Communications and Media Authority (ACMA) to be undertaken by almost half of Australians as a form of "defensive inaccuracy" designed to protect a digital identity (ACMA, 2013, p. 6). Whilst these mistakes or exaggerations may seem inadvertent and minor, when looked at through the lens of mass data-matching and big data analytics it becomes feasible a taxpayer may have their own, wholly compliant records matched with that of a serial fraudster as a result of a simple mistake.

Inaccuracy may also arise in the linkage between certain observed behaviors with corresponding risk factors (that is the use of data analytics requires an inherent acceptance of causal *if-then* links between an observed behavior and a risk posed). Consider the following scene from the popular movie *Minority Report* (Twentieth Century Fox, 2002):

WITWER: '*But it's not the future if you stop it. Isn't that a fundamental paradox?*'
ANDERTON: '*Yes, it is. You're talking about predetermination, which happens all the time.*'
(Anderton rolls the ball towards Witwer who catches it just as it's about to go off the table).
ANDERTON: '*Why did you catch that?*'
WITWER: '*Because it was going to fall.*'
ANDERTON: '*You're certain?*'
WITWER: '*Yes.*'
ANDERTON: '*But it didn't fall. You caught it. The fact that you prevented it from happening doesn't change the fact that it was going to happen.*'

Therefore, a taxpayer who fails to disclose the income they earned from being an Uber or Lyft driver in their spare time must surely have decided to intentionally hide that from the tax administration (*Uber BV v Commissioner of Taxation*, 2017). Correspondingly, the taxpayer who over-claims their allowable deductions despite being warned by a computer program they were at risk of being audited justifies a higher penalty. Additionally, a taxpayer who has defaulted on three previous payment arrangements will surely default on a fourth. Unfortunately, these kinds of predictions can be wrong, irrespective of whether historical or future analytics are undertaken. The behaviors observed by the tax administration may be linked to risky behavior such as tax avoidance, but they also may not be, as current analytics programs usually take no notice of psychological motivations or narratives (Rouvroy, 2012). Analytics also requires the correct inputs be selected and validated in order to produce proper outputs, a concept widely recognized by the computer science maxim 'garbage in-garbage out'. In Australia, the ATO's focus on work-related expenses can and often do produce substantial amendments to pre-lodgement claims for work-related expenses, but require the taxpayer to select the correct occupation code, otherwise the analytics risks comparing the deductions of butchers with hairdressers, or doctors with miners (Veit, 2019).

The consequences of incorrect data matching, analytics and predictions can be catastrophic. In Australia, the social security agency, Centrelink, launched a new Online Compliance Intervention (OCI) system in 2016 to assist in recovering debts of overpaid allowances. Client data held by Centrelink payments was matched with historical tax information supplied by the ATO to identify where Centrelink clients were earning a wage whilst earning a disability or unemployment payment. In such cases, a debt was automatically raised and processed for collection via Centrelink's powers under Australia's social security laws. However, the OCI failed in a number of respects to correctly verify income with taxpayers and resulted in certain absurd circumstances such as the pursuit of debt owed by a deceased taxpayer and pursuit of debts that had been fully repaid (Commonwealth Ombudsman, 2017).

In Australia, judicial scrutiny of inaccuracy in tax analytics has been scant—the Commissioner is not required to identify how he or she came to select a taxpayer for audit (*Industrial Equity Ltd v Deputy Commissioner of Taxation*, 1990), nor are they required to give reasons for what information is selected or checked (*Federal Commissioner of Taxation v Citibank*, 1989) and they may obtain such information from any parties they see fit (*Southwestern Indemnities Ltd v Bank of New South Wales & Federal Commissioner of Taxation*, 1973). Furthermore, the Commissioner has significant evidentiary powers in proceedings, where certain documents produced under s. 350-10 of sch. 1 of the *Taxation Adminis-tration Act 1953* (Cth) are considered *prima facie* evidence that the matters are correct. Despite this, there is some obiter in *Denlay v Commissioner of Taxation* (2011), *Deputy Commissioner of Taxation v Bonaccorso* (2016) and *Deputy Commissioner of Taxation v Armstrong Scalisi Holdings Pty Ltd* (2019), where the Court accepted evidence from a taxation officer relating to the use of data analytics within the course of their normal duties which may have evidenced certain inaccuracies relevant to the course of the litigation. However, in counterpoint to these cases, in *Sgardelis and Commissioner of Taxation* (2007), the Administrative Appeals Tribunal seemed to accept that an "audit" under s. 995-1 of the *Income Tax Assessment Act 1997* (Cth) had commenced once the ATO case officer had downloaded a case from an Automated Work Allocation (AWA) system, and no further inquiry was deemed to be necessary by the learned Tribunal. Perhaps in such circumstances what is needed is an acceptance by the tax administra-tion that observations of potential risks need to be validated through the use of different datasets, or perhaps just an acknowledgement that the findings of the algorithm are informative rather than probative.

The Honourable Justice Melissa Perry (2019, p. 4) wrote extra-judicially that we must:

Be cautious of the human tendency to trust the reliability of computers... Legal advisers and decision-makers must therefore be alert to the risk of assuming the correctness of information provided by au-tomated processes and to take steps to ensure an understanding of the way in which such material has been produced. It may not be enough to assume that the "bottom line" is correct.

Privacy

Privacy is a substantial challenge for data analytics, where the concepts pertaining to big data already create tensions between both individual and collective privacy on the one hand, and the potential benefits to the greater good of society on the other. These tensions are important when considering individual and collective privacy can be interfered with when tax administrations are conducting big data analytics, either in a direct way (e.g., an individual's tax records being reviewed by an algorithm where no officer has formed a reasonable suspicion of wrongdoing) or in an indirect way (e.g., where the inadvertent disclosure of non-tax information, such as on social media or blogs, permits inferences to be drawn regarding taxable affairs).

Therefore, it is important to recognize privacy is a substantial concern when massive amounts of data are being collected, stored, matched and analyzed by government agencies (especially the tax administra-tions) in circumstances where the individual to whom that information relates may not have consented or even been aware of the information becoming available. There are also substantial protections in place relating to the privacy of tax information—in Australia, these are recognized in both the *Privacy Act 1988* (Cth) (the Privacy Act) and the *Taxation Administration Act 1953* (Cth). Similar protections exist in the US (e.g. *Internal Revenue Code of 1986* [US] §. 6103) and the United Kingdom (UK) and Europe (e.g. statutory tax acts but, more broadly, the General Data Protection Regulation 2016/679 (GPDR)).

In the European Union (EU), one of the widespread data protections enshrined in the GPDR was first enunciated by Viviane Reding, the European Commissioner for Justice, Fundamental Rights and Citizen-ship when she described the "right to be forgotten" (Rosen, 2012, p.89). The Commissioner described the right to be forgotten falling under circumstances where "[if] an individual no longer wants his personal data to be processed or stored by a data controller, and if there is no legitimate reason for keeping it, the data should be removed from their system" (Rosen, 2012, p. 89). In the literature, Commissioner Reding's sentiments are reflected in the academic commentary that establishes generally accepted requirements for information collection and privacy involve notice and consent—that is, the individual must be aware their information is being collected and the purpose/s for collection, and be given the opportunity to consent or refuse consent for those purposes (Cate & Mayer-Schonberger, 2013; Solove, 2013).

Both of these concepts (the right to be forgotten and the awareness/consent paradigm) have relevance to Australia because of the "growing power asymmetries between institutions that accumulate data, and the individuals who generate it" (Campolo, Sanfilippo, Whittaker & Crawford, 2017, p. 28). The OAIC has clearly recognized this connection, having made several submissions to government and regulatory discussion papers which call for recognition of the EU's approach to the right to be forgotten in the age of data analytics (OAIC, 2019a; OAIC, 2019b). The right to be forgotten and awareness/consent also speak directly to obligations imposed on entities under Australia's privacy framework, which at a Commonwealth level is regulated by the Privacy Act containing the Australian Privacy Principles (APP). Compliance with the Privacy Act is overseen by the OAIC. Each of the States and Territories handles the protection of personal information in different ways which creates a somewhat difficult patchwork of laws to navigate.

Under s.6 of the Privacy Act, personal information is defined as:

information or an opinion about an identified individual, or an individual who is reasonably identifiable (a) whether the information or opinion is true or not; and (b) whether the information or opinion is recorded in a material form or not.

Entities covered by the Act (including Commonwealth agencies and organizations) must comply with the APPs, including APP1 (open and transparent management of personal information), APP5 (notification of the collection of personal information) and APP6 (use or disclosure of personal information). Generally, small businesses with an annual turnover of less than $3 million are exempt for the Act. These obligations impose a number of obligations in a tax environment generally discharged by obtaining consent from taxpayers during lodgment or physical interaction, having open and public data handling and processing procedures, and allowing human intervention to correct errors (whether taxpayer-initiated or audit-initiated).

However, consent can be a nebulous or even moot issue when it comes to the administration of public revenue due in many instances to tax administrations having lawful rights to access the information they do. Under Australian law, the Commissioner of Taxation is permitted full and free access to any documents and places for the purposes of the taxation laws (*Taxation Administration Act 1953* (Cth), div. 353, sch. 1), and similar sweeping access provisions exist in other common law jurisdictions (e.g., §. 7602 of the *Internal Revenue Code* (US) or the HMRC's automatic exchange of information agreements).

From a taxation perspective at least, there is a presumption for taxation administrations to have access to the information they need to protect the public revenue (see *Bloemen v Commissioner of Taxation*, 1980; *Deputy Commissioner of Taxation v Richard Walter Pty Ltd*, 1994; *Commissioner of Taxation v Futuris Corporation Ltd*, 2008). This has been reflected in common law in cases such as *Commissioner of Taxation v Warner* (2015), where the statutory duty of a liquidator to keep records confidential unless ordered by the Court is overridden by the Commissioner's right to free and full access to documents. In the US, third-party sellers such as eBay and PayPal have been ordered to turn over records of sales to catch taxpayers out in under-declaring their income (*Orellana v Commissioner*, 2010; *U.S. v Wilson*, 2014). In the UK, a proposal is currently underway to consider whether to remove requirements for approval by the First-tier Tribunal (Tax Chamber) before Her Majesty's Revenue and Customs (HMRC) can issue compulsory information-gathering notices to financial institutions (HMRC, 2015; Register & Adams, 2017). In *Deputy Commissioner of Taxation v Zeqaj* (2019), the Victorian Supreme Court rejected allegations that the Commissioner had improperly violated the appellant's privacy by seeking, and subsequently using, information from Victorian Police regarding his alleged involvement in the cultivation of cannabis. Finally, and most recently, in *Glencore International AG & Ors v Commissioner of Taxation of the Commonwealth of Australia & Ors* (2019), the High Court established the Commissioner may, in the course of his or her duties of assessing the taxation liabilities of any person, use whatever material which happens to come to the ATO or be in the public domain, including material which may have been gathered illegally or subject to legal professional privilege.

There may be valid reasons for privacy considerations being waived or ignored in a number of contexts in the taxation administration. First, the mere knowledge of scrutiny can be sufficient to change behavior. If a person is notified or informed they are being investigated, this may be enough to cause them to shift their behavior—particularly the case for serious offences involving theft, money laundering, tax evasion or fraud. This type of behavior was clearly contemplated by Zarsky (2013, p. 1555) when he stated that, "with full transparency [of analytics], monitored individuals will sidestep proxies even while still engaging in risk-generating behavior". This perhaps stands as an answer to why certain approaches, such as the release of certain source codes of analytical programs to public websites under a black box tinkering model, are considered to be inappropriate in ensuring transparency of state-sanctioned data analytics (Perel & Elkin-Koren, 2017).

Even where we have given consent to the collection, use or disclosure of our personal information, there are still circumstances where we remain blind to the effect of inadvertent disclosures and the effects on our privacy. For example, when we sign up for rewards programs in retail stores, we agree to marketing agencies potentially selling our data; we eSign collection statements on websites without reading them; and we agree that our phones can store our passwords in keychains or virtual lockers (van Dijsck, 2014). Zuboff (2015, p. 75) called this phenomenon "surveillance capitalism", the idea that we appear more than happy to trade our individual privacy for monetary gain, non-financial rewards or some other kind of convenience. There is no strict legislative barrier preventing a tax administration, either under a statutory information-gathering power or by purchasing the dataset on the open market, from obtaining this information for tax administration purposes. On this point, Professor Karen Yeung (2016, p. 56) was acerbic in her comments when she stated that "we suspend our privacy rights in return for new technology built with our data and the convenience and efficiency that they offer".

Privacy considerations also come to the fore in circumstances where tax administrations overstep their bounds in relation to compliance or audit activity—often taxpayer sentiment is quick to question whether a tax administration that does not have its own house in order should have the right to access such confidential information. Whilst, thankfully, these instances are relatively few in number, they go a long way in undermining the legitimacy of administrations and the credibility to engage in what may otherwise be lawful compliance activity. Globally, Houser and Sanders (2016) detail the politicization of the Internal Revenue Service (IRS) audit by previous Presidential administrations, and Freedman and Vella (2011) discuss the common law treatment of the HMRC where auditors have acted contrary to the principles of good administrative decision-making and either acted *ultra vires* or contravened a legitimate expectation. Thankfully, Australia's experience with similar instances appears brief. A recent review by the Inspector-General of Taxation (IGT) was conducted into the ATO's use of garnishee notices, a powerful debt recovery tool forcing entities that may owe a taxpayer money to pay those funds to the

Commissioner instead, and is usually used to "dock" earnings of taxpayers who do not meet their debt obligations and have the capacity to repay them (Inspector-General of Taxation, 2019b). Whilst found no misconduct by the ATO was found, the IGT nevertheless concluded there were several improvements that could be made to the ATO's garnishee and debt recovery program.

The privacy landscape also changes if the shift in data analytics pushes tax assessments towards source-based rather than taxpayer-based assessments of income. Where the tax administration can obtain information on matters such as wages, contractor payments, deductions, sales taxes and other financial data directly from retailers or employers (Ibrahim & Pope, 2011), this reduces the need to directly obtain information from the taxpayer. Income can be verified with the entity that pays it, rather than requiring the taxpayer to prove the income and calculating revenue on that basis. In the UK, the HMRC is already transitioning to a fully pre-filled system of data analytics and employer-obligation reporting which would see individual taxpayers not needing to lodge a tax return—they would simply receive a notice of assessment indicating whether a debt or refund has been raised. Under these circumstances, tax administrations are relying on third-party information which may have been gathered without the taxpayer's notice or consent. This raises potential concerns regarding the disclosure obligations of third-parties of that information, but also whether the taxpayer has a right to provide information that may change their tax assessment prior to such a determination being made.

Privacy will likely remain a key consideration for tax administrations well into the future. However, the individual rights of privacy appear largely undisturbed by big data analytics, where it seems to have effected a change more in form than in substance. Privacy regulators may have concerns with the expansion of programs into areas of data being used for taxation purposes (OVIC, 2018; OAIC, 2018a; OAIC, 2018b; OAIC, 2019c; OAIC, 2019d), but it appears on evidence that these actions are consistent with the ATO's broader statutory mandates to protect public revenue. Even in circumstances where the Commissioner or his or her delegates are engaging in a fishing expedition and hoping to catch an errant taxpayer, there are grounds to consider the collection of such personal information for assessing a tax liability is within the scope of legal authority.

Opacity

Opacity is an interlinked, but distinct, concept from privacy and covers the "black box" nature of analytics programs (Pasquale, 2016). For example, opacity occurs when we cannot answer questions such as how do tax administrations' analytics programs reach the conclusions they do? How do these programs weigh or assess the data they are fed? What things/situations/facts do they consider more relevant than others? Opacity, therefore, is a term with two potential meanings, as follows:

- *Opacity-by-understanding.* This concept describes opacity relating to the technical know-how needed to read computer code and data science, to interpret what the code does and how it works.
- *Opacity-at-law.* This form of opacity creates a blanket of secrecy over the data analytics program, either by reference to the tax information the program deals with or the analytics program code itself (opacity-by-law).

Opacity-by-understanding hinges on the basis of a technical argument—that is, the skills to decipher complex coding languages are highly complex, and even the creators of algorithms can struggle to define how they work (Burrell, 2015). However, this concern is somewhat temporal in nature. Whilst the skills of computer coding and data science are currently specialized, society is very quickly reacting to data analytics, algorithms and even AI, to the extent these skills are considered highly desirable by modern business recruiters and computer coding is now a common inclusion in most school curricula. There is also evidence to suggest opacity-by-understanding is limited only by the willingness of the party examining the analytics program. In 2019, investigative journalists successfully reversed-engineered a Chinese Government algorithm, proving it racially segregated the minority Uighur population for targeting by police and national security officers (Human Rights Watch, 2019). Opacity-by-understanding also has limited application to machine learning and AI programs, where even understanding of the algorithm itself will not necessarily demonstrate what it has learned and how it applies the requisite business rules to making decisions (Desai & Kroll, 2017). This is widely known in the computing community as the "interpretability problem", and requires that humans adopt alternative approaches more akin to psychology in dealing with machine learning or AI programs (Anannay & Crawford, 2018, p. 4).

Opacity-by-understanding also has the potential to exacerbate or contribute to substantial information asymmetries between governments and taxpayers. In the EU, the GPDR includes a somewhat limited right of explanation, under which an affected individual can seek explanations from governments as to how a computer program made decisions using their personal data and covers any entity that "controls" or "processes" personal data (GPDR, art. 4, 12 and 22). However, there is a growing concept in the academic and computing literature for explainability (Pasquale, 2017), where a black box algorithm becomes a "white box" and allows "people [to] scrutinise and understand how the algorithms make decisions, and judge the algorithms that judge us" (Loke, 2019, pp. 25). Explainability builds on the explicit or implicit requirements for entities conducting data analytics to provide reasoning for their decisions when those decisions are based on analytics, such as under the GPDR (Casey, Farhangi & Vogl, 2019).

Whilst Australia lacks a similar provision, there remains a requirement (and avenue of remedy) under the *Administrative Decisions (Judicial Review) Act 1977* (Cth) for aggrieved persons to seek the reasons for why a particular decision is made, including those made by a computer (*Re Minister for Immigration and Multicultural Affairs; Ex parte Palme*, 2003). There may also be valid reasons for information asymmetries between the regulator and regulated. Most regulators (including tax administrations) strive for more information than their subjects or targets, making their decisions more effective and better tailored to the regulated environment. In some cases, it can also enable covert assessments or activities which may catch offending red-handed (Lim, Hagendorff, & Armitage, 2016; Loftus, 2019).

On the other hand, opacity-by-law creates circumstances of secrecy or confidentiality around the workings of a data analytics program, and is often cited in the literature as a foreign entity to the principles of transparency, open government, and accountability (e.g., see the various works by Professor Brownsword referenced in this chapter). Opacity-by-law has an even greater scope of application in the taxation spaces due to the highly sensitive nature of taxpayer information such administrations deal with. Sandvig (2014, p. 9) and Burrell (2015, p. 4) describe a "right to look" as a claim by right of consumers to see and understand how algorithms used by private enterprise receive, sort, assess and rank data to ensure the results are not being unfairly skewed by players in given markets.

In the Australian tax administration space, there are strong provisions regarding the disclosure of information related to the tax affairs of an individual, which is generally considered as protected information (see *Taxation Administration Act 1953* (Cth), subdiv. 355-B, sch. 1). However, the source code for a data analytics tool which simply reads or analyses this protected information and produces an output may not necessarily be protected in and of itself. Yet other agencies have had some judicial consideration of their own approach to data analytics and the use of algorithms. In *Cordover v Australian Electoral Com-*

mission (2015), the Administrative Appeals Tribunal determined the Australian Electoral Commission (AEC) was correct in its decision not to hand over the source code for vote-counting software known as 'Easycount'. The Tribunal accepted the grounds that the software was a "trade secret", that is it met the terms under *Searle Australia v PIAC* (1992) of having commercial value and steps being taken to limit or control its dissemination and also having commercial value that would be destroyed if disclosed.

However, the aforementioned 'right to look' is not as relevant in a tax administration context. There are valid reasons why data analytics and algorithms assessing various forms of taxpayer behavior should remain hidden (or, at least, the nature of the algorithm's internal workings). As described earlier, when taxpayers are aware of the 'red flags' their behavior can trigger with tax administrations, they are more likely to modify their behaviors to avoid detection. It would also be hard to argue a person or class of people suspected of being involved in a criminal enterprise has a 'right to look' at the algorithms which may detect them. Assume for a moment the ATO builds an algorithm to analyze a series of inputs (e.g., banking information, travel documents, social media posts) and provides a single output—that is, an individual's risk score of engaging in tax evasion. If the precise nature of the inputs was made public, it would be possible to game the algorithm by tailoring behavior to avoid detection via those inputs. Yet, in this circumstance, the penalty is not defaulting on a loan but a substantial risk to the public revenue. There are also certain classes of criminal investigation that occur in the taxation world which are only possible under a blanket of secrecy, cast either by the tax statutes themselves or associated legislation relating to terrorism, money laundering, serious organized crime or national security (e.g., the ATO's experience in Project Wickenby; see also Numerato, 2016; Baldwin & Gadboys, 2016). These tensions between an open society and secret government have always involved the balance between rights of citizens engaging in lawful activity and "foreign spies, terrorists and criminals when they pry, plot and steal" (Moore & Rid, 2016, p. 9).

However, the purpose of this chapter is not to argue that data analytics should be shrouded in absolute secrecy. Instead, what is necessary is a careful reframing of our arguments around secrecy. One option is to utilize open-source software as the algorithmic base, but then to vary the inputs to information only available to law enforcement. The actual work being undertaken by the algorithm in terms of ranking and sorting can easily be understood, but the dataset on which the algorithm runs remains (rightfully) secret. Buiten (2019) proposes perhaps a more useful version of transparency, one that considers transparency on the inputs (what data is fed to the algorithm), transparency of the decision-making process and transparency of the outcomes (where counterfactuals, being the measurement of different outcomes based on a single variable input, become relevant in assessing accuracy). Another option would be the establishment of an effective governance-within-governance framework, such as oversight by an ombudsman-style body or review by a judge. This type of overview is already contemplated in the Australian context, including the IGT established under the *Inspector-General of Taxation Act 2003* (Cth), the Commonwealth Ombudsman established by the *Ombudsman Act 1976* (Cth), as well as Parliamentary scrutiny via the House of Representatives Standing Committee on Tax and Revenue and the Senate Standing Committee on Economics. In this manner, the secrecy of an algorithm could remain protected whilst providing opportunities for independent review, investigation and amendment.

Bias

The use of analytics can also suffer from bias. Although analytical programs as computer constructs are inherently bias-neutral, they also currently lack the relative insight of an objective human decision-maker who may take into account certain matters not easily interpreted by data. Barocas and Selbst explain that, depending on where in the decision-making process a term of bias arises, data analytics create the potential for a "disproportionately adverse impact on protected classes" (2016, p. 5). In taxation administration, these can be substantially problematic, especially when data analytics may be used for assessments of qualitative rather than quantitative matters. For example, how does an analytical program determine if someone is "fit and proper" in the terms used in s. 126A(3) of the *Superannuation Industry (Supervision) Act 1993* (Cth) (SISA)? Though there are pathways for disqualification for contraventions of the SISA, subs. 126A(3) permits that "the Regulator may disqualify an individual if satisfied that the individual is otherwise not a fit and proper person". How does the analytics program properly evaluate qualitative matters for honesty, knowledge and ability as set out in Australia's seminal cases of *Hughes and Vale Pty Ltd v State of New South Wales* (1955) and *Australian Broadcasting Tribunal v Bond & Ors* (1990)?

Assuming it can do so, how do analytics weigh honesty, knowledge and ability against other matters which may count against them? Indeed, the Courts have stipulated that for such matters there is no "neat arithmetical algorithm or a guide which is able to be used mechanically" (*Australian Securities & Investments Commission v Lindberg*, 2012, para. 89).

Data analytics can therefore be biased on a number of different counts. First, the data being used for analysis may have been deliberately or inadvertently swayed due to pre-existing bias in the data collection. The deployment of predictive policing analytics in the US has been marred in several states by predilections of over-representation of risk scores for African-American and Latino communities (Ferguson, 2017). Data analytics based on policing data may be drawing correlations based on arrests made as far back as the 1950s, a time in which racial profiling and segregation by police was a common sight. Chiao (2019, p. 129) describes this effect as follows: "where upstream decisions exert significant influence over downstream ones, if for no other reason than that they determine the profile of the population over which downstream decisions operate". For gang membership, persons of color inevitably associate with other race-similar groups, feeding "associational suspicion" amongst minority members of the target population. Geographically-oriented analytics programs used by police have also associated high crime risks with poor socio-economic neighborhoods which disproportionately feature these same African-American and Latino communities, leading to increased policing scrutiny (and, of course, more policing data, reinforcing the vicious cycle; Ferguson, 2017). In tax administration, certain classes of individuals may be targeted for audit either deliberately or inadvertently on the basis of certain misconceptions regarding how their wealth may have been accrued or how those classes respond to taxation audits (Sharkey & Murray, 2016; Henricks & Seamster, 2017). As outlined earlier, the IGT review into the ATO's use of garnishee notices found a number of small businesses were disproportionately targeted for the issue of enduring garnishee notices, resulting in the IGT making recommendations regarding the way the ATO analytics selected taxpayers for the issue of enduring garnishee notices (Inspector-General of Taxation, 2019a).

The data itself may also be the source of bias, where the data may have been preferentially selected, collected, entered or transformed prior to analysis. For example, if tax auditors over-select their targets from 'working professionals' and achieve a 100 per cent strike rate for over claiming a certain deduction, this may permit the inference that all working professionals are over claiming (even though there is actually no correlation between those two characteristics). If the datasets used are not sufficient, complete or lack cohesive detail, the analytics program may be selecting characteristics that have no bearing on the behavior sought to be regulated. This can result when the datasets reflect existing social biases (e.g., a data analytics program which selects on wages earned will preferentially select men, because women earning high wages are underrepresented in the target population). Where a test environment is used to train a data analytics program (e.g., an algorithm or machine learning system) which is not representative of the wider society, the selection will necessarily be biased. In a recent study, an algorithm was built to distinguish huskies from wolves and worked perfectly under laboratory settings but failed to work in field tests (Ribeiro, Singh, & Guestrin, 2016). After further work it was found the algorithm, which had been trained on photographs of wolves and huskies, was selecting on the presence or absence of snow in the backgrounds. In tax administration, there is a body of work showing young taxpayers between the ages of 18 to 30 are disproportionately represented in tax audits due to their *laissez faire* attitudes to tax obligations and reporting requirements (see an excellent example in Braithwaite, Reinhart, & Smart, 2010).

The linkages between entities (particularly in the context of tax administration) may also be of questionable veracity. Associational analytics can be used to identify co-actors in complex networks of interrelationship; yet, when these types of associational analytics are used in practice—such as by police to identify gang membership—they inevitably tar innocent individuals with the same brush based on loose connection. US police in the cities of New Orleans, Kansas City, Chicago and New York City used similar programs to identify people they believed were involved in gang violence or gun crime, and implemented risk treatment strategies for those with top scores according to their risk models, even if these persons had never been the subject of police attention previously (Ferguson, 2017). Where associational analytics is used in tax administrations, such as in analyzing the relationship between egregious taxpayers and tax advisors or agents who offer them advice on how to avoid or evade their lawful obligations, innocent taxpayers who also use that advisor or agent may be caught up by the audit or enforcement activity. In much the same way, credit card companies have been known to limit or downgrade the credit scores of individuals on the basis they visited the same establishments as others who demonstrated a poor repayment history (Lepri et al., 2017).

The questions on how analytics might respond to biased data requires a nuanced response. The first step is to recognize that analytics programs, at least at the level currently utilized, should be considered indicative and not probative without further review. A set of human eyes is always important in validating whether the selections of the dataset are achieving the aims for which the analytics program was initially established. Second, where data analytics programs show a tendency towards bias or unfair weightings, this must be incorporated into feedback structures to foster continuous improvement of the selection models. Third, data analytics based on associational dynamics between individuals should be carefully managed to ensure that racial, social or sexual biases do not arise inadvertently. Finally, analytics programs can be designed (particularly in a tax administration context) to utilize multiple decision trees to identify and minimize the occurrence of bias.

Fairness and Due Process

Where decisions are made by computer programs—even relatively simple decisions such as which taxpayers to audit, or which taxpayer debts may be more easily recovered—and the source code of the data analytics is not publicly available, it can be difficult to challenge how that decision was made in a court or tribunal. Fairness and due process challenges in analytics can present in two interesting scenarios: (1) an algorithm is not as objective as a human being; and (2) an algorithm is diametrically opposed where analytics are *too* objective, and interprets the data with no interpretation of the subjective 'vibe' of the matter.

Legally, the protections for fairness and due process in data analytics are difficult to articulate. Generally, there is a long line of authority dictating administrative decision-makers must afford "procedural fairness" to those whose interests are or may be affected by their decisions (see *X v The Minister for Immigration & Multicultural Affairs*, 1999, para. 92). However, from a tax perspective, where analytics may have been used to find a tax liability, there appears little ground for legal challenge to the tools employed. Rather, the focus is usually on the basis of the Commissioner's assessment and there remains an equally long line of clear authority for the proposition that recovery of tax owed is preferable to considering a taxpayer's challenge to the Commissioner's assessment (see *Deputy Commissioner of Taxation v Mackey*, 1982; *Uratoriu v Commissioner of Taxation*, 2008; *Queensland Maintenance Services Pty Ltd v Commissioner of Taxation*, 2011; *Rossi v Commissioner of Taxation*, 2015). It is worth noting that an element of caution is necessary. For example, as the Full Federal Court decided in the Pintarich case that a decision by computer lacked "both a mental process of reaching a conclusion and an objective manifestation of that conclusion" (*Pintarich v Deputy Commissioner of Taxation*, 2018, [140]), there is no confidence that Australian jurists would be willing to entertain data analytics decisions without a decision from a superior court.

Fairness is also a double-sided concept, as binding on the Commissioner as on the taxpayer. In circumstances where the tax authority has access to much greater, more accurate and more real-time reporting of data from taxpayers and third parties, the window for error is reduced. Taxpayers will (quite understandably) be more likely to hold tax administrations to account if their information is wrong or outdated, and trust in the ATO will be eroded as taxpayers' dispute more and more of their individual assessments. Given the extensive use by the ATO for data analytics for debt, lodgement, refunds, compliance activities and future strategic planning of tax policy, there is an equally binding obligation on the ATO to use this information fairly, honestly and as transparently as the legislation permits. Should the ATO (or any other tax administration) seek to move to fully automated tax reporting and completely remove the need for an individual or small business taxpayer to lodge a return by pre-filling and by third-party data validation, this would be a considerable savings initiative and reduce a substantial amount of regulatory burden. However, there are a number of downstream effects on professional advisors to give tailored and specific advice, as well as on the ATO to ensure it continued its focus on taxpayer assistance rather than taxpayer deterrence such that fairness under tax algorithms is "a right they will pursue in Australia, to ensure global competitive equality" (Bentley, 2019, p. 712).

The additional challenges to analytics in tax regulation and enforcement involving issues of wrong or unfair decisions could also be ameliorated by the adoption of constant feedback and self-orientation. Zweig, Wenzelburger & Krafft (2018) describe a need for algorithms in use in national security environments to be embedded in social oversight (either by systems internal to the security organization, or externally as a community ombudsman or other surveillant organization) as a way of ensuring quality decision-making and eliminating racial and ethnic bias. The constant feedback and repositioning required in a systemic design framework would inevitably need this degree of algorithmic tweaking to ensure ongoing accuracy and viability. Zweig et al. (2018) also describe a need for effective counterfactuals and being transparent about where algorithms or analytics feed predictions into decision-making.

CONCLUSION

The prospect of data analytics, particularly in the arena of tax administration, is an exciting development in the fields of data science and governmental regulation. In Australia, where tax liability is determined and pursued by the Commissioner of Taxation and the ATO, data analytics has enabled taxation officers to make decisions with better access to evidence and more processing power to make the correct calculations of tax liability. However, the use of powerful analytical programs to mine the gems out of 'big data' raises a series of interrelated and complex concerns relating to privacy, opacity, inaccuracy, fairness, bias and due process which apply to individuals as well as whole classes of taxpayers across entire segments of society. Additionally, the tax policy and regulatory environment is changing every day and requires adaptation of data analytics programs to both support the Commissioner's statutory objectives and align with contemporary societal values.

On individual cases, there is a danger to accept that a computer program will detect more than the human eye, a danger that will only increase as we develop ever more sophisticated models of analytics which blur the line between algorithms, machine learning and full AI. This danger extends well into the hazards of our own ignorance, engendered by a reliance on machines to do the work for us where law or policy does not clearly delineate where a machine may make a decision and where it cannot, or at what point in an automated decision-making tree a human should intervene to respond. Therefore, data analytics in tax administrations offer significant promise, as long as we respect that decision-making occurs "under condition of paying adequate respect to human rights, offering choice, providing for transparency, and adhering to accountability" (Leenes, 2011, p. 159).

Yet for all the risks, there are substantial benefits to be had. The use of data analytics, machine learning and AI will likely only increase in the future. Therefore, the potential issues regarding privacy, opacity, inaccuracy, fairness, bias and due process need to be duly considered when systems are designed to take advantage of our technological strength. Privacy can live side-by-side with compulsive investigation; opacity can exist with qualification; and, inaccuracy, fairness and bias can be appropriately managed and treated with proper respect for the checks and balances of the legal system, parliamentary debate and adherence to the commonality of human rights.

REFERENCES

Administrative Decisions (Judicial Review) Act 1977 (Cth).

Anannay, M., & Crawford, K. (2018). Seeing without knowing: Limitations of the transparency ideal and its application to algorithmic accountability. *New Media & Society, 20*(3), 981. doi:10.1177/1461444816676645

ASIC v Westpac Banking Corporation [2019] FCA 1244.

Attorney-General's Department. (2004). *Automated assistance in administrative decision making*. Canberra: Administrative Review Council.

Australian Broadcasting Tribunal v Bond & Ors (1990) 170 CLR 321.

Australian Communications & Media Authority (ACMA). (2013). *Managing your digital identity: Digital footprints and identities research short report.* Canberra, Australia: Commonwealth Government Printer. Retrieved from https://apo.org.au/node/36376

Australian Government Information Management Office (AGIMO). (2007). *Automated assistance in administrative decision-making: Better practice guide.* Canberra, Australia: Department of Finance and Deregulation.

Australian Law Reform Commission (ALRC). (1998). *Secrecy & open government in Australia* (Report 112). Retrieved from https://www.alrc.gov.au/publication/secrecy-laws-and-open-government-in-australia-alrc-report-112/14-frameworks-for-effective-information-handling/data-matching/

Australian National Audit Office (ANAO). (2008). *The Australian taxation office's use of data matching and analytics in tax administration.* Retrieved from https://www.anao.gov.au/work/performance-audit/australian-taxation-offices-use-data-matching-and-analytics-tax

Australian Securities & Investments Commission v Lindberg [2012] VSC 332.

Australian Taxation Office. (2019). *Australian tax gaps - an overview.* Retrieved from https://www.ato.gov.au/About-ATO/Research-and-statistics/In-detail/Tax-gap/Australian-tax-gaps-overview/?page=1#Tax_gap_research_program

Baldwin, F., & Gadboys, J. (2016). The duty of financial institutions to investigate and report suspicions of Fraud, financial crime, and corruption. In M. Dion, D. Weisstub, & J.-L. Richet (Eds.), Financial crimes: Psychological, technological, and ethical Issues (pp. 83-104). Cham, Switzerland: Springer. doi:10.1007/978-3-319-32419-7_4

Barocas, S., & Selbst, A. (2016). Big data's disparate impact. *California Law Review, 104*(3), 671–732.

Bentley, D. (2019). Timeless principles of taxpayer protection: how they adapt to digital disruption. *eJournal of Tax Research, 16*(3), 679-713.

Bloemen v Commissioner of Taxation (1980) 147 CLR 360.

Braithwaite, V., Reinhart, M., & Smart, M. (2010). Tax non-compliance among the under-30s: Knowledge, obligation or scepticism? In J. Alm, J. Martinez-Vazquez, & B. Torgler (Eds.), *Developing alternative frameworks for explaining tax compliance.* London, UK: Routledge.

Brotherton, E. A. (2012). Big brother gets a makeover: Behavioural targeting and the third-party doctrine. *Emory Law Journal, 61*(3), 555–558.

Brownsword, R. (2004). What the world needs now: Techno-regulation, human rights and human dignity. In R. Brownsword (Ed.), Global governance and the quest for justice: Volume 4 human rights (pp. 203-234). Oxford, UK: Hart Publishing.

Brownsword, R., & Harel, A. (2019). Law, liberty and technology: Criminal justice in the context of smart machines. *International Journal of Law in Context, 15*(2), 107–125. doi:10.1017/S1744552319000065

Brownsword, R., & Yeung, K. (2008). *Regulating technologies: Legal futures, regulatory frames and technological fixes.* Oxford, UK: Hart Publishing.

Buiten, M. (2019). Towards Intelligent Regulation of Artificial Intelligence. *European Journal of Risk Regulation, 10*(1), 41–59. doi:10.1017/err.2019.8

Burrell, J. (2015, Jan.). How the machine "thinks": Understanding opacity in machine learning algorithms. *Big Data & Society*, 1–12. doi:10.2139srn.2660674

Campolo, A., Sanfilippo, M., Whittaker, M., & Crawford, K. (2017). *AI now 2017*. Retrieved from https://ainowinstitute.org/AI_Now_2017_Report.pdf

Carltona Ltd v Commissioners of Works [1943] 2 All ER 560.

Casey, B., Farhangi, A., & Vogl, R. (2019). Rethinking explainable machines: The GDPR's right to explanation debate and the rise of algorithmic audits in enterprise. *Berkeley Technology Law Journal, 34*(1), 143–188.

Cate, F., & Mayer-Schonberger, V. (2013). Notice and consent in a world of big data. *International Data Privacy, 3*(2), 67–73. doi:10.1093/idpl/ipt005

Chiao, V. (2019). Fairness, accountability and transparency: Notes on algorithmic decision-making in criminal justice. *International Journal of Law in Context, 15*(2), 126–139. doi:10.1017/S1744552319000077

Cohen, J. E. (2012). *Configuring the Networked Self*. New Haven, CT: Yale University.

Commissioner of Taxation v Futuris Corporation Ltd (2008) 237 CLR 146.

Commissioner of Taxation v Warner (2015) FCA 659.

Commonwealth Ombudsman. (2017). *Centrelink's automated debt raising and recovery system*. Retrieved from https://www.ombudsman.gov.au/__data/assets/pdf_file/0022/43528/Report-Centrelinks-automated-debt-raising-and-recovery-system-April-2017.pdf

Cordover v Australian Electoral Commission (2015) AATA 956.

Data-matching Program (Assistance and Tax) Act 1990 (Cth).

Denlay v Commissioner of Taxation (2011) FCAFC 63.

Deputy Commissioner of Taxation v Armstrong Scalisi Holdings Pty Ltd (2019) NSWSC 129.

Deputy Commissioner of Taxation v Bonaccorso (2016) NSWSC 595.

Deputy Commissioner of Taxation v Mackey [1982] 13 ATR 547.

Deputy Commissioner of Taxation v Richard Walter Pty Ltd (1994) 183 CLR 168.

Deputy Commissioner of Taxation v Zeqaj (2019) VSC 194.

Desai, D., & Kroll, J. (2017). Trust but verify: A guide to algorithms and the law. *Harvard Journal of Law & Technology, 31*(1), 1–64.

Elvery, S. (2017). How algorithms make important government decisions — and how that affects you. *ABC News*. Retrieved from https://www.abc.net.au/news/2017-07-21/algorithms-can-make-decisions-on-behalf-of-federal-ministers/8704858

Federal Commissioner of Taxation v Citibank [1989] 89 ATC 4268.

Fellmeth, A. (2005). Civil and criminal sanctions in the constitution and courts. *The Georgetown Law Journal, 94*(1), 1–15.

Ferguson, A. G. (2017). Illuminating black data policing. *Ohio State Journal of Criminal Law, 15*(2), 503–525.

Fertik, M., & Thompson, D. (2015). *The reputation economy: How to optimize your digital footprint in a world where your reputation is your most valuable asset.* Danvers, MA: New York Crown Business.

Freedman, J., & Vella, J. (2011). *HMRC's management of the UK tax system: The boundaries of legitimate discretion.* Oxford, UK: Oxford University Centre for Business Taxation. Retrieved from https://ora.ox.ac.uk/objects/uuid:869d0c16-7748-489d-9a74-

Glencore International AG & Ors v Commissioner of Taxation of the Commonwealth of Australia & Ors (2019) HCA 26.

Henricks, K., & Seamster, L. (2017). Mechanisms of the racial tax state. *Critical Sociology, 43*(2), 169–179. doi:10.1177/0896920516670463

Her Majesty's Revenue & Customs (HMRC). (2015). *Tax administration: regulations to implement the UK's automatic exchange of information agreements.* London, UK: HMRC. Retrieved from https://www.gov.uk/government/publications/tax-administration-regulations-to-implement-the-uks-automatic-exchange-of-information-agreements

Hill, K. (2012, February 16). How Target figured out a teen girl was pregnant before her father did. *Forbes.* Retrieved from https://www.forbes.com/sites/kashmirhill/2012/02/16/how-target-figured-out-a-teen-girl-was-pregnant-before-her-father-did/

Hogan-Doran, D. (2017). Computer says "no": Automation, algorithms and artificial intelligence in Government decision-making. *The Judicial Review, 13*, 1–39.

Houser, K., & Sanders, D. (2016). The use of big data analytics by the IRS: Efficient solutions or the end of privacy as we know it. *Vanderbilt Journal of Entertainment & Technology Law, 19*(4), 817–872.

Hughes and Vale Pty Ltd v State of New South Wales (1955) 93 CLR 127.

Human Rights Watch. (2019, 1 May). *China's algorithms of repression: Reverse engineering a Xinjiang police mass surveillance app.* Retrieved from https://www.hrw.org/report/2019/05/01/chinas-algorithms-repression/reverse-engineering-xinjiang-police

Ibrahim, I., & Pope, J. (2011). The viability of a pre-filled income tax return system for Malaysia. *Journal of Contemporary Issues in Business and Government, 17*(2), 85–89.

Income Tax Assessment Act 1997 (Cth).

Industrial Equity Ltd v Deputy Commissioner of Taxation [1990] 89 ATC 5316.

Inspector-General of Taxation. (2019a). *The future of the tax profession.* Canberra, Australia: Australian Government Printer.

Inspector-General of Taxation. (2019b). *Review into the Australian Taxation Office's use of garnishee notices*. Canberra, Australia: Australian Government Printer.

Inspector-General of Taxation Act 2003 (Cth).

Internal Revenue Code of. (1986). *Title 26*. USC.

Leenes, R. (2011). Framing techno-regulation: An exploration of state and non-state regulation by technology. *Legisprudence, 5*(2), 159. doi:10.5235/175214611797885675

Lepri, B., Staiano, J., Sangokoya, D., Letouze, E., & Oliver, N. (2017). The tyranny of data? The bright and dark sides of data-driven decision making for social good. In T. Cerquitelli, D. Quercia, & F. Pasquale (Eds.), *Transparent data mining for big and small data* (pp. 2–22). Dordrecht, Germany: Springer. doi:10.1007/978-3-319-54024-5_1

Lim, I., Hagendorff, J., & Armitage, S. (2016). Regulatory monitoring, information asymmetry and accounting quality: Evidence from the banking industry. *EFMA 25th Annual Meeting*. Retrieved from https://efmaefm.org/0efmameetings/efma%20annual%20meetings/2016-Switzerland/papers/EFMA2016_0504_fullpaper.pdf

Loftus, B. (2019). Normalizing covert surveillance: the subterranean world of policing. *British Journal of Sociology, 70*(5), 2070-2091. http://doi-org/ doi:10.1111/1468-4446.12651

Loke, S. (2019). *Achieving ethical algorithmic behaviour in the internet-of-things: A review*. Retrieved from https://arxiv.org/pdf/1910.10241.pdf

Maciejewski, M. (2016). To do more, better, faster and more cheaply: using big data in public administration. *International Review of Administrative Sciences, 83*(IS), 120-135. doi:10.1177/0020852316640058

Moore, D., & Rid, T. (2016). Cryptopolitik and the darknet. *Global Politics and Strategy, 58*(1), 7–38. doi:10.1080/00396338.2016.1142085

National Consumer Credit Protection Act 2009 (Cth).

Numerato, D. (2016). Corruption and public secrecy: An ethnography of football match-fixing. *Current Sociology, 64*(5), 699–717. doi:10.1177/0011392115599815

Nunn, S. (2003). Seeking tools for the war on terror: A critical assessment of emerging technologies in law enforcement. *Policing, 26*(3), 454–472. doi:10.1108/13639510310489494

Office of the Australian Information Commissioner (OAIC). (2014). *Guidelines on data matching in Australian Government administration*. Retrieved from https://www.oaic.gov.au/privacy/guidance-and-advice/guidelines-on-data-matching-in-australian-government-administration/

Office of the Australian Information Commissioner (OAIC). (2018a). *The ATO's administrative approach to the disclosure of tax debt information to credit reporting bureaus — submission to the Australian Taxation Office*. Canberra, Australia: OAIC.

Office of the Australian Information Commissioner (OAIC). (2018b). *Guide to data analytics and the Australian Privacy Principles*. Canberra, Australia: OAIC.

Office of the Australian Information Commissioner (OAIC). (2019a). *Artificial Intelligence: Australia's Ethics Framework – Submission to the Department of Industry, Innovation and Science and Data 61 discussion paper*. Canberra, Australia: OAIC.

Office of the Australian Information Commissioner (OAIC). (2019b). *Developing Standards for Artificial Intelligence: Hearing Australia's Voice — submission to Standards Australia*. Canberra, Australia: OAIC.

Office of the Australian Information Commissioner (OAIC). (2019c). *Handling of personal information — Department of Human Services PAYG data matching program*. Canberra, Australia: OAIC.

Office of the Australian Information Commissioner (OAIC). (2019d). *Handling of personal information — Department of Human Services NEIDM data matching program*. Canberra, Australia: OAIC.

Office of the Victorian Information Commissioner (OVIC). (2018). *Artifical intelligence and privacy: issues paper*. Melbourne: OVIC.

Ombudsman Act 1976 (Cth).

Orellana v Commissioner, No. 8950-08S, 2010 WL 1568447 [T.C. Apr. 20, 2010].

Pasquale, F. (2011). Restoring Transparency to Automated Authority. *Journal on Telecommunications & High Technology Law*, 9, 235–254. Retrieved from http://digitalcommons.law.umaryland.edu/cgi/viewcontent.cgi?article=2357&context=fac_pubs

Pasquale, F. (2016). *Black Box Society: The Secret Algorithms That Control Money and Information*. Harvard University Press.

Pasquale, F. (2017). Toward a Fourth Law of Robotics: Preserving Attribution, Responsibility, and Explainability in an Algorithmic Society. *Ohio State Law Journal*, 78, 1243–1255. Retrieved from https://kb.osu.edu/bitstream/handle/1811/85768/OSLJ_V78N5_1243.pdf

Perel, M., & Elkin-Koren, N. (2017). Black Box Tinkering: Beyond Disclosure in Algorithmic Enforcement. *Florida Law Review*, 69, 181–221. Retrieved from https://scholarship.law.ufl.edu/cgi/viewcontent.cgi?article=1348

Perry, M. (2019). iDecide: Digital pathways to decisions. *Federal Judicial Scholarship*, 3. Retrieved from http://www.austlii.edu.au/cgi-bin/sinodisp/au/journals/FedJSchol/2019/3.html

Pintarich v Deputy Commissioner of Taxation [2018] FCAFC 79.

Privacy Act 1988 (Cth).

Queensland Maintenance Services Pty Ltd v Commissioner of Taxation [2011] FCA 1443.

Re Minister for Immigration and Multicultural Affairs; Ex parte Palme [2003] 216 CLR 212.

Register, D., & Adams, H. (2017). Extending HMRC's civil information powers. *Tax Journal*. Retrieved from https://www.taxjournal.com/articles/extending-hmrc-s-civil-information-powers-30082018

Ribeiro, M. T., Singh, S., & Guestrin, C. (2016). Why should I trust you? Explaining the predictions of any classifier. *Proceedings of the 22nd ACM SIGKDD international conference on knowledge discovery and data mining*, 1135-1144. Retrieved from https://arxiv.org/pdf/1602.04938.pdf

Rosen, J. (2012). The right to be forgotten. *Stanford Law Review*, *64*, 88–92. Retrieved from https://review.law.stanford.edu/wp-content/uploads/sites/3/2012/02/64-SLRO-88.pdf

Rossi v Commissioner of Taxation [2015] AATA 601.

Rouvroy, A. (2012). The end(s) of critique: data-behaviourism vs. due-process. In M. Hildebrandt & K. De Vries (Eds.), *Privacy, due process and the computational turn: Philosophers of law meet philosophers of technology* (pp. 142–168). Abingdon, UK: Routledge.

Sandvig, C. (2014). Seeing the sort: The aesthetic and industrial defense of the algorithm. *Journal of the New Media Caucus*, *10*(3). Retrieved from http://median.newmediacaucus.org/art-infrastructures-information/seeing-the-sort-the-aesthetic-and-industrial-defense-of-the-algorithm/

Savas, E. S., Fite, H. H., Schumacher, B. G., Kanter, J., Bowen, H. R., & Mangum, G. L. (1969). Computers in public administration. *Public Administration Review*, *29*(2), 225–231. doi:10.2307/973708

Searle Australia v PIAC [1992] 108 ALR 163.

Sgardelis and Commissioner of Taxation (2007) 68 ATR 963.

Sharkey, N., & Murray, I. (2016). Reinventing administrative leadership in Australian taxation: Beware the fine balance of social psychological and rule of law principles. *Australian Tax Forum*, 63.

Social Security (Administration) Act 1999 (Cth).

Solove, D. (2013). Privacy self-management and the consent dilemma. *Harvard Law Review*, *126*, 1880–1893.

Southwestern Indemnities Ltd v Bank of New South Wales & Federal Commissioner of Taxation [1973] 73 ATC 4171.

Superannuation Industry (Supervision) Act 1993 (Cth).

Taxation Administration Act 1953 (Cth).

Twentieth Century Fox. (2002). *Minority Report*.

Uber BV v Commissioner of Taxation (2017) FCA 110.

Uratoriu v Commissioner of Taxation [2008] FCA 1531.

U.S. v Wilson, 593 F. Appendix 942 [11th Cir. 2014].

van Dijsck, J. (2014). Datafication, dataism and dataveillance: Big Data between scientific paradigm and ideology. *Surveillance & Society*, *12*(2), 199–208. doi:10.24908s.v12i2.4776

Veit, A. (2019). Swimming upstream: leveraging data and analytics for taxpayer engagement - an Australian and international perspective. *eJournal of Tax Research, 16*(3), 474-499.

X v The Minister for Immigration & Multicultural Affairs [1999] 92 FCR 524.

Yeung, K. (2016, October). Algorithmic regulation and intelligent enforcement. In M. Lodge (Ed.), *Regulation scholarship in crisis? LSE discussion paper No 84* (p. 56). London: London School of Economics.

Zarsky, T. (2013). Transparent predictions. *University of Illinois Law Review, 4,* 1503–1570.

Zuboff, S. (2015). Big other: Surveillance capitalism and the prospects of an informal Civilization. *Journal of Information Technology, 30*(1), 75–89. doi:10.1057/jit.2015.5

Zweig, K., Wenzelburer, G., & Krafft, T. D. (2018). On chances and risks of security related algorithmic decision-making systems. *European Journal for Security Research, 3*(2), 181–203. doi:10.100741125-018-0031-2

ADDITIONAL READING

Coglianese, C., & Lehr, D. (2017). Regulating by robot: Administrative decision-making in the machine-learning era. *The Georgetown Law Journal, 105,* 1147–1223.

Danaher, J. (2016). The threat of algocracy: Reality, resistance and accommodation. *Philosophy & Technology, 29*(3), 245–268. doi:10.100713347-015-0211-1

European Commission. (2016). *General Data Protection Code, Regulation (EU) 2016/679 of the European Parliament and of the Council of 27 April 2016 on the protection of natural persons with regard to the processing of personal data and on the free movement of such data, and repealing Directive 95/46/EC.* Retrieved from https://publications.europa.eu/en/publication-detail/-/publication/3e485e15-11bd-11e6-ba9a-01aa75ed71a1/language-en

Ferguson, A. G. (2017). *The rise of big data policing: Surveillance, race, and the future of law enforcement.* New York: NYU Press. doi:10.2307/j.ctt1pwtb27

Hannah-Moffat, K. (2018). Algorithmic risk governance: Big data analytics, race and information activism in criminal justice debates. *Theoretical Criminology, 13,* 1–20. doi:10.1177/1362480618763582

Hildebrandt, M., & Koops, B. (2010). The challenges of ambient law and legal protection in the profiling era. *The Modern Law Review, 73*(3), 428–460. doi:10.1111/j.1468-2230.2010.00806.x

Holzinger, L. A., & Biddle, N. (2016). *Behavioural insights of tax compliance: An overview of recent conceptual and empirical approaches.* Canberra, Australia: Crawford School of Public Policy.

Martin, F. (1991). The audit power of the commissioner of taxation: Sections 263 and 264 of the income tax assessment Act 1936. Queensland University of Technology Law Journal, 7, 67-80.

Organization for Economic Cooperation and Development (OECD). (2017a). *The changing tax compliance environment and the role of audit.* Paris, France: OECD. Retrieved from https://www.oecd.org/ctp/the-changing-tax-compliance-environment-and-the-role-of-audit-9789264282186-en.htm

Organization for Economic Cooperation and Development (OECD). (2017b). *Tax Administration 2017.* Paris: OECD. Retrieved from https://www.oecd.org/tax/administration/tax-administration-23077727.htm

Sales, N. (2007). Secrecy and national security investigations. *Alabama Law Review, 58,* 811–884.

Walker-Munro, B. (2019). Disruption, regulatory theory and China: What surveillance and profiling can teach the modern regulator. *Journal of Governance & Regulation, 8*(1), 23–40. doi:10.22495/jgr_v8_i2_p3

Yeung, K. (2018). Algorithmic regulation: A critical interrogation. *Regulation & Governance, 12*(4), 505–523. doi:10.1111/rego.12158

KEY TERMS AND DEFINITIONS

Analytics: The mining, research, or examination of large-scale datasets to yield evidence of past, present or future behavior.

Artificial Intelligence (AI): Any system of computing capable (in part or in whole) of simulating the decision-making capability of a human being.

Big Data: The concept that near-infinite storage and computer processing has permitted the mass collection and storage of information about every aspect of our lives.

Data Matching: The comparison of two or more data sets to identify matches and anomalies in both.

Machine Learning: Where a computer program or algorithm 'learns' how to select or filter input data by assessing previous cases or instances and making correlations or judgements.

Chapter 6
The Regulation of Blockchain in Africa:
Challenges and Opportunities

Michael Casparus Laubscher
https://orcid.org/0000-0001-7825-5650
Faculty of Law, North-West University, South Africa

Muhammed Siraaj Khan
https://orcid.org/0000-0002-4270-8264
Faculty of Law, North-West University, South Africa

ABSTRACT

Blockchain and blockchain technology have captured the imagination of the world. It is being used increasingly more in business and has found its way into the legal profession as well. Blockchain as such has immense potential and can certainly be extremely beneficial. However, since it is such a dynamic, innovative, and recent development, there is a need for regulation of this phenomenon. Regulation will bring more clarity, protection, and assurance. One of the main objectives of a blockchain, however, is to move away from centralised control, so the issue of regulation is a sensitive and complex one. Regulators and policymakers find it difficult to maintain the balance between effective regulation and allowing blockchain to fulfil its potential.

INTRODUCTION

Blockchain and blockchain technology has opened up a whole new world - a world of possibilities for business and law. Businesses and law firms are increasingly looking at utilising this technology and some have already implemented it.

DOI: 10.4018/978-1-7998-3130-3.ch006

Andries Verschelden, a partner at Armanino, an accounting and business consultancy firm in the United States, when referring to blockchain, goes as far as to say "what if someone told you that a new technology would significantly impact every law firm within the next 10 years - and would influence how your firm gets paid, the types of services it offers, and everything in between?" (Verschelden, 2019, para. 1).

Verschelden (2019) is referring to smart contracts, automated security and payments via digital assets, which are all examples how blockchain technology will feature prominently in the legal industry.

Whether one agrees with such bold statements or not, the fact remains, blockchain and blockchain technology is here to stay, in the same manner as social media. Social media has changed the way the world does business, and while it is difficult to say whether blockchain will have such a far-reaching influence, suffice to say it will definitely have a significant influence in business and law.

Africa is no exception to the influence of blockchain and many countries on the continent have considered the use of it. It has the potential to change the way people do business and practice law, and because of that it is vital that the legal sector acknowledges blockchain and blockchain technology, and provide measures aimed at regulating this potentially powerful market driver.

With a focus on the African continent and specifically South Africa, this chapter provides an overview of blockchain, explaining how the technology works and what opportunities it provides in business and law. It concludes with a discussion on how blockchain should be regulated.

DEFINITION OF BLOCKCHAIN

There is no consensus as to what the exact definition of blockchain is. It has been described as similar to a bookkeeping system which securely and reliably captures and stores data on a network in a sophisticated manner (Cuccuru, 2017). On a very basic level, it offers various and wide-spread recorded information wherein the parties to the blockchain can then share this information (Rajput, Singh, Khurana, Bansal, & Shreshtha, 2019). Once the data is captured, it will never be erased or removed and the blockchain then has "an explicit and clear record of each and every exchange whenever created" (Rajput et al., 2019, p. 909). So this data structure or list of transactions are all put together in blocks and then cryptographically secured and linked together on a specific chain, hence the name blockchain (Crosby, Pattanayak, Verma, & Kalyanaraman, 2016). Technology such as this has the advantage in that it is regarded as tamper-resistant and can provide immutable records of transactions (Crosby et al., 2016).

Not all blockchain constructions are the same. On a very basic level, a distinction is made between different kinds of blockchains, as for instance, permissioned and permission-less blockchains (Mattila, 2016). With regard to the permissioned blockchain, the implication is that the participants in the specific network are known and that they can be trusted to act honestly, so co-operation is assumed and incentives to ensure co-operation are not introduced. On the other hand, permission-less blockchains offer complete open access to everyone and the participants do not need to first attain permission to join the network. The participants are also not known to each other and trust is established from using game-theoretical incentives (Bürer, de Lapparent, Pallotta, Capezzali, & Carpita, 2019).

BLOCKCHAIN BASICS

A blockchain consists of two parts; the block body (which contains the transactions) and the block header which contains the hash. Hashing basically involves putting a data item through a hash function. This function then creates a string of digits which are all of a set and fixed length, and which are unique to the input data item (Bacon, Michels, Millard, & Singh, 2018). The output that is then produced is called a hash value (Knuth, 2014). The value of this lies in the fact that is it virtually impossible for two different data items to "hash to the same value" (Bacon et al., 2018, p. 19) which means the data enjoys an extreme high level of protection and integrity (Bacon et al., 2018).

Should the original input be altered in any way, even by a character or a space; the hash function will produce a totally unrelated hash (Narayanan, Bonneau, Felten, Miller, & Goldfeder, 2016). The hash value must then be visible to external observers in order to prevent tampering. If observers note no change to the hash value, they can be confident that the input data has not been tampered with (Pavlou & Snodgrass, 2008).

Additional hash values can be used to ensure that a data structure of multiple data items can be tamper-evident, and this is done by using hash pointers (Yaga, Mell, Roby, & Scarfone, 2018). Hash pointers assist to prove the integrity of a string of data items, and this will be connected to the contents and their sequence (Yaga et al., 2018). This happens when hash pointers link together a series of items. Each item's data is combined with the hash value of the previous item and put into a hash function. This creates that specific item's hash value, which is then included in the next item. So for example, 'item 5's' hash value is based on data of 'item 5' and the hash of 'item 4', and it forms part of the chain (Bacon et al., 2018).

If someone wants to change the data of 'item 5', they must change its hash value. Such an attempt to change and re-hash an item will break the link between the items because 'item 5's' hash is contained in 'item 6' (Bacon et al., 2018). This causes a chain reaction and all of the blocks in the chain would have to be re-hashed to reconstruct the chain. If this is attempted in a fraudulent manner, external observers can spot such tampering (Bacon et al., 2018).

Blockchains can record and store a vast number of transactions in a ledger (database) by placing individual transaction records together into a block, and then chaining these blocks together by utilizing hash pointers, and not just linking single data items (Nakamoto, 2008). As noted above, a block consists of two parts; the block body which contains the transactions that the block records, as well as the block header which includes the hash locks of the previous block and also some metadata such as a timestamp (Khan & Salah, 2018). Blocks are hashed as a whole, which means that both the header and the body are used as input data for the hash function (Nakamoto, 2008). This means that the hash value of a block will include the data that contains the hash of the previous block. Block hash pointers are then used to construct a blockchain (Nakamoto, 2008).

In order to record a transaction or other data items in a secure manner, the authenticity of the relevant parties has to be established before it can be stored in a database that will be able to display evidence of tampering (Olshansky & Wison, 2018). If this does not happen, it will be very easy to simply pose as a different party and then affect transactions in a fraudulent manner (Olshansky & Wison, 2018).

The authenticity is achieved by means of a public key infrastructure (PKI) which allows users to generate a key pair which will consist of a public and a private key, and will be used to sign a data item, as well as to validate whether a digital signature is correct (Yaga et al., 2018). If data has been encrypted by such a public key, the only way in which it can be decrypted is by means of the private key, information only the holder of the private key should have (Schneier, 2015).

The public key is used to represent the individual or entity holding the corresponding private key, therefore the need for a pair of keys which correspond – private and public (Yaga et al., 2018). The public key is used to decrypt the data, which then proves that the sender is in possession of the private key – so the keys 'communicate' and work in unison in order to ensure authenticity and protection of identity (Yaga et al., 2018). Transactions are signed by using this private key before being included in blocks. In this way, it indicates that the transaction must have originated from the owner of the public key, or it has been stolen or has been shared by the owner with someone else (Yaga et al., 2018).

Blockchain should offer participants assurances and confidence that the transactions encrypted in the blockchain are protected and that evidence of tampering will be displayed should it occur. This leads to the question – who controls the blockchain? Initially with early cryptocurrency blockchain a trust-less environment was used with no centralized control and anyone was allowed to store a copy of the blockchain (Nakamoto, 2008). However, there has a been a move towards incorporating platforms which will have an entity, often called the 'trusted third party' or TTP, usually a small group of participants which then operate the blockchain (Mattila, 2016).

Blockchain has evolved into a system that has endless possibilities and one that offers aspects such as authenticity, practicality, trust and accessibility. It stretches across geographical borders and has definite advantages and a myriad of possible applications – very much like the internet when it first arrived a few decades ago. However, as is often the case with something which is so complex, it also opens the doors for abuse and exploitation. It cannot become a law unto its own, and this is where regulation is essential.

The original vision of promoters and disciples of cryptocurrencies has been to operate in a financial space and environment that is free from government control and stringent regulations (Cryptohound, 2019). However, in order for cryptocurrencies to be accepted by society and to be able to compete with traditional finance systems, it may be that cryptocurrencies must receive legal recognition and be subject to regulation.

THE POTENTIAL OF BLOCKCHAIN IN BUSINESS AND LAW

Blockchain offers immense potential and opportunities worldwide. Mattila (2016, p. 4) believes:

[i]t has the potential to impact all sectors and layers of society in a multitude of combined ways – whether it is completely novel solutions, to interacting over the internet, or with increased efficiencies in pre-existing industrial systems, there are benefits to reap in all playing fields.

Blockchain technology's flagship has been cryptocurrencies such as Bitcoin and Ethereum. In August 2018 Bitcoin had a market capitalisation of $121.5 billion (Taskinsoy, 2018). However, blockchain technology has far more to offer than just cryptocurrencies. It has been described as technology which "is an apparently mundane process that has the potential to transform how people and businesses co-operate" (Berkeley, 2015, para. 11). In 2016, it was reported that more than $4.5 billion in private funds were invested in blockchain around the world (McWaters, Bruno, Galaski, & Chaterjee, 2016). Between 2014 and 2015, blockchain related start-ups raised more than $800 million (Higginson, Lorenz, Münstermann, & Olesen, 2017).

In Estonia, blockchain technology is being used in helping to maintain the integrity of data and transactions with regard to national health, judicial, and other public services (Adams, 2018). It offers an excellent way in which to keep and maintain inventory and is ideal for record-keeping and energy contracts (Düdder & Ross, 2017).

Swan refers to blockchain as the way forward, essentially as a blueprint for establishing a new economy (Swan, 2015). Swan (2015) lists a vast range of areas where blockchain can be used such as; transactions, contracts, private equity, bonds, mutual funds, derivatives, identification (passports or driver's licences) private records (signatures, wills or trusts) and intangible assets such as intellectual property rights (trademarks or copyright).

Blockchain has immense potential in Africa as well. It can help to construct an infrastructure for Africa's financial markets. In Ghana, a company called Bitland does exactly that. The company puts individuals and organizations in the position to record deeds and survey land on the Bitshares blockchain (Lee & Mueller, 2019). Bitcoin is seen as an alternative payment system in the rural areas of South Africa, by making use of mobile phones (Dlamini, Scott, & Nair, 2016).

A Kenyan-based blockchain startup, AgriLedger, enables farmers to know their buyers and what the market prices are; BitPesa is an online payment platform that facilitates bitcoin transactions, while TwigaFoods takes the form of a logistics start-up and it connects farmers to kiosks and markets in Kenya, and has recently struck up a partnership with IBM (Giuliani, n.d.).

Another example of the use of blockchain technology in Africa, and especially South Africa, is StudEx, piloted by Tumelo Ramaphosa, son of the current president of South Africa, Cyril Ramaphosa, in partnership with IBM and Cardano. StudEx uses the Internet of Things (IoT) to combat illegal poaching by tracking the location of the animal, monitoring their heart rate, and keep record of other significant activity, using blockchain technology (Koffman, 2019).

In the legal field, blockchain also has massive potential. An obvious example is the use of smart contracts. The latter refers to a set of terms and conditions which can be automated using blockchain technology. Smart contracts can record changes in ownership, and has the potential to automate laws and statutes which can help to improve government services and the legal work (Treleaven, Brown, & Yang, 2017).

Blockchain technology has the ability to store and record events for a long period of time, which is often needed in the field of law, for example intellectual property claims and even criminal procedures (Legal Executive Institute, 2019). Other examples are estate planning, funding litigation by means of tokenized payments and creation of alternative dispute resolution (ADR) platforms for online dispute resolution (Di Mariani, 2019). Blockchain technology offers various advantages such as: anonymity, self-determination (the participants control their own data), transparency (the ledgers are distributed), immutability (records are kept and stored), collaboration (direct transacting between parties), and disintermediation (no central controlling authority to manage transactions) (Grech & Camilleri, 2017).

BLOCKCHAIN TECHNOLOGY IN AFRICA

In Africa, the use of blockchain technologies tends to suggest that many potential uses could disrupt whole sectors of the economy (United Nations Economic for Africa, 2017). This technology, which will be attractive to financial institutions and entrepreneurs, makes financial services open to more Africans and reduces counterparty risk (United Nations Economic for Africa, 2017). For example, in Ghana and Kenya, "traditional banking institutions invest heavily and collaborate to develop blockchain technology and explore its new possible implementations" (United Nations Economic for Africa, 2017, p. 18).

However, with that said, "there are very few concrete cases of the use of or adoption of blockchain technology" (United Nations Economic for Africa, 2017, p. 18).

Solutions are created within the confines of a poor understanding and knowledge of the technology generally, particularly in sectors besides banking (United Nations Economic for Africa, 2017). In Africa, many areas lack extensive infrastructure, "advanced financial institutions, a high degree of political stability and/or large pools of capital" (United Nations Economic for Africa, 2017, p. 26). As a growing technology, the distributed ledger will encounter many challenges in three major aspects, namely: technical, regulatory and institutional (United Nations Economic for Africa, 2017). Furthermore, at an institutional level, there is resistance on the deployment of blockchain (United Nations Economic for Africa, 2017),

Perumall, Selfe & Jen (2019, p.4) noted that "[t]he Bank of Botswana has not released any regulation on cryptocurrencies or the use of blockchain technology and has reportedly stated that it currently has no intention of regulating cryptocurrencies". The Bank of Ghana has stated that the trading and use of cryptocurrency in Ghana is not yet considered legal because (similar to the position in South Africa) it is not yet considered to be a legitimate form of currency (Perumall et al., 2019).

It must be noted however, that the "Bank of Ghana has drafted the Ghanaian Bill to regulate cryptocurrency through electronic money issuers" (Perumall et al., 2019, p. 21). Despite this, Laghmari (2019) reports that in the Kumasi metropolitan region of Southern Ghana, Bitland (a start-up company specializing in blockchain technology) registered land titled in a public blockchain for 28 communities, and that the start-up has intentions of expanding this project to a national or even a continental scale with a view of eradicating corruption and unlocking billions in fixed capital for infrastructure development. Kenya does not yet have a regulatory framework in place for blockchains but their National Land Commission uses a blockchain network to establish transparency in land ownership, as they are of the view that it will alleviate potential fraudulent sales of land, and confusion over title to land (Perumall et al., 2019). The Government of Namibia has not yet released any promulgation on the regulations of cryptocurrencies in their country, with The Bank of Namibia strongly voicing its objections to the use of same (Perumall et al., 2019).

In early 2017, the Central Bank of Nigeria warned financial institutions not to use, hold or trade virtual currencies pending "substantive regulation or decision by the (Central Bank of Nigeria) as they are not legal tender in Nigeria" (Perumall et al., 2019, p. 8). Further, the Central Bank of Nigeria stated that banks who trade in cryptocurrencies do so at their own risk. The Central Bank of Nigeria cited its scepticism of cryptocurrencies on the possible exploitation of Nigerian citizens by criminals and terrorists. Despite these warnings, a bitcoin-related Ponzi scheme reportedly resulted in almost 2 million Nigerian residents losing a combined USD 50 million in early 2017 (Perumall et al., 2019).

Not all African countries are opposed to the use of blockchain. Tunisia, for example, is "reportedly partnering with the Locus Chain Foundation to apply blockchain technology as its settlement currency and service platform" (Perumall et al., 2019, p. 16). The position in Senegal and Sierra Leone also leads one to believe that they lend support to use and implementation of blockchain technology. In October 2017, the President of Sierra Leone announced his intentions to establish Sierra Leone as the world's first 'Smart Country' (Perumall et al., 2019).The first step in this programme was to establish a nationwide economic identification service which will provide all Sierra Leonean citizens with digital credentials, thereby increasing their access to services offered by the Sierra Leone Government as well as promoting financial inclusion. This announcement elevated Sierra Leone to the position of reportedly being the first country to use blockchain technology in its national election, whereby the Agora platform (a blockchain based digital voting solution) was used to record and verify the votes cast during the election (Perumall et al., 2019).

THE NEED FOR REGULATION

Should Blockchain Be Regulated?

Blockchain at its heart strives for decentralization and moving away from control being seated in a singular entity. Regulation, on the other hand, in many ways wants to achieve the exact opposite. The environment of fast-paced technology, such as blockchain, runs ahead of regulation (Peters, Panayi, & Chapelle, 2015). Due to blockchain's decentralized nature, it lends itself to be beyond the reach of direct regulation, monetary policy and oversight (Peters et al., 2015). Further, there seems to be no uniform or unified approach to the regulation of blockchain technologies such as virtual currencies (Peters et al., 2015). In Kenya, one of the attractions of blockchain technology is the low threat of governmental regulation, which on the flipside, can lead to an increase in crime (Nseke, 2018).

Walch highlights the classic dilemma regarding the regulation of innovative technologies and their practices when she refers to "just the right moment" (2016, p. 717) to regulate, which remains an age-old question. On the one hand, regulation offers protection which might be needed immediately by parties, but if it occurs too early, regulation can be inappropriate, irrelevant and inefficient since more time is needed to identify issues within the specific field and how it functions and operates in a legal context (Walch, 2016).

Walch admits regulation is necessary but highlights the fact that since there is such a great deal of uncertainty regarding the blockchain lexicon, regulation of it will be problematic and can lead to inconsistent regulation across jurisdictions (Walch, 2016). Ducas and Wilner (2017), when referring to the Canadian situation, are of the view that the Canadian government should play a definitive role in promoting innovation while concurrently bolstering regulations when it comes to blockchain. In China, the banking industry realises that while the potential of blockchain is immense, regulation is essential and there is a call for regulation and the development of industry standards (Guo & Liang, 2016).

It is submitted that "the use of technology combined with the necessary consumer safeguards are part of the requirements for a successful assault on financial exclusion. It is further observed that customers' needs must be addressed for this success to materialize" (Singh, 2013, p. 53). It is further submitted that regulators need to be conscious of 'enablement' and that a balance needs to be struck between the regulation that is flexible enough to allow for innovation while at the same time providing trust in the system and maintaining consumer protection (Singh, 2013). "Enabling regulation will be part of increasing financial inclusion" (Singh, 2013, p. 63).

The lack of enabling regulation and the general uncertainty and complexity regarding a regulatory framework for blockchain, has been highlighted in a recent case in the Supreme Court of India.

In April 2018, the Reserve Bank of India (RBI) issued a circular in which it banned regulated financial institutions from providing services to crypto businesses. The High Court of India was required to investigate whether the central bank has the power to impose such a ban. The court analysed the provisions of the *RBI Act of 1934* and the *Banking Regulation Act of 1949*, as well as the circular that the bank had released. It was argued by the counsel for the crypto exchanges that the RBI action to restrict banks from offering crypto businesses necessary services is a smokescreen and not in the interest of the consumer as RBI claims. They further submit that RBI can only exercise its power in the public interest within the ambit of the law, and that this ambit does not extend to crypto businesses (Helms, 2019a).

The second issue the court addressed related to the Indian government's policy on cryptocurrency. An inter-ministerial committee (IMC) was formed in 2017 to investigate all aspects of cryptocurrencies. In 2019, it published its recommendation together with a draft bill entitled *Banning of Cryptocurrency and Regulation of Official Digital Currency Bill* 2019. Although the committee states it is receptive and supportive of ledger technologies (such as bitcoin and cryptocurrencies), the committee seems to regard cryptocurrencies as having no real value and fraught with danger (Helms, 2019a). They cite extreme fluctuations in prices as one of the worrying aspects, and therefore suggest a law which bans the cryptocurrencies in India and criminalizing carrying on of any activities connected with it in India (Helms, 2019a).

Soon after the publication of this report, the Minister involved with this was moved to another position in the cabinet. During the Supreme Court case, the government requested a postponement until January 2020, since they claimed that they would have introduced the bill in Parliament during the winter session and would therefore in January be in a better position to address the matter. The case has subsequently been postponed again (Helms, 2019b). The uncertainty drags on and the cryptocurrency market suffers, but it is clear that there are still many hurdles to cross in order to achieve a satisfactory situation.

The RBI case in India illustrated that some governments seem to be very unsure as to how to deal with blockchain technology and this hampers the implementation of effective, balanced regulation of blockchain.

Regulation of Blockchain in South Africa

At this stage, there is no specific regulation with regard to blockchain technology in South Africa. However, regulators have displayed positive responses when it comes to regulation for cryptocurrencies, for example, and seem to be keen to cooperate with the fintech and banking industries in order to identify the most effective, relevant and appropriate way to regulate cryptocurrencies in South Africa (Perumall, 2019).

There has been some movement on the regulation front, one example being the *National Treasury's Taxation Laws Amendment Bill 2018* which proposed amendments to tax legislation, including the way in which cryptocurrencies are classified in South Africa. The South African Reserve Bank (SARB) published its review of the *National Payment Systems Act, 78 of 1998* in December 2018 for public comment (The South African Reserve Bank, 2018). This specific legislation regulates systems used by South Africans for payment settlement, and the SARB apparently aims to completely overhaul the present regulation by 2020 (Perumall, 2019).

It is clear that the SARB understands and realizes that there might be a striking resemblance between domestic and international payments. They realize the potential of using similar digital currencies as part of the national payment system, which has the potential to lead to a South African fiat currency (A. Perumall, 2019).

The need for law to adapt to rapidly evolving technologies is self-explanatory. In the context of gaming law, rather than virtual currencies per se, the slow nature of its laws and inability to adequately cater for the advancement in technology have left the United States (US) in a less than ideal position to cater for the monetization of the retail video games industry (Castillo, 2019).

In 2014, the SARB published a *Position Paper on Virtual Currencies* (the Paper) (The South African Reserve Bank - National Payment System Department, 2014), wherein it inter alia dealt with the Reserve Bank's stance on virtual currencies (specifically in terms of the Bank's mandate and responsibilities), clarifying concepts related to the virtual currency discussion, and the categorization of virtual currencies. The Paper highlights the risks associated with virtual currency and the bank's obligations thereof. The Paper also highlights the fact that virtual currencies are not immune from being exploited for unlawful or ambiguous purposes (The South African Reserve Bank - National Payment System Department, 2014). Such innovations simultaneously provide a platform for, inter alia, money laundering and the financing of terrorism, and introduce a new set of risks to consumers as decentralised convertible virtual currencies (DCVC) are susceptible to misuse and at the very worst, have the ability to disrupt the financial system (The South African Reserve Bank - National Payment System Department, 2014).

It is self-evident that regulations are needed to address the above, but even if one were to temporarily ignore the potential of criminal activities, and focus on the logistics of dealing with virtual currencies in day to day activities, regulations are required. One of the most important considerations is whether virtual currencies are considered as legal tender under South African Law?

In early 2018, a combined working group was created under the auspices of the Intergovernmental Fintech Working Group (IFWG) to specifically consider crypto assets (Perumall, 2019). The Working Group consisted of members from the National Treasury (NT), the South African Reserve Bank (SARB), Financial Sector Conduct Authority (FSCA), South African Revenue Service (SARS) and Financial Intelligence Centre FIC. (The South African Reserve Bank, 2019). The aim of the IFWG is to create a general understanding among regulators and policymakers of fintech developments, as well as highlight policy and regulatory effects for the financial sector and economy as a whole. The IFWG offers an ideal opportunity and stage for regulators and policymakers to engage and consult with industry in order to follow a united and coordinated approach to regulation (Perumall, 2019).

In 2019, the IFWG released a consultation paper on crypto assets. The aim of the paper was to provide background and further provides the scope of the crypto activities assessed. At the time of issuing of the statement, two crypto assets use cases were analysed – specifically the buying and selling of crypto assets, as well as making use of crypto assets to make payments (South African Reserve Bank 2019; A. Perumall, 2019)

It is clear to see that South Africa is not oblivious to the advancement in technology, and the need to sufficiently respond thereto, but with the same breath, the lack of legislation specifically catering for same is glaringly obvious. This clearly indicates that while the South African government is willing to embrace blockchain technology, there is also a very definite realization that the latter offers challenges, legal and regulatory challenges which are currently not being met.

The South African Perspective – Bitcoin

Bitcoin is probably the phenomenon that comes to mind when one thinks of virtual currency in South Africa. Bitcoin is underpinned by blockchain technology (Mitchell, 2017). Bitcoin in its early stages had a novel idea of how financial transactions in the future would be facilitated (Nieman, 2015) However, in early 2013 it had proved itself to be a legitimate and viable form of currency, and the use of bitcoin expanded (Nieman, 2015). The growing acceptance of bitcoin on a global scale might suggest that the currency is here to stay. This means that governments cannot simply ignore it (Nieman, 2015). This in turns highlights the need for regulatory developments. Nieman is of the view that "regulatory response from the South African regulators has been limited" (Nieman, 2015, p. 1988). Nieman further observes that there is "no primary or secondary legislation pertaining to virtual currencies that have been promulgated in South Africa" (Nieman, 2015, p. 1988).

As of March 2020, virtual currencies are not considered legal tender in South Africa. Legal tender is defined in the *South African Reserve Bank Act 90 of 1989*. Section 17 provides as follows:

1) A tender, including a tender by the Bank itself, of a note of the Bank or of an outstanding note of another bank for which the Bank has assumed liability in terms of section 15(3) (c) of the Currency and Banking Act or in terms of any agreement entered into with another bank before or after the commencement of this Act, shall be a legal tender of payment of an amount equal to the amount specified on the note. (2) A tender, including a tender by the Bank itself, of an undefaced and unmutilated coin which is lawfully in circulation in the Republic and of current mass, shall be a legal tender of payment of money- (a) in the case of gold coins, in settlement of any amount, and the value of each gold coin so tendered shall be equal to the net amount at which the bank is prepared to purchase that gold coin on the day of such tender thereof; and (b) in the case of other coins, in settlement, per individual transaction, of a total amount not exceeding- (i) fifty rand, where coins of the denomination of one rand or higher are so tendered; (ii) five rand, where coins of denominations of ten cents up to and including fifty cents are so tendered; (iii) fifty cents, where coins of the denomination of five cents or less are so tendered, and the value of each coin so tendered shall be equal to the amount specified on that coin.

The wording of the section is not broad enough to include the definition of virtual currencies, and a cursory view of the date the Act was promulgated easily explains why this is probably the case.

REGULATION OF BLOCKCHAIN IN MALTA

In July 2018, Malta became the first country in the world to "provide an official set of regulations for operators in the blockchain, cryptocurrency and DLT (distributed ledger technology) space" (Wolfson, 2018, para. 1). The Maltese Parliament did this by officially passing three bills into law; *The Malta Digital Innovation Authority Act* (MDIA Act), *Innovative Technology Arrangement and Services Act* (ITAS Act) and the *Virtual Financial Assets Act* (VFA Act) (Wolfson, 2018). The goal with the passing of these laws was to create a regulated platform and environment for companies and equip them with the necessary tools to successfully function in a digital environment (Wolfson, 2018).

The MDIA Act establishes the Malta Digital Innovation Authority and certifies DLT platforms. The focus is on the establishment of internal governance arrangements and it outlines the duties and responsibilities of the Authority to certify DLT platforms (Wolfson, 2018). The aim is to ensure credibility and provide legal certainty to users that utilise a DLT platform (Wolfson, 2018).

The ITAS Act deals with DLT arrangements and certifications of DLT platforms. Here the focus is the establishment of exchanges as well as other companies which operate in the cryptocurrency market (Wolfson, 2018). While VFA Act creates a regulatory framework which governs entities such as initial coin offerings (ICOs), cryptocurrency exchanges and wallet providers (Wolfson, 2018).

The Maltese government's approach to the regulation of blockchain technologies has been refreshing since it displays a robust technological perspective as well as a flexibility with regard to the laws that they have passed. The government focusses on an approach that places principles first and is willing to adapt the laws as it deems necessary and fitting, which given the fact that it regulates technology (a dynamic, ever-changing and progressive field) makes a lot of sense (Wolfson, 2018). This has meant that high-profile exchanges like Binance, Bittrex and Bitbay have either moved to Malta, or have expanded their operations to the crypto-friendly island (Bester, 2019).

However, despite Malta's revolutionary and progressive approach to blockchain technology, there have been issues with banks not being keen to grant crypto start-ups business accounts before these start-ups have not officially been licensed with the MFSA (Malta Financial Services Authority) (Bester, 2019). Such a process can take up to six months just to receive a first-round response, which is proving to be problematic (Bester, 2019).

According to the VFA Act, those who wish to act as agents in a field that involves cryptocurrencies and ICOs are obliged to complete a short training course as well as pass an exam based on the content of the course (Helms, 2018). After the first round of exams, which included candidates who practise as lawyers, accountants and auditors, a pass rate of only 39 percent was achieved. This led to the MFSA, which regulates admission of the candidates, to propose adding a number of additional rules for the prospective candidates to comply with. These include increased capital requirements and also regulatory fees; introducing strenuous assessment of competencies and a compulsory requirement which ensures continuous professional education (Helms, 2018). This clearly shows that the MFSA realises that there are definite issues regarding the practicality, expertise and effective regulation of trading and transacting with regard to blockchain technology.

However, the acts that have been passed, although robust, are a step in the right direction. The mere fact that companies have to obtain a licence from the financial regulator (MFSA) in order to operate already creates a sound foundation for effective regulation. The process to achieve this is clear, but not necessarily cheap or easy and definitely has its challenges, but it sends the message that the Maltese government is serious about the regulation of blockchain technology (Cryptohound, 2019).

Blockchain technology offers virtually limitless opportunities and has the potential to improve people's lives, therefore African governments should embrace this phenomenon. If African countries and governments shun or ignore blockchain technology it will be short-sighted and detrimental. However, blockchain technology cannot be allowed to operate without any control, regulations or good governance principles. A country such as South Africa should therefore follow the example of Malta and in a meaningful, progressive and sensible manner tackle the regulation of blockchain technology.

FURTHER RESEARCH DIRECTIONS

As discussed, blockchain technology has faced some opposition from some countries including African countries but is being encouraged by some governments such as Malta and Estonia. A comparative survey of all national approaches to the technology would be an important area for further research, together with some in-depth case studies evaluating the success or otherwise of national regulatory approaches.

CONCLUSION

Blockchain and blockchain technology features in business and law and will continue to do so at an increasing rate. However, regulatory bodies and governments must also acknowledge the need for regulation. This regulation must be sensible, practical and relevant regulation that does not stifle the growth of blockchain but also does not allow it to roam unhindered and unchecked. Finding this balance is thwart with challenges and difficulties, although some countries, like Malta, are attempting to meet the challenge.

There is a lot of uncertainty when it comes to blockchain technology; the terminology and language that surrounds it; the legal issues with regard to this ever-changing field, but it is a challenge the legal profession, regulatory bodies and governments need to address. These challenges have been highlighted recently when First National Bank South Africa announced that they will be closing the bank accounts of major crypto currency exchanges such as Luno, ICE3X and VLR as of the end of March 2020 (McKane, 2019). The reasons provided by First National Bank to discontinue their services were based on their "risk appetite" and that regulation around the industry requires clarification (McKane, 2019, para. 2). This seems to underline the issues regarding a lack of proper regulation with regard to blockchain technology in South Africa and the Africa continent as a whole.

REFERENCES

Adams, C. (2018). *Estonia, a blockchain model for other countries?* Retrieved from https://www.investinblockchain.com/estonia-blockchain-model/

Bacon, J., Michels, J. D., Millard, C., & Singh, J. (2018). Blockchain demystified: A technical and legal Introduction to Distributed and Centralized Ledgers. *Richmond Journal of Law & Technology*, *25*(1), 1–106.

Banking Regulation Act of 1949 (India).

Banning of Cryptocurrency and Regulation of Official Digital Currency Bill. (2019). India.

Berkeley, J. (2015, 31 October). The promise of the blockchain the trust machine. *The Economist*. Retrieved from https://www.economist.com/leaders/2015/10/31/the-trust-machine

Bester, N. (2019, 3 March). Malta might be 'blockchain island' but don't try opening a crypto bank account. *Bitcoin.com*. Retrieved from https://news.bitcoin.com/malta-might-be-blockchain-island-but-dont-try-opening-a-crypto-bank-account/

Bürer, M. J., de Lapparent, M., Pallotta, V., Capezzali, M., & Carpita, M. (2019). Use cases for blockchain in the energy industry opportunities of emerging business models and related risks. *Computers & Industrial Engineering*, *137*, 1–9. doi:10.1016/j.cie.2019.106002

Castillo, D. (2019). Unpacking the loot box: How gaming's latest monetization system flirts with traditional gambling methods. *Santa Clara Law Review*, *59*(1), 165–201.

Crosby, M., Pattanayak, P., Verma, S., & Kalyanaraman, V. (2016). Blockchain technology: Beyond bitcoin. *Applied Innovation Review*, *2*(June), 6–19.

Cryptohound, O. (2019). *Tough, but worth it: Pros and cons of blockchain regulation in Malta.* Retrieved from https://cryptodigestnews.com/tough-but-worth-it-pros-and-cons-of-blockchain-regulation-in-malta-c337a5906025

Cuccuru, P. (2017). Beyond bitcoin: An early overview on smart contracts. *International Journal of Law and Information Technology*, 25(3), 179–195. doi:10.1093/ijlit/eax003

Di Mariani, C. (2019, 7 February). Blockchain for law firms: Revolutionizing escrow, contracts, and more. *D!gitalist.* Retrieved from https://www.digitalistmag.com/digital-economy/2019/02/07/blockchain-for-law-firms-revolutionizing-escrow-contracts-more-06196152

Dlamini, N., Scott, M., & Nair, K. K. (2016). *A bitcoin framework: an alternative payment system for rural areas of South Africa using low-end mobile phones.* Paper presented at the 2016 Southern Africa Telecommunications Networks and Applications Conference (SATNAC), George, South Africa.

Ducas, E., & Wilner, A. (2017). The security and financial implications of blockchain technologies: Regulating emerging technologies in Canada. *International Journal (Toronto, Ont.)*, 72(4), 538–562. doi:10.1177/0020702017741909

Düdder, B., & Ross, O. (2017). *Timber tracking: Reducing complexity of due diligence by using blockchain technology* (Publication no. SSRN 3015219). https://papers.ssrn.com/sol3/papers.cfm?abstract_id=3015219

Giuliani, D. (n.d.). *Blockchain in Africa: Assessing opportunities and feasibility.* Retrieved from https://briterbridges.com/blockchain-in-africa-assessing-opportunities-and-feasibility

Grech, A., & Camilleri, A. F. (2017). Blockchain in education. Luxembourg: European Commission. doi:10.2760/6064

Guo, Y., & Liang, C. (2016). Blockchain application and outlook in the banking industry. *Financial Innovation*, 2(1), 24. doi:10.118640854-016-0034-9

Helms, K. (2018). Only 39 percent pass Malta's cryptocurrency exam. *Bitcoin.com.* Retrieved from https://news.bitcoin.com/maltas-cryptocurrency-exam/

Helms, K. (2019a). Indian Supreme Court heard crypto case in depth. *Bitcoin.com.* Retrieved from https://news.bitcoin.com/indian-supreme-court-heard-crypto-case-in-depth/

Helms, K. (2019b). Indian Supreme Court postpones crypto case to November, new date confirmed. *Bitcoin.com.* Retrieved from https://news.bitcoin.com/indian-supreme-court-postpones-crypto-case-to-november/

Higginson, M., Lorenz, J., Münstermann, B., & Olesen, P. (2017). *The promise of blockchain.* Retrieved from https://www.mckinsey.com/industries/financial-services/our-insights/the-promise-of-blockchain

Innovative Technology Arrangement and Services Act. (2018). Malta.

Khan, M. A., & Salah, K. (2018). IoT security: Review, blockchain solutions, and open challenges. *Future Generation Computer Systems*, 82, 395–411. doi:10.1016/j.future.2017.11.022

Knuth, D. E. (2014). Art of computer programming: Vol. 2. *Seminumerical algorithms* (3rd ed.). Boston, MA: Addison-Wesley Professional.

Koffman, T. (2019, 4 April). Blockchain - Africa rising. *Forbes Magazine*. Retrieved from https://www.forbes.com/sites/tatianakoffman/2019/04/04/blockchain-africa-rising/#36d767817711

Laghmari, S. (2019). *The upsurge of blockchain market in Africa.* Retrieved from https://infomineo.com/the-upsurge-of-blockchain-market-in-africa

Lee, C., & Mueller, J. (2019). Can blockchain unlock the investment Africa needs? *Innovations: Technology, Governance, Globalization, 12*(3-4), 80–87. doi:10.1162/inov_a_00277

Legal Executive Institute. (2019). *The application of blockchain in the legal sector.* Retrieved from https://blogs.thomsonreuters.com/legal-uk/2019/01/04/the-application-of-blockchain-in-the-legal-sector/

Malta Digital Innovation Authority Act 2018.

Mattila, J. (2016). *The blockchain phenomenon–the disruptive potential of distributed consensus architectures* (ETLA working paper 38). Helsinki, Finland: The Research Institute of the Finnish Economy.

McKane, J. (2019). *FNB shut down South African cryptocurrency-linked bank accounts.* Retrieved from https://mybroadband.co.za/news/cryptocurrency/328355-fnb-shuts-down-south-african-cryptocurrency-linked-bank-accounts.html

McWaters, R. J., Bruno, G., Galaski, R., & Chaterjee, S. (2016). *The future of financial infrastructure: An ambitious look at how blockchain can reshape financial services.* Retrieved from http://www3.weforum.org/docs/WEF_The_future_of_financial_infrastructure.pdf

Mitchell, K. (2017). Bitcoin: the business of blockchain. *Without Prejudice, 17*(9), 10-11.

Nakamoto, S. (2008). *Bitcoin: A peer-to-peer electronic cash system.* Retrieved From https://bitcoin.org/bitcoin.pdf

Narayanan, A., Bonneau, J., Felten, E., Miller, A., & Goldfeder, S. (2016). *Bitcoin and cryptocurrency technologies: A comprehensive introduction.* Princeton, NJ: Princeton University Press.

National Payment Systems Act, 78 of 1998.

National Treasury's Taxation Laws Amendment Bill 2018.

Nieman, A. (2015). A few South African cents' worth on Bitcoin. *Potchefstroom Electronic Law Journal/Potchefstroomse Elektroniese Regsblad, 18*(5), 1978-2010.

Nseke, P. (2018). How crypto-currency can decrypt the global digital divide: Bitcoins a means for African emergence. *International Journal of Innovation and Economic Development, 3*(6), 61–70. doi:10.18775/ijied.1849-7551-7020.2015.36.2005

Olshansky, S., & Wison, S. (2018). *Do blockchains have anything to offer identity?* Retrieved from https://www.internetsociety.org/resources/doc/2018/blockchain-identity/

Pavlou, K. E., & Snodgrass, R. T. (2008). Forensic analysis of database tampering. *ACM Transactions on Database Systems, 33*(4), 30. doi:10.1145/1412331.1412342

Perumall, A. (2019). *Blockchain and cryptocurrency regulation in Africa*. Retrieved from https://www.dailymaverick.co.za/article/2019-04-08-blockchain-and-cryptocurrency-regulation-in-africa/

Perumall, A., Selfe, E., & Jen, S. (2019). *Blockchain and cryptocurrency in Africa: A comparative summary of the reception and regulation of blockchain and cryptocurrency in Africa*. Retrieved from https://www.bakermckenzie.com/-/media/files/insight/publications/2019/02/report_blockchainandcryptocurrencyreg_feb2019.pdf

Peters, G., Panayi, E., & Chapelle, A. (2015). Trends in cryptocurrencies and blockchain technologies: A monetary theory and regulation perspective. *Journal of Financial Perspectives*, *3*(3), 1–46.

Rajput, S., Singh, A., Khurana, S., Bansal, T., & Shreshtha, S. (2019). *Blockchain technology and cryptocurrenices*. Paper presented at the 2019 Amity International Conference on Artificial Intelligence (AICAI), Dubai, UAE. 10.1109/AICAI.2019.8701371

Reserve Bank of India Act of 1934.

Schneier, B. (2015). *Applied cryptography, protocols algorithms and source code in C*. Brisbane, Australia: John Wiley and Sons.

Singh, S. (2013). *Globalization and money: A global south perspective*. Lanham, MD: Rowman & Littlefield.

South Africa, The National Treasury's Taxation Laws Amendment Bill (2018).

South African Reserve Bank Act 90 of 1989, (1989).

Swan, M. (2015). *Blockchain Blueprint for a new economy*. Sebastopol, CA: O'Reilly Media.

Taskinsoy, J. (2018). B*itcoin mania: An end to the US dollar's hegemony or another cryptocurrency experiment destined to fail?* Retrieved from https://papers.ssrn.com/sol3/papers.cfm?abstract_id=3311989

The South African Reserve Bank. (2018). *Review of the national payment system Act 78 of 1998 policy paper*. Retrieved from http://www.treasury.gov.za/publications/other/NPS%20Act%20Review%20Policy%20Paper%20-%20final%20version%20-%2013%20September%202018.pdf

The South African Reserve Bank. (2019). *Statement on crypto assets*. Retrieved from https://www.resbank.co.za/Lists/News%20and%20Publications/Attachments/9037/Joint%20media%20statement_crypto%20assets%20consultation%20paper.pdf

Treleaven, P., Brown, R., & Yang, D. (2017). Blockchain technology in finance. *Computer*, *50*(9), 14–17. doi:10.1109/MC.2017.3571047

United Nations Economic for Africa. (2017). *Blockchain technology in Africa*. Retrieved from https://www.uneca.org/sites/default/files/images/blockchain_technology_in_africa_draft_report_19-nov-2017-final_edited.pdf

Verschelden, A. (2019). *Get ready: Blockchain will transform the legal industry*. Retrieved from https://www.moore-global.com/insights/articles/get-ready-blockchain-will-transform-the-legal-indu

Virtual Financial Assets Act, 2018 (Malta).

Walch, A. (2016). The path of the blockchain lexicon (and the law). *Review of Banking and Financial Law*, *36*(2), 713–765.

Wolfson, R. (2018). Maltese parliament passes laws that set regulatory framework for blockchain, cryptocurrency and DLT. *Forbes Magazine*. Retrieved from https://www.forbes.com/sites/rachelwolfson/2018/07/05/maltese-parliament-passes-laws-that-set-regulatory-framework-for-blockchain-cryptocurrency-and-dlt/#6ef3ab49ed2f

Yaga, D., Mell, P., Roby, N., & Scarfone, K. (2018). *Blockchain technology overview*. Retrieved from arxiv.org/ftp/arxiv/papers/906/906.1078.pdf

ADDITIONAL READING

Batog, C. (2015). Blockchain: A proposal to reform high frequency trading regulation. *Cardozo Arts and Entertainment Law Journal*, *33*(3), 739–770.

Brookes, A. (2018). US regulation of blockchain currencies: A policy overview. *U.S Regulation Blockchain Currencies*, *9*(2), 75-104.

Fulmer, N. (2018). Exploring the legal issues of blockchain applications. *Akron Law Review*, *52*(2), 161–192.

Yeoh, P. (2017). Regulatory issues in blockchain technology. *Journal of Financial Regulation Compliance*, *25*(2), 196–208. doi:10.1108/JFRC-08-2016-0068

KEY TERMS AND DEFINITIONS

Blockchain: An electronic system that securely and reliably stores data on a specific network.

Blockchain Technology: The technology that supports and enables the blockchain to operate effectively.

Contract: An agreement between parties which the obligations; duties; responsibilities and rights of each party.

Cryptocurrency: A digital, virtual currency which is exchanged and used by means of encryption techniques.

Ledger: A specific database relating to blockchain technology.

Malta: Island in the Mediterranean Sea often referred to as 'the blockchain island'.

Regulation: The process of designing and implementing rules, regulations and laws in order to govern and regulate actions, activities, duties.

South Africa: Country at southern tip of Africa, one of the most developed countries in Africa which boasts one of the strongest economies in the region.

Chapter 7
Smart Contracts:
An Overview

Michael Laubscher
https://orcid.org/0000-0001-7825-5650
Faculty of Law, North-West University, South Africa

Muhammed Siraaj Khan
https://orcid.org/0000-0002-4270-8264
Faculty of Law, North-West University, South Africa

ABSTRACT

When Nick Szabo pioneered the idea of a smart contract in the 1990s, the economic and communications infrastructure available at that time could not and did not support the protocols needed to execute and apply smart contracts. While smart contracts may be viewed as an example of the use of blockchain and blockchain technology which offers great opportunities to the field of law; others are more sceptical. The use of smart contracts in law is anything but straightforward, but this should not deter jurists from investigating the opportunities this instrument offers. This chapter aims to provide an overview of smart contacts, explaining how they work, the ways they differ from written contracts, their legal status, and the advantages and disadvantages associated with using them. Finally, it identifies the main challenges facing businesses and the legal profession with regard to the expanding use of smart contacts.

INTRODUCTION

At the time that Nick Szabo initiated the notion of a smart contract back in the 1990's, the economic and communications infrastructure of the time did not have the capability or capacity to support the protocols which are needed to execute and apply smart contracts (Omohundro, 2014). Times have changed, and today the necessary infrastructure is available which has led to a wide range of industries, including the field of law, leading the way in the testing, development and implementation of smart contracts (Giangaspro, 2017).

DOI: 10.4018/978-1-7998-3130-3.ch007

The idea and concept of a smart contract can be traced back to the 1990s (Hu et al., 2019). A computer engineer named Wei Dai has been credited with the formulation of the concept when he "created a post on anonymous credits, which described an anonymous loan scheme with redeemable bonds and lump sum taxes to be collected at maturity" (Hu et al., 2019, p. 2). Szabo is considered the father of smart contracts. He stated that "smart contracts utilize protocols and user interfaces to facilitate all steps of the contracting process. This gives us new ways to formalize and secure digital relationships which are far more functional than their inanimate paper-based ancestors" (Szabo, 1997, para. 10).

He believes smart contracts reduce mental and computational transaction costs, and sees smart contracts as a major force in the merger of law and computer security.

As De Caria observes, a search for the term 'smart contract' results in a plethora of definitions (De Caria, 2019). Szabo's definition is probably the most user friendly – he defines it as "a computerized protocol that executes the terms of a contract" (De Caria, 2019, p. 734). Essentially, a smart contract is "a computer program which verifies and executes its terms upon the occurrence of predetermined events" (Giansparo, 2017, p. 3).

Tan argues that we cannot speak about smart contracts without considering 'Etherum', which he considers to be the "mother of all smart contracts" (Tan, 2018, para. 1). He submits that 'Etherum' was the project which attracted the public's attention to the implementation of smart contracts (Tan, 2018). While the application and implementation of smart contracts is not a new phenomenon, the term and its applications have only received exploration in relatively recent times.

The use of public smart contracts (PSC) has been limited. Nevertheless, it is pointed out that large organizations such as Microsoft, IBM and JPMorgan (to name a few) have tapped into "providing consulting services and building private consortium blockchains in a number of industries to build smart contracts on" (Tan, 2018, para. 9). Many parties are investigating the best way to utilize block chain infrastructure to mould the next phase of technology. It is further submitted by Tan that the use of smart contracts will continue to gain momentum, as more parties seek ways in which to make the most of them (Tan, 2018).

While smart contracts may be viewed as an example of the use of blockchain and blockchain technology which offers great opportunities to the field of law; others are more sceptical (Ruhl, 2019; De Caria, 2019). The use of smart contracts in law is anything but straightforward, but this should not deter jurists from investigating the opportunities this instrument offers.

This chapter aims to provide an overview of smart contacts, explaining how they work, the ways they differ from written contracts, their legal status, and the advantages and disadvantages associated with using them. The chapter concludes by identifying the prime challenges facing businesses and the field of law with regard to the increasing use of smart contracts.

DEFINITION OF A SMART CONTRACT

A major challenge with regard to smart contracts is the fact that when parties refer to smart contracts, it can mean different things. When dealing with contracts, language becomes vital. The consistency of such language and consensus regarding smart contracts and what these entail should be considered (Murphy & Cooper, 2016). A smart contract in its basic form refers to "computer programs that secure, enforce and execute settlement of recoded agreements between people and organisations" (Tapscott & Tapscott, 2018, p. 126). These programmes can then set out and define the terms, conditions and consequences of the agreement in similar fashion as a traditional contract does (Roux, 2017). However, where smart contracts really become 'smart' is that they can absorb information, process it by making use of the rules defined in the contract and then self-execute specific terms of the contracts if certain conditions are fulfilled (Roux, 2017). This automation does not automatically occur with traditional contracts. So the smart contract actually enforces the rules of the contract and therefore controls the assets that are being transferred, as occurs in the operation of Bitcoin (Roux, 2017).

The main objective or function of a smart contract seems to be quite obvious; it enables a transfer at minimal cost and automates payments and transfer assets when certain negotiated conditions have been met. A simple and practical example would be if a firm places an order for goods and then pays the supplier for the goods as soon as these goods arrive. A smart contract can be executed automatically (once the negotiated conditions have been met) and it can all happen efficiently with minimal cost (Lansiti & Lakhani, 2017).

THE EXECUTION OF SMART CONTRACTS

When it comes to a smart contract, all the parties to the specific agreement are involved in the management and supervision of the computers and the computer programme which automates the transactions. The smart contract has custody of the assets of the specific contract and the terms of the contract will control the movement of the assets based on whether the conditions have been met (Roux, 2017).

Smart contracts offer many benefits, since the contracts are written, coded and programmed in such a manner that no single party can halt the operation and execution of the contract since no single party has full control of the contract (Roux, 2017). Smart contracts can bridge the gap between legal and commercial arrangements and legal compliance can be added to the programme logic which can maximise operational efficiency and curb costs and risk (Lansiti & Lakhani, 2017; Roux, 2017).

There is a wide range of smart contracts. Since smart contracts are in actual fact computer programmes, they can be programmed using different languages either imperative or declarative languages (Governatori et al., 2018). With a smart contract that uses imperative language, the programmer writes what should be done and how to perform the procedural language (Governatori et al., 2018). What makes this challenging is that with imperative smart contracts, the order of the instructions will not be the same as the natural order of contract clauses in traditional contracts. It is the job of the programmer to come up with an order and work out how a specific trigger changes the normative provisions (i.e. obligations, permissions and prohibitions) and then how to effect the changes to their meaning. The programmer must understand and anticipate the legal reasoning which is implied by the contract clauses (Governatori et al., 2018).

With a declarative smart contract, the programmer incorporates a logic component which indicates what should be done and a control component which indicates how it should be done (Governatori et al., 2018). So here the programmer does not have to explain clearly and explicitly what has to happen, just describe what should be done without specifying how it should be done (Governatori et al., 2018). The advantage of such contracts is that if it is seen that the programme's set of the specifications are correct and thus logical, sound and complete, then the programme will correctly execute its functions (Governatori et al., 2018). A declarative smart contract will then usually specify which semantics should be used, and then the inference system executes this. This would mean that the implemented inference system must be correct with regard to the semantics (Governatori et al., 2018).

Most smart contracts seem to be using an imperative approach and the smart contract then directly states the computational operations which should be performed in order to implement the contract. However, Governatori et al. (2018) believes that a declarative approach should be followed as this approach states the legal arrangements that the parties have agreed to and abstracts these from the computations which are needed in order to implement these arrangements (Governatori et al., 2018). The declarative approach is closer to natural language and understanding and offers a more succinct representation (Governatori et al., 2018).

There are different approaches to the use of smart contracts. There are those who are in favour of "the 'code is contract' approach (that is, the entirety of the natural language can be encoded)" in a contract by a computer programme (i.e. smart contract) (Murphy & Cooper, 2016, p. 4). Others consider smart contracts as instruments that consist of "digitising the performance of business logic (for example, payment) which may or may not be associated with a natural language contract" (Murphy & Cooper, 2016, p. 4). Then, between these two opposite approaches, there are also a number of other permutations and options. An example of the latter would be a so-called "'split' smart contract model [where] natural language contract terms are [linked] to computer code [by using certain] parameters (a smart contract template, for instance)" and this is then incorporated into a computer system so that execution can take place (Murphy & Cooper, 2016, p. 4).

SMART CONTRACTS AND TRADITIONAL CONTRACTS

Smart contracts are similar to traditional contracts because obligations can be defined and consequences for non-conformance can be determined. Users can define and determine rules regarding the execution of the contract. For instance, time frames can be incorporated and conditions such as requiring multiple signatures in order for the transaction to be processed (Roux, 2017).

A smart contract may or may not have legal significance. In the first case, often a separate agreement, expressed in ordinary fashion and in natural language, can exist between parties and then the smart contract is used to automatically effect the implementation of the contract. So the smart contract functions to confirm the existence of the contract and its content (Governatori et al., 2018). In the second instance, when no other document exists recording the agreement of the parties, the smart contract itself embodies the binding expression of that agreement, so in this case, the smart contract itself is meant both to have certain legal effects and to implement them automatically.

A contract is legally binding and causes a change in the legal positions of the parties to the contract (Governatori et al., 2018). Professor Giesela Rühl, Professor of Private International Law and Co- Director of the Centre for European Studies at the Friedrich Schiller University in Jena, believes that smart contracts, just like any other contracts, are subject to the law. The more important question according to her is – which law will smart contracts be subjected to? (Rühl, 2019).

Thus, a smart contract which has legal effect is basically "a computer program that both performs certain operations and expresses, by specifying such operations, the intention to create the legal results (obligations and entitlements) that are presupposed by such an operation" (Governatori et al., 2018, pp. 384-385).

Many of these smart contracts can be seen as 'real contracts' since they have legal effect, but they differ from traditional contracts which are expressed in natural language. There can be various reasons for this, for example, certain parts of the smart contract may not have equivalent terms in the traditional contract which uses traditional language (Governatori et al., 2018). Some terms in the smart contract may explicitly refer to details that are implicitly contained in the traditional contracts. Conversely, the traditional contract might contain certain clauses that are not to be found in the smart contract because automation is not necessary or desirable or even possible. A good example of this might be where standards are involved that cannot be determined easily such as undue delay, or that will not be relevant or applicable in the context of a smart contract (Governatori et al., 2018).

ARE SMART CONTRACTS LEGALLY BINDING CONTRACTS?

In South African law, there are five requirements that must be met in order for a valid and legally binding contract to be established. These are; consensus, contractual capacity, legality, physical possibility, certainty and formalities (Nagel, 2016).

Consensus forms the basis of all contracts. There must be clear consensus between the parties with regard to the proposed contract, together with a serious intention of concluding the specific contract and committing to its juristic consequences (Nagel, 2016). Contractual capacity refers to the fact that the parties must have the necessary capacity to conclude the contract (Nagel, 2016).

Legality deals with the fact that the contract must be legal, it cannot be contrary to common law, legislation, public policy or good morals (Nagel, 2016). At the time of the conclusion of the contract, the parties must be able to perform or execute the terms of the contract. The terms must be determinable and objectively possible (Nagel, 2016). Lastly, the contract must comply with the formalities as prescribed by law (the formalities usually refer to the external visible form of the contract) (Nagel, 2016).

If one considers the five elements applicable to establishing a legally binding contract in South African law, smart contracts certainly meet the requirements of the element consensus in the creation of the contract. The parties agree to some form of contractual terms before the computer ware is actually employed (Raskin, 2017). The parties to a smart contract have to exchange certain private information (Durovic & Janssen, 2018). For instance, parties will submit their cryptographic private keys in order to add resources to a smart contract that has a block-chain basis (Kaulartz & Heckmann, 2016). This reflects consensus and commitment. If one looks at transactions regarding a cryptocurrency such as Bitcoin, the fact that one party places the contract on the blockchain and the other party accepts it by entering the cryptographic key, can be seen as an offer and acceptance of the offer (Durovic & Janssen, 2018). Acceptance of the offer can occur either by performance or by the fact that the transfer is authorized by the specific party when it submits the special cryptographic key (i.e. the password) (Jaccard, 2017). There seems to be very little doubt that if a party enters into a smart contract in a commercial setting, there is an intention to create a legal relationship, and that a rebuttable presumption exists that the intention by the parties is to create legal and juristic consequences (Durovic & Janssen, 2018).

The requirement of contractual capacity can be problematic. Blockchain platforms such as Bitcoin do not ascertain if parties possess full legal capacity. Basically, anyone can open an account without possessing sufficient capacity to do so, which means technically that an intoxicated person, a minor or any other person who does not have full legal capacity can be a party to a smart contract (Durovic & Janssen, 2018). In some cases, transfers of assets can be invalidated after the transferral in a legal manner by an action of unjust enrichment or even by reversing the transaction (Schrey & Thalhofer, 2017).

Smart contracts offer a further challenge in the sense that there can be uncertainty as to what the contractual terms constitute and if these terms are comprehensive enough (Murphy & Cooper, 2016).

This consideration can be a vital and critical factor if one wants to establish if a legally binding contract has been established (Murphy & Cooper, 2016). Another problem is that because smart contracts "purely digitise a particular process but do not include, or operate in conjunction with, contractual terms (express or implied) [they] may not satisfy such requirements" (Murphy & Cooper, 2016, p. 4).

Parties to a smart contract place a huge amount of faith and trust in the system that operates the smart contract. Furthermore, variations to a contract, unlike with a traditional contract, cannot easily be incorporated or achieved with smart contracts (Roux, 2017). So amendments to a smart contract can be problematic.

Walch (2016) indicates that the uncertain and flexible lexicon surrounding blockchain technology can be problematic for regulators. Walch (2016) refers to the fact that one of the reasons people prefer blockchain technology is because of its status as being "immutable", yet the meaning of this word is not that clear. If any variation of the technology takes place, can it still be said that the blockchain creates an "immutable" record (Walch, 2016). The implications of this for the interpretation of contracts can be crucial.

The aspect of formalities can also be an issue since certain jurisdictions call for certain technical requirements or formalities for a contract to be legally binding contract (Murphy & Cooper, 2016). Legal enforceability of the contract is a further concern (Murphy & Cooper, 2016). Smart contracts use technology in order to execute the contract and this can cause a problem if one considers the so-called 'permissionless' distributed ledger. These types of smart contract typically do not have a central administering authority which can settle a dispute, therefore, it is possible that there may be no obvious defendant, and enforcement of a court judgment or arbitration award with regard to a certain transaction can be problematic (Murphy & Cooper, 2016).

FUTURE RESEARCH DIRECTIONS

The advent of smart contracts focuses attention on the role of the legal profession. Generally, with legal contracts, lawyers are either involved in preparing the contract or are involved in advising on the terms and conditions and legality of it, particularly if a dispute arises. In the latter case, with a smart contract, the lawyer may not have been involved in its negotiation and preparation. As discussed above, the identity of the authors of a smart contract may be unknown, as well as whether or not the code has been altered. The creators of the contract may not have adequately considered issues around cross border implementation. Misrepresentations may have been made and incorporated into the code governing the contract with unanticipated results and it may not be possible to prevent a smart contract once it has commenced.

The technology skills (or lack thereof) of lawyers who may be asked to have input into drafting or advising on smart contracts are a huge challenge facing the legal profession (Bacina, 2017). One approach to overcoming this problem is being trialled in Australia. Three organizations, Herbert Smith Freehills, IBM and Data61 have joined together to set up a platform which will enable companies "to use digitised contracts, exchange data and confirm the authenticity and status of legal contracts" (CSIRO, 2018, para 1). The platform will be available to all Australian businesses and will comply with Australian law. If the pilot is successful, the platform may be extended to other jurisdictions.

CONCLUSION

The advent of technology and the rise of blockchain technology have firmly established smart contracts in modern business. The field of law has also welcomed the use and application of smart contracts and it would have been short-sighted not to do so. Smart contracts constitute progress in law and has a definite place in the field of law.

However, to unequivocally embrace the use of smart contracts in law without a level-headed approach to the challenges that the use of smart contracts pose, would be irresponsible and unacceptable. From a legal perspective, there are definite issues regarding jurisdiction, consent, terminology and legal formalities, to name a few, and the lack of proper and effective regulation with regard to smart contracts also raises concerns. Despite this, there should be an increase in the use of smart contracts in law, and the jurists should pave the way in creating greater insight into this phenomenon and assisting in offering it as an effective instrument to be used in the field of law. Many see smart contracts as a vehicle to replace traditional contracts and predict that lawyers who will become experts in this field will benefit richly from such knowledge due to more and more companies using smart contracts (Verschelden, 2019).

REFERENCES

Bacina, M. (2017). *Smart contracts in Australia: just how clever are they?* Retrieved from https://piper-alderman.com.au/insight/smart-contracts-in-australia-just-how-clever-are-they/

CSIRO. (2018, 29 August). *New blockchain-based smart legal contracts for Australian businesses.* Retrieved from https://www.csiro.au/en/News/News-releases/2018/New-blockchain-based-smart-legal-contracts

De Caria, R. (2019). The legal meaning of smart contracts. *European Review of Private Law, 6,* 731–752.

Durovic, M., & Janssen, A. (2018). The formation of blockchain-based smart contracts in the light of contract law. *European Review of Private Law, 26*(6), 753–771.

Giangaspro, M. (2017). Is a 'smart contract' really a smart idea? Insights from a legal perspective. *Computer Law & Security Review, 33*(6), 1–23. doi:10.1016/j.clsr.2017.05.007

Governatori, G., Idelberger, F., Milosevic, Z., Riveret, R., Sartor, G., & Xu, X. (2018). On legal contracts, imperative and declarative smart contracts, and blockchain systems. *Artificial Intelligence and Law, 26*(4), 377–409. doi:10.100710506-018-9223-3

Hu, Y., Liyanage, M., Manzoor, A., Thilakarathna, K., Jourjon, G., & Seneviratne, A. (2019). *Blockchain-based smart-contracts-applications and challenges.* Retrieved from https://arxiv.org/abs/1810.04699

Jaccard, G. (2017). Smart contracts and the role of law. *Jusletter IT, 23,* 1–25. doi:10.2139srn.3099885

Kaulartz, M., & Heckmann, J. (2016). Smart contracts-anwendungen der blockchain-technologie. *Computer und Recht (Köln), 32*(9), 618–624. doi:10.9785/cr-2016-0923

Lansiti, M., & Lakhani, K. R. (2017). The truth about blockchain. *Harvard Business Review, 95*(1), 118–127.

Murphy, S., & Cooper, C. (2016). *Can smart contracts be legally binding contracts?* Retrieved from https://www.nortonrosefulbright.com/-/media/files/nrf/nrfweb/imported/norton-rose-fulbright--r3-smart-contracts-white-paper-key-findings-nov-2016.pdf

Nagel, C. (2016). *Commercial law*. Johannesburg, South Africa: LexisNexis.

Omohundro, S. (2014). Cryptocurrencies, smart contracts, and artificial intelligence. *AI Matters*, *1*(2), 19–21. doi:10.1145/2685328.2685334

Raskin, M. (2017). The law and legality of smart contracts. *Georgetown Law Technology Review.*, *1*(2), 304–341.

Roux, S. (2017). Smart contracts. *Without Prejudice, 17*(2), 28-29.

Rühl, G. (2019). *The law applicable to smart contracts, or much ado about nothing?* Retrieved from https://www.law.ox.ac.uk/business-law-blog/blog/2019/01/law-applicable-smart-contracts-or-much-ado-about-nothing

Schrey, J., & Thalhofer, T. (2017). Rechtliche aspekte der blockchain. *Neue Juristische Wochenschrift: NJW, 70*(20), 1431–1436.

Szabo, N. (1997). *Formalizing and securing relationships on public networks*. Retrieved from https://nakamotoinstitute.org/formalizing-securing-relationships/

Tan, E. (2018). *The evolution of smart contracts*. Retrieved from hackernoon.com/are-smart-contracts-the-future-1d9028f49743

Tapscott, D., & Tapscott, A. (2018). *Blockchain revolution: how the technology behind bitcoin and other cryptocurrencies is changing the world*. London, UK: Portfolio.

Verschelden, A. (2019). *Get ready: Blockchain will transform the legal industry*. Retrieved from https://www.moore-global.com/insights/articles/get-ready-blockchain-will-transform-the-legal-indu

Walch, A. (2016). The path of the blockchain lexicon (and the law). *Review of Banking and Financial Law, 36*(2), 713–765.

ADDITIONAL READING

Al Khalil, F., Butler, T., O'Brien, L., & Ceci, M. (2017). Trust in smart contracts is a process, as well. In A. Kiayias (Ed.), *International Conference on Financial Cryptography and Data Security* (pp. 510-519). Cham: Switzerland: Springer. 10.1007/978-3-319-70278-0_32

Eenmaa-Dimitrieva, H., & Schmidt-Kessen, M. J. (2017). Regulation through code as a safeguard for implementing smart contracts in no-trust environments. *EUI Department of Law Working Paper 2017/13*. San Domenico di Fiesole, Italy: European University Institute.

Lauslahti, K., Mattila, J., & Seppala, T. (2017). Smart contracts - how will blockchain technology affect contractual practices? *Etla Reports*, (68). Retrieved from https://www.etla.fi/wp-content/uploads/ETLA-Raportit-Reports-68.pdf

Savelyev, A. (2017). Contract law 2.0: 'Smart' contracts as the beginning of the end of classic contract law. *Information & Communications Technology Law*, 26(2), 116–134. doi:10.1080/13600834.2017.1301036

Staples, M., Chen, S., Falamaki, S., Ponomarev, A., Rimba, P., Tran, A. B., ... Zhu, J. (2017). *Risks and opportunities for systems using blockchain and smart contracts*. Sydney, Australia: CSIRO; doi:10.4225/08/596e5ab7917bc

KEY TERMS AND DEFINITIONS

Blockchain: An electronic system that securely and reliably stores data on a specific network.

Blockchain Technology: The technology that supports and enables the blockchain to operate effectively.

Contract: An agreement between parties which the obligations; duties; responsibilities and rights of each party.

Cryptocurrency: A digital, virtual currency which is exchanged and used by means of encryption techniques.

Formalities: Requirements which must be complied with in order to constitute as valid contract.

Regulation: The process of designing and implementing rules, regulations and laws in order to govern and regulate actions, activities, duties.

Smart Contract: A computer programme that automates certain actions based on set codes and parameters and agreements between parties to the agreement.

South Africa: Country at southern tip of Africa, one of the most developed countries in Africa which boasts one of the strongest economies in the region.

Chapter 8
Robots:
Regulation, Rights, and Remedies

Migle Laukyte
Faculty of Law, Pompeau Fabra University, Spain

ABSTRACT

More and more often legal scholars notice that developments in robotics are becoming increasingly relevant from a legal point of view. This chapter critically assesses the current debate in the regulation of artificial intelligence (AI)-based robotics, whose scope should be seen as part of a wider debate that concerns AI. Indeed, what interests legal scholars are those robots that are able to act autonomously and intelligently, that is, robots embedded with AI. The chapter looks at such robots from the twofold perspective: on the one hand, robot as a product (and therefore the chapter refers to consumer protection) and, on the other hand, robot as entity (and therefore it addresses robot rights). The chapter also includes a brief overview of some of the initiatives to regulate AI and robotics interpreting the nuances so as to extract some ideas on national priorities in this regard.

INTRODUCTION

Developments in robotics are becoming increasingly relevant from a legal point of view,[1] and even though there is still no consensus about what falls under the term 'robot', we instinctively feel that robotics is going to give rise to many legal nuisances and Gordian knots. This chapter provides an overview of the current legal debate concerning robotics, understood here as those virtual and physical robots that are able to act autonomously and intelligently, that is, robots embedded with artificial intelligence (AI). These AI-based robots represent a paradigmatic change that could mark not only the evolution of legal thought but could also widely impact social arrangements and equilibriums: the change from robot as a thing (product) to robot as an entity (a person in law).

A question immediately arises: why are these, and not other topics being addressed in this work? The author has no doubts that there are many legal and social issues related to AI and robotics – the terms that will be used interchangeably in this chapter unless specified otherwise – and much work has been already done to understand, question, analyze and share them.[2] Yet usually these works focus on very

DOI: 10.4018/978-1-7998-3130-3.ch008

specific questions, such as civil liability, contracts or intellectual property (IP) protection. This chapter has a different goal: it aims to provide a more general and panoramic vision of the main legal questions related to AI and robotics.

Only such a general vision can help to reveal the Janus-faced nature of AI, where each position (AI as a product or AI as an entity) challenges the established legal concepts and legal frameworks differently. The overall challenge then is not related to specific questions, but rather to the whole legal system, because what lawyers and legal scholars fail to see is that AI is different from any other technology: it escapes our legal ontologies and shows an out-of-datedness. Consequently, the legal concepts that until so recently were clearly defined and immovable (within certain limits), are now becoming more fluid and shapeless. As imperfect and far from complete the author's account may be, this chapter attempts to provide a more complete and all-embracing vision of how AI is challenging the law and how legal scholars still have not worked out sufficiently clear and exhaustive answers to these challenges.

The chapter is organized as follows. The first section focuses on robots as things or products, and therefore on problems and challenges that robots might cause to consumers (Hartzog, 2015). As a part of this, robots can affect a wide array of legal and social goods, such as human rights, in particular, the right to privacy, data protection, but also consumer trust, and security. This section argues that robots reveal consumer vulnerability more than any other technologies have done so far, and it seems that legislators have not yet fully understood their impact.

The second section presents a different perspective: having looked at robots as products and their real and potential impact on consumers, the author changes the focus completely and looks at them as entities in their own right and accordingly focuses on the rights of robots. The idea of robot rights is not a new one, but it has been gaining ground, and new paradigms have been introduced, such as the development of computational law applications that could provide legal advice to machines (Kahana, 2018). This section shows that the debate on robot rights is not only taking a clear path leading to straightforward, all-encompassing arguments for or against robot rights, but that there also is a shift underway towards a more nuanced discussion focused on specific rights, such as the previously suggested example of a right to legal advice.

The third section is dedicated to legal and regulatory initiatives that are being undertaken in Europe and elsewhere. The author argues that there are no norms specifically designed for robots, just preliminary work that will be functional for future regulation. This preliminary work, in the forms of strategies and initiatives, varies among countries. Thus, for example, European Union (EU) lawmakers are promoting a human-centric approach (High Level Expert Group, 2019), while Canadian researchers in the *Montreal Declaration* (University of Montreal, 2017) have advanced a slightly different position, being among the first to admit that human relation with robots could be a relationship to protect. This chapter analyzes EU, United States (US) and Canadian approaches and draws some preliminary conclusions on what these approaches establish as their priorities. The chapter ends with a few closing remarks.

Before starting, the author provides a working idea of what the robot is for the purposes of this chapter. There are many things, tools and programs, that can be - and actually are - called robots: from vacuum cleaners to flight booking systems. We are surrounded by them, and yet not all of these tools and services are robots. The author uses the term robot to represent all those tools and services that imbue robots with some sort of autonomy, that is, robots that can act without human intervention and control and could exercise any kind of (human-like) intelligent behavior (World Commission on the Ethics of Scientific Knowledge and Technology, 2017). This is why the terms robot and AI will be used interchangeably throughout this chapter, unless stated differently, and it is also why a flight booking system would not qualify as a robot, whereas Sophia robot, Bina 48 or Mitsuku chatbot could.[3] The overall idea is to keep the definition of robot broad and inclusive: the goal of this chapter is to draft some common issues that could be applicable to as much types of robots as possible, nevertheless, in specific cases, the author refers to particular robots that help to illustrate the case at hand.

ROBOT AS A THING: CONSUMER PROTECTION

The current debate on legal issues related to robotics is characterized by the attempt to 'pour the new wine' of robotics and AI into the 'old bottles' of existing legal categories, at the same time keeping an eye on the novel challenges that robotics bring into being for such social goods as human rights and, in particular, privacy, but also others such as security and data protection. While there are many more legal issues related to robotics, nevertheless, they are still to some extend vague and ill-defined, such as the progress around standardization and national certification of robots. Indeed, the research in robotics presents society with a variety of possibilities, but for consumers, the interesting ones are those which bring people in direct contact with the robots: for example, social robotics, that is robotics that interact with other robots, with people, and the surrounding environment. Social robots can be physical and can touch, move, lift things and do many other tasks that we, humans, can: they perceive and are aware of their surroundings, which makes them the most apt tools for domestic or generally human environments, such as hospitals, schools, postal offices, and other public and private spaces. Social robots can also be virtual (see the aforementioned Mitsuku): as research shows (Ligthart and Truong, 2015), the sociability of robot is what matters most to the majority of people, whereas its form depends on the circumstances.

Consumer Vulnerability

But consumers will not interact only with these social robots, but will have to deal with other kinds of robots that are not necessarily so social (or rather their sociality is different), such as autonomous cars. This variety of forms and kinds of sociability means that the consumers will have to face and learn how to deal with different levels of automation, intelligence, autonomy, complexity and technological sophistication: all these features will give a new meaning to the fact that the consumer is defined by the weakness of his or her position with respect to the supplier (manufacturer, seller, or any other party representing business). The more intelligent and autonomous a machine is, the weaker the consumer becomes because of the difference in levels of knowledge.

This position - the position that the consumer is a weaker party - is debatable though: for instance, Ryan cites Julian Smith, an analyst for Jupiter Research, who argues that consumers (2016, p.15):

are better informed through the increased ability to access and sift an abundance of information anytime, anywhere. They are better connected through the ability to instantaneously communicate with others across time zones and social strata. They are more communicative through the ability to publish and share their ideas and opinions.

This may be so in the case of the digital market but AI-based applications (including robots) are taking this market to a different level and perhaps what is true for the digital world might no longer be true in the AI world.

Take, for example, the information asymmetry that exists between a supplier (manufacturer) and a consumer: people are used to see this asymmetry between these two players, but the challenge is that, thanks to AI, rather than two players, there might be three players: supplier (manufacturer), consumer and autonomous and intelligent robot that also possesses information that is either inaccessible or unavailable to the consumer and which substantially exceeds the knowledge of the supplier (manufacturer). Furthermore, there might not be just one robot involved but a network of robots that "know" more than the consumer does, and who can use this knowledge against the consumer. The measures proposed by legislators to level this asymmetry might not work for AI and it might be necessary to explore new ways to deal with this problem.

Going even further and taking into account consumer profiling, it cannot be excluded that the machines and suppliers (manufacturers) would not only know more than consumers do, but could also know what the consumers know and what they do not know. This provokes a complete imbalance of information and knowledge among the parties and so far it seems that the AI will work to benefit the supplier (manufacturer) rather than the consumer. In this scenario, the consumer data that businesses will be able to collect with or without the help of the AI is key, and privacy and personal data protection could be a game changer not only for individuals as such, but especially for individuals as consumers.

The European Commission (2018) thinks in this direction too (p.16):

The large-scale use of AI-enabled tools in business-to-consumer transactions needs to be fair, transparent and compliant with consumer legislation. Consumers should receive clear information on the use, features and properties of AI-enabled products.

Furthermore, the EU is also adopting the idea that human beings should be informed about whether they are interacting with a machine or with a human, and should be offered the opportunity to talk to a human if need be (High Level Expert Group, 2019). From the consumer perspective, this idea provides additional means to ensure that a consumer is not 'left' to interact with the AI alone and can turn to a human in cases when the decision taken by the AI alone is unsatisfactory. What remains unclear is how the guarantee of human intervention relates to product liability rules.

Additional questions arise in the possible role of AI systems in promoting unfair, that is, misleading or aggressive, commercial practices against consumers. According to the *Directive 2005/29/EC*, misleading practices are defined as practices that contain "false information [...] or in any way, including overall presentation, deceives or is likely to deceive the average consumer, even if the information is factually correct, in relation to one or more of [such] elements, [...]" as existence or nature of product, its characteristics, [...], additional services related to maintenance or repair, etc. (art. 6). Aggressive commercial practices are those that involve harassment, physical force, coercion or undue influence (art. 8).

AI could give a new meaning and content to these practices. For example, AI systems could easily deceive or mislead a person but could also manipulate the consumer to take decisions that do not reflect his or her real intentions or that he or she would not have taken were these practices not used. Indeed AI systems, trained to use these misleading practices, should have no difficulties in providing incorrect information relating to robot maintenance or repair, omitting important updates that need to be made or cases in which the robot should necessarily be revised by the supplier (manufacturer). Furthermore, an AI can be aggressive in its persistent attempts to influence the consumer to change their decision (especially with virtual systems that can send continuous emails, alerts, warnings and other unsolicited information) through use of abusive language or exploitation of knowledge about the consumer against them. Legal norms are in place to deal with misleading or aggressive commercial practices against the consumers but it is not clear whether these norms could be applied to AI and how. Furthermore, the consumer deception could be easier to achieve in the case of humanoid robots: that is especially relevant in the case of elderly or intellectually impaired consumers who have more difficulty in distinguishing a humanoid from a human. This kind of deception highlights the vulnerability of already vulnerable social groups and the question is whether such kind of products should exist at all: should not the goal be a completely different one, that is, to strengthen these social groups?

As already mentioned above, the EU considers that people should be told whenever they are dealing with an AI so this technique could also work to deal with the (malicious) use of AI against consumers, especially if it is the case of online or telephonic conversations. Kerr (2004) has observed that many businesses use virtual assistants, bots and other interactive programs as the primary source of information for consumers, and that they use what this author calls "slick form of misdirection" (Kerr, 2004, p. 288) and obstructs consumers from making decisions freely and on their own. Kerr calls this phenomenon a *californication of commerce* and what might be different today with respect to 2004, is that the same processes would leave the virtual world and could enter the real, AI-based world: then the discussion would be about the *californication* of households, hospitals or other places where consumers could be misled by the machines. Looking at these examples and the evolution of trends - from virtual bot to real robot—are consumers becoming more vulnerable? Are they continuously losing their freedom and autonomy both as consumers and as individuals?

Consumer Trust

There is also a big question related to consumer trust: people anthropomorphize things and have always done so, but the machines are the tools people usually trust so much more than other human beings, if not in everything, but at least in letting them handle their personal information (Sundar & Kim, 2019). Human trust is also the reason why humans are vulnerable (Hartzog, 2015). It is not only about the robots being able to manipulate people or make people believe that they know everything, but it is also human beings that need to trust and often trust without any sound reason for it. Hartzog (2015) explains the origins of this trust in robots as a kind of trust by proxy or because the supplier (manufacturer) uses certain cognitive techniques to induce feelings of trust in the consumers.

However, trust is the enabler of any human to robotic interaction as it is in any human to human interaction: the levels of trust affects human acceptance of the information the robot is providing and the probability that the consumer will follow its suggestions (Hancock et al., 2011). While it is not that crucial in the case of an assistant robot for entertainment, it could become a life threatening issue in security, elderly assistance or hospital settings. Morality and other social norms and conventions are the ways to encourage trustworthy behavior (Kuipers, 2018) of human or non-human entities, and this is why the ability of robots to follow human social norms is so important. Indeed, a recent study by PEGA (PEGA, 2019) shows that the majority of US consumers do not believe that machines can tell right from wrong and more than 50 percent do not believe it could be possible at all, and only a small percentage think that they have had an interaction with a machine that has showed some sort of empathy towards them.

Another related question is whether a robot's appearance influences a human's ability to trust. If humans have more trust in robots that look like humans (the aforementioned, humanoid robots), should we oppose their development and explicitly require that suppliers (manufacturers) do not produce machines that pretend to be something more than machines? The question is tricky, because, at least in the western world, a common image of how 'a friendly robot' looks like have been already formed by mass culture. These common images do not refer to robots that look like humans or at least not always: just think about R2-D2 or C-3PO depicted in 'Star Wars'. R2-D2 and C-3PO are cute, everybody likes them, because these robots have always been nice, friendly and helpful to humans. A non-fictional robot, that is somewhat similar to these fictional robots, could be JIBO, which is described by its developers in such terms as 'authentically charming', 'seems downright human' and it is referred to as 'he' rather than 'it'.[4] As Hartzog (2015, p. 93) puts it: "[popular movies, books and other aspects of pop culture] makes marketing robots a ripe opportunity for deception because consumers are primed to believe".

Product Liability

There is an enormous debate on the liability regimes that should be applied in the case of autonomous and intelligent robots: who is liable is not a real question, because the supplier (manufacturer) is strictly liable at least within the EU, but now consumers and legislators are beginning to understood that perhaps the supplier (manufacturer) liability - although still one of the most powerful legal instrument to ensure consumer protection - cannot be the only solution, so much so that the exemptions of this kind of liability - in particular, those related to the compliance of the product with mandatory regulations or the state of scientific and technical knowledge that did not permit identification of the defect in a product - are playing in favor of companies. Probably the focus should not be on liability attribution, but on its distribution among the stakeholders, because AI-based robotics require levels of complexity that one single supplier is no longer neither able nor willing to assume. The supplier (manufacturer) needs to know that its liability for the actions that autonomous and intelligent robots might take will not destroy their business, because otherwise what is the value of investing millions in robots if a company could be easily ruined by a single unforeseen and unforeseeable action? Many authors reject the need for new liability regimes (Shaerer, Kelley & Nicolescu, 2009; Barfield, 2018), but this author agrees with those who think that it remains an important question that needs to be tackled in a constructive and open manner, because this problem will become more urgent as robot autonomy and intelligence grows constantly: humans no longer question the possibility of AI, but rather argue about the approximate date when it will be developed (Wagner, 2018).

The switch from the attribution to the distribution of liability adds to other liability-related questions that AI and robotics are giving rise to, such as the changing nature of machines and programs that are continuously learning new things, thanks to self-learning. This changing nature of a robot as a product clashes with the legal assumption that the product once put on the market no longer changes besides its natural operation (Turner, 2019). The static nature of product is also the foundation of its safety, whereas there is nothing static in AI. How will it be possible to address this drawback (or advantage) of AI and at the same time guarantee consumer protection and safety?

Hence, what is necessary are new liability schemes and arrangements that, on the one hand, would protect consumers, and, on the other hand, would ensure the investments in technology and the development of new services that we, as a human society, desperately need. AI-based robotics may lead to new meanings of such legal concepts as negligence, prudence ("reasonably prudent AI standard" suggested by Barfield, 2018, p. 198), duty of care, intention, product and many others. The role of the consumer in causing an accident involving a robot is also a question not sufficiently explored in the academic literature on robotic liability. To what extent does technological literacy play a role in inappropriate or dangerous use of robots? Should there be particular cases when robots could be sold only to those users who provide evidence that they underwent some kind of training on the functioning of particular robots? Will human have to train people not to make robots misbehave?

An additional factor that always has to be taken into account is the possibility of hackers' attacks that could lead a machine to act in a dangerous or harmful way. this is not specific to robots, as any digital technology, connected to wifi, is subject to the same threat. Perhaps nowadays these digital threats are already assumed and do not scare the customers as they used to scare just two decades ago. Supposedly, the hacker threat is limited because both the technological safety and security has increased, but also because society feels relatively more secure and no panic related to hackers has been observed in commercial settings.

So to conclude this section, the most important point is to stress that nobody questions the advantages that AI is going to bring about in the business sector, but there are still many doubts about the price consumers will probably be asked to pay to get these benefits as well. The business world shows that the benefits exist, but there is also a probability that these benefits will not reach consumers, that consumers may be used as a means to (commercial or business) ends but not as ends in themselves. This is particularly true in the case of personal data, which robots need to develop new services, learn new things and better adapt to the human environment.

Privacy

Probably the most important concept related to privacy is the consent given by the data subject, in this particular case, the consumer. The General Data Protection Regulation (GDPR) (European Union, 2016) of the EU clearly states that this consent must be given freely, and should be unambiguous, specific and informed. These terms might be difficult to achieve, especially as concerns AI and robots. Indeed as argued by Bester, Cole and Kodish (2016), humans already face many situations when they have to give an informed consent, but because of the complexity and volume of information - or as the authors call it, 'informational overload' - cannot really give it. There can be too much and too complicated information, but there also can be intellectual inability to handle this information and inability to access the choices that this information is putting in front of the consumer. There is still an open question about how to ensure informed consent in many spheres of human life, and robotics adds to this list of further unknowns. The difference lies in the fact that many times a person is given time to make a decision and decides on whether or not to consent, whereas in the case of AI and robotics, they could be induced to think they have to give consent 'right now and right here'; in such cases whether that consent could be considered to be given freely is a big question.

Furthermore, coming back to the idea of information asymmetry, any legitimate consent seems to be out of question. The supplier (manufacturer) should be able to inform the consumer about what kind of data the robot is going to record, how it is going to store it, for how long, who is going to have an access to it, how the security and integrity of this data is going to be ensured and how individual rights to access, to rectify, to modify or to delete personal data will be guaranteed. It is an enormous burden for the supplier (manufacturer), but these are the requirements in Europe for those who want to access the EU market. A good solution could be that any data recorded by the robot be immediately anonymized or the personal data (such as name, address, the IP address of family's personal computers) should not be recorded at all. This could be a privacy-by-design or also privacy-by-default choice of robotic architecture that prevents the privacy problem in the first place. This strategy seems to be the choice of SoftBank Robotics (the company producing social robot Pepper)[5]. The company's privacy policy announces that with regard to dialogue data, that is, data that the robot gets as a result of talking to humans, its recording will not be carried out without the consent of that person.

However, humans should also bear in mind that as robots are not yet sophisticated enough to understand natural language at a 100 percent level, if the robot does not understand what the human is telling it, it will translate the human commands into text and send that text to the third party that provides voice recognition; the company asks the humans to bear this possibility in mind and also offers the possibility to deactivate this feature. Nonetheless, with this feature deactivated, the interaction with the robot is much more complicated. One possible interpretation of this could be that if a human wants a robot to understand him or her, a human should give the third party access to his or her personal data.

In this section, robots were considered as an example of a complicated product that could make the lives of consumers more complicated instead of making them easier. In the next section, a different perspective is provided; it looks at robots no longer as mere products, but as entities with their own rights.

ROBOT PERSON: QUESTION OF RIGHTS

In this section, the author looks at robots from a completely different perspective. If, in the previous section, the goal was to look at the challenges robots and AI are about to introduce for consumers, this section deals with robots as entities in their own right and accordingly focuses on the rights of robots.

The idea of robot rights is still somewhat speculative and science fiction-based, and yet to think that it is not possible is not an acceptable answer. Although the idea of robot rights is not new (Gunkel, 20007; Koops, Hildebrandt & Jaquet-Chiffelle, 2010), lately it has evolved and gained ground thanks to the development of computational law applications that could provide legal advice to machines (Kahana, 2018). This section examines the debate on robot rights which involves both straightforward, all-encompassing arguments for or against robot rights, and a more nuanced discussion focused on specific rights, such as the previously suggested example of a right to legal advice.

What Do We Mean by Robot Rights?

The matter of robot rights is sometimes called "the last socially accepted moral prejudice" (Gunkel, 2007, p. 174). Nobody can deny that human beings are extending the list of those entities that have ethical entitlements to consider and, most importantly, legal rights that grant them protection; the last but probably not the least among them is the environment or nature - in the form of rivers, forests, or other parts of nature - and the ensuing movement of environmental personhood which stems and gets inspiration from corporate personhood, the first non-human entity recognized by law (Gordon, 2017). The human history of granting rights is a continuous sequence of arguments to include those under scrutiny for the rights: the approach has moved from anthropocentrism, that included all the people (of all sexes, races, ages) to animiocentrism, that included not only humans but animals as well (human and non-human animals), then to biocentrism that expands the list of right holders to cover all who (and that) are alive on this earth, and then to ontocentrism, which advocates for the inclusion of everything and everyone that exists (Gunkel, 2007), and, consequently, robots as well.

What is important in this later development of environmental personhood, is not so much the idea of the rights of rivers, national parks or ecosystems, but the idea of how these rights change the human right of ownership and property. From the right to use and exploit, humans are moving to recognize the right of these other entities to be respected and protected from exactly this use and exploitation. And this is where the link between environmental and robotic personhood lies; both, nature and robots, are or were considered to be things, but humans are slowly acknowledging that there might be a different kind of relationship, and that this relationship should not be forced into an ownership-possession-(ab) use-exploitation framework.

Against Legal Personhood of Robots

The EU Parliament in its Resolution issued in 2017 has admitted the possibility that humans might need to create a new legal status for autonomous robots, a status that would grant them electronic personhood (EU Parliament, 2017). The exact wording was that the future might ask us to think about (p. 18):

creating a specific legal status for robots in the long run, so that at least the most sophisticated autonomous robots could be established as having the status of electronic persons responsible for making good any damage they may cause, and possibly applying electronic personality to cases where robots make autonomous decisions or otherwise interact with third parties independently

The voices against this idea were and still are numerous (Bryson, Diamantis &Grant, 2017; Schafer, 2016). An example of the opposition to the personhood of robots, and perhaps the one that 'harmed' the cause of robot personhood most, was the open letter that many prominent scholars and researchers have signed (Robotics Open Letter, n.d.). This letter showed their position against the personhood of robots, because this idea was considered to be impossible and inacceptable technically, legally and ethically. From the technical perspective, the objection is based on the overestimation of advancements in robotics and distortions, produced by the mass media and science fiction, of human perceptions of what robots can do. What is surprising though is that if such sophisticated and autonomous robots cannot exist technically, then the attack on the idea of their personhood is not justified: if these robots are not possible, their personhood should not bother humans either. And yet the open letter continues with ethical and legal reasons why this kind of personhood cannot exist. These reasons are based on personhood models; natural person, legal entity and Anglo-Saxon trust. The reasons why any of these model could work for machines, is as follows:

- the first is impossible to apply to robots because it would clash with human rights;
- the second implies that there are human beings behind the technology, who should be accountable, and in case of robots, this may not be so;
- the third model is too complex to use, would not solve the liability issue, and would also imply participation of humans.

It may be that many of the critics simply misunderstood what the EU Parliament really had in mind, which is a hypothetical possibility about the future: none of the wording of the Resolution suggests that robots should be granted (human or corporate) rights right away. Reactions however - and the open letter is just one of many examples - do not seemed to be directed against an idea, but against a concrete legislative strategy and yet there was no intention to promote any strategy whatsoever. Furthermore, all the arguments against have their flaws: for example, the EU Parliament never talked about a concrete model of personhood nor ever proposed to grant human rights to robots. The idea of personhood was just what it was, an idea, which was left for the EU to elaborate if need be: which kind of personhood is a question that might be necessary to answer, but so far there was no need to do that.

There are further arguments against (any kind of) personhood - and consequently, against any kind of rights - to robots. They do not have consciousness, they are not human, and they do not have a soul (van der Hoven van Genderen, 2018). The question however is twofold: one is whether the robots *could* have rights, whereas the second is whether they *should* have rights. The first question is legal, whereas the second is ethical. Many times the answer to the second is also the answer to the first, that is, if robot rights are unethical and incompatible with human values, then there should be no legal recognition of these rights. Nevertheless, then a question could arise, namely, whether corporate rights should exist. Although many would agree that they should not, they do exist. Then, why couldn't they exist for machines?

The biggest problem is that scholars often forget that granting rights also means deciding what kind of rights to recognize. Rights should not be taken as a unique package of rights, that cannot be opened and should be adopted only as a whole. People decide what rights to recognize to whom, when and why. Furthermore, many times the debate about robot rights turns into debate about whether we should grant robots *human* rights, and, consequently, any rational and constructive debate ends. But 'rights' is not a synonym of 'human rights', and if the first can be discussed, elaborated, changed, eliminated or ended, human rights can be changed and updated (for instance, new generations of human rights), but they cannot be cancelled nor ended. Robot rights should have a start and should have an end and should not be seen as in any way comparable or in competition with human rights. Having this in mind could help scholars discuss the possibility of robot rights without prejudice and fear.

In Favor of Legal Personhood of Robots

According to Turner (2019), there are three basic reasons to protect the rights of those who (or what) are not humans; ability to suffer, compassion, and value to humans. There is also a fourth reason, which is completely and exclusively robotics and AI-oriented, namely, the cases in which AI and human being are combined (human enhancement with the help of AI), but this later point is still a discussion about how far humans could be modified technologically and still remain human, and therefore the author will not address this reason here.

The first reason - namely, the ability to suffer - is very much related to consciousness and is one of the reasons why humans started recognizing rights to animals and prohibiting their torture. So far, no AI-based robot is known to show any features of consciousness, for example, no robot could show any ability to perceive oneself and its existence. The ability to suffer right now does not apply to machines, because to date humans have not succeeded in building some kind of artificial consciousness, although many attempts (and associative neural networks is but one of many examples) have been made to achieve it (Haikonen, 2019). The problem with consciousness is that humans do not really know how consciousness works, and in many ways consciousness remains a mystery. Van den Hoven van Genderen (2018) puts this mystery in the following questions that humans have no answers for (p. 238):

[…] what is consciousness? Is 'cogito ergo sum' […] from Descartes proof that the mere act of thinking sufficient to define one's existence as rational being? Is consciousness part of, or something separate from, a human being? Or any being for that matter? […] How would the consciousness of AI be established?.

Ability to suffer is what usually helps human beings to distinguish conscious forms of life from those which are not, but the researchers Johannes Kuehn and Sami Haddadin from the Leibniz University in Hannover argue that this is a question of time. Their work on artificial robot nervous systems involves teaching robots how to feel pain as a tool of self-preservation (Ackerman, 2016), and scholars should start wondering whether their research could change human conception of suffering and its link to consciousness.

The second reason - human compassion - is related to suffering too. If an entity (human or animal) can convince humans that they suffer, humans will feel compassion, and this leads - in some but surely not all cases - to legal measures that stop it. Hence, human compassion might take the form of legal norms; humans legalize their empathy and make a rule out of it. What really matters in feeling compassion and empathy for robots is the way they look: Sophia robot and JIBO robot are very different and give rise to different feelings. In the case of Sophia or Ava, an avatar created by Soul Machines,[6] some of the people will feel rejection (the 'uncanny valley syndrome') because it is perceived as creepy and scary, however, the robots can change that with the help of their behavior or people can easily get used to uncommon appearances (Złotowski, Sumioka, Nishio, Glas, Bartneck & Ishiguro, 2018). Hence human feelings of compassion are flexible and can be induced or manipulated, the way people feel about a particular robot could be changed with the help of additional features that the robot might not show during the first encounter, for example, humans might feel nothing towards Asimo robot, but feelings can change if Asimo says that it recognizes a particular person, calls them by name, touches a person or walks with them hand-in-hand (Honda, 2020).

The third reason - value to humans - means that treating robots as if they were entities and not simple tools could provide higher human safety in a human-robotic society. The Confucian principle of not doing unto others what you do not want to be done unto you could be applied to justify this statement. Another interpretation of this value is that there are things that have value for humanity as such, for instance, the environment and nature. Natural entities, such as the Whanganui river in New Zealand, have been granted rights, because otherwise the rights of everybody to enjoy them might be harmed due to private or public interests that destroys rather than preserves nature. The environmental personhood shows that humans are moving from exploitation-oriented relations with the world to preservation-oriented ones and it seems that the concept of (private or public) ownership is becoming an outdated paradigm for this relationship. Robots could be the next in line in this process. In the next section, the author introduces computational law applications that advise robots in legal matters and, in the author's opinion, represent a small step toward the realization that not only are legal support and advice no longer only human-oriented, but also that the robot rights debate could be pushed with the help of computational law and other applications that entitle robots to similar products and services as humans.

The Impact of Computational Law

A paradigmatic change in our vision of autonomous and intelligent robotics is represented by the emergence of what is called computational law, that is, a branch of legal informatics that aims to codify legal norms and regulations (Genesereth, 2015). The overall aim of computational law is to make law understandable (and legal tools available) to everyone everywhere, and, in addition, it goes a little bit beyond that; *everyone* in this context is no longer only a human being, but also a machine. This is why the computational law is so important for the discussion about robot rights. Due to computational law, robots will be able to understand law and use law, because computational law basically extends the list of those who can raise a legal question or have a legal interest. Furthermore, the computational law changes the paradigm in another way; whereas earlier technology was used as a *means* to deal with law and its complexities, now, thanks to computational law, the technology (and in particular, AI programs and robots) is an *end*, because it too, just as human beings, has to understand and use legal regulations for the aims it has.

Undeniably, this is the next step in the research and development of computational law applications. Right now the idea is to make these applications available to autonomous and connected vehicles, that is, drones, cars, and other means of transportation, but in the future more sophisticated applications could be available for much smarter and much more autonomous technologies, such as robots that will perform many of the tasks and jobs that today are exclusively human (for example nursing or driving). Of course, this does not mean to push people to abandon these jobs, but it is also true that many people would prefer (or are more talented) to do other things.

If these computational law applications become available for machines, it would also mean that the machines would be compliant with the law and it would increase their trustworthiness (Kahana, 2018), which is a very important goal for the whole industry of - and research on - AI and robotics and another kind of 'by design' feature, such as privacy-by-design, that the AI development is pushed by normative frameworks to develop.

An additional idea is to use computational law to work out a code of conduct (or ethical code) for robots, because besides legal behavior, robots should also behave ethically (Wolfram, 2016). Computational law - perhaps together with computational ethics - then could not only ensure that we have robots aware of legal norms and requirements, but also robots aware of ethical norms and practices. This legal and ethical awareness could be another step towards recognition of robot rights.

COMPASS OF NATIONAL STRATEGIES: WHERE ARE WE HEADING?

In this section, the author looks at several international initiatives dedicated to social aspects of AI and robotics: needless to say, that positive law is not available yet, but the preparatory work - in the form of strategies, plans and other proposals - can give insights on the directions some of the countries (or, as is the case of EU, union of countries) are currently undertaking.

These of course are not the only initiatives that have been launched around AI, however, they are outside the purview of this work: the author looks at some - but not all - of the actions of the EU, Canada and the US and will point out particularities that the author consider to be important.

European Union

The EU is promoting what it calls a EU approach to AI, which is based on three pillars: (a) being ahead of technological advancements and boosting this advancement both on public and private levels; (b) being ready to deal with socio-economic challenges that the arrival and application of AI will doubtlessly cause; and (c) making sure that the ethical and legal frameworks are in place for the arrival of AI.

As already mentioned above, there are many more initiatives, guidelines and calls for action that exist on a EU level on AI, but the author will look only at some of the actions that EU has undertaken. In particular, the author focuses on "The Ethical Guidelines for Trustworthy AI" elaborated by the High Level Expert Group (HLEG), nominated by the European Commission (High Level Expert Group, 2019).

The Ethical Guidelines to Trustworthy AI

The Ethical Guidelines to Trustworthy AI (Ethical Guidelines) is the most recent EU policy document on AI, and envisions AIs as lawful, ethical and technologically robust. The Ethical Guidelines deal with ethics and robustness, but leaves the lawfulness outside of its scope. The Ethical Guidelines link the achievement of such AI to seven principles (High-Level Expert Group, 2019):

1. Human agency and oversight, including fundamental rights.
2. Technical robustness and safety, including safety, security, resistance to attacks, accuracy, reliability and reproducibility.
3. Privacy and data governance, including integrity and access to data.
4. Transparency, which means traceability, explainability and communication.
5. Diversity, non-discrimination and fairness, including unbiased technology, accessibility, universal design, and stakeholder involvement.
6. Societal and environmental well-being, including environmental-friendly and sustainable technology, and positive social and democratic impacts.
7. Accountability, including auditability, minimisation and reporting of negative impact, trade-offs and redress.

These principles currently have been turned into an assessment list and many business companies are testing it within their organizations so as to provide the HLEG with valuable feedback. This list helps practitioners to understand and check whether their work with AI is compliant with the EU vision. By answering the questions in the checklist, companies can realize and discover aspects of AI development that have escaped their risk prevention and management instruments and also verify whether they are potentially going against the EU strategy as if not today, then tomorrow being contrary to EU policy on AI could be a wrong strategy if one wants to compete in the EU market.

What the EU argues to be its distinctive trademark in dealing with AI and robotics is its human-centric approach to AI, namely, that AI should not be developed to substitute for humans or in any other way cause harm or displace humans from the focus of scientific and technological research. On the contrary, AI should help, support and provide humans with new forms of empowerment. This human-centricity is articulated through the aforementioned principles: human oversight of AI should guarantee that AI is developed in line with human values and interests; privacy and personal data protection should ensure that this data is not used against humans; transparency should protect humans from arbitrary or biased algorithmic decisions; accessibility should provide for inclusive society where everyone could have equal opportunities and possibilities to enjoy the technological advancements; and environment protection should guard against negative impact related to the growth of technological industry. In this way, the EU is communicating that it is not interested in AI as such, but in AI that serves to improve human lives within the EU; the technological supremacy, if not accompanied by a human-centric approach, is not worthwhile pursuing. This is why the EU has singled out the feature of trustworthiness: AI that EU is promoting should be trustworthy to realize and support human values and human paramountcy, otherwise it cannot be trusted with human lives and the future of European society.

United States

The US has always been ahead of other countries in relation to technological development, so it is no surprise then the biggest innovation companies, that have conquered not only the US market but have gone global, such as Google, Facebook, Amazon, Apple, Microsoft, are all from the US. There are many initiatives being undertaken[7] but the author will focus on one of the latest attempt to provide a vision of what the US sees as its future with AI.

Artificial Intelligence for the American People

The national strategy, set out in Executive Order 13859, signed by President Trump in 11 February 2019, is based on five pillars (United States White House, 2019):

1. Promote continuity in AI R&D investment.
2. Use federal AI resources.
3. Remove obstacles to AI innovation.
4. Invest into workers by providing AI-focused education and training opportunities.
5. Work on an international environment that is supportive of American AI innovation and its responsible use

These pillars alone show the different approach to AI from the European Ethical Guidelines. The US strategy is business-oriented and US-oriented, because it sees the international environment not as valued in its own right but as functional to the realization of the national AI objectives. Another quite specific feature of this document is the focus on education and training.

Throughout the whole document, the reader can observe a continuous reference to job market, workers, occupations and other issues related to AI challenges to employment. The focus on industrial applications of AI is also intense; from transportation to healthcare, from financial services to manufacturing, the whole of US industry is being oriented to meet the challenges and possibilities of AI.

The section on American values - such as freedom, IP, the rule of law, human rights and others - is probably the most interesting part for the purposes of this chapter: AI, compliant with these values, must be understandable, trustworthy, robust (these two latter characteristics shared with the EU), and safe (Whitehouse.gov. 2019). These features also include explainability and fairness. Curiously enough, the word "ethics" is used only twice, one in reference to military ethics. Indeed, there is a greater emphasis on national security and the government reveals its plans to invest substantial resources in military AI.

The question remains whether humans will be able to build machines that would respect these values. Opinions might differ, but, for example, the OpenAI initiative (Irving & Askell, 2019) argues that humans might build machines that are reliably aligned to human values, if they collaborate in explaining what these values mean; the problem is not the technology, but humans whose emotions and biases provide uncertain or incomplete data in training AI. Therefore, the challenge is to study humans rather than machines so as to make AI able to respect these values.

In November 2019, the National Security Commission on Artificial Intelligence (NSCAI) released an *Interim Report*. Although the Commission focused on the security and defense aspects, it did consider economic competitiveness "as a component of national security, including the strength of our [US] scientific community and our [US] larger workforce" (NSCAI, 2019, p. 4). Even though it is an interim and not a final report (due to be released in 2021), the NSCAI stressed that there are divergent views about personal data protection with respect to the EU, and these differences are 'significant hurdles' which may eventually stand in the way of common standards for ethical AI.

Canada

The initiative to develop the Montreal Declaration for a Responsible Development of Artificial Intelligence (*The Montreal Convention*) started in 2017 and involved not only research institutions, but also experts, public policymakers, industry stakeholders and members of society. The Declaration was launched in 2018 and is based on ten principles: well-being; autonomy; intimacy and privacy; solidarity; democracy; equity; inclusion; caution; responsibility and environmental sustainability. Unlike other documents on AI, this *Declaration* does not represent a government's position: it is the outcome of an academic initiative (University of Montreal, 2017) and is an interesting example of what kind of AI civic society and Canadian academia have envisaged for the future.[8]

The Montreal Declaration is also an initiative that is signed not only by Canadian research organizations, individual researchers and citizens, but also by the research institutions from other countries, such as the UK and Hong Kong. Many business entities and professional associations, such as the dentists' association of Quebec, have signed it too. What it means is that *The Montreal Declaration* crossed national boundaries and became a kind of international multi-stakeholder agreement, without actually being an international treaty or covenant: this fact contributed to increasing the author's interest in its contents.

Indeed, what perhaps distinguishes the Canadian strategy the most from the other strategies seen so far, is that it was the first to involve the business and professional communities: that might also be the reason why it was signed by so many non-academic and not technological industry actors, and succeeded in getting public attention much more that the other strategies.

The Montreal Declaration

What is the most interesting thing about *The Montreal Declaration* is some of the norms that it establishes; first of all, it establishes a solidarity principle. According to the Declaration, humans should not treat robots that physically resemble - or act similarly to - human beings or non-human animals, cruelly. Curiously, no such duty exists in cases where robots do not resemble living beings.

Another idea, established by this Declaration, is to ensure that human freedom is not being locked into people's profiles (diversity inclusion principle). Algorithms should not decide for humans who they are, otherwise humanity risks ending up in what Davidow (2014) calls algorithmic prisons. Being in such a prison means that the algorithms - and not an individual - decides who he or she is, how he or she behaves, how he or she spend money and how often, and many other aspects of human lives. The worse of all this is that once the algorithms decide who a person is, that person is treated accordingly to this decision: many things that the particular person might need or be interested in, might fall outside his or her reach, simply because the bars of this algorithmic prison will keep that person from getting away.

The Montreal Declaration has also anticipated the solution to the dilemma about whether to share a potentially dangerous AI program. According to the Declaration, if public health or security is at stake, such a program should not be shared and should not become public (Prudence principle). The issues around such sharing are illustrated by a recent decision by OpenAI, a non-profit organization that supports open-source research on AI that is based on sharing, in order to avoid agglomeration of AI in the hands of selected few. OpenAI has just recently developed an AI program that was very useful for translations, but at the same time was also extremely useful for generating fake news. Faced with the dilemma whether to go against its own principles of openness and prevent the possibility that fake news would become much easier to create and spread, or to be loyal to its own principles, OpenAI has chosen the middle and has made public only a part of code (Hao, 2019). *The Montreal Declaration* is silent about partial release of code, but probably it would not allow it: the logic seems to be that the greatest good of the greatest number is what matters most (utilitarianism).

Responsibility - one of the most important aspects of AI and robotics - is also a focus in *The Montreal Declaration*; it clearly establishes that development and use of AI should not affect human responsibility. In other words, humans should not try to discharge their responsibility by passing their (in)actions onto the systems. AI should not be seen as an alternative solution to free oneself from a duty to respond for one's choices, negligence or ignorance.

Similarly to the EU, the Montreal Declaration is human-centric without explicitly saying so. *The Declaration* states that AI should help humans, improve their wellbeing in terms of work, health, personality, autonomy and other features that make human life fulfilling: in other words, AI will be an integral part of human life. All the principles in one way or the other should empower the human being as employee, as citizen, as part of democratic structure of the country, as part of vulnerable social group and in many other roles.

Comparative Approach

Having briefly glanced at the national (or regional in the case of EU) initiatives, the following table summarizes the main issues that were discovered. To be sure the differences are not so clearly cut and represent the author's interpretation. A review of all the documentation on AI that these countries have issued so far, rather than these three documents, could change the contents of this table.

First of all, the approaches differ in that the EU and Canadian positions focus on the living being (human or sentient being), whereas the US strategy focuses on industry, medicine, transportation, defense, business. According to the US strategy, if the government guarantees the advancements of AI in these sectors, the benefits for humans will be automatic. Nevertheless, this position is very different from the aforementioned EU and Canadian position; humans (or sentient beings) come first and only once the human rights and dignity are in place, then the industrial advancements could follow.

The approach these strategies adopt, that is human-centric (EU), industry-centric (US) and sentient being-centric (Canada), also reflect their focus. The EU focuses on human rights and values, the US on national competitiveness and technological primacy, whereas Canada takes a more inclusive approach by focusing on paving the path for new form of social coexistence between humans and machines.

The methodologies to achieve the objectives are very different; the EU is asking its members to comply with the list of requirements that are inspired by EU values, whereas the US consider that the way to achieve its objectives is through education and training, which means that additional investment in education is foreseen. The Canadian initiative adopts the least rigid idea of how to realize its objectives by assuming that adherence stands for compliance and if the stakeholder supports *The Montreal Declaration*, it means the stakeholder commits himself (herself or itself in case of a company or other institution) to make the objectives come true within the limits of one's possibilities.

Another comparison that can be made is their strength. the privacy and personal data protection is what differentiates the EU strategy, whereas the completeness and concreteness of the US strategy makes it the most viable at least at the first glance. Finally, the Canadian initiative is the only that strongly relies on civil society and a variety of stakeholders that supported and adhered to it.

Table 1. Particularities of national initiatives

Particularities	The Ethics Guidelines (EU)	AI for American People (USA)	Montreal Declaration (Canada)
1st: approach	*Human-centric*	*Industry-centric*	*Sentient beings-centric*
2nd: methodology to achieve the objectives	*Assessment list of compliance*	*Training and education*	*International consensus to a non-governmental initiative*
3rd focus:	*Human values*	*Employment, national security, competitiveness*	*Human-robot coexistence*
4th: strengths:	*Privacy and personal data protection*	*Completeness of issues addressed*	*Independence and openness to all the (national and international) stakeholders*

There are many issues that overlap in the documents analyzed above, although these documents were drafted by nations (and unions of nations in case of EU), with many similarities and also many differences. For example, the EU and Canada have both highlighted the importance of ensuring that wherever a human being interacts with AI, they have to be informed about it, as already mentioned in the section on consumer protection. At the current state of technological advancement, it means, for example, that the person talking on the phone should be informed that they are talking to an AI system, if that is the case (*The Montreal Declaration* explicitly refers to chatbots), but in the future the humans might face the same problem with humanoid machines that might look similar or identical to humans.

Furthermore, the EU and Canada share their involvement in the sustainable and environment protection-oriented use of AI, the USA do not seem to share this commitment. It seems then that EU and Canada have much more in common than the EU and US or Canada and US regarding the way AI and robotics should be developed on their territories, but this hypothesis should be verified by analyzing all the documents related to national strategies on AI.

FURTHER RESEARCH DIRECTIONS

There is already considerable research being conducted internationally on robots and AI technology and on how to control, regulate and/or monitor their activities. It is important that a common approach to creating an appropriate ethical framework for AI be reached because, as shown above, some differences in national approaches are already emerging. As suggested, further research is needed on analyzing the different strategies being adopted by different nations around AI developments.

Legal personhood for robots and AI and all the different interpretations of what this entails now and in the future remains a key area for further research as does the identification of where liability for loss or damage resulting from the actions of robots and AIs should be assessed and shared.

CONCLUSION

In the previous sections, the author has briefly introduced the reader to AI-based robots as products and discussed the challenges that robotic and AI-based products pose for consumers. The author addressed different scenarios that showed the complexity of robotic challenges to human consumption practices, such as challenges to consumer trust, product liability frameworks and new forms of consumer vulnerability.

The author also analyzed the possibility that one day robots could become entities with rights and entitlements. The goal of this section was not only to show how the debate on such a possibility is balancing between different positions (positions 'yes' and positions 'no' to robot rights), but also to show that the debate on robot rights is slowly taking different shapes, such as computational law applications, thanks to which, without even raising any question on rights and personhood, humans build applications that only recently were directed only for human use.

Many things have been left outside this brief overview of the current debate on autonomous and intelligent robots, and the author invites the readers to continue reading on these constantly changing technologies and the legal debates that result. Although representatives of academia, business and industry, and civil society do not agree either on what robot is, nor what kind of machines humanity should concentrate on building, it is important that all interested parties remain aware of developments and changes in AI and robotics, and also continuously question the impact of these changes on legal frameworks.

The final part of this chapter provided a very short overview of some of the most important documents in which the US, Canada, and the EU have revealed their main preoccupations about AI. As short as this overview is, it permitted the author to discuss a few insights and look at these initiatives from a comparative point of view: comparing these strategies also permitted the author to speculate on the priorities of each of them. Whether these speculations are correct or how much they diverge from the reality, are all the questions that only the future can tell. In the meantime, the most important thing is to continue debate, carry out the research and do not forget that it is humans who shape AI and robots and not the other way round.

REFERENCES

Ackerman, E. (2016). Researchers teaching robots to feel and react to pain. *IEEE Spectrum*. Retrieved from https://spectrum.ieee.org/automaton/robotics/robotics-software/researchers-teaching-robots-to-feel-and-react-to-pain

Barfield, W. (2018). Liability for autonomous and artificially intelligent robots. *Paladyn: Journal of Behavioral Robotics*, 9(1), 193–203. doi:10.1515/pjbr-2018-0018

Bester, J., Cole, C. M., & Kodish, E. (2016). The limits of informed consent for an overwhelmed patient: Clinicians' role in protecting patients and preventing overwhelm. *AMA Journal of Ethics*, 18(9), 869–886. doi:10.1001/journalofethics.2016.18.9.peer2-1609 PMID:27669132

Bryson, J. J., Diamantis, M. E., & Grant, T. D. (2017). Of, for, and by the people: The legal lacuna of synthetic persons. *Artificial Intelligence and Law*, 25(3), 273–291. doi:10.100710506-017-9214-9

Davidow, B. (2014, 20 February). Welcome to algorithmic prison: The use of big data to profile citizens is subtly, silently constraining freedom. *The Atlantic*. Retrieved from https://www.theatlantic.com/technology/archive/2014/02/welcome-to-algorithmic-prison/283985/

Directive 2005/29/EC Concerning Unfair Business-to-Consumer Commercial Practices in the Internal Market (Unfair Commercial Practices Directive).

European Commission. (2018). *Artificial intelligence for Europe*. Retrieved from https://eur-lex.europa.eu/legal-content/EN/TXT/PDF/?uri=CELEX:52018DC0237&from=EN

European Parliament. (2017). *European Parliament resolution of 16 February 2017 with recommendations to the Commission on Civil Law Rules on Robotics (2015/2103(INL))*. Retrieved from https://www.europarl.europa.eu/doceo/document/TA-8-2017-0051_EN.html

European Union. (2016). *General data protection regulation* Retrieved from https://gdpr-info.eu/

Genesereth, M. (2015). Computational law: The cop in the backseat (White Paper). *CodeX - The Stanford Center for Legal Informatic*. Retrieved from http://logic.stanford.edu/publications/genesereth/complaw.pdf

Gordon, G. J. (2017). *Environmental personhood*. Retrieved from https://papers.ssrn.com/sol3/papers.cfm?abstract_id=2935007

Gunkel, D. J. (2007). Thinking otherwise: Ethics, technology and other subjects. *Ethics and Information Technology*, *9*(3), 165–177. doi:10.100710676-007-9137-3

Haikonen, P. O. (2019). *Consciousness and robot sentience*. Singapore: World Scientific. doi:10.1142/11404

Hancock, P. A., Billings, D. R., Schaefer, K. E., Chen, J. Y., de Visser, E. J., & Parasuraman, R. (2011). A meta-analysis of factors affecting trust in human-robot interaction. *Human Factors*, *53*(5), 517–527. doi:10.1177/0018720811417254 PMID:22046724

Hao, K. (2019, 29 August). OpenAI has released the largest version yet of its fake-news-spewing AI. *MIT Technology Review*. Retrieved from https://www.technologyreview.com/s/614237/openai-released-its-fake-news-ai-gpt-2/

Hartzog, W. (2015). Unfair and deceptive robotics. *Maryland Law Review (Baltimore, Md.)*, *74*(4), 785–829.

High Level Expert Group (HLEG). (2019). *Ethics guidelines for trustworthy AI*. Retrieved from https://ec.europa.eu/digital-single-market/en/news/ethics-guidelines-trustworthy-ai

Honda. (2020). *Asimo*. Retrieved from https://asimo.honda.com/

Irving, G., & Askell, A. (2019). *AI safety needs social scientists*. Retrieved from https://distill.pub/2019/safety-needs-social-scientists/

Kahana, E. (2018). *Providing legal advice to machines: The application-to-machine paradigm in a CAV setting*. Retrieved from https://law.stanford.edu/2018/10/06/providing-legal-advice-to-machines-the-application-to-machine-paradigm-in-a-cav-setting/

Kerr, I. R. (2004). Bots, babes and the Californication of commerce. *University of Ottawa Law and Technology Journal, 26*(1), 284–324.

Koops, B.-J., Hildebrandt, M., & Jaquet-Chiffelle, D.-O. (2010). Bridging accountability gap: Rights for new entities in the information society? *Minnesota Journal of Law, Science & Technology, 11*(2), 497–561.

Kuipers, B. (2018). How can we trust a robot? *Communications of the ACM, 61*(3), 86–95. doi:10.1145/3173087

Ligthart, M., & Truong, K. P. (2015). Selecting the right robot: Influence of user attitude, robot sociability and embodiment on user preferences. In *Proceedings of 2015 24th IEEE International Symposium on Robot and Human Interactive Communication (RO-MAN)*. Kobe, Japan: IEEE. 10.1109/ROMAN.2015.7333598

National Security Commission on Artificial Intelligence (NSCAI). (2019). *Interim report.* Retrieved from https://www.epic.org/foia/epic-v-ai-commission/AI-Commission-Interim-Report-Nov-2019.pdf

PEGA. (2019). *Consumers failing to embrace AI benefits, says research: PEGA study highlights the need for greater empathy in artificial intelligence systems.* Retrieved from https://www.pega.com/about/news/press-releases/consumers-failing-embrace-ai-benefits-says-research

Robotics Open Letter. (n.d.). *Open letter to the European Commission: AI and robotics.* Retrieved from http://www.robotics-openletter.eu/

Ryan, D. (2016). *Understanding digital marketing: Marketing strategies for engaging the digital generation.* London, UK: KoganPage.

Schaerer, E., Kelley, R., & Nicolescu, M. (2009). Robots as animals: A framework for liability and responsibility in human-robot interactions. In *Proceedings of The 18th IEEE International Symposium on Robot and Human Interactive Communication (RO-MAN 2009)*. Toyama, Japan: IEEE. 10.1109/ROMAN.2009.5326244

Schafer, B. (2016). Closing Pandora's box? The EU proposal on the regulation of robots. *The Journal of the Justice and the Law Society of the University of Queeensland, 19*, 55–68.

Sundar, S. S., & Kim, J. (2019). Machine heuristic: When we trust computers more than humans with our personal information. In *Proceedings of the 2019 CHI Conference on Human Factors in Computing Systems* (CHI '19). New York, NY: ACM. 10.1145/3290605.3300768

Turner, J. (2019). *Robot rules: Regulating artificial intelligence.* Cham, Switzerland: Palgrave Macmillan. doi:10.1007/978-3-319-96235-1

United States White House. (2019, 11 February). *Maintaining American Leadership in Artificial Intelligence.* Executive Order 13859. Retrieved from https://www.whitehouse.gov/ai/executive-order-ai/

University of Montreal. (2017). *The Montreal Declaration for a responsible development of Artificial Intelligence.* Retrieved from https://docs.wixstatic.com/ugd/ebc3a3_c5c1c196fc16475 6afb92466c-081d7ae.pdf

Van den Hoven van Genderen, R. (2018). Legal personhood in the age of artificially intelligent robots. In W. Barfield & U. Pagallo (Eds.), *Research Handbook on the Law of Artificial Intelligence* (pp. 213-250). Cheltenham, UK: Edward Elgar Publishing.

Wagner, G. (2018). *Robot liability*. Retrieved form https://ssrn.com/abstract=3198764

WhiteHouse.gov. (2019). *Artificial intelligence for the American people*. Retrieved from https://www.whitehouse.gov/ai/

Wolfram, S. (2016). Computational law, symbolic discourse, and the AI constitution. *Wired*. Retrieved from https://www.wired.com/2016/10/computational-law-symbolic-discourse-and-the-ai-constitution/

World Commission on the Ethics of Scientific Knowledge and Technology. (2017) *Report of COMEST on robotics ethics*. Retrieved from https://unesdoc.unesco.org/ark:/48223/pf0000253952

Złotowski, J. A., Sumioka, H., Nishio, S., Glas, D. F., Bartneck, C., & Ishiguro, H. (2018). Persistence of the uncanny valley: the influence of repeated interactions and a robot's attitude to its perception. *Frontiers in Psychology*. Retrieved from https://www.frontiersin.org/articles/10.3389/fpsyg.2015.00883/full

ADDITIONAL READING

BEUC. (2018). *Automated decision making and Artificial Intelligence – a consumer perspective*. Rtrieved from https://www.beuc.eu/publications/beuc-x-2018-058_automated_decision_making_and_artificial_intelligence.pdf

Corrales, M., Fenwick, M., & Forgó, N. (Eds.) (2018). Robotics, AI and the Future of Law. Singapore: Springer.

Director of National Intelligence. (2019). *The aim initiative: A strategy for augmenting intelligence using machines*. Retrieved from https://www.dni.gov/files/ODNI/documents/AIM-Strategy.pdf

European Commission. EU Science Hub. (2018). *Artificial intelligence: European perspective*. Retrieved from https://ec.europa.eu/jrc/en/publication/artificial-intelligence-european-perspective

European Commission. (2018). *Made in Europe*. Retrieved from https://ec.europa.eu/digital-single-market/en/news/coordinated-plan-artificial-intelligence

European Commission. (2019). *Communication: Building trust in human centric artificial intelligence*. Retrieved from https://ec.europa.eu/digital-single-market/en/news/communication-building-trust-human-centric-artificial-intelligence

European Commission. Expert Group on Liability and New Technologies - New Technologies Formation (2019). *Liability for artificial intelligence and other emerging technologies*. Retrieved from https://ec.europa.eu/transparency/regexpert/index.cfm?do=groupdetail.groupmeetingdoc&docid=36608)

European Commission. EU Science Hub. (2020*). Robustness and explainability of artificial intelligence*. Retrieved from https://ec.europa.eu/jrc/en/publication/robustness-and-explainability-artificial-intelligence

Inclusive Robotics for a Better Society (INBOTS). (2019). *Preliminary white paper on standardisation and interactive robots*. Retrieved from http://inbots.eu/wp-content/uploads/2019/07/Attachment_0-3.pdf

Pagallo, U. (2013). *The Laws of robots: crimes, contracts, and torts*. Dordrecht, Netherlands: Springer. doi:10.1007/978-94-007-6564-1

US Government. (2019). *2016-2019 progress report: Advancing artificial intelligence R&D*. Retrieved from https://www.whitehouse.gov/wp-content/uploads/2019/11/AI-Research-and-Development-Progress-Report-2016-2019.pdf

US Government. (2020). *Ensuring American leadership in automated vehicle technologies, automated vehicles 4.0*. Retrieved from https://www.transportation.gov/sites/dot.gov/files/docs/policy-initiatives/automated-vehicles/360956/ensuringamericanleadershipav4.pdf

KEY TERMS AND DEFINITIONS

Artificial Intelligence (AI): The creation of programs designed to perform tasks generally performed by humans.

Computational Law: A branch of legal informatics that aims to codify legal norms and regulations (Genesereth, 2015).

Human-Centric: Places people at the centre of whatever product, solution, or technique is being designed or planned.

Legal Personhood: Granting a being or entity similar legal rights to those granted to humans.

Robot: A programmable machine imbued robots with some sort of autonomy, that is, robots that can act without human intervention and control and could exercise any kind of (human-like) intelligent behavior (World Commission on the Ethics of Scientific Knowledge and Technology, 2017).

ENDNOTES

1   The number of academic articles, reports and books on law and (of, for, against, etc.) AI and robotics is a proof to this relevance. It is not the aim of the author to discuss them all, but a list of recent publications is contained in the additional reading section of this chapter.

2   Although oriented more towards technical issues (that is, AI for law and not law for AI), the "Artificial Intelligence and Law Journal" (https://www.springer.com/journal/10506) and its archives are an excellent place to observe the evolution of issues that the lawyers discovered in time with relation to AI and related technologies.

3   Sophia robot is a robot of Hanson Robotics, more information is available on its webpage at https://www.hansonrobotics.com/sophia/;information about about Bina 48, see https://www.hansonrobotics.com/bina48-9/, whereas for more on Mitsuku, follow https://www.pandorabots.com/mitsuku/.

4   More about JIBO, at https://www.jibo.com/

5   For more about SoftBank robot Pepper, see https://www.softbankrobotics.com/corp/robots/

6   Ava is an avatar created by Soul Machines: how it looks like can be seen at https://www.youtube.com/watch?v=mKZ84O1666g

7   These have been included in the additional reading section of the chapter.

8   For more about Canadian AI initiatives, see http://www.canada.ai/industry/policy-ethics

Chapter 9
Regulating AI

Margaret A. Jackson
RMIT University, Australia

ABSTRACT

Artificial intelligence (AI) is already being used in many different sectors and industries globally. These areas include government (help desks, sending demand letters), health (predicative diagnosis), law (predicative policing and sentencing), education (facial recognition), finance (for share trading), advertising (social media), retail (recommendations), transport (drones), smart services (like electricity meters), and so on. At this stage, the AI in use or being proposed is 'narrow' AI and not 'general' AI, which means that it has been designed for a specific purpose, say, to advise on sentencing levels or to select potential candidates for interview, rather than being designed to learn and do new things, like a human. The question we need to explore is not whether regulation of AI is needed but how such regulation can be achieved. This chapter examines which existing regulations can apply to AI, which will need to be amended, and which areas might need new regulation to be introduced. Both national and international regulation will be discussed; Australia is the main focus.

INTRODUCTION

Artificial Intelligence (AI) involves the creation of programs designed to perform tasks generally performed by humans. As the Office of the Victorian Information Commissioner (OVIC) explains in its 2018 issues paper *Artificial Intelligence and Privacy* (OVIC, 2018, p.1):

These tasks can be considered intelligent, and include visual and audio perception, learning and adapting, reasoning, pattern recognition and decision-making. 'AI' is often used as an umbrella term to describe a collection of related techniques and technologies including machine learning, predictive analytics, natural language processing and robotics.

Artificial Intelligence (AI) is already being used in many different sectors and industries globally. These areas include government (help desks, sending demand letters); health (predicative diagnosis), law (predicative policing and sentencing), education (facial recognition), finance (for share trading),

DOI: 10.4018/978-1-7998-3130-3.ch009

advertising (social media), retail (recommendations), transport (drones), smart services (electricity meters) and so on. At this stage, the AI in use or being proposed is 'narrow' AI and not 'general' AI. This means that it has been designed for a specific purpose, say, to advise on sentencing levels or to select potential candidates for an interview, rather than being designed to learn and do new things, like a human. This does not mean that 'narrow' AI, generally non-conscious systems, may not be able to replicate human consciousness in recognising patterns (Harari, 2016) as AI systems excel at identifying patterns in large amounts of data.

While some of the development and the deployment of AI systems is happening at a state or national level, for instance, self-driving cars, there are concerns being expressed that AI development and ownership will be dominated by the large global companies such as Google, Facebook, Apple, Microsoft and Amazon (Nemitz, 2018). Paul Nemitz cites four bases of digital power to watch – lots of money; control of "infrastructure of public discourse", collection of personal data and profiling, and the algorithms in a "black box; not open to public scrutiny" (Nemitz, 2018, pp. 3-4). All of these bases of power are possessed by the global companies and they are investing considerably in AI development. What this means is that, unless the international community is proactive in working together to create an acceptable and consistent framework of AI regulation which can be adapted by individual nations, there is a risk that commercial interests will set the AI agenda and regulatory responses, at both an international and national level, will largely be reactive.

This chapter examines what is an appropriate regulatory framework for dealing with AI, one which will be able to handle future developments in AI technology. Ethical principles, guidelines, standards and legislation all form part of a regulatory framework. The focus of the chapter is on Australian regulation. It discusses the role of ethical codes and standards in handling AI challenges. It then explores existing regulation to determine if it will apply to AI, whether it will need to be amended and whether there are areas which will require new regulation to be introduced.

ETHICAL GUIDELINE PROPOSALS AND STANDARDS

Ethical Guidelines

There is no shortage of ethical guidelines for AI systems being proposed, some by specific professional and industry groups (IEEE, 2019), others by individual countries (UK House of Lords, 2018), the EU (European Commission High-Level Expert Group on Artificial Intelligence (AIHLEG), 2019), and by large global technology companies (Microsoft, n.d.). It is clear that there is national and international agreement that such guidelines will be vital for protection of human rights, including the rights to be free of discrimination and bias. There are some slight differences in the ethical approaches being proposed, as pointed out by Laukyte (forthcoming), but generally, the principles aim to protect human rights.

The European Commission High-Level Expert Group on Artificial Intelligence (AIHLEG) released draft *Ethics Guidelines for Trustworthy AI* in 2018, with a final version in April 2019. These AIHLEG guidelines propose a human-centric approach, with the key question to be asked: how will this AI help humans? Humans will need to be able to trust the AI. To achieve 'trustworthy' AI, three components must be satisfied throughout the AI's entire life cycle. First, the AI must be "lawful, complying with all applicable laws and regulations, second, it should be ethical, adhering to ethical principles and values, and, third, it must be robust from a technical and social perspective" (European Commission AIHLEG,

2019, p 7). The guidelines are intended to be voluntary and to provide a broad and general horizontal framework, which should be supplemented by sectorial approaches, say, in areas such as medical health.

Both the draft and final versions of the AIHLEG guidelines have been used by other organisations as the basis for their own ethical guidelines. One such example is *The European Group on Ethics in Science & New Technologies Statement on AI*, released in 2018 (European Commission, European Group on Ethics in Science & New Technologies, 2018). The AI 4People's *Ethical Framework for a Good AI Society* project has five principles derived from a survey of 37 different sets of ethical principles, including from the AIHLEG (AI 4People, 2019).

The AI Group of Experts at the Organisation for Economic Co-operation and Development (OECD) (AIGO) developed a set of recommendations about guidelines for AI which were approved by the OECD Ministerial Council Meeting in 2019. In the *Recommendation on Artificial Intelligence (AI)* (OECD, 2019), the Council recommends that member countries should implement the suggested national policies and engage in international co-operation using the following five principles (OECD, 2019, Background information section):

- Inclusive growth, sustainable development and wellbeing
- Human-centred values and fairness
- Transparency and explainability
- Robustness, security and safety
- Accountability.

As at May 2019, 42 countries, including Australia and the G20 (the Group of 20 comprising government representatives from 19 countries and the EU) have adopted AI principles based on the OECD Principles (OECD, 2019).

In Australia, Data61, a division of the CSIRO, released a draft paper, *Artificial Intelligence: Australia's Ethics Framework,* which summarised the relevant legislation and ethical principles relating to AI, both at an Australian and international level, as well as setting out eight core principles for AI (Data61, 2019). It provided a number of case studies illustrating issues with possible AI bias in decision-making, automated data decisions in government settings, transparency issues and the need for human oversight, and predictive systems in health, policing and insurance. The paper proposed eight core principles for an ethical AI framework, however, after requesting public submissions, these principles were amended to (Department of Industry, Innovation and Science, 2019, p. 1):

- Human, social and environmental wellbeing: Throughout their lifecycle, AI systems should benefit individuals, society and the environment.
- Human-centred values: Throughout their lifecycle, AI systems should respect human rights, diversity, and the autonomy of individuals.
- Fairness: Throughout their lifecycle, AI systems should be inclusive and accessible, and should not involve or result in unfair discrimination against individuals, communities or groups.
- Privacy protection and security: Throughout their lifecycle, AI systems should respect and uphold privacy rights and data protection, and ensure the security of data.
- Reliability and safety: Throughout their lifecycle, AI systems should reliably operate in accordance with their intended purpose.

- Transparency and explainability: There should be transparency and responsible disclosure to ensure people know when they are being significantly impacted by an AI system, and can find out when an AI system is engaging with them.
- Contestability: When an AI system significantly impacts a person, community, group or environment, there should be a timely process to allow people to challenge the use or output of the AI system.
- Accountability: Those responsible for the different phases of the AI system lifecycle should be identifiable and accountable for the outcomes of the AI systems, and human oversight of AI systems should be enabled.

These eight principles are very vague and general, unlike the original principles proposed, and use much softer language. For instance, an original draft principle proposed was: "There will [underline added] be a process to contest decisions" (Data61, 2019, p. 6). This wording has been softened to stating that there should be a process (Department of Industry, Innovation and Science, 2019). The word 'should' suggests that this is what might occur rather than what must occur.

These voluntary principles are now being trialled by five large corporations in Australia – National Australia Bank, Commonwealth Bank, Telstra, Microsoft and Flamingo AI (Andrews, 2019).

All the ethical guidelines developed or being developed are intended to be voluntary non-binding guidelines. Some are aimed at professional groups, others are documents intended for national or international impact. Human rights and data privacy are mentioned as key rights in all of the ethical guidelines as is the need for transparency (or explicability).

While the effectiveness of non-legally binding ethical principles at an international level can be questioned, there are a number of examples of internationally agreed ethical guidelines which have achieved global impact and have resulted in legislative adoption by a number of countries. Such examples are the 1980 OECD Guidelines on the Protection of Privacy and Transborder Flows of Personal Data (OECD Guidelines) which were incorporated into the Privacy Act 1988 (Cth) and the 1995 European Union Directive on the protection of individuals with regard to the processing of personal data and on the free movement of such data and which influenced all relevant data protection legislation enacted by nations.

Another example of a set of international guidelines that eventually led to widespread adoption is those relating to research ethics. Starting with the *1947 Nuremberg Code for research on human subjects*, formulated by the American judges sitting on the Nuremberg Tribunal, and leading to the *1964 Declaration of Helsinki* developed by the World Medical Association to govern medical research, ethical principles governing the conduct of medical, biomedical and social science research involving human subjects apply to research activities in most countries (Williams, 2008). The international acceptance and adoption of research ethics involving human subjects has been a longer and more tortuous journey than that of data protection, and is still continuing, but it does illustrate the need for initial international expression of what is acceptable.

In areas of important social and economic change which will have a global impact, such as is occurring with AI systems and technology, ethical frameworks offer a way to introduce agreed principles that support the introduction and implementation of the technological change whilst at the same time setting acceptable standards to lessen any negative impact of humans. The frameworks that have been proposed by the various international bodies and organizations are necessary to provide a readily understood context for individuals to accept that there are constraints within which AI development and implementation will occur. As noted above, there are numerous AI ethical frameworks being proposed. Fortunately, there is considerable overlap in the principles comprising each framework. The next stage in development of an AI ethical framework is international agreement on one set of principles.

Standards

As with ethical principles, technical standards relating to AI are being developed by accredited international and national bodies. The International Organization of Standardization (ISO) and the International Electrotechnical Commission (IEC), through their Joint Technical Committee 1 (JTC 1), created Subcommittee 42 – artificial intelligence (SC42) in 2017 to work on AI regulation. It has published three ISO standards and has 11 ISO standards under development (ISO, 2019). Whilst its standards are voluntary, ISO standards are usually considered by courts to be best practice. Standards Australia is involved with some of these developments and in 2019, it published a discussion paper, *Developing Standards for Artificial Intelligence: Hearing Australia's Voice* (Standards Australia, 2019).

The Institute of Electrical and Electronics Engineers (IEEE) has identified 11 areas for standardisation, including one on data privacy and another on transparency of AI systems (IEEE, 2019).

Both Google and Microsoft are both active in creating guidelines for AI development, with both taking a fairly broad approach. Google has published some very broad *Responsible AI Practices* (Google, n.d.) while Microsoft has published two publications covering AI and the future (Microsoft, 2019).

WHAT CURRENT LEGAL REGULATION APPLIES?

Until there is an agreed international set of ethical principles on AI, it is necessary to understand what current regulation at a national level might apply to AI. Laws are remarkably flexible and can often apply to new technology without the need for significant amendments. When computer technology was first introduced, only a few sections of the existing Australian criminal legislation were amended or strengthened, to ensure that stealing information from a computer was theft of property, deceiving a machine like an ATM into giving you money was fraud and changing data stored on a computer was forgery (Jackson, 2001). The notion of computer trespass was criminalised through offences such as unauthorised access to a machine or destroying data without authority with intent to commit a crime (Jackson, 2001). Eventually, after international agreement on what was needed in this area, specific 'cybercrime' legislation was introduced. For example, the *2001 Council of Europe Convention on Cybercrime* and the *Criminal Code Act 1995* (Cth), (Criminal Code). Part 10.7 of the Criminal Code addresses growing concerns about hacking and denial of service activities once it was clear where the existing law was deficient.

Some laws introduced since the advent of computer technology are designed to be technology neutral, such as the *Privacy Act 1988* (Cth) (Privacy Act) and state and territory acts like the *Privacy and Data Protection Act 2014* (Vic) (PDP Act), so that developments in new technology do not require new legislation to deal with any problems. Many laws, such as the *Competition and Consumer Act 2010* (Cth) (CAA) which contains the *Australian Consumer Law* (ACL) focuses on the injury or loss suffered by the consumers due to actions of the seller, rather than on the type of technology sold by the seller which may have led to that injury. Under the ACL, manufacturers bear the responsibility for loss or damage. As well, the users of computer systems such as banks, transport companies, airlines, hospitals, and so on, bear the risks for damage caused to their customers. They in turn may seek redress from suppliers of the product. This should not change if an AI is involved in providing the service or is part of the goods or products being sold, although there may be difficulty in integrated products in identifying which part of the supply chain – the designers, developers, or manufacturers of the different components – was the cause of the problem.

In some instances, the main approach to handling AI issues is to use current regulation with some amendments as far as possible as discussed below. However, with other areas of law, such as consumer protection law, some clarification of terminology and reach of operation may be needed.

Drones and Driverless Cars

Computer technology has been used for years in the automotive and aeronautics industries to provide assistance to drivers and pilots to improve safety. AI technology is enabling developers to replace humans completely or partially in operating drones, and driverless and self-driving cars. In the first instance, governments are dealing with both drones and driverless cars through amendments to existing legislation. With drones, in Australia, Part 101 of the *Civil Aviation Safety Regulations 1998*, which specifically regulates unmanned aircraft, was amended in 2016 to introduce new rules about licensing, necessary permissions and notifications. In July 2018, the Commonwealth Government released a *Report on Regulatory Requirements that Impact on the Safe Use of Remotely Piloted Aircraft Systems, Unmanned Aerial Systems and Associated Systems*, which reviewed the success of the new amendments and recommended new processes for dealing with risks (Commonwealth of Australia, 2018). In 2019, *Project US 18/09 Remotely Piloted Aircraft* (RPA), a scheme which is working on RPA registration and RPAS operator accreditation, commenced (CASA, 2019). In July 2019, the *Civil Aviation Safety Amendment (Remotely Piloted Aircraft and Model Aircraft—Registration and Accreditation) Regulations 2019*, which adopted the recommendations of the 2018 Commonwealth report, were approved (CASA, 2019).

While the work around dealing with the growth of RPAs is primarily at a national level, it should be noted that it fits within the context of the international framework for civil aviation, as established by the United Nations International Civil Aviation Organization (ICAO).

A similar approach to using existing legislation is being taken with autonomous (driverless) cars and self-driving cars (in which a human driver is still in the car). Unlike RPAs, the regulatory approach involves both Commonwealth and State interaction. The National Transport Commission (NTC) which is funded by the Commonwealth, State and Territory Governments, has released guidelines for trialling semi-autonomous vehicles as well as discussion papers exploring issues around their use and the use of fully autonomous vehicles. These issues included options for amending existing legislation to cover autonomous vehicles, including trains, and approaches to providing appropriate motor accident injury insurance (NTC, 2019). It announced that agreement was reached in August 2019 by Commonwealth, State and Territory transport ministers about a national approach to insurance for automated vehicles that requires existing motor accident injury insurance schemes to provide cover for automated vehicle crash injuries (NTC, 2019). Three states (South Australia, Victoria and New South Wales) have introduced regulations to assist with trialling of autonomous car.[1]

Again, the discussion around how to handle the issues caused by autonomous vehicles is informed by similar investigations being undertaken globally, particularly in the United Kingdom (UK), the United States of America (US) and the European Union (EU). The US Department of Transport and the National Highway Traffic Safety Administration (NHTSA) introduced a voluntary *Federal Automated*

Vehicles Policy in 2016, which has since been updated twice (NHTSA, 2019). The majority of US states have introduced some form of regulation addressing autonomous vehicles (Dentons, 2019). Germany in particular has developed ethical guidelines for automated and connected driving (Federal Ministry of Transport and Digital Infrastructure, 2017). In the UK, the Centre for Connected and Driverless Cars in 2019 released a new *Code of Practice* on automated vehicle trialling (Centre for Connected and Driverless Cars, 2019). There are also international groups such as the UN Global Forum for Road Traffic Safety, of which Australia is a member, which are examining rules for autonomous vehicles, having released a revised framework document on automated/autonomous vehicles in mid 2019 (UNECE, 2019). Most countries expect that autonomous cars will be produced for commercial and domestic use after 2020 and it is clear that regulations will be in place to deal with this event.

Consumer Protection

As noted above, the ACL is nationwide legislation covering the sale of goods to consumers which will apply to many aspects of AI systems involved in such sales. The ACL applies to goods like computer software which are provided to a consumer, either directly or by being embedded in a product provided to them. The consumer guarantees in s. 138 of the ACL include the requirement that goods are fit for the purpose and that they are of acceptable quality which includes a requirement that the goods be reasonably 'safe'. Customers who are injured or who suffer property damage as a result of unsafe goods can be compensated by manufacturers without having to prove that the manufacturer was negligent.

However, at present, the ACL does offer the manufacturer some statutory defences, including in s. 142 which provides that if there was no defect in the goods when they were supplied, or that the state of scientific and technical knowledge at the time of supply did not enable the supplier or the manufacturer to discover the defect, or a cause independent of human control occurred after the goods left the manufacturer's control, then the manufacturer may not be liable for the defect. This would mean that if manufacturers or designers claim that the pre-release testing of the AI system showed it worked as expected but that the problem that led to the injury or damage to a consumer developed after the release in a way that was not expected, then they might be able to avail themselves of the defences provided by s. 142. Whether this defence is appropriate for AIs is discussed in the section on new proposals for laws to handle AI issues below.

Many countries are reviewing whether existing product liability laws will apply to AI devices. The European Commission, for instance, produced a paper *Liability for emerging digital technologies* in 2018 which examined whether the *Product Liability Directive (*85/374/EEC) and the *Machinery Directive* (2006/42/EC) adequately covered issues with AI (European Commission, 2018). Both of these directives provide for strict liability if there was loss or damage. Generally, the paper decided that the Directives were adequate for the current state of development in technology but that further examination was needed in particular around defectiveness and the burden of proof, and the management of risk (European Commission, 2018). Product liability legislation also covers 'goods', 'products', 'services' and 'manufacturers' and it needs to be clarified whether these terms will apply to self-conscious AI in particular or whether different terminology may be needed. This issue is discussed further below.

Government AI Decisions

The section above focused on consumer protection issues but most of the legal cases that have arisen to date involving AIs have not arisen in the consumer context. They have primarily involved the use of AI by government departments. In Australia, there are already a number of instances where human decision makers have delegated decision making to computers. For example, s. 495A(1) of the *Migration Act 1958* (Cth) states that the "Minister may arrange for the use, under the Minister's control, of computer programs for any purposes for which the Minister may, or must … make a decision; or exercise any power…". Another 22 sections in a range of acts allow government departments to deem a decision by a computer system to be a decision made by a designated officer. For instance, s. 7C(2) of the *Therapeutic Goods Act 1989* (Cth) and s. 6A of the *Social Security (Administration) Act 1999* (Cth) (Hogan-Doran, 2019; Elvery, 2017).

Decisions made by Australian Government ministers, departments and agencies can be reviewed by the Administrative Appeals Tribunal if allowed for under the relevant Commonwealth legislation. Similar State and Territory bodies such as the Victorian Civil and Administrative Appeals Tribunal fulfil similar roles. As well, the Commonwealth Human Rights Commission and its State and Territory counterparts can investigate complaints alleging discriminatory actions by government departments in some cases. Complaints against public sector decisions can also be lodged with the Commonwealth Ombudsman (or State and Territory counterparts if the decision being complained about is made under State or Territory legislation) as occurred with the 2016 Centrelink Robodebt project, designed to check for overpayment of social services by matching data with the Australian Taxation Office, which resulted in 20,000 people being falsely accused of fraud. The Federal Ombudsman investigated numerous complaints and issued two reports containing recommendations for improvements to be implemented by the Departments of Human Services and Social Services. According to the Ombudsman, the purpose of the system was not well thought out[2] and risk management, communication and overall planning was poor (Commonwealth Ombudsman, 2017, 2019).

Courts provide further avenues for appeal. Some appeals against penalty assessments raised by the Robodebt project have been lodged with the Federal Court. Twice the government department responsible for the program, Centrelink, withdrew the assessment before the appeals were heard (Henriques-Gomez, 2019). On 15 November 2019, a class action against Centrelink was announced (Gordon Legal, 2019). On 19 November 2019, the Federal Government announced a change to the scheme in identifying debts by averaging a person's income using tax office data only will cease (Tillet, 2019). All cases involved such averaging will also be reviewed. On 27 November, an appeal against a Robodebt bill was successful in the Federal Court (Karp, 2019).

Anti-Competitive Behaviour

Section 18L of the ACL makes it an offence for a person to deceive or mislead a consumer or a business. A similar section in the CCA, s. 131, applies to the conduct of companies in trade and commerce. No intent is needed to be shown in a case of misleading behaviour. It is arguable that the actions of an AI system could fall under these sections. AI systems can fabricate and manipulate data either because of their programming or due to the data they have been fed or have collected.

AI systems may also be involved in anti-competitive behaviour, particularly for making and monitoring pricing decisions of competitors. In 2015, the US Department of Justice prosecuted a seller in the

Amazon marketplace for collusion with other sellers to fix the price of posters sold online, by sharing and jointly implementing dynamic pricing algorithms (Department of Justice, 2015). While no similar cases have occurred in Australia, the Australian Competition and Consumer Commission (ACCC) Chair, Rod Sims, in a 2017 address titled *The ACCC's approach to colluding robots*, stated that he considered the anti-competitive provisions of the CCA would able to handle cases involving price algorithms and collusion (Sims, 2017). Mr Sims referred in particular to two new provisions in the CCA, ss. 45(1)(c) and s. 46. Section 45(1)(c) of the CCA, the 'concerted practices' provision, provides that a corporation may not "…engage with one or more persons in a concerted practice that has the purpose, or has or is likely to have the effect, of substantially lessening competition". Section 46 prohibits a firm with a substantial degree of market power from engaging in conduct that has the purpose, effect or likely effect of substantially lessening competition in a market. Mr Sims (2017) believes these two new sections would give the ACCC the appropriate powers to address collusion by AI systems.

Privacy Protection Legislation

The privacy protection legislation in Australia is designed to be technology neutral and should apply to AI. This may be the case but there are a few issues with protection of personal data that will need attention. The first area is that of 'big data'. Privacy legislation in Australia and internationally has struggled a little to cope with the advent of 'big data', that is, the enormous amounts of data collected by organisations and governments, much of it generated by individuals online. Many of the difficulties with big data have arisen because the organisations that are using it are not necessarily the same as the organisations that collected it, so that informed consent, an important requirement in privacy legislation, becomes difficult if not impossible to obtain. However, as the Office of the Victorian Information Commissioner (OVIC) has pointed out, there are many circumstances in which the lawful collection, use and disclosure of personal information can occur without the need for individuals' consent (OVIC, 2019). As well, much of the personal information in big data sets has been consciously disclosed by individuals through social media or via online websites, or it has been collected through CCTV and similar surveillance technology or through online cookies. Often, any consent, let alone informed consent, is not possible due to the processes used to collect the personal data.

Organisations and governments have often struggled to process big data due to its size and complexity. AI systems, however, have the capacity to analyse big data and are able to recognise patterns in data which will include identifying individuals from the data analysed. The UK Information Commissioner and the Australian Information Commissioner have released guides to assist organisations and government with big data analysis (UK OIC, 2017; OAIC, 2018b). These guides focus on embedding "privacy-by-design" into the early stage of AI development, rather than "unpredictability by design" which can result if data are fed into algorithms without pre-defined queries (UK OIC, 2107, p. 10). The guides state the importance of privacy impact assessments at the beginning of AI projects, for transparency about processing and for minimisation in data collection.

While there have been some amendments to privacy legislation to strengthen the law in the light of the ongoing growth in the collection of vast amounts of personal data, the effectiveness of such amendments is not yet clear. For instance, the EU *General Data Protection Regulation* (GDPR) 2016 (European Union, 2016) is designed to be technology neutral as well and so applies to new technology such as AI. It focuses on informed consent, more protections around the collection of sensitive data, breach notification and two new rights for individuals – the right to be forgotten and the right to data portability, although these two new rights became gradually weaker as the lengthy negotiations over the new GDPR took place. It can now impose heavy penalties on organisations and governments that breach its provisions. However, doubts have been raised about the applicability of the new GDPR to AI technology with its associated issues such as a lack of transparency about decision-making and obtaining consent (UK OIC, 2017).

The Australian Federal government has announced that it will strengthen the Privacy Act by increasing penalties for serious and repeated interference with an individual's privacy, introducing a right so that individuals can ask technology and social media companies to cease using and disclosing their personal information and introducing a new code of conduct for social media and online platforms covering the collection and use of personal information (Lexology, 2019). These amendments will address some of the issues relating to big data and social media but do not appear to be addressing specific AI-related issues such as how to ensure that the human rights of individuals whose data is being collected and used by AI system is protected as obtaining consent from the individuals becomes more impracticable.

Another issue with the privacy legislation is that new government legislation relating to big data use may lessen the protections for personal information in the Privacy Act, either through a widening of the exemptions for government security and policing activities under the Act or through moving privacy protection outside the operation of the Act. This can be seen with recently proposed surveillance and facial recognition legislation.

As mentioned, big data sets can comprise large amounts of personal data or forms of identification data taken from numerous sources including surveillance technology. Algorithms can use data collected from sources such as CCTVs, radio frequency identification (RFID) tagging, mobile phone location technology and social media activity to identify individuals. Surveillance technology is generally accepted as providing significant benefits in areas such as crime prevention and national security, but such activities can also result in significant loss of privacy.

The *Surveillance Devices Act 2004* (Cth) governs the use of surveillance technology by government agencies. The States and Territories have similar legislation which applies to the private sector as well as government agencies. The *Telecommunications (Interception and Access) Act 1979* (Cth) also addresses interception of private telecommunications. As well, over the last decade, there has been an increase in Commonwealth initiatives aimed at identifying and preventing national security breaches but these initiatives, such as the document verification service (DVS), also extends the exemptions for law enforcement agencies under the Privacy Act.

One particular area of surveillance technology that is raising concern is the growing use of facial recognition, particularly by police and other government departments, and the lack of regulation around its use. This concern is deepened by the fact that exemptions in the Privacy Act apply to such activities (Law Council of Australia, 2018). In Australia, the Federal Government attempted to introduce two bills on identity-matching by government departments which would have consolidated and expanded government facial recognition activities considerably, by allowing the use of the data for a broad range of activities, including locating missing persons and promoting road safety activities, as well as allowing non-government entities to access the created face recognition database. These bills were the Identity-matching Services Bill 2019 and the Australian Passports Amendments (Identity-matching Services) Bill 2019.

Whilst the government departments and private organisations which were to be empowered by the Acts if passed were supposed to comply with the Privacy Act, there were criticisms that the proposed legislation would lessen the protections for personal information in the Act and would permit matching to be used for relatively minor issues (Law Council of Australia, 2018). Much of the privacy protection for individuals was to be included in formal participation agreements and data-sharing arrangements (OAIC, 2018a). It was pointed out by the OAIC that while the bills contained governance, protections and oversight mechanisms which had been built upon existing identity and security initiatives, such as the DVS, the risks of unauthorised access to personal information in such legislation were limited and governance arrangements in place were proportionate to the risk (OAIC, 2018a). The same could not be said about the proposed legislation.

The Bills were reviewed by the Parliamentary Joint Committee on Intelligence and Security (PJCIS) in October 2019 and it recommended that the Identity-matching Services Bill be re-drafted with a focus on privacy and transparency and that it be subject to robust safeguards (PJCIS, 2019). The Australian Passports Amendments Bill was to be amended and was to be reviewed again once the re-drafting of the Identity-matching Bill was completed (PJCIS, 2019).

PROPOSALS FOR NEW SPECIFIC AI REGULATION, PARTICULARLY RELATED TO GENERAL AI

The previous section has shown that some existing laws as they stand or with amendments can regulate certain areas of AI and that using existing legislative approaches to broaden the operation of the law is possible. It still needs to be explored, though, whether there are ways in which AI systems are so different from other software and computer related technology, that new approaches and specific legislation is needed to deal with any safety and security issues that might arise? Three stages have been proposed as possible areas that need addressing with AI – specification, robustness, and assurance (Otega, Maini & DeepMind Safety Team, 2018):

- Stage one, specification, covers the design of the AI system. Was the design appropriate for the purpose it was intended to fulfil? However, while the initial stage of AI design, deciding the purpose of it, is not particularly different from designing any computer system, the architectural design of AI software involves the selection of appropriate data and tuning and training of a neural network, rather than coding in a programming language. However, the algorithm may then develop in ways not intended or expected from the original intent (Otega, Maini & DeepMind Safety Team, 2018).
- Robustness, the second stage proposed, is also expected of the design and implementation of any computer system. Has the designer built into the system appropriate ways to deal with risk, to incorporate margins of acceptable unpredictability, and adequate failsafe mechanisms? However, the main challenge with AI systems, particularly those intended to be dynamic, is understanding how and why the AI acted as it did, if its actions or decisions were not what was anticipated (Otega, Maini & DeepMind Safety Team, 2018).
- The third stage, assurance, covers monitoring the performance of the system and enforcing the controls and safeguards built into the system, including interrupting the system and closing it down. Again, this would be expected in any computer system design. However, again, with AI, while the design objective might be appropriate, the data as accurate as possible and the neural network fully trained, the results may not be what was expected or intended, or able to be explained or even foreseen (Otega, Maini & DeepMind Safety Team, 2018).

It appears, therefore, that the challenges for appropriate regulation of some aspects of AI arise around AI behaviour that is unexpected, unforeseen or unexplained, unintended and unexpected. Linked to these behaviours is the fact that AI sustems are intended to learn, develop and improve. Ethical principles address these areas but these may not be adequate/

Explainability and Foreseeability

The questions of 'explainability' and 'foreseeability' of actions by AI sustems are therefore two key issues to be considered. Machine learning AI systems, for example, are a result of the provision of data, training and tuning in how to analyse the data, resulting in an algorithm which is then used, say, to predict share prices. The algorithm may change as new or different data is received. From this starting point, the system develops its own conclusions about the data analysis. Despite testing, it is not always possible to foresee if the AI algorithm will operate as expected. For example, in 2016, Microsoft developed an AI called Tay to 'engage and chat with people'. It appeared on Twitter but after 16 hours online, Tay was making racist and inflammatory statements as a result of online interaction with other tweeters (Hunt, 2016).

At present, as discussed earlier, risks relating to injury or damage are borne by the owners or implementers of an AI system. They in turn may seek redress from suppliers of the product. A statutory defence in the ACL is available to manufacturers who may claim that while the product, the AI, worked as designed when tested before release, it was beyond the control of the manufacturer/producer to foresee all it might do when in operation. At this stage, it is possible for the manufacturer to claim that they have shown 'reasonable care' in designing an AI system. But is 'reasonable care' or avoidance of foreseeable harm in designing an autonomous AI an adequate standard? Is a different test required and should a specific liability regime be established for AI? Is, in fact, an AI a 'product' at all? If ACL does not apply because an AI system is not considered to be a product, then the applicability of common law areas such as negligence and vicarious liability, and contract law need to explored (Dodd, 2019).

The difficulty in understanding how many algorithms operate has been described as the 'black box' problem. The 'black box problem' (Pasquale, 2015) is a response by some AI developers/owners to why they cannot explain how the AI operates and why it did what it did. This issue of 'explainability' is also relevant when considering how consent for the use of their personal data can be obtained from individuals. If the developers and users of AI cannot understand how it works, it is almost impossible for an individual to consent to something that cannot be understood.

Another argument offered is that the algorithm is commercial in confidence and cannot be disclosed to other. This argument was successfully used in *Wisconsin v Loomis* (2016) and unsuccessfully in *Houston Federation of Teachers vs Houston Independent School District* (2017). In *Cordover and Australian Electoral Commission* (2015), the Administrative Appeals Tribunal upheld the Australian Electoral Commission's (AEC) refusal to release the computer program code which it used to read and count Senate ballot papers as it claimed that the code was a 'trade secret', used for the AEC's fee-for-service function (Miller, 2016).

The argument that AI actions might not be foreseeable, understandable or accessible has led to calls for transparency around algorithms. Both the US Congress and Senate introduced a Federal *Algorithmic Accountability Act* in April 2019. Applying only to companies earning over $USD50 million per year, it would make the Federal Trade Commission (FTC) responsible for evaluating automated systems that had been classified as 'highly sensitive'. As well, companies would be required to evaluate algorithms for a range of issues such as bias, discrimination and/or security and privacy risks. While the US Senate, which is currently controlled by the Republican Party, is unlikely to approve the bill for political reasons at this time, the issue will remain on the national agenda, particularly as some US states and cities are trying respond to concerns by their citizens. .

The New York City Council passed an algorithm transparency bill in 2017 (*Local Law 49*) which mandated that a task force be established (*Local Law 49*, s. 1(b)) to study the use of algorithms by New York agencies and to develop recommendations about how information on agency automated decision systems might be shared with the public (*Local Law 49*, s. 3(e)) and how agencies can address any harm caused (*Local Law 49*, s. 3(d)). Progress to date by the task force has been slow due to the complexity of the issues being dealt with (Lecher, 2019). Washington State has also drafted algorithmic accountability bills (*HB1655* and *SB5527*) which, if passed, would require algorithms to be made available by vendors of AI systems for government agency or third party testing, auditing or research (Pangburn, 2019).

Unintended and Unconscious Bias

As noted above, issues associated with a lack of transparency lead to concerns about bias and discrimination by AI systems. Bias can arise in two ways with AI systems. The first is when bias, conscious or unconscious, is incorporated into the design of the AI system and the algorithm that it will use. The second is when the data that is provided to the AI contains biases. Amazon provides an example of the importance of ensuring that the data provided to an AI is not biased. Amazon had developed a recruitment tool but found that its AI was biased against women and was more inclined to select males rather than female applicants. The AI had been provided with the resumes of successful applicants over the previous ten year period but this data reflected the dominance of males working in information technology. This AI is no longer used by Amazon (Reuters Business News, 2018).

AI systems are being used widely in employment recruitment, in setting penalties in lower courts, in checking for fraud in government payments, for facial recognition in areas such as education and policing, and in legal advice work. The private sector offers more challenges than the public sector as there are limited avenues to process complaints. In recruitment situations, appeals by non-employers against decisions made to interview or appoint applicants are generally not available. In some cases, anti-discrimination laws (such as the *Age Discrimination Act 2014* (Cth) and the *Sex Discrimination Act 2004* (Cth) and state and territory equivalents) might be used.

The UK's Centre for Data Ethics and Innovation (CDEI), created by the UK government to advise on AI, has announced that one of its first activities will be to undertake reviews into bias in a number of sectors, starting with the finance sector, and moving onto local government, recruitment, and crime and justice over the next two years (CDEI, 2019). The use of AI systems for decision-making in all these areas has the potential to adversely affect individuals if bias is embedded in the algorithms being used.

One regulatory solution to concerns about bias with AI decision making that has been proposed is that there should be human involvement in decisions by AI which affect human rights. The EU GDPR provides a right to individuals "not to be subject to a decision based solely on processing" (GDPR, art. 22) so that some human contribution to the decision making is needed. However, this right, which was originally described as a 'right to explanation', was reduced after lengthy compromises and its operation is fairly restricted. It does not apply if the individual gives explicit consent. As well, it does not apply if the decision is necessary for entering into a contract, say, for employment (GDPR, Art 22(2a,c)). However, Australia's Privacy Act does not even include a similar right.

Electronic Personality

There have been suggestions made that a solution to the problem of foreseeability and lack of transparency is to recognise some form of 'electronic personality' for AI and robots (European Parliament, 2015; Republic of Estonia, 2018). These suggestions are pragmatic and are an attempt to address the related issues of liability, rather than an attempt to grant legal human status to AI systems. For instance, while Estonia had announced in early 2019 that it was considering granting legal status to robots, or kratts,[3] it was doing so in the context of allocating liability for damages, having rejected introducing sector based liability regulation and "opting for algorithmic liability instead" (Republic of Estonia, 2018, p. 1; Kaevats, 2018; ABA Journal, 2017). Similarly the European Parliament approved a *Resolution on 16 February 2017 with recommendations to the Commission on Civil Law Rules on Robotics* (European Parliament, 2015). Article 59(f) of that Resolution states that the EU should consider:

creating a specific legal status for robots in the long run, so that at least the most sophisticated autonomous robots could be established as having the status of electronic persons responsible for making good any damage they may cause, and possibly applying electronic personality to cases where robots make autonomous decisions or otherwise interact with third parties independently...

With this approach, it is envisaged that awarding some form of legal status to an AI would enable a specific compensation scheme for loss and damage caused by the AI to be established. This could mean separating it from the company that developed the AI or initiated it. There is no doubt that, as AI technology develops, there will be a need for new forms of accountability and liability for business and consumer related damages and injuries resulting from AI activity but whether it takes to form of legal personhood will require much more debate.

Strict Liability

Another suggestion has been to introduce strict liability (no fault) laws (European Commission, 2018; Barfield, 2018)). Unlike the EU, the product liability laws in Australia have limited strict liability. Often, a remedy for damages is sought under tort law. It applies if a person suffers injury or loss as a result of the negligent actions of another. For negligence to be proven, the injured person has to show that the other party owed them a duty of care, that they failed in that duty, that the risk of harm was reasonably foreseeable and that the injury was caused by the failure of the person (Oxford Australian Law Dictionary, 2010). However, it is only in cases where the activities that led to injury to a person could be called 'ultra-hazardous' activities, such as those involving fire, hazardous materials and so on, that the injured person does not have to prove negligence, as found in *Burnie Port Authority v General Jones Pty Ltd* (1994). If strict liability is extended to cover all AI activities, then it may be that insurance cover will be needed, creating compensation pools funded by developers and implementers of AI. Examples of similar compensation pools are the Victorian Motor Car Traders Guarantee Fund, established by an Act, funded by motor car trader licence fees, and intended to compensate individuals who suffer loss due to actions of car sellers (Consumer Affairs Victoria, 2019) or the various worker's compensation insurance schemes in Australia which are funded by employers to cover employees' work injuries (Victorian WorkSafe Scheme, n.d.).

Intellectual Property

Apart from issues around liability for loss and damage, and bias, questions around intellectual property (IP) also arise. New IP might be created once the AI system is operational. For instance, the developer of an AI system may provide the technical expertise, while the user of the system may provide the data without which the AI cannot operate. New IP may then be created. In Australia, under the *Copyright Act 1968* (Cth), s 32(4), copyright exists in a works resulting from human intellectual effort, not from computer generated works. Some countries, like the UK and New Zealand, have amended their copyright law to grant ownership of computer generated works for copyright purposes to the person who made the arrangements for the work to be undertaken (Allens, 2019).

FURTHER RESEARCH DIRECTIONS

Future research will need to be undertaken on whether AI systems will be considered to be products under the ACL and whether amendments need to be made to the product liability framework. The effectiveness of the existing privacy legislation to deal with the activities of AI systems in the collection, use and disclosure of data will need to be reviewed as will the application of the IP laws to the creations of AI systems.

CONCLUSION

Regulation of AI has already commenced. Challenges associated with certain types of AI currently being tested and introduced, like driverless cars and drones, are being addressed through amendments to existing national and state legislation, but with input from global forums and working groups.

As well, many countries are reviewing their laws around product liability and consumer protection in particular to determine whether any amendments might be needed to address AI-related issues. Governments and industry both have key roles to establish clear frameworks for developers, deployers and users and to determine gaps in existing regulation.

The growth in the uses of AI by governments is generally been handled by appropriate legislation. The private sector, too, has expanded its use of AI as well. In many cases, this growth has been built on the understanding that there are protections for misuse of personal data contained in privacy acts, however, the exceptions and the breadth of the rights contained in the extended uses of personal data appear to have weakened those protections. This will need to be addressed by regulators.

However, the lack of transparency about how AI systems operate and the associated issues around 'foreseeability' of AI decisions are the biggest challenges for regulating AI and these issues are unlikely to be dealt with without the introduction of new legislation. General AI involves bigger challenges to those posed by narrow AI, particularly as machine consciousness develops. There will be increasing problems of foreseeability, from what is developed to how it evolves. It will be vital that human rights and the rule of law are protected.

While the manufacturer/developer might argue that at the time of placing the AI on the market or providing the system to the user, no vulnerability with the AI was known or that they do not control the algorithms, it is likely that the concept of strict liability for damage or loss may need to be extended.

Insurance and compensation pools will also be needed. Control and liability issues will need to be addressed as more advanced AI is developed. It is unlikely to be one single regulatory solution, rather a layered approach to AI regulation is needed at various levels. Ethical guidelines will also be an important part of that framework as will the involvement of human oversight in decisions made by AI.

Ethical AI principles and guidelines are being developed at all levels, international, national and industry. While there is considerable overlap in the principles being developed, there does need to be international support for universally agreed principles.

What is missing with the AI ethical principles, which occurred with the OECD Data Protection Guidelines and research ethics, is a clear international leader. With data protection, the OECD, which now represents 34 members plus 16 adherents but had lower membership numbers in the 1970s and 80s, took that role. At this stage, the EU AI ethical principles appear to be the most developed and have been incorporated into other proposed frameworks but the approval of the *Recommendation on AI* by the OECD may see this change.

There are considerable challenges facing Australia and the rest of the world in ensuring that the concepts embedded in the various ethical principles, such as transparency, explainability, impact assessments, risk assessment and review processes of AI, and avenues for recourse against decisions by AI, are operationalized effectively and appropriately. The future advent of AI systems that achieve consciousness lends urgency to these endeavours.

AI developments offer the potential for quite destructive and detrimental impacts on the lives of individuals globally. A workable and globally accepted AI regulation and ethical framework should be able to restrict the harm to individuals and society without stifling developments that can benefit the same groups with advances in health and security, and in ensuring economic security and stability. Regulation does not need to be a barrier to developments but it does need to be consistent.

REFERENCES

ABA Journal. (2017, 20 October). *Estonia considering new legal status for artificial intelligence.* Retrieved from https://www.abajournal.com/news/article/estonia_considering_new_legal_status_for_ai

ActCopyright 1968 (Cth).

ActMigration 1958 (Cth).

ActPrivacy 1988 (Cth).

Age Discrimination Act 2014 (Cth).

AI 4People. (2019). *Ethical framework for a good AI society.* Retrieved from https://www.eismd.eu/wp-content/uploads/2019/02/Ethical-Framework-for-a-Good-AI-Society.pdf

Algorithmic Accountability Act. (2019). US.

Allens. (2019). *AI toolkit.* Retrieved from https://www.allens.com.au/datadrivenbusiness/AI-toolkit/

Amendment, T. L. (Automated Vehicle Trials and Innovation) Act 2017 (NSW).

Andrews, K. (2019, 7 November). *Businesses ready to test AI ethics principles*. Press Release. Retrieved at https://www.minister.industry.gov.au/ministers/karenandrews/media-releases/businesses-ready-test-ai-ethics-principles

Australian Consumer Law (Competition and Consumer Act 2010 (Cth), sch. 2).

Australian Government, Department of Industry, Innovation & Science. (2019, November). *AI ethics principles*. Retrieved from https://www.industry.gov.au/data-and-publications/building-australias-artificial-intelligence-capability/ai-ethics-framework/ai-ethics-principles

Barfield, W. (2018). Liability for autonomous and artificially intelligent robots. *De Gruyter, 9,* 193-203. Retrieved from https://www.degruyter.com/downloadpdf/j/pjbr.2018.9.issue-1/pjbr-2018-0018/pjbr-2018-0018.pdf

Burnie Port Authority v General Jones Pty Ltd (1994) HCA 13.

Centre for Connected and Driverless Cars. (2019, February). *Code of practice: automated vehicle trialling*. Retrieved from https://assets.publishing.service.gov.uk/government/uploads/system/uploads/attachment_data/file/776511/code-of-practice-automated-vehicle-trialling.pdf

Centre for Data Ethics and Innovation (CDEI). (2019, 21 March). *Two year strategy*. Retrieved from https://www.gov.uk/government/publications/the-centre-for-data-ethics-and-innovation-cdei-2-year-strategy/centre-for-data-ethics-cdei-2-year-strategy

Civil Aviation Safety Authority (CASA). (2019). *Project US 18/09*. Retrieved from https://www.casa.gov.au/standard-page/project-us-1809-remotely-piloted-aircraft-rpa-registration-and-rpas-operator-accreditation-scheme

Civil Aviation Safety Regulations 1988 (Cth).

Commonwealth of Australia. (2018). *Regulatory requirements that impact on the safe use of remotely piloted aircraft systems, unmanned aerial systems and associated systems*. Retrieved from https://www.aph.gov.au/Parliamentary_Business/Committees/Senate/Rural_and_Regional_Affairs_and_Transport/Drones/Report

Competition and Consumer Act 2010 (Cth).

Consumer Affairs Victoria. (2019). *Motor car traders guarantee fund*. Retrieved from https://www.consumer.vic.gov.au/about-us/who-we-are-and-what-we-do/funds-we-administer/motor-car-traders-guarantee-fund

Cordover and Australian Electoral Commission, 2015] AATA 956.

2001. Council of Europe Convention on Cybercrime.

Criminal Code Act 1995 (Cth).

Data61. (2019, 5 April). *Artificial intelligence: Australia's ethics framework*. Retrieved from https://consult.industry.gov.au/strategic-policy/artificial-intelligence-ethics-framework/supporting_documents/ArtificialIntelligenceethicsframeworkdiscussionpaper.pdf

Dentons. (2019). *Autonomous vehicles: US legal and regulatory landscape.* Retrieved from http://www.thedriverlesscommute.com/wp-content/uploads/2019/08/Dentons-US-Autonomous-Vehicles-Whitepaper-August-1-2019.docx.pdf

Department of Industry, Innovation and Science. (2019). *Artificial intelligence: Australia's ethics framework.* Retrieved from https://consult.industry.gov.au/strategic-policy/artificial-intelligence-ethics-framework/

Department of Justice. (2015, 6 April). Former e-commerce executive charged with price fixing in the antitrust division's first online marketplace prosecution. *Justice News of the US Department of Justice.* Retrieved from https://www.justice.gov/opa/pr/former-e-commerce-executive-charged-price-fixing-antitrust-divisions-first-online-marketplace

DirectiveMachinery (2006/42/EC).

Directive 95/46/EC of the European Parliament and of the Council of 24 October 1995 on the protection of individuals with regard to the processing of personal data and on the free movement of such data.

Dodd, A. (2019). *"I'm sorry, Dave. I'm afraid I can't do that": Legal liability in the age of artificial intelligence.* Retrieved from https://www.fieldfisher.com/en/insights/i%E2%80%99m-sorry,-dave-i%E2%80%99m-afraid-i-can%E2%80%99t-do-that%E2%80%9D-legal

Elvery, S. (2017). How algorithms make important government decisions. *ABC News.* Retrieved from https://www.abc.net.au/news/2017-07-21/algorithms-can-make-decisions-on-behalf-of-federal-ministers/8704858

European Commission, European Group on Ethics in Science & New Technologies. (2018). *Statement on artificial intelligence, robotics and 'autonomous' systems.* Retrieved from https://ec.europa.eu/jrc/communities/en/community/humaint/useful-link/statement-artificial-intelligence-european-group-ethics-science-and

European Commission. (2018). *Liability for emerging digital technologies.* Retrieved from https://ec.europa.eu/digital-single-market/en/news/european-commission-staff-working-document-liability-emerging-digital-technologies

European Commission High-Level Expert Group on Artificial Intelligence (AIHLEG). (2019). *Ethics guidelines for trustworthy AI.* Retrieved from https://ec.europa.eu/digital-single-market/en/news/ethics-guidelines-trustworthy-ai

European Parliament. (2015). *Civil laws for robotics (2015/2103(INL).* Retrieved from http://www.europarl.europa.eu/doceo/document/TA-8-2017-0051_EN.html?redirect

European Union. (2016). *General data protection regulation article 22.* Retrieved from https://eur-lex.europa.eu/legal-content/EN/TXT/?qid=1528874672298&uri=CELEX%3A32016R0679

Federal Ministry of Transport and Digital Infrastructure. (2017). *Automated and connected driving.* Retrieved from https://www.bmvi.de/SharedDocs/EN/publications/report-ethics-commission.pdf?__blob=publicationFile

Google. (n.d.). *Responsible AI practices.* Retrieved from https://ai.google/responsibilities/responsible-ai-practices/

Gordon Legal. (2019). *Robodebt class action.* Retrieved from https://gordonlegal.com.au/robodebt-class-action/

Harari, Y. N. (2016). *Homo deus: A brief history of tomorrow.* New York, NY: Vintage Digital.

Henriques-Gomez, L. (2019). Centrelink robodebt scheme faces second legal challenge. *The Guardian.* Retrieved from https://www.theguardian.com/australia-news/2019/jun/12/centrelink-robodebt-scheme-faces-second-legal-challenge

Hogan-Doran, D. (2017). Computer says "no": Automation, algorithms and artificial intelligence in government decision-making. *Judicial Review: Selected Conference Papers: Journal of the Judicial Commission of New South Wales, 13*(3), 345–382.

Houston Federation of Teachers vs Houston Independent School District, Amended Summary Judgment Opinion, 4 May 2017, US District Court of Southern District of Texas.

Hunt, E. (2016, March 24). Tay, Microsoft's AI chatbox, gets a crash course in racism from Twitter. *The Guardian.* Retrieved from https://www.theguardian.com/technology/2016/mar/24/tay-microsofts-ai-chatbot-gets-a-crash-course-in-racism-from-twitter

Identity-matching Services Bill (Cth) 2018.

Institute of Electrical and Electronics Engineers (IEEE). (2019). *Ethically aligned design: A vision for prioritizing human well-being with autonomous and intelligent systems first edition.* Retrieved from https://ethicsinaction.ieee.org/

International Standards Organization (ISO). (2019). *Artificial intelligence.* Retrieved from https://www.iso.org/committee/6794475.html

Jackson, M. (2001). *Hughes on data protection in Australia* (2nd ed.). Sydney, Australia: Lawbook Co.

Kaevats, M. (2018) *AI and the Kratt momentum.* Retrieved from https://investinestonia.com/ai-and-the-kratt-momentum/

Karp, P. (2019). Government admits robodebt was unlawful as it settles legal challenge. *The Guardian.* Retrieved from https://www.theguardian.com/australia-news/2019/nov/27/government-admits-robodebt-was-unlawful-as-it-settles-legal-challenge

Laukyte, M. (forthcoming). Robots: Regulation, rights and remedies. In M. Jackson & M. Shelly (Eds.), *Legal regulations, implications and issues surrounding digital data.* Hershey, PA: IGI Global.

Law Council of Australia. (2018). *Submission to the review of the identity-matching services bill 2018.* Retrieved from https://www.lawcouncil.asn.au/media/news/review-of-the-identity-matching-services-bill-2018

Lecher, C. (2019, April 15). *New York's algorithm task force is fracturing.* Retrieved from https://www.theverge.com/2019/4/15/18309437/new-york-city-accountability-task-force-law-algorithm-transparency-automation

Lexology. (2019). *Australia's privacy and consumer laws to be strengthened.* Retrieved from https://www.lexology.com/library/detail.aspx?g=4fbb5191-1fb2-4e5f-8d2d-f9a6aaf3754c

Microsoft. (2019). *Future computed: AI & manufacturing.* Retrieved from https://news.microsoft.com/futurecomputed/

Microsoft. (n.d.). *Microsoft AI principles.* Retrieved from https://www.microsoft.com/en-us/ai/our-approach-to-ai

Miller, K. (2016). The application of administrative law principles to technology-assisted decision-making. *AIAL Forum, 86*, 20-34.

National Highway Traffic Safety Administration (NHTSA). (2019). *Automated vehicles for safety.* Retrieved from https://www.nhtsa.gov/technology-innovation/automated-vehicles-safety

National Transport Commission (NTC). (2019). *Automated vehicles in Australia.* Retrieved from https://www.ntc.gov.au/transport-reform/automated-vehicle-program

Nemitz, P. (2018). *Constitutional democracy and technology in the age of artificial intelligence.* Retrieved from https://royalsocietypublishing.org/doi/abs/10.1098/rsta.2018.0089

1980. OECD Guidelines on the Protection of Privacy and Transborder Flows of Personal Data (OECD Guidelines).

Office of the Australian Information Commissioner (OAIC). (2018a). *Submission 13, submission to the review of the identity-matching services bill 2018 and the Australian passports amendments (identity-matching services) bill 2018.* Retrieved from https://www.aph.gov.au/Parliamentary_Business/Committees/Joint/Intelligence_and_Security/IMSBill/Submissions

Office of the Australian Information Commissioner (OAIC). (2018b, March). *Guide to data analytics and the Australian privacy principles.* Retrieved from https://www.oaic.gov.au/resources/agencies-and-organisations/guides/guide-to-data-analytics-and-the-australian-privacy-principles.pdf

Office of the Victorian Information Commissioner (OVIC). (2018, June). *Artificial intelligence and privacy.* Retrieved from https://ovic.vic.gov.au/wp-content/uploads/2018/08/AI-Issues-Paper-V1.1.pdf

Office of the Victorian Information Commissioner (OVIC). (2019). *Submission to the artificial intelligence: Australia's ethic framework discussion paper.* Retrieved from https://ovic.vic.gov.au/wp-content/uploads/2019/06/OVIC-submission-to-DIIS-AI-Ethical-Framework-Discussion-Paper-V1.0-.pdf

Ombudsman, C. (2017, July). *Centrelink's automated debt raising and recovery system.* Retrieved from https://www.ombudsman.gov.au/__data/assets/pdf_file/0022/43528/Report-Centrelinks-automated-debt-raising-and-recovery-system-April-2017.pdf

Ombudsman, C. (2019, April). *Centrelink's automated debt raising and recovery system: Implementation report.* Retrieved from https://www.ombudsman.gov.au/__data/assets/pdf_file/0025/98314/April-2019-Centrelinks-Automated-Debt-Raising-and-Recovery-System.pdf

Organisation for Economic Co-operation and Development (OECD). (2019). *Recommendation on artificial intelligence (AI).* Retrieved from https://legalinstruments.oecd.org/en/instruments/OECD-LEGAL-0449

Otega, P. A., Maini, V., & DeepMind Safety Team. (2018, Sept 27). *Building safe artificial intelligence: specification, robustness, and assurance.* Retrieved from https://medium.com/@deepmindsafetyresearch/building-safe-artificial-intelligence-52f5f75058f1

Oxford Australian Law Dictionary. (2010). Sydney, Australia: Oxford University Press.

Pangburn, D. J. (2019, February 8). *Washington could be the first state to rein in automated decision-making.* Retrieved from https://www.fastcompany.com/90302465/washington-introduces-landmark-algorithmic-accountability-laws

Parliamentary Joint Committee on Intelligence and Security (PJCIS). (2019, October). *Advisory report on the identity-matching services bill 2019 and the Australian passports amendment (identity-matching services) bill 2019.* Retrieved from https://www.aph.gov.au/Parliamentary_Business/Committees/Joint/Intelligence_and_Security/Identity-Matching2019/Report/section?id=committees%2freportjnt%2f024343%2f27801

Pasquale, F. (2015). *The black box society: The secret algorithms that control money and information.* Cambridge, MA: Harvard University Press. doi:10.4159/harvard.9780674736061

Perry, M. (2019). *Idecide: Digital pathways to decision.* Retrieved from https://www.fedcourt.gov.au/digital-law-library/judges-speeches/justice-perry/perry-j-20190321

Privacy and Data Protection Act. (2014). Vic.

Product Liability Directive (85/374/EEC).

Republic of Estonia. (2018). *Estonia will have an artificial intelligence strategy.* Retrieved from https://www.riigikantselei.ee/en/news/estonia-will-have-artificial-intelligence-strategy

Reuters Business News. (2018, October 10). *Amazon scraps secret AI recruiting tool that showed bias against women.* Retrieved from https://www.reuters.com/article/us-amazon-com-jobs-automation-insight/amazon-scraps-secret-ai-recruiting-tool-that-showed-bias-against-women-idUSKCN1MK08G

Safety, R. (Automated Vehicles) Act 2018 (Vic).

Sex Discrimination Act 2004 (Cth).

Sims, R. (2017). *The ACCC's approach to colluding robots.* Retrieved from https://www.accc.gov.au/speech/the-accc%E2%80%99s-approach-to-colluding-robots

Social Security (Administration) Act 1999 (Cth).

Standards Australia. (2019). *Developing standards for artificial intelligence: Hearing Australia's voice discussion paper.* Retrieved from https://www.standards.org.au/getmedia/aeaa5d9e-8911-4536-8c36-76733a3950d1/Artificial-Intelligence-Discussion-Paper-(004).pdf.aspx

Surveillance Devices Act 2004 (Cth).

Telecommunications (Interception and Access) Act 1979 (Cth).

Therapeutic Goods Act 1989 (Cth).

Tillet, A. (2019). Federal government backs down on 'robo-debt' scheme. *Australian Financial Review*. Retrieved from https://www.afr.com/politics/federal/government-backs-down-on-robo-debt-scheme-20191119-p53bz4

UK House of Lords. (2018). *AI in the UK: Ready, willing and able?* Retrieved from https://publications. parliament.uk/pa/ld201719/ldselect/ldai/100/100.pdf

UK Office of the Information Commissioner (OIC). (2017). *Big data, artificial intelligence, machine learning and data protection.* Retrieved from https://ico.org.uk/media/for-organisations/documents/2013559/big-data-ai-ml-and-data-protection.pdf

United Nations Economic Commission for Europe (UNECE). (2019, June). *Revised framework document on automated/autonomous vehicles.* Retrieved from https://www.unece.org/fileadmin/DAM/trans/doc/2019/wp29/ECE-TRANS-WP29-2019-34-rev.1e.pdf

Vehicles, M. (Trials of Automotive Technologies) Amendment Act 2016 (SA).

Victorian WorkSafe Scheme. (n.d.). *How to register for WorkCover insurance.* Retrieved from https://www.worksafe.vic.gov.au/how-register-workcover-insurance

Williams, J. R. (2008). The declaration of Helsinki and public health. *Bulletin of the World Health Organization*, *86*(8), 577–656. doi:10.2471/BLT.08.050955 PMID:18797627

Wisconsin v Loomis, 881 NW 2d 749 (Wis, 2016).

ADDITIONAL READING

Chae, Y. (2020). U.S. AI regulation guide: Legislative overview and practical considerations. *The Journal of Robotics. Artificial Intelligence and Law*, *3*(1), 17–40. Retrieved from https://www.bakermckenzie.com/-/media/files/people/chae-yoon/rail-us-ai-regulation-guide.pdf

European Commission. (2020). *Shaping Europe's digital future.* Retrieved from https://ec.europa.eu/info/strategy/priorities-2019-2024/europe-fit-digital-age/shaping-europe-digital-future_en

Library of Congress. (2019a). *Regulation of artificial intelligence: The Americas and the Caribbean.* Retrieved from https://www.loc.gov/law/help/artificial-intelligence/americas.php

Library of Congress. (2019b). *Regulation of artificial intelligence in selected jurisdictions.* Retrieved from https://www.loc.gov/law/help/artificial-intelligence/regulation-artificial-intelligence.pdf

KEY TERMS AND DEFINITIONS

Artificial Intelligence (AI): The creation of programs designed to perform tasks generally performed by humans. AI can be 'narrow' AI which means that it has been designed for a specific purpose and 'general' AI which are designed to replicate human consciousness.

Regulation: Mechanisms of social control, usually based in law, and resulting in the establishment of frameworks, policies, standards and laws.

Standards: Usually technical specifications which set out levels of quality, performance, safety or dimensions relating to a product or process.

ENDNOTES

[1]   Motor Vehicles (Trials of Automotive Technologies) Amendment Act 2016 (SA); Transport Legislation Amendment (Automated Vehicle Trials and Innovation) Act 2017 (NSW); Road Safety (Automated Vehicles) Act 2018 (Vic).

[2]   The algorithm methodology itself may be flawed, as was found by a Senate Review Committee hearing into the 'Robo-debt' program used by the Departments of Human Services and Social Security.

[3]   Kratts are part of Estonia folklore and are servants built from hay or old household items.

Chapter 10
A Matter of Perspective:
Discrimination, Bias, and Inequality in AI

Katie Miller
Deakin University, Australia

ABSTRACT

The challenge presented is an age when some decisions are made by humans, some are made by AI, and some are made by a combination of AI and humans. For the person refused housing, a phone service, or employment, the experience is the same, but the ability to understand what has happened and obtain a remedy may be very different if the discrimination is attributable to or contributed by an AI system. If we are to preserve the policy intentions of our discrimination, equal opportunity, and human rights laws, we need to understand how discrimination arises in AI systems; how design in AI systems can mitigate such discrimination; and whether our existing laws are adequate to address discrimination in AI. This chapter endeavours to provide this understanding. In doing so, it focuses on narrow but advanced forms of artificial intelligence, such as natural language processing, facial recognition, and cognitive neural networks.

INTRODUCTION

An Aboriginal woman is refused housing.

A man with a disability is refused a contract for a phone service.

A woman is denied employment as a pilot.

Each of these examples involve discrimination. But discrimination by whom? Can you distinguish the case where the discrimination is caused by a human and the case where the discrimination is caused by artificial intelligence (AI), meaning computers doing tasks that, when humans do them, require thinking (Walsh, 2019)?

DOI: 10.4018/978-1-7998-3130-3.ch010

This is the challenge presented in an age when some decisions are made by humans, some are made by AI and some are made by a combination of AI and humans. For the person refused housing, a phone service or employment, the experience is the same – but the ability to understand what has happened and obtain a remedy may be very different if the discrimination is attributable to, or contributed by, an AI system.

The questions posed above are, of course, trick questions. Each of the examples given have resulted from discrimination by humans in the past (see for example Australian Human Rights Commission, 2002; Australian Human Rights Commission, 2009; Solonec, 2000). Each of the examples given could, or already have, resulted from the use of AI systems. Each of the examples given can result from direct discrimination on the basis of race, gender or parental responsibilities, or indirectly through discrimination on the basis of criminal record, employment status or mental health status. One of the challenges presented by AI systems is that we increasingly do not know why decisions are made or how traditionally protected attributes factor into AI decisions, recommendations and advice.

If we are to preserve the policy intentions of our discrimination, equal opportunity and human rights laws, we need to understand how discrimination arises in AI systems; how design in AI systems can mitigate such discrimination; and whether our existing laws are adequate to address discrimination in AI. This chapter endeavours to provide this understanding. In doing so, it focuses on narrow, but advanced, forms of artificial intelligence, such as natural language processing, facial recognition and cognitive neural networks.

ARE WE SPEAKING THE SAME LANGUAGE?

The challenge of discrimination, bias and equality in AI involves the intersection of multiple domains of law, sociology and technology, each with their own experts and language. In order to have a shared understanding of the issues and possible solutions, we must first ensure that we are speaking the same language. In particular, we need to know what we mean by 'discrimination' and 'bias'. While the same words may be used across domains, they can have different meanings and connotations within different domains.

In everyday speech, to 'discriminate' is to "note or observe a difference; distinguish" (Dorner, Blair & Bernard, 1998, Discriminate entry) and 'discrimination' is "the process of differentiating between persons or things possessing different properties" (*Street v Queensland Bar Association*, 1989, p. 570). Understood in this sense, an AI system is a discriminating machine. The ability to discriminate, quickly and over large data sets, is one of AI's greatest strengths and a large part of the reason for its adoption and incorporation into so much of our daily lives. For example, AI assistants such as Cortana, Siri and Alexa rely on natural language processing, speech recognition and deep learning algorithms that can differentiate between words (or the sounds we use to represent words) and the contexts in which they are used (Krywko, 2017).

In a legal sense, 'discrimination' involves treating, or proposing to treat, someone unfavourably because of a personal characteristic protected by law (Rees, Rice & Allen, 2018). For example, refusing a person a job because of their gender, racial background, disability or sexual orientation constitutes an unlawful form of discrimination.

Considerations of discrimination in AI involve questions about the types of discrimination that are acceptable, desirable and intended. Discriminating between cancer cells (Toratani et al., 2018) may be acceptable, desirable and intended. Discriminating against women of colour (Buolamwini & Gebr, 2018) may not be acceptable or desirable – and, depending on the design of the AI system, such discrimination may not be intended. The challenge for designers, users and subjects of AI is that cancer cells are clearly something we want to discriminate against – they are objectively 'bad'. People are more complex – and so too the questions of when it is acceptable or desirable to discriminate against them.

The legal concepts of direct and indirect discrimination are both important and helpful to the discussion about discrimination in AI systems. Understanding these concepts can assist in designing AI systems that are lawful because they comply with discrimination laws. More fundamentally, they are helpful in ascertaining if the discrimination undertaken by an AI system is acceptable or desirable.

Direct discrimination occurs when a person is treated less favourably *because of* an attribute that is protected by law, such as race, gender, religious belief or (dis)ability. Laws prohibiting direct discrimination are based on the idea that a person's protected attribute must be an irrelevant consideration when dealing with that person (Rees et al., 2018). Discrimination is prohibited not just on the actual protected attribute (such as a person's gender), but also characteristics that are stereotypically attributed to persons of the protected group. Such imputed characteristics can include the susceptibility of married women to the influence of their spouses and the clothing and grooming preferences of persons of particular sexual orientations (*Daniels v Hunter Water Board*, 1994; *Waterhouse v Bell*, 1991).

Indirect discrimination is directed towards activities that are "fair in form but discriminatory in outcome" (Rees et al., 2018, p. 53). It requires consideration of how an ostensibly neutral action affects people with one or more protected attributes. For example, preferring to employ people who can attend work at 8am may indirectly discriminate against parents who have child care responsibilities for young or school-aged children. Indirect discrimination is not automatically unlawful; it requires consideration of the reasonableness of that requirement (Rees et al., 2018).

This distinction between direct and indirect discrimination finds an analogy in algorithms and mathematics, where a distinction is made between direct and indirect variables. Direct variables are specific characteristics that the algorithm is programmed to recognise and consider; indirect variables or 'proxies' are statistical correlations between one attribute (such as postcode) and another attribute – which may or may not be protected (such as race or social class) (O'Neil, 2016).

If and when an AI system is challenged for breaching discrimination laws, there will be complex and novel arguments about whether an AI system is engaged in direct discrimination and/or whether it can be said that an AI system involves a 'requirement condition or practice' constituting indirect discrimination (*Equal Opportunity Act 2010* (Vic), s. 9(1); Rees et al., 2018). This chapter does not engage with these complex arguments, which will no doubt depend on the particular circumstances of the AI system and discriminatory effect alleged. Instead, it is sufficient for now to distinguish between the AI system coded to rely or use directly protected attributes such as gender, race, (dis)ability; and the ostensibly neutral AI systems that operate in a discriminatory way.

Understanding the meaning of 'bias' is arguably more straight forward. While used in different ways between law and technology, the mechanism is generally accepted across domains. 'Bias' refers to a predisposition, prejudgment or distortion. In law, this often refers to a prejudice, inclination or prejudgment of a question (Aronson & Groves, 2013). In technology and mathematics, 'bias' may refer to a "systemic distortion of a statistical result due to a factor not allowed for in its derivation" (Hughes, Michell & Ramson, 1992, Bias entry). Across the domains of law and technology, bias implies that some parts of the picture are being preferred and others being ignored. Bias is generally recognised as a problem to be managed and something that can affect the integrity and quality of the final result – whether it be a decision by a government official or the ability of an AI system to recognise and match a face accurately. We strive for unbiased AI systems because we implicitly understand and accept that a biased decision is less desirable than an unbiased decision.

Yet there is a tension in our desire for unbiased AI systems because every AI system has some inherent bias. Any AI system is limited, in the sense that it is merely a model or representation of a real world situation (O'Neil, 2016). In designing and implementing the model, choices are made about what to include or exclude. Just as we are becoming increasingly aware of the inherent, unconscious biases that all humans have (Office of Diversity and Outreach, n.d.), so too must we be open to the presence of inherent bias in any AI system or model.

Related notions of 'fairness' and 'equality' are much more complicated – and always have been. There are different formulations and understandings of both 'fairness' and 'equality' across societies, cultures, socioeconomic divides (Office of the Victorian Information Commissioner, 2019). Our understanding of what is fair or equal can change depending on whether we consider it from our position as an individual or between groups; and when we consider the extent to which we can control or influence particular outcomes (Friedler, Scheidegger & Venkatasubramanian, 2016).

Both law and technology offer responses to the philosophical questions of 'what is fair' and 'what is equal', which are informed by and applied within their respective domains. For example, in administrative law, a distinction is drawn between substantive and procedural fairness – the latter attracts remedies in administrative law, whereas the former does not (Aronson & Groves, 2013; Groves, 2017). In discrimination law, a distinction is drawn between equality of outcome and equality of opportunity; some advocate that laws should be directed towards equality of outcome whereas others argue that equality of opportunity is sufficient (Rees et al., 2018). Within the domain of artificial intelligence, 'fairness' can refer to notions of parity between data sets, classifiers and outcomes (see for example Chen, Johansson & Sontag, 2018; Kim, Ghorbani & Zou, 2018; Lahoti, Weikum & Gummadi, 2018; Whittaker et al., 2018). Each of these definitions is workable within the respective domain. However, they necessarily represent particular perspectives which ignore many facets of fairness and equality which may be provided by other perspectives, such as cultural or philosophical perspectives. The difference in language, which in turn is based on a difference of conceptual understanding, makes any discussion about whether an AI system is 'fair' or produces 'equal' results challenging. For present purposes, it is sufficient to note that real differences in language exist and encourage AI users and designers to be transparent about how they define fairness and equality when using such terms.

THE PROMISE OF AI

AI is not the only machine that can discriminate. The human brain has also evolved to be a highly effective discriminating machine, filtering irrelevant information and creating mental heuristics to discriminate quickly between friend and foe, in and out groups. While useful to our early survival in ensuring we could quickly identify a threat and respond to it, these heuristics also inform the stereotypes and quick judgments that underpin or lead to discrimination (Bodenhausen, 1990; Dale, 2015).

We are increasingly aware of the role that unconscious bias and human fallibility play in human decision making and discrimination. Humans segregate prisoners with HIV/AIDS from other prisoners (see *NC v Queensland Corrective Services Commission*, 1997). Humans refuse to make adjustments for people who use different languages, such as refusing to provide an interpreter for a person with a hearing impairment who uses Auslan (see *Woodforth v Queensland*, 2017). Humans have a long history of, and continue to treat female employees unfairly when they are pregnant (Australian Human Rights Commission, 2014). Humans are less inclined to grant parole immediately before lunch than after (Danziger, Levav & Avnaim-Pesso, 2011)[1], are more likely to perceive male candidates as competent and worthy of higher salaries (Moss-Racusin, Dovidio, Brescoll, Graham & Handelsman, 2012) and more likely to prefer names that don't 'sound foreign' (Banerjee, Reitz, & Oreopoulos, 2018; Booth, Leigh, & Varganova, 2012; Chohan, 2016). We suffer from the 'halo effect' (for example, we assume good looking people are also intelligent) and confirmation bias, whereby we look for information that confirms our existing biases and decsions while discarding information that contradicts them. We can become more discriminatory the more objective we think we are (Lattice, 2019; Uhlmann & Cohn, 2007).

Mental heuristics assist us in rendering complex information simple, distinguishing between relevant and irrelevant information and making decisions quickly. Yet these are also the conditions in which an AI system will excel. An AI system can process large amounts of data quickly, differentiating between the relevant and irrelevant and rendering the complex simple.

AI systems may therefore present opportunities to replace or support fallible human decision makers with objective, rational technology systems, thereby reducing the risk of discrimination. AI systems have been used to increase diversity in employment practices (Cowgill, 2018) and select members for company boards (Erel, Stern, Tan, & Weisbach, 2018) as well as increasing access to financial services by traditionally underrepresented consumer cohorts (Gates, Perry & Zorn, 2002).

Replacing humans with AI systems enables data to be sorted and differentiated at high speed and with access to a greater range of data and evidence than humans could process efficiently. AI can be programmed to exclude certain matters from the data set or algorithm more cheaply and effectively than training humans not to have regard to such matters or enforcing laws that prohibit them from doing so. AI does not get tired, hungry or distracted by the challenges of their personal lives.

Even where humans remain in control, AI can inform, support and assist our decisions and functions. AI provides insights and identifies patterns that humans could not effectively or efficiently do alone. AI replaces the gut instincts and reliance on personal experience that often inform human efforts to predict risk with "deep context and … pertinent patterns in data" (Eggers, Schatsky & Viechnicki, 2017, Cognitive insights: Better predictive capabilities section, para, 1).

AI can also promote less discriminatory policy by analysing big data to identify trends, norms and outliers in our social practices and policies. Regulators could use AI systems to understand and monitor how different groups within society are treated in the provision of goods and services and to identify outliers who may be discriminating directly or indirectly. For example, analysing payroll tax, employment data and data about maternity leave payments could reveal insights about which employers have employees end their employment in close proximity to pregnancy or birth, which may in turn invite consideration of whether the employer's policies and practices are directly or indirectly discriminating against women on the basis of pregnancy or status as a parent.

One of the harms inherent with discrimination is that it treats an individual according to the characteristics of the group to which they belong or are assumed to belong, rather than treating the individual on their own merits (Khaitan, 2015). For decades, both policy makers and businesses have sought to decrease their reliance on broad-brush generalisations and potentially discriminatory stereotypes by increasing their understanding of individuals within groups through surveys, statistics and customer research (Henman, 2004). AI systems carry the allure and promise of perfecting targeting and matching, thereby allowing governments and businesses to meet the individual's personal needs – whether it be in the context of social services or music preferences.

Improved targeting of individuals could result in people who are eligible for social security payments being identified and paid their entitlements – 'no more and no less' (Lane, 2017). It could also improve risk-based approaches to the use of state power, reducing the bureaucratic burden on those who are not a risk while focusing resources on those identified as a risk (Henman, 2004). This could reduce the time the average traveller spends at an airport by focusing on persons identified as being a higher risk of infringing immigration requirements (Ajana, 2015; Tay, 2012). Implemented well, such systems carry the promise of reducing friction – for both government and citizen – in the administration of government schemes and functions.

THE DARK SIDE OF AI

AI carries the promise of decreased discrimination and enhanced efficiency. But is that promise always realised?

The Australian Human Rights Commission and World Economic Forum have identified several ways in which AI is susceptible to discriminating and operating unfairly (Australian Human Rights Commission & World Economic Forum, 2019):

- AI is designed by human beings who possess inherent biases and is often trained with data that reflects the imperfect world that we live in.
- Training AI systems with data that is not representative, or using data that reflects bias or prejudice (for example, sexism or racism), can lead to an AI-supported decision that is unfair, unjust, unlawful or otherwise wrong.
- AI's algorithms can include discriminatory variables (for example, including a variable for private school attendance in a loan application algorithm) that results in further discrimination.
- Where users do not understand AI's limitations, especially if they assume AI's predictions to be more accurate and precise (and thus more authoritative) than those made by people, this can result in unfairness.
- AI can be deployed in an inappropriate context (for example, deploying a model in a different cultural context from that in which it was originally trained).
- Personal data is the 'fuel' for AI. It can be at risk when deployed in machine learning models, as hackers can often threaten individual privacy by reverse-engineering algorithms, which could allow access to the personal data the algorithm is trained on.

As AI systems become more prevalent around the world, more examples of discrimination in AI are being discovered, including:

- Amazon's experimental hiring tool, which used AI to review resumes and give job applicants' resumes a score from one to five stars. The experiment was discontinued after Amazon realised that the tool was biased towards men. The data used to train the AI tool was 10 years' worth of resumes submitted to Amazon, most of which came from men because men still represent the vast majority of employees in the technology industry (Dastin, 2018).

- Centrelink's Robodebt algorithm was more likely to raise a disputed or unfair debt for a person with inconsistent income and work hours because it relies on averaging annual income reported to the Australian Taxation Office across 26 fortnights and using that average as evidence of an overpayment in a given fortnight (The Senate Community Affairs References Committee, 2017). This averaging process was later declared by the Federal Court of Australia to be unlawful (Carney, 2019).
- Companies advertising housing on Facebook were permitted to exclude persons of particular races from seeing the advertisements (Angwin & Parris Jr, 2016).
- A US immigration algorithm used to assist immigration officials deciding whether to detain or release a person pending deportation was modified to remove the system recommendation of 'release' – resulting in the only possible answer being 'detain' (Sonnad, 2018).
- Online targeted advertising through popular search engines and email services can change depending on whether the names used in association with those searches and email services are associated with particular racial backgrounds (Pasquale, 2015).
- AI systems used to predict a person's risk of recidivism underestimate the recidivism risk of white people while overestimating the recidivism risk of black people – and ultimately are no more accurate than random human decision makers (Angwin, Larson, Mattu, & Kirchner, 2016).
- Voice recognition software appears to respond more accurately to male voices than female and people with certain accents and first languages (Bajorek, 2019).
- An algorithm used in the US health care system assigned the same level of risk to white and black patients, even when the black patients were objectively sicker than the white patients. This reduced the number of black patients referred for extra care (Obermeyer, Powers, Vogeli & Mullainathan, 2019).

In some of these examples, the cause of discrimination was identified. Often, the data used to train the AI system was found to be biased, which in turn affected the bias of the AI system. In many, but not all of these examples, the discrimination was unintended. Understanding the cause of any discriminatory outcome often requires access to the AI system itself, the data used to train the system and the data used by the AI system when operating. The causes for discrimination are more readily identifiable when the system is subjected to scrutiny eiter by the developer (as was the case with the Amazon experimental hiring tool) or independent researchers (as was the case with the US health care system algorithm).

We readily recognise discrimination in an AI system when we can identify that a person has been unfairly denied a service, opportunity or resource or, alternatively, has been unfairly targeted for scrutiny, investigation or suspicion. This form of harm is described as "allocative harm" (Whittaker et al., 2018, p. 25). It is the type of harm that most aligns with our understanding of direct discrimination – a person denied or targeted for something based on an attribute or characteristic that is unrelated to the outcome. The bail and sentencing algorithms are recognised as being unfair and discriminatory when they produce outcomes that are more influenced by a person's racial background than the crimes they have committed, or are alleged to have committed. The Amazon resume algorithm is recognised as unfair because it gives too much weight to being male without any evidence that men develop better software than women.

Discrimination in AI systems can also produce an additional, systematic harm, known as "representational harm", which involves the reproducing and application of harmful stereotypes (Whittaker et al., 2018, p. 25). Targeted online advertising algorithms are harmful not just because they result in people of colour being targeted for some services (such as exploitative loan and debt recovery services) or missing opportunities for other services (such as housing or certain types of jobs), but because they reinforce stereotypes about people of colour. The AI systems in turn absorb the lessons of these reinforced stereotypes, producing even more discrimination in the AI system. This phenomenon can be seen in Microsoft's chatbot, Tay, which, without the intention of its designers, learnt to be racist. Designed to learn from the tweets it was sent, Tay was vulnerable to learning (and did learn) to be racist after it was sent tweets containing intentionally racist and offensive content (Metz, 2016).

The interaction between human and AI systems can contribute to representational harms becoming allocative harms by converting, over time, an ostensibly neutral and objective AI system into one with discriminatory effect. For example, an AI system may identify (or 'flag') a child at risk of abuse using non-discriminatory characteristics. A human acts on this flag to conduct an investigation into the circumstances of the child and their family. The investigation produces more data about the family, which is fed back into the AI system – enhancing the specificity of the algorithm in respect of the investigated family and families with similar characteristics. As a result, more children in similar situations are flagged – not necessarily because they are more at risk of abuse, but because there is more data about children like them in the AI system. The effect is discriminatory, without the design necessarily being so (Eubanks, 2018; Whittaker et al., 2018).

Like all discrimination, representational harm is not the sole province of AI. Representational harm can also be seen in the discriminatory practices of humans and cultures of "deep-seated, pervasive prejudice that lingers" (Rice, 2013, p. 6). Discrimination laws have traditionally not addressed or dealt with representational harm, preferring instead to focus on individual acts, harms and "overt, explicit and formal inequality" (Rice, 2013, p. 6). This preference for the overt and tangible discrimination is reflected in discussions about reducing discrimination in AI, which focus is on the reduction of allocative harm, rather than representational harm (Whittaker et al., 2018).

DETECTING DISCRIMATION IN AI SYSTEMS

Identifying that discrimination has occurred has always been a difficult task. In the words of Justice Kirby of the High Court of Australia, "human motivation is complex, [d]iscriminatory conduct can rarely be ascribed to a single "reason" or "ground"' … and "much discrimination occurs unconsciously, thoughtlessly or ignorantly" (*IW v City of Perth,* 1997, pp. 59, 63). A person alleging discrimination is at a disadvantage, because the information relevant to whether discrimination has occurred or not is held by the alleged discriminator – who may be under no obligation to explain their decision and may not even be aware of the full reasons for their decision (Allen, 2009).

These problems are present and compounded in the case of AI systems. AI systems allow a fragmentation of responsibility for any particular decision or action. The person designing the AI system is likely to be different to the person using the AI system. When the user of the AI system is asked for an explanation, the most common response will be "because the computer said so" (O'Neil, 2016, p. 8).

Furthermore, technologists have focused much of their developments and research efforts on refining the outputs of AI systems, rather than explaining why those outputs are produced. The problem of 'explainability' has attracted more research attention in recent years, but researchers are playing catch up (Nunes & Jannach, 2017).

For a person who has been the subject of AI discrimination, the following barriers exist to understanding what has occurred:

1. The individual affected may not realise that an AI system has been used in making the decision or taking the action that affects them.
2. The user of the AI system may not be obliged to provide an explanation. This is generally the case where the decision or action is taken in a commercial setting. While there is a limited obligation to provide reasons in respect of some government decisions,[2] that obligation may not extend to assistance provided by an AI system, e.g. where a risk assessment is provided to a human who ultimately makes the decision.
3. The AI system may not be capable of producing an explanation. Increasingly advanced forms of artificial neural networks are producing outcomes based on correlations and patterns that are unseen to the human eye. From the perspective of data analytics, this is one of the key strengths of advanced neural networks. From an explainability perspective, it is a significant barrier.
4. The designer of the AI system may resist disclosing the AI system's reasoning process in order to maintain commercial and competitive advantages and secrecy. This is described as the 'black box' problem (Pasquale, 2015, Whittaker et al., 2018).
5. While the AI system may be able to produce an audit trail of the factors considered, such a trail may not extend to identifying why those factors have been marked as relevant to the decision or recommendation made by the AI system (Nunes & Jannach, 2017; Pasquale, 2017). Given that the power of an AI system is to identify and learn patterns drawn from large datasets over time, the answer to a question about the relevance of a particular feature may lie in millions of algorithmic cycles.

Technology can assist in helping disparate individuals understand that they share the experience of adverse action from an AI system. Social media in particular is an effective way of individuals sharing their experiences and 'connecting the dots' (Miller, 2017) to understand that they have been subject to an algorithm. For example, our collective understanding of the technology system utilised by Centrelink to automatically raise debts (colloquially described as 'Robodebt') owes, in large part, to social media. The issue first came to mainstream attention after individuals posted on social media that they had received debt notices which they did not understand. Social media helped similarly affected individuals to realise that they were subject to an automated system, rather than traditional, individualised human decision making. Social media facilitated the spread of understanding of how the system operated and tools and techniques to challenge it. Social media connected affected individuals with experts and advisors and created a community of sufficient size to attract attention from the media, politicians and oversight bodies. Following the Federal Court's declaration that debts were unlawful where they were based on a process of averaging, social media has continued to spread information about the scope and implications of the Court's decision and to connect affected individuals with resources to deal with their specific debt (Carney, 2019).

Acting on this shared experience can be difficult due to the problem of explainability. In Europe, art. 22 of the General Data Protection Regulation (GDPR) attempts to remedy this by introducing rights in respect of automated decision making, requiring safeguards that may include a right to obtain an explanation of a decision reached and to receive meaningful information about the logic involved in automated decision-making (Kaminski, 2019). Such protections are limited in operation and have not been introduced into Australian law.

ADDRESSING DISCRIMINATION

Although some anti-discrimination bodies have the power to consider systemic discrimination, Australia's discrimination laws are still based on a model of individuals making complaints about specific incidents of discrimination (Rees et al., 2018). Given the barriers to individuals identifying that they have been discriminated against by an AI system or understanding how that discrimination has occurred, the model of individual complaint is ill-equipped to effectively address discrimination in AI systems.

Technologists are aware of the problems posed by discrimination, bias and inequality in AI systems. The pursuit of 'fairness' in AI systems is increasingly a field of research. Researchers are posing different algorithms, mathematical techniques and definitions of 'fairness' to counter biases in datasets or discriminatory outcomes (See for example Chen, Johansson & Sontag, 2018; Kim, Ghorbani & Zou, 2018; Lahoti, Weikum & Gummadi, 2018; Whittaker et al., 2018).

It is unlikely that the problem of discrimination in AI systems will be solved by mathematics alone. Humans remain the designers, trainers and operators of AI systems – they are made in our image and reflect our own imperfect biases and prejudices. For mathematical solutions to fairness to be effective, they must be developed within 'a framework that accounts for social and political contexts and histories'. Without such a framework, mathematical 'solutions' may "serve to paper over deeper problems in ways that ultimately increase harm or ignore justice" (Whittaker et al., 2018, p. 8).

The benefits of AI systems – such as increased efficiency and insights – largely accrue to the operators of AI systems who implement them within existing business or government practices. Just as a company or government agency would be responsible for any discriminatory actions of their staff, policies or procedures, so too should they be responsible for any discriminatory actions or decisions made by the AI systems they implement. This imperative is made stronger by the increasing understanding of the risks of discrimination in AI systems. If a body knowingly imports such risk into their services and practices, it is not fair to then outsource the costs of those risks occurring to customers, citizens and the public.

For Victorian public authorities, the obligation to consider the potentially discriminatory effects of an AI system is even clearer. The *Charter of Human Rights and Responsibilities Act 2006* (Vic) (Charter) obliges public authorities to consider and act compatibly with human rights. One of those rights is the right to recognition and equality before the law, which includes the right to equal and effective protection against discrimination.

Operators of AI systems should review and monitor their AI systems for indicators of discrimination, bias and inequality. This requires consideration across the 'full stack supply chain' of an AI system, encompassing the "origins and use of training data, test data, models, application program interfaces (APIs) and other infrastructural components over a product life cycle" (Whittaker et al., 2018, p. 5). In particular, an operator of an AI system should:

- Ask the vendor of the AI system about how it has been programmed and trained to counter potentially discriminatory actions;
- Consider the effects of choices made in designing the model expressed in the AI system;
- Consider and test for potential discrimination embedded in any training data;
- Supervise machine learning to detect early if the AI system is learning to be discriminatory in process or outcome; and
- Test regularly the outcomes of AI systems to identify if it is producing unequal results that may reflect discrimination and/or bias.

Discovering that your AI system is discriminatory after it has been implemented costs time, money and public trust and confidence. Remedying or retraining a discriminatory AI system is rarely a matter of 'tweaking' and often requires abandoning an existing system and developing a new one (Office of the Victorian Information Commissioner, 2019). Taking a proactive approach by involving affected communities can assist designers of AI systems to better understand the problem the AI system is trying to solve, the data on which the AI system is to be trained and the effects of the AI system (Whittaker et al., 2018).

CALIBRATING AI WITH HUMAN RIGHTS

Just as a mathematical understanding of fairness is not adequate alone to address discrimination in AI, the lens of discrimination alone is inadequate to understanding equality.

Laws against discrimination ensure that people are not treated unequally on the basis of protected attributes. However, laws prohibiting discrimination alone are insufficient to ensure that everyone is treated equally. As discussed above, concepts like 'equality' and 'fairness' are understood differently depending on our social, cultural, philosophical and ideological standpoints. In a liberal democracy, we accept some forms of inequality (such as those based on income), while prohibiting others (such as those based on gender) (Haack & Sieweke, 2018). Even when discrimination is prohibited, inequality can remain due to the complex interaction of social, economic and legal practices. Pay discrimination on the basis of gender has been illegal since the 1970s, yet a gender pay gap remains (Workplace Gender Equality Agency, 2019). Understanding 'equality' requires us to understand how much and which types of inequality we accept and are prepared to justify.

Within the legal context, attempts have been made to reframe the contest about what constitutes 'equality' by understanding equality as fundamental to human dignity and protected to a minimum standard when rights and freedoms which are recognised as common to all humans and integral to human dignity are respected. In Victoria, those rights and freedoms find expression in the Charter.[3]

AI systems engage human rights directly and indirectly; that is, both through the direct operation of AI systems and indirectly by affecting the ability and confidence of persons to exercise their human rights.

THE RIGHT TO EQUALITY BEFORE THE LAW

Given the preceding discussion about discrimination in AI systems, it is clear that AI systems engage the right to recognition and equality before the law, which expressly includes the right to protection from discrimination.

The right to equality before the law "prohibits treatment based on distinctions between persons which are arbitrary, in the sense of lacking objective justification, in the application and administration of the law" (*Re Lifestyle Communities Ltd (No 3)*, 2009a, para. 137-141; *Re Lifestyle Communities Ltd (No 3)*, 2009b, para. 287-288). In developing AI systems to apply and administer the law, there is a real question about whether distinctions drawn by AI based on group characteristics, correlations and imperfect data can be considered as having 'objective justification' and are therefore not arbitrary.

The right to equal protection of the law without discrimination and equal and effective protection against discrimination requires equality in both the content and outcome of the law. It is not sufficient to ensure that the processes or opportunities are equal; the outcome or the law in action must also be similar across different types of people. As such, both the process and outcomes produced by an AI system must be non discriminatory. The right to equal protection of the law protects against the possibility that discriminatory outcomes of an AI system – such as disproportionately misidentifying black faces or targeting for audit or inspection women of child-bearing age – cannot be ignored or excused on the basis that the code was not designed to be discriminatory.

THE RIGHT TO PRIVACY

The right to privacy is most obviously engaged by AI. It is a concept that 'defies precise definition' (Pound & Evans, 2019). With each new era of technology comes a new concept of privacy. The existing paradigm that underpins most privacy legislation in Australia is 'information privacy', which is closely related to the concept of 'data protection' and was developed when computerised databases and ecommerce were the new technologies challenging our sense of privacy. The growth of cloud computing and algorithmic search functions has prompted debates about our right to be forgotten (Belbin, 2018). AI, combined with drones, CCTV networks and digital tracking, provokes debates about spatial privacy, the right to be left alone and the right to obscurity (Selinger & Hartzog, 2014).

Implicit in these concepts about privacy is a recognition that privacy has traditionally been protected by practical limitations. It was once very expensive to undertake widespread surveillance and it was therefore unnecessary to express legal protections in great detail. Advances in technology, including AI, have made surveillance cheap and access to it universal and easy. Our laws have not adapted to recognise this reality and our debates about the privacy impact of AI continue to be characterised by a legal standard developed for a less invasive form of technology.

Under the Charter, the right to privacy is expressed as a right not to have your privacy, family, home or correspondence unlawfully or arbitrarily interfered with; and not to have your reputation unlawfully attacked (*Charter of Human Rights and Responsibilities Act*, 2006, s. 13). Arbitrary interferences with privacy may include interferences that are "capricious and not based on any identifiable criterion or criteria" (*WBM v Chief Commissioner of Police*, 2010, para. 51-57) and interferences that are "unreasonable in the sense of not being proportionate to a legitimate aim sought" (*WBM v Chief Commissioner of Police*, 2010, para. 202; see Pound & Evans, 2019).[4] AI systems involve potentially arbitrary interferences with privacy. For many computer scientists, the answer to poor AI outcomes is often 'more data'. Yet the more data collected, the more the data collection approaches capriciousness and is disproportionate to the end sought. As AI advances, it is capable of taking more actions that cannot be explained by the humans programming the system. As the criteria on which actions are taken become less identifiable, the more AI systems start to act in ways that seem capricious and unreasonable.

FREEDOMS OF ASSOCIATION, EXPRESSION AND MOVEMENT

AI systems may also indirectly engage some of the 'freedom' rights, such as the freedom of movement, freedom of expression and freedom of association. While an algorithm per se does not stop a person moving about Victoria, expressing their views verbally or in print, or joining groups, AI systems do facilitate the surveillance of such activities. AI systems regularly use data from devices that we carry with us daily, especially our mobile phones and tablets. AI system are fed and can produce data about where we are and with whom. We are already familiar with advertising targeted to particular mobile devices in particular locations. It is just as possible that such technology could be used in ways that deter people from exercising their freedoms.

When the machine can know us better than we know ourselves – know when we are pregnant (Hill, 2012), seeking mental health services or associating with people who may be seen as undesirable – we are each compelled to take evasive action on a daily basis, never knowing when our actions may be captured by the AI system and rendered meaningful. The feeling of being watched may alone be sufficient to deter people – especially those from marginalised or minority groups – from feeling truly free to exercise their human rights. People with characteristics flagged as 'risky' and subjected to increased monitoring may find themselves needing to 'do more to prove and justify themselves simply because they 'look' like past transgressors' (Henman, 2004).

Some European authorities have found that storage of personal information on registers as a means of surveillance constituted an unjustified interference with the rights of freedom of assembly and expression, even where it had not been established that the person's exercise of their rights had in fact been hindered (*Segerstedt-Wiberg v Sweden,* 2006; *Segerstedt-Wiberg v Sweden,* 2007). In Victoria and the UK, courts and tribunals have been less willing to accept that collection and storage alone will constitute an unjustified interference without evidence that there has, in fact, been a 'chilling effect' and persons in fact deterred from exercising their freedoms (see for example *Caripis v Victoria Police*, 2012, [76] ; *R (Countryside Alliance) v Attorney General*, 2007, [17]; *R (Countryside Alliance) v Attorney General*, 2008).

FURTHER RESEARCH DIRECTIONS

A problem with understanding the extent of discrimination that might result from decisions by AIs is the lack of data that exists about AI decision making processes. Current attempts to ensure AI and algorithmic accountability, for example, the 2019 US Algorithmic Accountability Bill, the New Jersey Algorithmic Accountability Act, and the Californian and Washington State bills, seek to make AI users conduct impact assessments about issues such as bias, discrimination, privacy, and security as well as regular audits (Chae, 2020). This proposed legislation is either not ratified or not implemented but one area of further research is to monitor and evaluate such attempts to ensure some measure of AI accountability.

CONCLUSION

AI systems are discriminating, data hoarding machines that provide the means for surveillance. While AI systems have the potential to both help or harm humans, they are not neutral. At every stage of their development and use, AI systems can discriminate in ways that adversely and unfairly affect humans. As with so many technological advances experienced in the 21st century, "trying to put it all into context [can be] overwhelming" (Frankl, 2017, para. 1).

Before we can (re-)act, we must first understand what is happening. We need to appreciate and recognise the different ways in which we understand and use the language of 'fairness', 'equality' and 'discrimination'. We need to understand how AI systems work technically, both generally and in specific applications. We also need to better understand the ways in which AI operates on a practical level, which includes understanding the experiences of people who are subject to AI systems.

We are well placed to appreciate and recognise our different concepts of 'fairness', 'equality' and 'discrimination'. Such concepts have been discussed, debated and developed for centuries and, from a legal perspective, especially so in the last 50 years as human rights and equal opportunity legislation has developed. Continuing to engage in these discussions, especially across domains of expertise and experience, will provide us with a shared language in which to discuss the larger challenges presented by AI systems.

Mullainathan (2019) has suggested that algorithmic bias and discrimination may be easier to solve than the human variety. However, this assumes that we have access to, and understanding of, the AI system in question. Our understanding of how AI systems work technically is hampered by both the pace of technological change and the proporietary nature of many AI systems. The proprietary interests of developers of AI systems are protected by copyright and contract laws, which may also need to be revisited to determine if the balance between commercial interests and transparency remains appropriate.

We have a limited understanding of how AI is operating on a practical level and the experiences of people subject to AI systems. Some institutions, such as the UK Parliament and the Australian Human Rights Commission, have sought to enhance our understanding with broad ranging inquiries into the social, ethical, economic and human rights implications of AI (UK Parliament, 2018; Australian Human Rights Commission & World Economic Forum, 2019). While such inquiries are to be welcomed, they will have limited effect on the direction of the law if governments do not respond to the issues identified and recommendations offered.

There are several barriers to individuals understanding when and how they have been affected by AI. Both designers of AI systems and lawmakers have a potential role to play in proactively monitoring the operation and effects of AI systems. Where existing laws and practice are inadequate to provide the necessary information, laws promoting or requiring transparency, monitoring and auditing of AI systems may need to be contemplated.

In their current form, laws that protect against discrimination and promote equal opportunity and human rights are likely to be too slow to prevent large-scale discrimination from AI systems. Laws that rely on individuals to identify discrimination and its cause and react to it are no match for high volume, high speed actions of AI systems.

AI systems are not neutral and neither are our laws. Whatever your perspective, the adequacy of our laws and the fairness of our AI systems needs increased attention and reform.

REFERENCES

Ajana, B. (2015). Augmented borders: Big data and the ethics of immigration control. *Journal of Information. Communication & Ethics in Society*, *13*(1), 58–78. doi:10.1108/JICES-01-2014-0005

Allen, D. (2009). Reducing the burden of proving discrimination in Australia. *The Sydney Law Review*, *31*(4), 579–605.

Angwin, J., Larson, J., Mattu, S., & Kirchner, L. (2016). Machine bias there's software used across the country to predict future criminals. And it's biased against blacks. *ProPublica*. Retrieved from https://www.propublica.org/article/machine-bias-risk-assessments-in-criminal-sentencing

Angwin, J., & Parris, T., Jr. (2016). Facebook lets advertisers exclude users by race. *ProPublica*. Retrieved from https://www.propublica.org/article/facebook-lets-advertisers-exclude-users-by-race

Aronson, M., & Groves, M. (2013). *Judicial Review of Administrative Action* (5th ed.). Pyrmont, Australia: Thomson Reuters.

Australian Human Rights Commission. (2002). *Annual report 2001-2002: Human rights and equal opportunity commission*. Retrieved from https://www.humanrights.gov.au/our-work/commission-general/publications/annual-report-2001-2002-human-rights-and-equal-opportunity

Australian Human Rights Commission. (2009). *DDA conciliation: Goods, services and facilities*. Retrieved from https://www.humanrights.gov.au/our-work/disability-rights/dda-conciliation-goods-services-and-facilities

Australian Human Rights Commission. (2014). *Supporting working parents: Pregnancy and return to work national review*. Retrieved from https://www.humanrights.gov.au/our-work/sex-discrimination/projects/supporting-working-parents-pregnancy-and-return-work-national

Australian Human Rights Commission & World Economic Forum. (2019). *Artificial intelligence: Governance and leadership*. Retrieved from https://tech.humanrights.gov.au/sites/default/files/2019-02/AHRC_WEF_AI_WhitePaper2019.pdf

Bajorek, J. P. (2019). Voice recognition still has significant race and gender biases. *Harvard Business Review*. Retrieved from https://hbr.org/2019/05/voice-recognition-still-has-significant-race-and-gender-biases

Banerjee, R., Reitz, J. G., & Oreopoulos, P. (2018). Do large employers treat racial minorities more fairly? An analysis of Canadian field experiment data. *Canadian Public Policy*, *44*(1), 1–12. doi:10.3138/cpp.2017-033

Belbin, R. (2018). When Google becomes the norm: The case for privacy and the right to be forgotten. *Dalhousie Journal of Legal Studies*, *26*, 17–35.

Bodenhausen, G. V. (1990). Stereotypes as judgmental heuristics: Evidence of circadian variations in discrimination. *Psychological Science*, *1*(5), 319–322. doi:10.1111/j.1467-9280.1990.tb00226.x

Booth, A. L., Leigh, A., & Varganova, E. (2012). Does ethnic discrimination vary across minority groups? Evidence from a field experiment. *Oxford Bulletin of Economics and Statistics*, *74*(4), 547–573. doi:10.1111/j.1468-0084.2011.00664.x

Buolamwini, J., & Gebru, T. (2018). Gender Shades: Intersectional accuracy disparities in commercial gender classification. *Proceedings of Machine Learning Research*, *81*, 1-15. Retrieved from http://proceedings.mlr.press/v81/buolamwini

Caripis v Victoria Police [2012] VCAT 1472.

Carney, T. (2019). Robodebt failed its day in court, what now? *The Conversation*. Retrieved from http://theconversation.com/robodebt-failed-its-day-in-court-what-now-127984

Chae, Y. (2020). U.S. AI regulation guide: Legislative overview and practical considerations. *The Journal of Robotics. Artificial Intelligence and Law*, *3*(1), 17–40. Retrieved from https://www.bakermckenzie.com/-/media/files/people/chae-yoon/rail-us-ai-regulation-guide.pdf

Charter of Human Rights and Responsibilities Act. (2006). Vic.

Chen, I., Johansson, F. D., & Sontag, D. (2018). Why is my classifier discriminatory? *Advances in Neural Information Processing Systems*, *31*, 3539–3550.

Chohan, U. W. (2016). Skin deep: Should Australia consider name-blind resumes? *The Conversation*. Retrieved from https://theconversation.com/skin-deep-should-australia-consider-name-blind-resumes-55503

Cowgill, B. (2018) *Bias and productivity in humans and algorithms: Theory and evidence from resume screening*. Retrieved from http://conference.iza.org/conference_files/MacroEcon_2017/cowgill_b8981.pdf

Dale, S. (2015). Heuristics and biases: The science of decision-making. *Business Information Review*, *32*(2), 93–99. doi:10.1177/0266382115592536

Daniels v Hunter Water Board (1994) EOC 92-626.

Danziger, S., Levav, J., & Avnaim-Pesso, L. (2011). Extraneous factors in judicial decisions. *Proceedings of the National Academy of Sciences of the United States of America*, *108*(17), 6889–6892. doi:10.1073/pnas.1018033108 PMID:21482790

Dastin, J. (2018). Amazon scraps secret AI recruiting tool that showed bias against women. *Reuters*. Retrieved from https://www.reuters.com/article/us-amazon-com-jobs-automation-insight-idUSKCN1MK08G

Dorner, J., Blair, D., & Bernard, J. R. L. (Eds.). (1998). *Macquarie pocket dictionary* (3rd ed.). Milton, Australia: John Wiley & Sons.

Eggers, W. D., Schatsky, D., & Viechnicki, P. (2017). AI-augmented government using cognitive technologies to redesign public sector work. *Deloitte Insights*. Retrieved from https://www2.deloitte.com/us/en/insights/focus/cognitive-technologies/artificial-intelligence-government.html

Equal Opportunity Act. (2010). Vic.

Erel, I., Stern, L. H., Tan, C., & Weisbach, M. S. (2018). Selecting directors using machine learning. *National Bureau* of *Economic Research*. Retrieved from https://www.nber.org/papers/w24435.pdf

Eubanks, V. (2018). *Automating inequality: How high-tech tools profile, police, and punish the poor.* New York, NY: St. Martin's Press.

Frankl, P. (2017). Legal technology developments are overwhelming. *Legal Practice Intelligence.* Retrieved from https://www.legalpracticeintelligence.com.au/legal-technology-developments-are-overwhelming-start-here

Friedler, S. A., Scheidegger, C., & Venkatasubramanian, S. (2016). *On the (im)possibility of fairness.* Retrieved from https://arxiv.org/abs/1609.07236

Gates, S. W., Perry, V. G., & Zorn, P. M. (2002). Automated underwriting in mortgage lending: Good news for the underserved? *Housing Policy Debate, 13*(2), 369–391. doi:10.1080/10511482.2002.9521447

Groves, M. (2017). The unfolding purpose of fairness. *Federal Law Review, 45*(4), 653–679. doi:10.22145/flr.45.4.8

Haack, P., & Sieweke, J. (2018). The legitimacy of inequality: Integrating the perspectives of system justification and social judgment. *Journal of Management Studies, 55*(3), 486–516. doi:10.1111/joms.12323

Henman, P. (2004). Targeted!: Population segmentation, electronic surveillance and governing the unemployed in Australia. *International Sociology, 19*(2), 173–191. doi:10.1177/0268580904042899

Hill, K. (2012). How Target figured out a teen girl was pregnant before her father did. *Forbes.* Retrieved from https://www.forbes.com/sites/kashmirhill/2012/02/16/how-target-figured-out-a-teen-girl-was-pregnant-before-her-father-did/#79bfe7d66668

Hughes, J. M., Michell, P. A., & Ramson, W. S. (Eds.). (1992). *The Australian concise Oxford dictionary* (2nd ed.). Melbourne, Australia: Oxford University Press.

IW v City of Perth (1997) 191 CLR 1.

Kaminski, M. E. (2019). The right to explanation, explained. *Berkeley Technology Law Journal, 34*(1), 189–218. doi:10.15779/Z38TD9N83H

Khaitan, T. (2015). *A theory of discrimination law.* Oxford, UK: Oxford University Press. doi:10.1093/acprof:oso/9780199656967.001.0001

Kim, M. P., Ghorbani, A., & Zou, J. (2018). *Multiaccuracy: Black-box post-processing for fairness in classification.* Retrieved from https://arxiv.org/abs/1805.12317

Krywko, J. (2017). Siri can't talk to me: The challenge of teaching language to voice assistants. *Ars Technica.* Retrieved from https://arstechnica.com/information-technology/2017/12/teaching-old-virtual-assistants-new-language-tricks/

Lahoti, P., Weikum, G., & Gummadi, K. P. (2018). *IFair: Learning individually fair data representations for algorithmic decision making.* Retrieved from https://arxiv.org/abs/1806.01059

Lane, S. (2017). Interview with Christian Porter minister for social services. *ABC AM*. Retrieved from https://formerministers.dss.gov.au/17352/radio-interview-abc-am/

Lattice. (2019). *How to reduce unconscious bias at work*. Retrieved from https://lattice.com/library/how-to-reduce-unconscious-bias-at-work

Metz, R. (2016). Why Microsoft's teen chatbot, Tay, said lots of awful things online. *MIT Technology Review*. Retrieved from https://www.technologyreview.com/s/601111/why-microsoft-accidentally-unleashed-a-neo-nazi-sexbot/

Miller, K. (2017). Connecting the dots: A case study of the robodebt communities.' *AIAL Forum, 89*, 50-58.

Moss-Racusin, C. A., Dovidio, J. F., Brescoll, V. L., Graham, M. J., & Handelsman, J. (2012). Science faculty's subtle gender biases favor male students. *Proceedings of the National Academy of Sciences of the United States of America, 109*(41), 16474–16479. doi:10.1073/pnas.1211286109 PMID:22988126

Mullainathan, S. (2019). Biased algorithms are easier to fix than biased people. *The New York Times*. Retrieved from https://www.nytimes.com/2019/12/06/business/algorithm-bias-fix.html

NC v Queensland Corrective Services Commission (1997) QADT 22.

Nunes, I., & Jannach, D. (2017). A systematic review and taxonomy of explanations in decision support and recommender systems. *User Modeling and User-Adapted Interaction, 27*(3-5), 393–444. doi:10.100711257-017-9195-0

O'Neil, C. (2016). *Weapons of math destruction: How big data increases inequality and threatens democracy*. New York, NY: Crown Publishers.

Obermeyer, Z., Powers, B., Vogeli, C., & Mullainathan, S. (2019). Dissecting racial bias in an algorithm used to manage the health of populations. *Science, 366*(6464), 447–453. doi:10.1126cience.aax2342 PMID:31649194

Office of Diversity and Outreach. (n.d.). *State of science on unconscious bias*. Retrieved from https://diversity.ucsf.edu/resources/state-science-unconscious-bias

Office of the Victorian Information Commissioner. (2019). *Submission to DIIS on artificial intelligence: Australia's ethics framework discussion paper*. Retrieved from https://ovic.vic.gov.au/resource/submission-to-diis-on-artificial-intelligence-australias-ai-ethics-framework-discussion-paper/

Parliament, U. K. (2018). *AI in the UK: ready, willing and able*. Retrieved from https://publications.parliament.uk/pa/ld201719/ldselect/ldai/100/100.pdf

Pasquale, F. (2015). *The black box society: The secret algorithms that control money and information*. Cambridge, MA: Harvard University Press. doi:10.4159/harvard.9780674736061

Pasquale, F. (2017). Toward a fourth law of robotics: Preserving attribution, responsibility, and explainability in an algorithmic society. *Ohio State Law Journal, 78*, 1243–1255.

Pound, A., & Evans, K. (2019). Annotated Victorian charter of rights (2nd ed.). Pyrmont, Australia: Thomson Reuters (Professional) Australia Limited.

R (Countryside Alliance) v Attorney General (2007) UKHL 52.

R (Countryside Alliance) v Attorney General (2008) AC 719.

Re Lifestyle Communities Ltd (No 3) (2009a) 31 VAR 286.

Re Lifestyle Communities Ltd (No 3) (2009b) VCAT 1869.

Rees, N., Rice, S., & Allen, D. (2018). *Australian anti-discrimination and equal opportunity law* (3rd ed.). Alexandria, Australia: Federation Press.

Rice, S. (2013). *Basic instinct: The heroic project of anti-discrimination law (Roma Mitchell oration)*. Retrieved from https://eoc.sa.gov.au/sites/default/files/inline-files/Rice_Basic%20Instinct_Roma%20 Mitchell%20Oration_0.pdf

Segerstedt-Wiberg v Sweden (2006) ECHR 597.

Segerstedt-Wiberg v Sweden (2007) 44 EHRR 2.

Selinger, E., & Hartzog, W. (2014). Obscurity and privacy (SSRN Scholarly Paper No ID 2439866). *Social Science Research Network*. Retrieved from https://papers.ssrn.com/abstract=2439866

Solonec, T. (2000). Racial discrimination in the private rental market: Overcoming stereotypes and breaking the cycle of housing despair in Western Australia. *Indigenous Law Bulletin*, *5*(2), 4–6.

Sonnad, N. (2018). US border agents hacked their "risk assessment" system to recommend detention 100% of the time. *Quartz*. Retrieved from https://qz.com/1314749/us-border-agents-hacked-their-risk-assessment-system-to-recommend-immigrant-detention-every-time/

Street v Queensland Bar Association (1989) 168 CLR 461.

Tay, L. (2012). Immigration targets 'problem travellers' with analytics. *Itnews*. Retrieved from https:// www.itnews.com.au/news/immigration-targets-problem-travellers-with-analytics-321562

The Senate Community Affairs References Committee. (2017). Design, scope, cost-benefit analysis, contracts awarded and implementation associated with the better management of the social welfare system initiative. *Commonwealth of Australia*. Retrieved from https://www.aph.gov.au/Parliamentary_Business/ Committees/Senate/Community_Affairs/SocialWelfareSystem/Report

Toratani, M., Konno, M., Asai, A., Koseki, J., Kawamoto, K., Tamari, K., ... Ishii, H. (2018). A convolutional neural network uses microscopic images to differentiate between mouse and human cell lines and their radioresistent clones. *Cancer Research*, *78*(23), 6703–6707. doi:10.1158/0008-5472.CAN-18-0653 PMID:30254144

Uhlmann, E. L., & Cohen, G. L. (2007). I think it, therefore it's true: Effects of self-perceived objectivity on hiring discrimination. *Organizational Behavior and Human Decision Processes*, *104*(2), 207–223. doi:10.1016/j.obhdp.2007.07.001

Walsh, T. (2019). Understanding AI. In Office of the Victorian Information Commissioner (Ed.), Closer to the machine: Technical, social and legal aspects of AI (pp. 7-22). Melbourne, Australia: Office of the Victorian Information Commissioner.

Waterhouse v Bell (1991) 25 NSWLR 99.

WBM v Chief Commissioner of Police (2010) 27 VR 469, VSC 219.

Whittaker, M., Crawford, K., Dobbe, R., Fried, G., Kaziunas, E., Mathur, V., … Schwartz, O. (2018). AI now report 2018. *AI Now Institute New York University*. Retrieved from https://ainowinstitute.org/AI_Now_2018_Report.pdf

Woodforth v Queensland (2017) QCA 100.

Workplace Gender Equality Agency. (2019). *Gender pay gap statistics*. Retrieved from https://www.wgea.gov.au/data/fact-sheets/australias-gender-pay-gap-statistics

ADDITIONAL READING

Alarie, B., Niblett, A., & Yoon, A. H. (2018). How artificial intelligence will affect the practice of law. *University of Toronto Law Journal, 68*(5supplement 1), 106–124. doi:10.3138/utlj.2017-0052

Chen, F., & Zhou, J. (2019). AI in the public interest. In Office of the Victorian Information Commissioner (Ed.), Closer to the machine: Technical, social and legal aspects of AI (pp. 63-77). Melbourne, Australia: Office of the Victorian Information Commissioner.

Dalenberg, D. (2018). Preventing discrimination in the automated targeting of job advertisements. *Computer Law & Security Review: The International Journal of Technology Law and Practice, 34*(3), 615–627. doi:10.1016/j.clsr.2017.11.009

Stern, S. (2018). Introduction: Artificial intelligence, technology, and the law. *University of Toronto Law Journal, 68*(supplement 1), 1–11. doi:10.3138/utlj.2017-0102

Sullivan, C. A. (2018). Employing AI. *Villanova Law Review, 63*(3), 395–429.

Weinshall-Margel, K., & Shapard, J. (2011). Overlooked factors in the analysis of parole decisions. *Proceedings of the National Academy of Sciences of the United States of America, 108*(42), E833–E834. doi:10.1073/pnas.1110910108 PMID:21987788

KEY TERMS AND DEFINITIONS

Artifical Intelligence: Involves the use of computers or software programs designed to perform tasks generally performed by humans.

Bias: Refers to a predisposition, prejudgment or distortion. In law, this often refers to a prejudice, inclination or prejudgment of a question (Aronson & Groves, 2013).

Direct Discrimination: Occurs when a person is treated less favourably *because of* an attribute that is protected by law, such as race, gender, religious belief or (dis)ability.

Discrimination: Involves treating, or proposing to treat, someone unfavourably because of a personal characteristic protected by law (Rees, Rice, & Allen, 2018).

Indirect Discrimination: Requires consideration of how an ostensibly neutral action affects people with one or more protected attributes. For example, preferring to employ people who can attend work at 8am may indirectly discriminate against parents who have child care responsibilities for young or school-aged children.

ENDNOTES

[1]	However the results have been disputed by Weinshall-Margel & Shapard (2011) who suggest that the legal representation of prisoners may have more influence than the hunger of parole officials.

[2]	For example, s 8 of the *Administrative Law Act 1978* (Vic) obliges some public officials to provide a statement of reasons in respect of certain decisions.

[3]	Similar Acts are found in the ACT and Queensland: see the *Human Rights Act 2004* (ACT) and *Human Rights Act 2019* (Qld).

[4]	The question of whether 'arbitrarily' should be given its ordinary English meaning or a meaning informed by human rights jurisprudence is an unresolved question.

Compilation of References

18. Stored Communications Act §§. 2701-2702 (US).

1980. OECD Guidelines on the Protection of Privacy and Transborder Flows of Personal Data (OECD Guidelines).

2001. Council of Europe Convention on Cybercrime.

ABA Journal. (2017, 20 October). *Estonia considering new legal status for artificial intelligence.* Retrieved from https://www.abajournal.com/news/article/estonia_considering_new_legal_status_for_ai

Ackerman, E. (2016). Researchers teaching robots to feel and react to pain. *IEEE Spectrum.* Retrieved from https://spectrum.ieee.org/automaton/robotics/robotics-software/researchers-teaching-robots-to-feel-and-react-to-pain

ActCopyright 1968 (Cth).

ActMigration 1958 (Cth).

ActPrivacy 1988 (Cth).

Adams, C. (2018). *Estonia, a blockchain model for other countries?* Retrieved from https://www.investinblockchain.com/estonia-blockchain-model/

Administration and Probate Act 1958 (Vic).

Administrative Decisions (Judicial Review) Act 1977 (Cth).

Affinity Internet Inc. v Consolidated Credit Counselling Services, No 4D05-1193 (Fla Dist. Ct App 4th Dist. 2006).

Age Discrimination Act 2014 (Cth).

AI 4People. (2019). *Ethical framework for a good AI society.* Retrieved from https://www.eismd.eu/wp-content/uploads/2019/02/Ethical-Framework-for-a-Good-AI-Society.pdf

Airbnb Inc. v City and County of San Francisco, 217 F. Supp. 3d 1066 (ND Cal. 2016).

Ajana, B. (2015). Augmented borders: Big data and the ethics of immigration control. *Journal of Information. Communication & Ethics in Society, 13*(1), 58–78. doi:10.1108/JICES-01-2014-0005

Alan Yazbek v Ghosn Yazbek & Anor [2012] NSWSC 594.

Algorithmic Accountability Act. (2019). US.

Allen, D. (2009). Reducing the burden of proving discrimination in Australia. *The Sydney Law Review, 31*(4), 579–605.

Allens. (2019). *AI toolkit.* Retrieved from https://www.allens.com.au/datadrivenbusiness/AI-toolkit/

Allow States and Victims to Fight Online Sex Trafficking Act 47 U.S.C. § 230(e) (1996).

Alston, R. (2000). The government's regulatory framework for Internet content. *The University of New South Wales Law Journal*, *23*(1), 192–197.

Amazon Australia Services. (2017). *Kindle store terms of use*. Retrieved from https://www.amazon.com.au/gp/help/customer/display.html?nodeId=201014950

Amendment, T. L. (Automated Vehicle Trials and Innovation) Act 2017 (NSW).

Anannay, M., & Crawford, K. (2018). Seeing without knowing: Limitations of the transparency ideal and its application to algorithmic accountability. *New Media & Society*, *20*(3), 981. doi:10.1177/1461444816676645

Andrews, K. (2019, 7 November). *Businesses ready to test AI ethics principles*. Press Release. Retrieved at https://www.minister.industry.gov.au/ministers/karenandrews/media-releases/businesses-ready-test-ai-ethics-principles

Angwin, J., & Parris, T., Jr. (2016). Facebook lets advertisers exclude users by race. *ProPublica*. Retrieved from https://www.propublica.org/article/facebook-lets-advertisers-exclude-users-by-race

Angwin, J., Larson, J., Mattu, S., & Kirchner, L. (2016). Machine bias there's software used across the country to predict future criminals. And it's biased against blacks. *ProPublica*. Retrieved from https://www.propublica.org/article/machine-bias-risk-assessments-in-criminal-sentencing

Antoine, H. (2016). Digital legacies: Who owns your online life after death? *The Computer & Internet Lawyer*, *33*(4), 15–20.

Apple. (2019). *Apple media services terms and conditions*. Retrieved from https://www.apple.com/legal/internet-services/itunes/au/terms.html#SERVICE

Ardia, D. (2010). Free speech savior or shield for scoundrels: An empirical study of intermediary immunity under section 230 of the Communications Decency Act. *Loyola of Los Angeles Law Review*, *43*, 373–506.

Arenas, A., Goh, J. M., & Podar, M. (2015). A work-systems approach to classifying risks in crowdfunding platforms: An exploratory analysis. In *Twenty-First Americas Conference on Information Systems (AMCIS 2015) Proceedings*. Fajardo, Puerto Rico: US Association for Information Systems.

Aronson, M., & Groves, M. (2013). *Judicial Review of Administrative Action* (5th ed.). Pyrmont, Australia: Thomson Reuters.

ASIC v Westpac Banking Corporation [2019] FCA 1244.

Attorney-General's Department. (2004). *Automated assistance in administrative decision making*. Canberra: Administrative Review Council.

Australian Broadcasting Tribunal v Bond & Ors (1990) 170 CLR 321.

Australian Charities and Not-for-profits Commission Act (2012) (Cth).

Australian Communications & Media Authority (ACMA). (2013). *Managing your digital identity: Digital footprints and identities research short report*. Canberra, Australia: Commonwealth Government Printer. Retrieved from https://apo.org.au/node/36376

Australian Communications and Media Authority (ACMA). (2019). *Avoid sending spam*. Retrieved from https://www.acma.gov.au/avoid-sending-spam#get-permission

Australian Competition and Consumer Commission v Allergy Pathway Pty Ltd (No 2) [2011] FCA 74.

Australian Competition and Consumer Commission v Allergy Pathway Pty Ltd [2009] FCA 960.

Australian Competition and Consumer Commission. (2019). *Digital platforms inquiry: Final report.* Retrieved from https://www.accc.gov.au/publications/digital-platforms-inquiry-final-report

Australian Consumer Law (Competition and Consumer Act 2010 (Cth), sch. 2).

Australian Government Information Management Office (AGIMO). (2007). *Automated assistance in administrative decision-making: Better practice guide.* Canberra, Australia: Department of Finance and Deregulation.

Australian Government, Department of Industry, Innovation & Science. (2019, November). *AI ethics principles.* Retrieved from https://www.industry.gov.au/data-and-publications/building-australias-artificial-intelligence-capability/ai-ethics-framework/ai-ethics-principles

Australian Government. (2019). *Government response and implementation roadmap for the digital platforms inquiry.* Retrieved from https://treasury.gov.au/publication/p2019-41708

Australian Human Rights Commission & World Economic Forum. (2019). *Artificial intelligence: Governance* and *leadership.* Retrieved from https://tech.humanrights.gov.au/sites/default/files/2019-02/AHRC_WEF_AI_WhitePaper2019.pdf

Australian Human Rights Commission. (2002). *Annual report 2001-2002: Human rights and equal opportunity commission.* Retrieved from https://www.humanrights.gov.au/our-work/commission-general/publications/annual-report-2001-2002-human-rights-and-equal-opportunity

Australian Human Rights Commission. (2009). *DDA conciliation: Goods, services and facilities.* Retrieved from https://www.humanrights.gov.au/our-work/disability-rights/dda-conciliation-goods-services-and-facilities

Australian Human Rights Commission. (2014). *Supporting working parents: Pregnancy and return to work national review.* Retrieved from https://www.humanrights.gov.au/our-work/sex-discrimination/projects/supporting-working-parents-pregnancy-and-return-work-national

Australian Law Reform Commission (ALRC). (1998). *Secrecy & open government in Australia* (Report 112). Retrieved from https://www.alrc.gov.au/publication/secrecy-laws-and-open-government-in-australia-alrc-report-112/14-frameworks-for-effective-information-handling/data-matching/

Australian National Audit Office (ANAO). (2008). *The Australian taxation office's use of data matching and analytics in tax administration.* Retrieved from https://www.anao.gov.au/work/performance-audit/australian-taxation-offices-use-data-matching-and-analytics-tax

Australian Securities & Investments Commission v Lindberg [2012] VSC 332.

Australian Taxation Office. (2019). *Australian tax gaps - an overview.* Retrieved from https://www.ato.gov.au/About-ATO/Research-and-statistics/In-detail/Tax-gap/Australian-tax-gaps-overview/?page=1#Tax_gap_research_program

Bacina, M. (2017). *Smart contracts in Australia: just how clever are they?* Retrieved from https://piperalderman.com.au/insight/smart-contracts-in-australia-just-how-clever-are-they/

Bacon, J., Michels, J. D., Millard, C., & Singh, J. (2018). Blockchain demystified: A technical and legal Introduction to Distributed and Centralized Ledgers. *Richmond Journal of Law & Technology, 25*(1), 1–106.

Bajorek, J. P. (2019). Voice recognition still has significant race and gender biases. *Harvard Business Review.* Retrieved from https://hbr.org/2019/05/voice-recognition-still-has-significant-race-and-gender-biases

Baldwin, F., & Gadboys, J. (2016). The duty of financial institutions to investigate and report suspicions of Fraud, financial crime, and corruption. In M. Dion, D. Weisstub, & J.-L. Richet (Eds.), Financial crimes: Psychological, technological, and ethical Issues (pp. 83-104). Cham, Switzerland: Springer. doi:10.1007/978-3-319-32419-7_4

Ballon, I. (2017). *E-commerce & internet law*. New York: Thomson Reuters.

Banerjee, R., Reitz, J. G., & Oreopoulos, P. (2018). Do large employers treat racial minorities more fairly? An analysis of Canadian field experiment data. *Canadian Public Policy*, *44*(1), 1–12. doi:10.3138/cpp.2017-033

Banking Regulation Act of 1949 (India).

Banning of Cryptocurrency and Regulation of Official Digital Currency Bill. (2019). India.

Barfield, W. (2018). Liability for autonomous and artificially intelligent robots. *De Gruyter*, *9*, 193-203. Retrieved from https://www.degruyter.com/downloadpdf/j/pjbr.2018.9.issue-1/pjbr-2018-0018/pjbr-2018-0018.pdf

Barfield, W. (2018). Liability for autonomous and artificially intelligent robots. *Paladyn: Journal of Behavioral Robotics*, *9*(1), 193–203. doi:10.1515/pjbr-2018-0018

Barocas, S., & Selbst, A. (2016). Big data's disparate impact. *California Law Review*, *104*(3), 671–732.

Barrett v Rosenthal, 146 P. 3d. 510 (Cal. 2006).

BBC News. (2018, 12 July). Facebook ruling: German court grants parents' rights to dead daughter's account. *BBC News*. Retrieved from https://www.bbc.com

Belbin, R. (2018). When Google becomes the norm: The case for privacy and the right to be forgotten. *Dalhousie Journal of Legal Studies*, *26*, 17–35.

Belleflamme, P., Lambert, T., & Schwienbacher, A. (2013). Crowdfunding: Tapping the right crowd. *Journal of Business Venturing*, *29*(5), 585–609. doi:10.1016/j.jbusvent.2013.07.003

Bentley, D. (2019). Timeless principles of taxpayer protection: how they adapt to digital disruption. *eJournal of Tax Research, 16*(3), 679-713.

Berkeley, J. (2015, 31 October). The promise of the blockchain the trust machine. *The Economist*. Retrieved from https://www.economist.com/leaders/2015/10/31/the-trust-machine

Berkson v Gogo, 97 F.Supp.3d 359 (E.D.N.Y. 2015).

Bester, N. (2019, 3 March). Malta might be 'blockchain island' but don't try opening a crypto bank account. *Bitcoin.com*. Retrieved from https://news.bitcoin.com/malta-might-be-blockchain-island-but-dont-try-opening-a-crypto-bank-account/

Bester, J., Cole, C. M., & Kodish, E. (2016). The limits of informed consent for an overwhelmed patient: Clinicians' role in protecting patients and preventing overwhelm. *AMA Journal of Ethics*, *18*(9), 869–886. doi:10.1001/journalofethics.2016.18.9.peer2-1609 PMID:27669132

Beyer, G. W. (2015). Web meets the will: Estate planning for digital assets. *Estate Planning*, *42*(3), 28–41.

Bloch, H., & Bhattacharya, M. (2016). Promotion of Innovation and Job Growth in Small- and Medium-Sized Enterprises in Australia: Evidence and Policy Issues. *The Australian Economic Review*, *49*(2), 192–199. doi:10.1111/1467-8462.12164

Bloemen v Commissioner of Taxation (1980) 147 CLR 360.

Bodenhausen, G. V. (1990). Stereotypes as judgmental heuristics: Evidence of circadian variations in discrimination. *Psychological Science*, *1*(5), 319–322. doi:10.1111/j.1467-9280.1990.tb00226.x

Booth, A. L., Leigh, A., & Varganova, E. (2012). Does ethnic discrimination vary across minority groups? Evidence from a field experiment. *Oxford Bulletin of Economics and Statistics*, *74*(4), 547–573. doi:10.1111/j.1468-0084.2011.00664.x

Braithwaite, V., Reinhart, M., & Smart, M. (2010). Tax non-compliance among the under-30s: Knowledge, obligation or scepticism? In J. Alm, J. Martinez-Vazquez, & B. Torgler (Eds.), *Developing alternative frameworks for explaining tax compliance*. London, UK: Routledge.

Brennan, R. (2016, June 13). Sick truth behind this bloke's GoFundMe appeal. *Courier-Mail*. Retrieved from https://www.couriermail.com.au/news/queensland/crime-and-justice/brisbane-man-diakko-santaali-guilty-of-fraud-after-gofundme-page-appeal/news-story/6fe077e6e3d6ec33b4f2b78442c57b0b

Brewster, S. (2017, April 19). Inside the glowing-plant startup that just gave up its quest. *Wired*. Retrieved from https://www.wired.com/story/inside-the-glowing-plant-startup-that-just-gave-up-its-quest/

Briggs, T. (2019, 12 December). Government to evaluate 'right to be forgotten' but privacy reforms still years away. *The Age*. Retrieved from http://theage.com.au

Brisciani v Piscioneri (No 4) [2016] ACTCA 32.

Brisciani v Piscioneri [2015] ACTSC 106.

Brisciani, A. [@zgeeks]. (2019). *ZGeek was a magical place full of turnips. From 2001 to 2015, a great community of 1.3 million Geeks. Laughs, fights and many shenanigans* [Tweet]. Retrieved from https://twitter.com/zgeek?lang=en

Broadcasting Services Act 1992 (Cth).

Broadcasting Services Amendment (Online Services) Act 1999 (Cth).

Brook, L. (2018). Evidencing impact from art research: Analysis of impact case studies from the REF 2014. *The Journal of Arts Management, Law, and Society*, *48*(1), 57–69. doi:10.1080/10632921.2017.1386148

Brooks, M., McMillan, C., & Surya Darma, I. G. M. (2011, December 13). Subak with art festival. *Pozible* [Crowdfunding platform]. Retrieved from https://pozible.com/project/4080

Brotherton, E. A. (2012). Big brother gets a makeover: Behavioural targeting and the third-party doctrine. *Emory Law Journal*, *61*(3), 555–558.

Brown, J. H., & Bruch, R. E. (2019). Online tools under RUFADAA: The next evolution in estate planning or a flash in the pan? *Probate and Property (Chicago, Ill.)*, *13*(2), 60–63.

Brownsword, R. (2004). What the world needs now: Techno-regulation, human rights and human dignity. In R. Brownsword (Ed.), Global governance and the quest for justice: Volume 4 human rights (pp. 203-234). Oxford, UK: Hart Publishing.

Brownsword, R., & Harel, A. (2019). Law, liberty and technology: Criminal justice in the context of smart machines. *International Journal of Law in Context*, *15*(2), 107–125. doi:10.1017/S1744552319000065

Brownsword, R., & Yeung, K. (2008). *Regulating technologies: Legal futures, regulatory frames and technological fixes*. Oxford, UK: Hart Publishing.

Bryson, J. J., Diamantis, M. E., & Grant, T. D. (2017). Of, for, and by the people: The legal lacuna of synthetic persons. *Artificial Intelligence and Law*, *25*(3), 273–291. doi:10.100710506-017-9214-9

Buiten, M. (2019). Towards Intelligent Regulation of Artificial Intelligence. *European Journal of Risk Regulation*, *10*(1), 41–59. doi:10.1017/err.2019.8

Buolamwini, J., & Gebru, T. (2018). Gender Shades: Intersectional accuracy disparities in commercial gender classification. *Proceedings of Machine Learning Research, 81*, 1-15. Retrieved from http://proceedings.mlr.press/v81/buolamwini

Bürer, M. J., de Lapparent, M., Pallotta, V., Capezzali, M., & Carpita, M. (2019). Use cases for blockchain in the energy industry opportunities of emerging business models and related risks. *Computers & Industrial Engineering, 137*, 1–9. doi:10.1016/j.cie.2019.106002

Burnie Port Authority v General Jones Pty Ltd (1994) HCA 13.

Burrell, J. (2015, Jan.). How the machine "thinks": Understanding opacity in machine learning algorithms. *Big Data & Society*, 1–12. doi:10.2139srn.2660674

Burshtein, S. (2017). The true story of fake news. *Intellectual Property Journal, 29*, 397–446.

Byrnes, J. E. K. (2012, December 15). SciFund in 3 Rounds. *#SciFund Challenge*. Retrieved from https://scifundchallenge.org/2012/12/15/scifund-in-3-rounds/

Callaway, E. (2013). Glowing plants spark debate. *NATNews, 498*(7452), 15. doi:10.1038/498015a PMID:23739402

Campolo, A., Sanfilippo, M., Whittaker, M., & Crawford, K. (2017). *AI now 2017*. Retrieved from https://ainowinstitute.org/AI_Now_2017_Report.pdf

Caripis v Victoria Police [2012] VCAT 1472.

Carltona Ltd v Commissioners of Works [1943] 2 All ER 560.

Carney, T. (2019). Robodebt failed its day in court, what now? *The Conversation*. Retrieved from http://theconversation.com/robodebt-failed-its-day-in-court-what-now-127984

Casey, B., Farhangi, A., & Vogl, R. (2019). Rethinking explainable machines: The GDPR's right to explanation debate and the rise of algorithmic audits in enterprise. *Berkeley Technology Law Journal, 34*(1), 143–188.

Castillo, D. (2019). Unpacking the loot box: How gaming's latest monetization system flirts with traditional gambling methods. *Santa Clara Law Review, 59*(1), 165–201.

Cate, F., & Mayer-Schonberger, V. (2013). Notice and consent in a world of big data. *International Data Privacy, 3*(2), 67–73. doi:10.1093/idpl/ipt005

Centre for Connected and Driverless Cars. (2019, February). *Code of practice: automated vehicle trialling*. Retrieved from https://assets.publishing.service.gov.uk/government/uploads/system/uploads/attachment_data/file/776511/code-of-practice-automated-vehicle-trialling.pdf

Centre for Data Ethics and Innovation (CDEI). (2019, 21 March). *Two year strategy*. Retrieved from https://www.gov.uk/government/publications/the-centre-for-data-ethics-and-innovation-cdei-2-year-strategy/centre-for-data-ethics-cdei-2-year-strategy

Centrebet Pty Ltd v Baasland [2013] NTSC 59.

Chae, Y. (2020). U.S. AI regulation guide: Legislative overview and practical considerations. *The Journal of Robotics. Artificial Intelligence and Law, 3*(1), 17–40. Retrieved from https://www.bakermckenzie.com/-/media/files/people/chae-yoon/rail-us-ai-regulation-guide.pdf

Chander, A. (2014). How law made Silicon Valley. *Emory Law Journal, 63*, 639–694.

Charter of Human Rights and Responsibilities Act. (2006). Vic.

Chen, I., Johansson, F. D., & Sontag, D. (2018). Why is my classifier discriminatory? *Advances in Neural Information Processing Systems*, *31*, 3539–3550.

Chiao, V. (2019). Fairness, accountability and transparency: Notes on algorithmic decision-making in criminal justice. *International Journal of Law in Context*, *15*(2), 126–139. doi:10.1017/S1744552319000077

Chohan, U. W. (2016). Skin deep: Should Australia consider name-blind resumes? *The Conversation*. Retrieved from https://theconversation.com/skin-deep-should-australia-consider-name-blind-resumes-55503

Chubb, J., & Reed, M. S. (2018). The politics of research impact: Academic perceptions of the implications for research funding, motivation and quality. *British Politics*, *13*(3), 295–311. doi:10.105741293-018-0077-9

Chubb, J., & Watermeyer, R. (2016). Artifice or integrity in the marketization of research impact? Investigating the moral economy of (pathways to) impact statements within research funding proposals in the UK and Australia. *Studies in Higher Education*, *42*(12), 2360–2372. doi:10.1080/03075079.2016.1144182

Citron, D., & Witts, B. (2017). The internet will not break: Denying bad samaritans § 230 immunity. *Fordham Law Review*, *86*(2), 401–423.

Civil Aviation Safety Authority (CASA). (2019). *Project US 18/09*. Retrieved from https://www.casa.gov.au/standard-page/project-us-1809-remotely-piloted-aircraft-rpa-registration-and-rpas-operator-accreditation-scheme

Civil Aviation Safety Regulations 1988 (Cth).

Cohen, J. E. (2012). *Configuring the Networked Self*. New Haven, CT: Yale University.

Commissioner of Taxation v Futuris Corporation Ltd (2008) 237 CLR 146.

Commissioner of Taxation v Warner (2015) FCA 659.

Commonwealth of Australia. (2017). *Assessing the engagement and impact of university research*. National Innovation and Science Agenda. Retrieved from https://www.innovation.gov.au/page/measuring-impact-and-engagement-university-research

Commonwealth of Australia. (2018). *Regulatory requirements that impact on the safe use of remotely piloted aircraft systems, unmanned aerial systems and associated systems*. Retrieved from https://www.aph.gov.au/Parliamentary_Business/Committees/Senate/Rural_and_Regional_Affairs_and_Transport/Drones/Report

Commonwealth Ombudsman. (2017). *Centrelink's automated debt raising and recovery system*. Retrieved from https://www.ombudsman.gov.au/__data/assets/pdf_file/0022/43528/Report-Centrelinks-automated-debt-raising-and-recovery-system-April-2017.pdf

Communications Decency Act 47 U.S.C. § 230 (1996).

Competition and Consumer Act 2010 (Cth), (Australia Consumer Law), sch. 2.

Competition and Consumer Act 2010 (Cth).

Consumer Affairs Victoria. (2019). *Motor car traders guarantee fund*. Retrieved from https://www.consumer.vic.gov.au/about-us/who-we-are-and-what-we-do/funds-we-administer/motor-car-traders-guarantee-fund

Consumer New Zealand. (n.d.) *Digital wills*. Retrieved from https://www.consumer.org.nz/articles/digital-wills

Cordover and Australian Electoral Commission, 2015] AATA 956.

Cordover v Australian Electoral Commission (2015) AATA 956.

Corporations Amendment (Crowd-sourced Funding for Proprietary Companies) Act (2018) (Cth).

Corporations Amendment (Crowd-sourced Funding) Act (2017) (Cth).

Cowgill, B. (2018) *Bias and productivity in humans and algorithms: Theory and evidence from resume screening*. Retrieved from http://conference.iza.org/conference_files/MacroEcon_2017/cowgill_b8981.pdf

Criminal Code Act 1995 (Cth).

Criminal Code Amendment (Sharing of Abhorrent Violent Material) Act 2019 (Cth).

Crosby, M., Pattanayak, P., Verma, S., & Kalyanaraman, V. (2016). Blockchain technology: Beyond bitcoin. *Applied Innovation Review*, *2*(June), 6–19.

Cryptohound, O. (2019). *Tough, but worth it: Pros and cons of blockchain regulation in Malta*. Retrieved from https://cryptodigestnews.com/tough-but-worth-it-pros-and-cons-of-blockchain-regulation-in-malta-c337a5906025

CSIRO. (2015). *Impact evaluation guide*. Retrieved from https://www.csiro.au/impact

CSIRO. (2018, 29 August). *New blockchain-based smart legal contracts for Australian businesses*. Retrieved from https://www.csiro.au/en/News/News-releases/2018/New-blockchain-based-smart-legal-contracts

Cuccuru, P. (2017). Beyond bitcoin: An early overview on smart contracts. *International Journal of Law and Information Technology*, *25*(3), 179–195. doi:10.1093/ijlit/eax003

Cui, Y., & Zeng, C. (2016). *Regulation of Equity Crowdfunding in China. DEStech Transactions on Economics*. Business and Management. doi:10.12783/dtem/icem2016/4035

Cullinane v Uber Technologies (2016) 4-14750-DPW.

Cumming, D. J., Leboeuf, G., & Schwienbacher, A. (2015). *Crowdfunding models: Keep-It-All vs. All-Or-Nothing*. Social Science Research Network. Retrieved from https://papers.ssrn.com/abstract=2447567

Cumming, D. J., Hornuf, L., Karami, M., & Schweizer, D. (2016). *Disentangling crowdfunding from fraudfunding*. Munich, Germany: Max Planck Institute for Innovation & Competition. doi:10.2139srn.2828919

Cummings, R. G. (2014). The case against access to decedents' e-mail: Password protection as an exercise of the right to destroy. *Minnesota Journal of Law, Science & Technology*, *15*(2), 898–947.

Dale, S. (2015). Heuristics and biases: The science of decision-making. *Business Information Review*, *32*(2), 93–99. doi:10.1177/0266382115592536

Daniels v Hunter Water Board (1994) EOC 92-626.

Danziger, S., Levav, J., & Avnaim-Pesso, L. (2011). Extraneous factors in judicial decisions. *Proceedings of the National Academy of Sciences of the United States of America*, *108*(17), 6889–6892. doi:10.1073/pnas.1018033108 PMID:21482790

Dastin, J. (2018). Amazon scraps secret AI recruiting tool that showed bias against women. *Reuters*. Retrieved from https://www.reuters.com/article/us-amazon-com-jobs-automation-insight-idUSKCN1MK08G

Data61. (2019, 5 April). *Artificial intelligence: Australia's ethics framework*. Retrieved from https://consult.industry.gov.au/strategic-policy/artificial-intelligence-ethics-framework/supporting_documents/ArtificialIntelligenceethicsframeworkdiscussionpaper.pdf

Data-matching Program (Assistance and Tax) Act 1990 (Cth).

Davidow, B. (2014, 20 February). Welcome to algorithmic prison: The use of big data to profile citizens is subtly, silently constraining freedom. *The Atlantic*. Retrieved from https://www.theatlantic.com/technology/archive/2014/02/welcome-to-algorithmic-prison/283985/

Davies, H. (2015, 12 December). Ted Cruz using firm that harvested data on millions of unwitting Facebook users. *The Guardian*. Retrieved from https://www.theguardian.com/us-news/2015/dec/11/senator-ted-cruz-president-campaign-facebook-user-data

De Caria, R. (2019). The legal meaning of smart contracts. *European Review of Private Law*, *6*, 731–752.

DeJohn v. TV Corp International, 245 F Supp 2d 913 (ND Ill 2003). eBay International AG v Creative Festival Entertainment Pty Ltd (2006) 170 FCR 450; [2006] FCA 1768.

Denlay v Commissioner of Taxation (2011) FCAFC 63.

Dentons. (2019). *Autonomous vehicles: US legal and regulatory landscape*. Retrieved from http://www.thedriverless-commute.com/wp-content/uploads/2019/08/Dentons-US-Autonomous-Vehicles-Whitepaper-August-1-2019.docx.pdf

Department of Communities and Justice. (2020). *Access to digital assets upon death or incapacity*. Retrieved from https://www.lawreform.justice.nsw.gov.au/Pages/lrc/lrc_current_projects/Digital%20assets/Project-update.aspx

Department of Education and Training. (2017). *2018 Higher Education Research Data Collection: Specifications for the collection of 2017 data*. Retrieved from https://docs.education.gov.au/node/44986

Department of Industry, Innovation and Science. (2019). *Artificial intelligence: Australia's ethics framework*. Retrieved from https://consult.industry.gov.au/strategic-policy/artificial-intelligence-ethics-framework/

Department of Justice. (2015, 6 April). Former e-commerce executive charged with price fixing in the antitrust division's first online marketplace prosecution. *Justice News of the US Department of Justice*. Retrieved from https://www.justice.gov/opa/pr/former-e-commerce-executive-charged-price-fixing-antitrust-divisions-first-online-marketplace

Department of Justice. (2019). *Access to digital assets upon death or incapacity*. Retrieved from https://www.lawreform.justice.nsw.gov.au/Pages/lrc/lrc_current_projects/Digital%20assets/Project-update.aspx

Deputy Commissioner of Taxation v Armstrong Scalisi Holdings Pty Ltd (2019) NSWSC 129.

Deputy Commissioner of Taxation v Bonaccorso (2016) NSWSC 595.

Deputy Commissioner of Taxation v Mackey [1982] 13 ATR 547.

Deputy Commissioner of Taxation v Richard Walter Pty Ltd (1994) 183 CLR 168.

Deputy Commissioner of Taxation v Zeqaj (2019) VSC 194.

Desai, D., & Kroll, J. (2017). Trust but verify: A guide to algorithms and the law. *Harvard Journal of Law & Technology*, *31*(1), 1–64.

Di Mariani, C. (2019, 7 February). Blockchain for law firms: Revolutionizing escrow, contracts, and more. *D!gitalist*. Retrieved from https://www.digitalistmag.com/digital-economy/2019/02/07/blockchain-for-law-firms-revolutionizing-escrow-contracts-more-06196152

Dippon, C. (2017). *Economic value of internet intermediaries and the role of liability protections*. Retrieved from https://internetassociation.org/wp-content/uploads/2017/06/Economic-Value-of-Internet-Intermediaries-the-Role-of-Liability-Protections.pdf

Directive 2005/29/EC Concerning Unfair Business-to-Consumer Commercial Practices in the Internal Market (Unfair Commercial Practices Directive).

Directive 95/46/EC of the European Parliament and of the Council of 24 October 1995 on the protection of individuals with regard to the processing of personal data and on the free movement of such data.

DirectiveMachinery (2006/42/EC).

Dlamini, N., Scott, M., & Nair, K. K. (2016). *A bitcoin framework: an alternative payment system for rural areas of South Africa using low-end mobile phones.* Paper presented at the 2016 Southern Africa Telecommunications Networks and Applications Conference (SATNAC), George, South Africa.

Dodd, A. (2019). *"I'm sorry, Dave. I'm afraid I can't do that": Legal liability in the age of artificial intelligence.* Retrieved from https://www.fieldfisher.com/en/insights/i%E2%80%99m-sorry,-dave-i%E2%80%99m-afraid-i-can%E2%80%99t-do-that%E2%80%9D-legal

Dorner, J., Blair, D., & Bernard, J. R. L. (Eds.). (1998). *Macquarie pocket dictionary* (3rd ed.). Milton, Australia: John Wiley & Sons.

Dow Jones & Co Inc. v Gutnick [2002] HCA 56.

Ducas, E., & Wilner, A. (2017). The security and financial implications of blockchain technologies: Regulating emerging technologies in Canada. *International Journal (Toronto, Ont.)*, *72*(4), 538–562. doi:10.1177/0020702017741909

Düdder, B., & Ross, O. (2017). *Timber tracking: Reducing complexity of due diligence by using blockchain technology* (Publication no. SSRN 3015219). https://papers.ssrn.com/sol3/papers.cfm?abstract_id=3015219

Durovic, M., & Janssen, A. (2018). The formation of blockchain-based smart contracts in the light of contract law. *European Review of Private Law*, *26*(6), 753–771.

Dzieza, J. (2013, August 18). *Plants that glow in the dark spark heated debate.* Retrieved from https://www.thedailybeast.com/articles/2013/08/18/plants-that-glow-in-the-dark-spark-heated-debate

Edwards, L., & Harbinja, E. (2013). What happens to my Facebook profile when I die? Legal issues around transmission of digital assets on death. In C. Maciel & V. C. Periera (Eds.), *Digital legacy and interaction: Post-mortem issues* (pp. 115–144). Cham, Switzerland: Springer International Publishing. doi:10.1007/978-3-319-01631-3_7

Eggers, W. D., Schatsky, D., & Viechnicki, P. (2017). AI-augmented government using cognitive technologies to re-design public sector work. *Deloitte Insights*. Retrieved from https://www2.deloitte.com/us/en/insights/focus/cognitive-technologies/artificial-intelligence-government.html

Ehrlich, P. (2002). Communications Decency Act 230. *Berkeley Technology Law Journal*, *17*(1), 402–419.

Eisenberg, J. (2000). Safety out of sight: The impact of the new online content legislation on defamation law. *The University of New South Wales Law Journal*, *23*, 232–237.

Electronic Communications Privacy Act 18 U.S.C. §§ 2510-2523 (1986).

Electronic Transactions Act 1999 (Cth).

Elvery, S. (2017). How algorithms make important government decisions—and how that affects you. *ABC News*. Retrieved from https://www.abc.net.au/news/2017-07-21/algorithms-can-make-decisions-on-behalf-of-federal-ministers/8704858

Elvery, S. (2017). How algorithms make important government decisions. *ABC News*. Retrieved from https://www.abc.net.au/news/2017-07-21/algorithms-can-make-decisions-on-behalf-of-federal-ministers/8704858

English, R. (2014). Rent-a-crowd? Crowdfunding academic research. *First Monday, 19*(1). doi:10.5210/fm.v19i1.4818

Equal Opportunity Act. (2010). Vic.

Equity Trustees v Levin [2004] VSC 203.

Erel, I., Stern, L. H., Tan, C., & Weisbach, M. S. (2018). Selecting directors using machine learning. *National Bureau of Economic Research*. Retrieved from https://www.nber.org/papers/w24435.pdf

Estate of Masters, Hill v Plummer (1994) 33 NSWLR 446.

Estate of Sheron Jude Ladduhetti (2013) unreported, Supreme Court of Victoria.

Estate of Stewart (1996) unreported, Supreme Court of NSW.

Eubanks, V. (2018). *Automating inequality: How high-tech tools profile, police, and punish the poor.* New York, NY: St. Martin's Press.

European Commission High-Level Expert Group on Artificial Intelligence (AIHLEG). (2019). *Ethics guidelines for trustworthy AI*. Retrieved from https://ec.europa.eu/digital-single-market/en/news/ethics-guidelines-trustworthy-ai

European Commission, European Group on Ethics in Science & New Technologies. (2018). *Statement on artificial intelligence, robotics and 'autonomous' systems*. Retrieved from https://ec.europa.eu/jrc/communities/en/community/humaint/useful-link/statement-artificial-intelligence-european-group-ethics-science-and

European Commission. (1995). *Directive 95/46/EC of the European Parliament and of the council of 24 October 1995 on the protection of individuals with regard to the processing of personal data and on the free movement of such data.* Retrieved from https://eur-lex.europa.eu/legal-content/en/TXT/?uri=CELEX%3A31995L0046

European Commission. (2013). *LIBE committee vote backs new EU data protection rules* (Press release). Retrieved from https://europa.eu/rapid/press-release_MEMO-13-923_en.htm

European Commission. (2016). *Regulation (EU) 2016/679 of the European Parliament and of the council of 27 April 2016 on the protection of natural persons with regard to the processing of personal data and on the free movement of such data, and repealing directive 95/46/EC (General Data Protection Regulation).* Retrieved from https://eur-lex.europa.eu/eli/reg/2016/679/oj

European Commission. (2016). *Regulation (EU) 2016/679 of the European Parliament and of the council of 27 April 2016 on the protection of natural persons with regard to the processing of personal data and on the free movement of such data, and repealing Directive 95/46/EC (General Data Protection Regulation).* Retrieved from https://publications.europa.eu/en/publication-detail/-/publication/3e485e15-11bd-11e6-ba9a-01aa75ed71a1/language-en

European Commission. (2018). *Artificial intelligence for Europe.* Retrieved from https://eur-lex.europa.eu/legal-content/EN/TXT/PDF/?uri=CELEX:52018DC0237&from=EN

European Commission. (2018). *Liability for emerging digital technologies.* Retrieved from https://ec.europa.eu/digital-single-market/en/news/european-commission-staff-working-document-liability-emerging-digital-technologies

European Parliament. (2015). *Civil laws for robotics (2015/2103(INL).* Retrieved from http://www.europarl.europa.eu/doceo/document/TA-8-2017-0051_EN.html?redirect

European Parliament. (2017). *European Parliament resolution of 16 February 2017 with recommendations to the Commission on Civil Law Rules on Robotics (2015/2103(INL)).* Retrieved from https://www.europarl.europa.eu/doceo/document/TA-8-2017-0051_EN.html

European Union. (2016). *General data protection regulation article 22*. Retrieved from https://eur-lex.europa.eu/legal-content/EN/TXT/?qid=1528874672298&uri=CELEX%3A32016R0679

European Union. (2016). *General data protection regulation* Retrieved from https://gdpr-info.eu/

Evans, A. (n.d.). Glowing plants: Natural lighting with no electricity [Crowdfunding campaign]. *Kickstarter*. Retrieved from https://www.kickstarter.com/projects/antonyevans/glowing-plants-natural-lighting-with-no-electricity

Evans, M. C., & Cvitanovic, C. (2018). An introduction to achieving policy impact for early career researchers. *Palgrave Communications*, *4*(1), 88. doi:10.105741599-018-0144-2

Facebook. (2019). *Terms of service*. Retrieved from https://www.facebook.com/terms.php

Facebook. (2019a). *What will happen to my Facebook account if I pass away?* Retrieved from https://www.facebook.com/help/103897939701143?helpref=related

Facebook. (2019b). *What is a legacy contact and what can they do with my Facebook account?* Retrieved from https://www.facebook.com/help/1568013990080948?helpref=faq_content

Fair Housing Council of San Fernando Valley v Roommates.Com LLC, 521 F. 3d. 1157 (9th Cir. 2008).

Fairfax v Ibrahim [2012] NSWCCA 125.

Faulkes, Z. (2012, December 15). SciFund in 3 rounds, part 2: Box plot fever. *#SciFund Challenge*. Retrieved from https://scifundchallenge.org/2012/12/15/scifund-in-3-rounds-part-2-box-plot-fever/

Faulkes, Z. (2014, March 18). #SciFund round 4 analysis. *#SciFund Challenge*. Retrieved from https://scifundchallenge.org/2014/03/18/scifund-round-4-analysis/

Federal Commissioner of Taxation v Citibank [1989] 89 ATC 4268.

Federal Ministry of Transport and Digital Infrastructure. (2017). *Automated and connected driving*. Retrieved from https://www.bmvi.de/SharedDocs/EN/publications/report-ethics-commission.pdf?__blob=publicationFile

Federal Trade Commission. (2019, May 6). *FTC charges operator of crowdfunding scheme*. Federal Trade Commission. Retrieved from https://www.ftc.gov/news-events/press-releases/2019/05/ftc-charges-operator-crowdfunding-scheme

Fellmeth, A. (2005). Civil and criminal sanctions in the constitution and courts. *The Georgetown Law Journal*, *94*(1), 1–15.

Ferguson, A. G. (2017). Illuminating black data policing. *Ohio State Journal of Criminal Law*, *15*(2), 503–525.

Fertik, M., & Thompson, D. (2015). *The reputation economy: How to optimize your digital footprint in a world where your reputation is your most valuable asset*. Danvers, MA: New York Crown Business.

Fields v Twitter Inc., 217 F. Supp. 3d 1116 (ND Cal. 2016).

Forrest v Verizon Communications Inc., 805 A2d 1007 (DC 2002).

Frankl, P. (2017). Legal technology developments are overwhelming. *Legal Practice Intelligence*. Retrieved from https://www.legalpracticeintelligence.com.au/legal-technology-developments-are-overwhelming-start-here

Franklin, Z. (2014). Justice for revenge porn victims: Legal theories to overcome claims of civil immunity by operators of revenge porn websites. *California Law Review*, *102*(5), 1303–1336.

Franzen, C. (2013, August 7). Kickstarter says it consulted scientists before banning genetically-modified organisms. *The Verge*. Retrieved from https://www.theverge.com/2013/8/7/4595876/kickstarter-founder-yancey-strickler-explains-ban-GMOs

Freedman, J., & Vella, J. (2011). *HMRC's management of the UK tax system: The boundaries of legitimate discretion.* Oxford, UK: Oxford University Centre for Business Taxation. Retrieved from https://ora.ox.ac.uk/objects/uuid:869d0c16-7748-489d-9a74-

Friedler, S. A., Scheidegger, C., & Venkatasubramanian, S. (2016). *On the (im)possibility of fairness.* Retrieved from https://arxiv.org/abs/1609.07236

Fteja v Facebook Inc., 841 F. Supp. 2d 829 (S.D.N.Y. 2012).

Fyk v Facebook Inc., No. C 18-05159 JSW (ND Cal. 2019).

Ganatra, J. H. (2015). When a Kickstarter stops: Exploring failures and regulatory frameworks for the rewards-based crowdfunding industry. *Rutgers University Law Review, 68*, 1425–1472.

Gates, S. W., Perry, V. G., & Zorn, P. M. (2002). Automated underwriting in mortgage lending: Good news for the underserved? *Housing Policy Debate, 13*(2), 369–391. doi:10.1080/10511482.2002.9521447

Genesereth, M. (2015). Computational law: The cop in the backseat (White Paper). *CodeX - The Stanford Center for Legal Informatic.* Retrieved from http://logic.stanford.edu/publications/genesereth/complaw.pdf

Gerber, E. M., & Hui, J. (2013). Crowdfunding: Motivations and Deterrents for Participation. *ACM Transactions on Computer Human Interaction, 20*(6), 34:1–34:32. doi:10.1145/2530540

Getachew v Google Inc., 491 F. App. 923 (10th Cir. 2012).

Giangaspro, M. (2017). Is a 'smart contract' really a smart idea? Insights from a legal perspective. *Computer Law & Security Review, 33*(6), 1–23. doi:10.1016/j.clsr.2017.05.007

Gill, J. (2014, December 3). Crowd-funded science: Thoughts after 185 people gave us $10,733 for research. *The Contemplative Mammoth.* Retrieved from https://contemplativemammoth.com/2014/12/03/crowd-funded-science-thoughts-after-185-people-gave-us-10733-for-research/

Giuliani, D. (n.d.). *Blockchain in Africa: Assessing opportunities and feasibility.* Retrieved from https://briterbridges.com/blockchain-in-africa-assessing-opportunities-and-feasibility

Glencore International AG & Ors v Commissioner of Taxation of the Commonwealth of Australia & Ors (2019) HCA 26.

Goddard v Google Inc., 640 F. Supp. 2d 1193 (ND Cal. 2009).

GoFraudMe. (2016, June 13). Australian man pleads guilty to gofundme fraud, insists he really does have cancer. *GoFraudMe.* Retrieved from http://gofraudme.com/australian-man-pleads-guilty-gofundme-fraud-insists-really-cancer/

Goldman, E. (2019a). An overview of the United States' section 230 internet immunity. In G. Frosio (Ed.), The Oxford handbook of intermediary liability online (pp. 1–15). Oxford, UK: Oxford University Press.

Goldman, E. (2012). Online user account termination and 47 U.S.C. § 230(c)(2). UC *Irvine. Law Review, 2*, 659–673.

Goldman, E. (2017). The ten most important section 230 rulings. *Tulane Journal of Technology and Intellectual Property, 20*, 1–10.

Goldman, E. (2019b). Why section 230 is better than the first amendment. *Notre Dame Law Review Online, 94*(4), 1–16. doi:10.2139srn.3351323

Goldman, E. (2019c). The complicated story of FOSTA and section 230. *First Amendment Law Review, 17*, 279–293.

Goldman, E. (2019d). Law and technology internet immunity and the freedom to code. *Communications of the ACM, 62*(9), 22–24. doi:10.1145/3349270

Gonzalez v Agoda Company Pte Ltd, [2017] NSWSC 1133.

Google Spain v Gonzalez, c-131/12 (2014).

Google. (2019). *About inactive account manager.* Retrieved from https://support.google.com/accounts/answer/3036546

Google. (2019). *Terms of service.* Retrieved from https://policies.google.com/terms?hl=en-US

Google. (n.d.). *Responsible AI practices.* Retrieved from https://ai.google/responsibilities/responsible-ai-practices/

Gordon Legal. (2019). *Robodebt class action.* Retrieved from https://gordonlegal.com.au/robodebt-class-action/

Gordon, G. J. (2017). *Environmental personhood.* Retrieved from https://papers.ssrn.com/sol3/papers.cfm?abstract_id=2935007

Governatori, G., Idelberger, F., Milosevic, Z., Riveret, R., Sartor, G., & Xu, X. (2018). On legal contracts, imperative and declarative smart contracts, and blockchain systems. *Artificial Intelligence and Law, 26*(4), 377–409. doi:10.100710506-018-9223-3

Grech, A., & Camilleri, A. F. (2017). Blockchain in education. Luxembourg: European Commission. doi:10.2760/6064

Groves, M. (2017). The unfolding purpose of fairness. *Federal Law Review, 45*(4), 653–679. doi:10.22145/flr.45.4.8

Guest, G., Bunce, A., & Johnson, L. (2006). How many interviews are enough?: An experiment with data saturation and variability. *Field Methods, 18*(1), 59–82. doi:10.1177/1525822X05279903

Gunkel, D. J. (2007). Thinking otherwise: Ethics, technology and other subjects. *Ethics and Information Technology, 9*(3), 165–177. doi:10.100710676-007-9137-3

Guo, Y., & Liang, C. (2016). Blockchain application and outlook in the banking industry. *Financial Innovation, 2*(1), 24. doi:10.118640854-016-0034-9

Haack, P., & Sieweke, J. (2018). The legitimacy of inequality: Integrating the perspectives of system justification and social judgment. *Journal of Management Studies, 55*(3), 486–516. doi:10.1111/joms.12323

Haikonen, P. O. (2019). *Consciousness and robot sentience.* Singapore: World Scientific. doi:10.1142/11404

Hancock, P. A., Billings, D. R., Schaefer, K. E., Chen, J. Y., de Visser, E. J., & Parasuraman, R. (2011). A meta-analysis of factors affecting trust in human-robot interaction. *Human Factors, 53*(5), 517–527. doi:10.1177/0018720811417254 PMID:22046724

Hao, K. (2019, 29 August). OpenAI has released the largest version yet of its fake-news-spewing AI. *MIT Technology Review.* Retrieved from https://www.technologyreview.com/s/614237/openai-released-its-fake-news-ai-gpt-2/

Harari, Y. N. (2016). *Homo deus: A brief history of tomorrow.* New York, NY: Vintage Digital.

Harms, M. (2007). *What drives motivation to participate financially in a crowdfunding Community?* (Masters Thesis). Vrije Universitaet Amsterdam. Retrieved from https://www.ssrn.com/abstract=2269242

Hartzog, W. (2015). Unfair and deceptive robotics. *Maryland Law Review (Baltimore, Md.), 74*(4), 785–829.

Heberling, A. (2013a, November 7). I feel like it's safe to discuss this publicly now. *Alexheberling*. Retrieved from https://alexheberling.tumblr.com/post/66288651102

Heberling, A. (2013b, November 8). Report: Kickstarter scammer 'Encik Farhan'—updated - the beat. *Alexheberling*. Retrieved from https://alexheberling.tumblr.com/post/66385162129

Heberling, A. (2018, May 19). We'll help resolve payment-card disputes. *Alexheberling*. Retrieved from https://alexheberling.tumblr.com/post/174069323037

Helms, K. (2018). Only 39 percent pass Malta's cryptocurrency exam. *Bitcoin.com*. Retrieved from https://news.bitcoin.com/maltas-cryptocurrency-exam/

Helms, K. (2019a). Indian Supreme Court heard crypto case in depth. *Bitcoin.com*. Retrieved from https://news.bitcoin.com/indian-supreme-court-heard-crypto-case-in-depth/

Helms, K. (2019b). Indian Supreme Court postpones crypto case to November, new date confirmed. *Bitcoin.com*. Retrieved from https://news.bitcoin.com/indian-supreme-court-postpones-crypto-case-to-november/

Henman, P. (2004). Targeted!: Population segmentation, electronic surveillance and governing the unemployed in Australia. *International Sociology*, *19*(2), 173–191. doi:10.1177/0268580904042899

Henricks, K., & Seamster, L. (2017). Mechanisms of the racial tax state. *Critical Sociology*, *43*(2), 169–179. doi:10.1177/0896920516670463

Henriques-Gomez, L. (2019). Centrelink robodebt scheme faces second legal challenge. *The Guardian*. Retrieved from https://www.theguardian.com/australia-news/2019/jun/12/centrelink-robodebt-scheme-faces-second-legal-challenge

Her Majesty's Revenue & Customs (HMRC). (2015). *Tax administration: regulations to implement the UK's automatic exchange of information agreements*. London, UK: HMRC. Retrieved from https://www.gov.uk/government/publications/tax-administration-regulations-to-implement-the-uks-automatic-exchange-of-information-agreements

Higginson, M., Lorenz, J., Münstermann, B., & Olesen, P. (2017). *The promise of blockchain*. Retrieved from https://www.mckinsey.com/industries/financial-services/our-insights/the-promise-of-blockchain

High Level Expert Group (HLEG). (2019). *Ethics guidelines for trustworthy AI*. Retrieved from https://ec.europa.eu/digital-single-market/en/news/ethics-guidelines-trustworthy-ai

Hill, K. (2012). How Target figured out a teen girl was pregnant before her father did. *Forbes*. Retrieved from https://www.forbes.com/sites/kashmirhill/2012/02/16/how-target-figured-out-a-teen-girl-was-pregnant-before-her-father-did/#79bfe7d66668

Hill, K. (2012, February 16). How Target figured out a teen girl was pregnant before her father did. *Forbes*. Retrieved from https://www.forbes.com/sites/kashmirhill/2012/02/16/how-target-figured-out-a-teen-girl-was-pregnant-before-her-father-did/

Hinchliffe, J. (2018, October 25). GoFundMe changes policy to protect donors from sham causes. *ABC News*. Retrieved from https://www.abc.net.au/news/2018-10-25/gofundme-policy-changes-protect-donors-from-shams/10428180

Hogan-Doran, D. (2017). Computer says "no": Automation, algorithms and artificial intelligence in government decision-making. *Judicial Review: Selected Conference Papers: Journal of the Judicial Commission of New South Wales*, *13*(3), 345–382.

Hogan-Doran, D. (2017). Computer says "no": Automation, algorithms and artificial intelligence in Government decision-making. *The Judicial Review*, *13*, 1–39.

Holomaxx Technologies v. Microsoft Corporation Inc., 783 F. Supp. 2d 1097 (ND Cal. 2011).

Honda. (2020). *Asimo*. Retrieved from https://asimo.honda.com/

Hopkins, J. (2013). Afterlife in the cloud: Managing a digital estate. *Hastings Science and Technology Law Journal*, *5*(2), 209–243.

Hornuf, L., & Schwienbacher, A. (2017). Should securities regulation promote equity crowdfunding? *Small Business Economics*, *49*(3), 579–593. doi:10.100711187-017-9839-9

Houser, K., & Sanders, D. (2016). The use of big data analytics by the IRS: Efficient solutions or the end of privacy as we know it. *Vanderbilt Journal of Entertainment & Technology Law*, *19*(4), 817–872.

Houston Federation of Teachers vs Houston Independent School District, Amended Summary Judgment Opinion, 4 May 2017, US District Court of Southern District of Texas.

Hu, Y., Liyanage, M., Manzoor, A., Thilakarathna, K., Jourjon, G., & Seneviratne, A. (2019). *Blockchain-based smart-contracts-applications and challenges*. Retrieved from https://arxiv.org/abs/1810.04699

Hubbert v Dell Corporation, 835 NE 2d 113 (Ill App Ct 2005).

Hughes and Vale Pty Ltd v State of New South Wale*s* (1955) 93 CLR 127.

Hughes, G., & Sharpe, A. (2012). *Computer contracts: Principles and precedents*. Sydney: Thomson Reuters.

Hughes, J. M., Michell, P. A., & Ramson, W. S. (Eds.). (1992). *The Australian concise Oxford dictionary* (2nd ed.). Melbourne, Australia: Oxford University Press.

Hui, J. S., & Gerber, E. M. (2015). Crowdfunding science: Sharing Research with an extended audience. In *Proceedings of the 18th ACM Conference on Computer Supported Cooperative Work & Social Computing*. New York, NY: Association for Computing Machinery. 10.1145/2675133.2675188

Human Rights Watch. (2019, 1 May). *China's algorithms of repression: Reverse engineering a Xinjiang police mass surveillance app*. Retrieved from https://www.hrw.org/report/2019/05/01/chinas-algorithms-repression/reverse-engineering-xinjiang-police

Humphries, M. (2018, 16 July). German court rules Facebook data can be inherited. *PC Mag Australia*. Retrieved from https://au.pcmag.com/

Hunt, E. (2016, March 24). Tay, Microsoft's AI chatbox, gets a crash course in racism from Twitter. *The Guardian*. Retrieved from https://www.theguardian.com/technology/2016/mar/24/tay-microsofts-ai-chatbot-gets-a-crash-course-in-racism-from-twitter

Ibrahim, I., & Pope, J. (2011). The viability of a pre-filled income tax return system for Malaysia. *Journal of Contemporary Issues in Business and Government*, *17*(2), 85–89.

Identity-matching Services Bill (Cth) 2018.

Ikkatai, Y., McKay, E., & Yokoyama, H. M. (2018). Science created by crowds: A case study of science crowdfunding in Japan. *Journal of Science Communication*, *17*(3), A06. doi:10.22323/2.17030206

In re Request for Order Requiring Facebook, Inc. to Produce Documents and Things, Case No: C 12-80171 LHK (PSG), 9/20/201.

Income Tax Assessment Act 1997 (Cth).

Industrial Equity Ltd v Deputy Commissioner of Taxation [1990] 89 ATC 5316.

Innovative Technology Arrangement and Services Act. (2018). Malta.

Inspector-General of Taxation Act 2003 (Cth).

Inspector-General of Taxation. (2019a). *The future of the tax profession.* Canberra, Australia: Australian Government Printer.

Inspector-General of Taxation. (2019b). *Review into the Australian Taxation Office's use of garnishee notices.* Canberra, Australia: Australian Government Printer.

Instagram. (2019a). *How do I report a deceased person's account on Instagram?* Retrieved from https://help.instagram.com/264154560391256/

Instagram. (2019b). *What happens when a deceased person's account is memorialized?* Retrieved from https://help.instagram.com/231764660354188

Institute of Electrical and Electronics Engineers (IEEE). (2019). *Ethically aligned design: A vision for prioritizing human well-being with autonomous and intelligent systems first edition.* Retrieved from https://ethicsinaction.ieee.org/

Internal Revenue Code of. (1986). *Title 26.* USC.

International Standards Organization (ISO). (2019). *Artificial intelligence.* Retrieved from https://www.iso.org/committee/6794475.html

Interpretation Act. (1954). QLD.

Irving, G., & Askell, A. (2019). *AI safety needs social scientists.* Retrieved from https://distill.pub/2019/safety-needs-social-scientists/

IW v City of Perth (1997) 191 CLR 1.

Jaccard, G. (2017). Smart contracts and the role of law. *Jusletter IT, 23,* 1–25. doi:10.2139srn.3099885

Jackson, M. (2001). *Hughes on data protection in Australia* (2nd ed.). Sydney, Australia: Lawbook Co.

Jones, M. M., Castle-Clarke, S., Manville, C., Gunashekar, S., & Grant, J. (2013). *Assessing research impact: An international review of the excellence in innovation for Australia trial* [Commissioned research]. Santa Monica, CA: RAND Corporation. doi:10.7249/RR278

Kaevats, M. (2018) *AI and the Kratt momentum.* Retrieved from https://investinestonia.com/ai-and-the-kratt-momentum/

Kahana, E. (2018). *Providing legal advice to machines: The application-to-machine paradigm in a CAV setting.* Retrieved from https://law.stanford.edu/2018/10/06/providing-legal-advice-to-machines-the-application-to-machine-paradigm-in-a-cav-setting/

Kaminski, M. E. (2019). The right to explanation, explained. *Berkeley Technology Law Journal, 34*(1), 189–218. doi:10.15779/Z38TD9N83H

Kappel, T. (2009). Ex ante crowdfunding and the recording industry: A model for the U.S. *Loyola of Los Angeles Entertainment Law Review, 29*(3), 375–385.

Karakashian, S. (2015). A Software Patent War: The Effects of Patent Trolls on Startup Companies, Innovation, and Entrepreneurship. *Hastings Business Law Journal, 11*(1), 119–156.

Karp, P. (2019). Government admits robodebt was unlawful as it settles legal challenge. *The Guardian.* Retrieved from https://www.theguardian.com/australia-news/2019/nov/27/government-admits-robodebt-was-unlawful-as-it-settles-legal-challenge

Kaulartz, M., & Heckmann, J. (2016). Smart contracts-anwendungen der blockchain-technologie. *Computer und Recht (Köln), 32*(9), 618–624. doi:10.9785/cr-2016-0923

Keller, D. (2017). *SESTA and the teachings of intermediary liability.* Retrieved from https://cyberlaw.stanford.edu/files/publication/files/SESTA-and-IL-Keller-11-2.pdf

Kerr, I. R. (2004). Bots, babes and the Californication of commerce. *University of Ottawa Law and Technology Journal, 26*(1), 284–324.

Khaitan, T. (2015). *A theory of discrimination law.* Oxford, UK: Oxford University Press. doi:10.1093/acprof:oso/9780199656967.001.0001

Khan, M. A., & Salah, K. (2018). IoT security: Review, blockchain solutions, and open challenges. *Future Generation Computer Systems, 82*, 395–411. doi:10.1016/j.future.2017.11.022

Kickstarter. (2010, December 3). *Community guidelines.* Retrieved from https://web.archive.org/web/20101203214618/http://www.kickstarter.com/help/guidelines

Kickstarter. (n.d.). Prohibited items. *Kickstarter.* Retrieved from https://www.kickstarter.com/rules/prohibited

Kim, M. P., Ghorbani, A., & Zou, J. (2018). *Multiaccuracy: Black-box post-processing for fairness in classification.* Retrieved from https://arxiv.org/abs/1805.12317

Klayman v Zuckerberg and Facebook, 753 F. 3d. 1354 (DC Cir. 2014).

Klonick, K. (2018). The new governors: The people, rules, and processes governing online speech. *Harvard Law Review, 131*, 1598–1670.

Knuth, D. E. (2014). Art of computer programming: Vol. 2. *Seminumerical algorithms* (3rd ed.). Boston, MA: Addison-Wesley Professional.

Koffman, T. (2019, 4 April). Blockchain - Africa rising. *Forbes Magazine.* Retrieved from https://www.forbes.com/sites/tatianakoffman/2019/04/04/blockchain-africa-rising/#36d767817711

Koops, B.-J., Hildebrandt, M., & Jaquet-Chiffelle, D.-O. (2010). Bridging accountability gap: Rights for new entities in the information society? *Minnesota Journal of Law, Science & Technology, 11*(2), 497–561.

Kosseff, J. (2017). The gradual erosion of the law that shaped the internet: Section 230's evolution over two decades. *The Columbia Science and Technology Law Review, 18*, 1–41.

Kosseff, J. (2019). *The twenty-six words that created the internet.* New York: Cornell University Press. doi:10.7591/9781501735783

Krippendorff, K. (2018). *Content analysis: An introduction to its methodology.* Thousand Oaks, CA: Sage Publications.

Krywko, J. (2017). Siri can't talk to me: The challenge of teaching language to voice assistants. *Ars Technica.* Retrieved from https://arstechnica.com/information-technology/2017/12/teaching-old-virtual-assistants-new-language-tricks/

Kuipers, B. (2018). How can we trust a robot? *Communications of the ACM, 61*(3), 86–95. doi:10.1145/3173087

Laghmari, S. (2019). *The upsurge of blockchain market in Africa.* Retrieved from https://infomineo.com/the-upsurge-of-blockchain-market-in-africa

Lahoti, P., Weikum, G., & Gummadi, K. P. (2018). *IFair: Learning individually fair data representations for algorithmic decision making*. Retrieved from https://arxiv.org/abs/1806.01059

Lamm, J. P., Kunz, C. L., Riehl, D. A., & Rademacher, P. J. (2014). The digital death conundrum: How Federal and State laws prevent fiduciaries from managing digital property. *University of Miami Law Review, 68*, 385–420.

Lane, S. (2017). Interview with Christian Porter minister for social services. *ABC AM*. Retrieved from https://former-ministers.dss.gov.au/17352/radio-interview-abc-am/

Lansiti, M., & Lakhani, K. R. (2017). The truth about blockchain. *Harvard Business Review, 95*(1), 118–127.

Lattice. (2019). *How to reduce unconscious bias at work*. Retrieved from https://lattice.com/library/how-to-reduce-unconscious-bias-at-work

Laukyte, M. (forthcoming). Robots: Regulation, rights and remedies. In M. Jackson & M. Shelly (Eds.), *Legal regulations, implications and issues surrounding digital data*. Hershey, PA: IGI Global.

Law Commission. (n.d.). *Wills*. Retrieved from https://www.lawcom.gov.uk/project/wills/#related

Law Council of Australia. (2018). *Submission to the review of the identity-matching services bill 2018*. Retrieved from https://www.lawcouncil.asn.au/media/news/review-of-the-identity-matching-services-bill-2018

Law Council of Australia. (2019). *Crowdfunding: Guidance for Australian legal practitioners*. Retrieved from https://www.lawcouncil.asn.au/policy-agenda/regulation-of-the-profession-and-ethics/crowdfunding-guidance-for-australian-legal-practitioners

Law, N. Z. (2019). *Protecting your digital assets*. Retrieved from https://nzlaw.co.nz/news/protecting-your-digital-assets/

Le Bras, T. (2015). O*nline overload – it's worse than you thought*. Retrieved from https://blog.dashlane.com/infographic-online-overload-its-worse-than-you-thought/

Lecher, C. (2019, April 15). *New York's algorithm task force is fracturing*. Retrieved from https://www.theverge.com/2019/4/15/18309437/new-york-city-accountability-task-force-law-algorithm-transparency-automation

Lee, C., & Mueller, J. (2019). Can blockchain unlock the investment Africa needs? *Innovations: Technology, Governance, Globalization, 12*(3-4), 80–87. doi:10.1162/inov_a_00277

Leenes, R. (2011). Framing techno-regulation: An exploration of state and non-state regulation by technology. *Legisprudence, 5*(2), 159. doi:10.5235/175214611797885675

Legal Executive Institute. (2019). *The application of blockchain in the legal sector*. Retrieved from https://blogs.thomsonreuters.com/legal-uk/2019/01/04/the-application-of-blockchain-in-the-legal-sector/

Lemley, M. (2007). Rationalizing internet safe harbours. *Journal on Telecommunications & High Technology Law, 6*, 101–120.

Leonard, P. (2010). Safe harbours in choppy waters – building a sensible approach to liability of Internet intermediaries in Australia. *Journal of International Media & Entertainment Law, 3*(2), 221–262.

Lepri, B., Staiano, J., Sangokoya, D., Letouze, E., & Oliver, N. (2017). The tyranny of data? The bright and dark sides of data-driven decision making for social good. In T. Cerquitelli, D. Quercia, & F. Pasquale (Eds.), *Transparent data mining for big and small data* (pp. 2–22). Dordrecht, Germany: Springer. doi:10.1007/978-3-319-54024-5_1

Lexology. (2019). *Australia's privacy and consumer laws to be strengthened*. Retrieved from https://www.lexology.com/library/detail.aspx?g=4fbb5191-1fb2-4e5f-8d2d-f9a6aaf3754c

Ligthart, M., & Truong, K. P. (2015). Selecting the right robot: Influence of user attitude, robot sociability and embodiment on user preferences. In *Proceedings of 2015 24th IEEE International Symposium on Robot and Human Interactive Communication (RO-MAN)*. Kobe, Japan: IEEE. 10.1109/ROMAN.2015.7333598

Lim, I., Hagendorff, J., & Armitage, S. (2016). Regulatory monitoring, information asymmetry and accounting quality: Evidence from the banking industry. *EFMA 25th Annual Meeting*. Retrieved from https://efmaefm.org/0efmameetings/efma%20annual%20meetings/2016-Switzerland/papers/EFMA2016_0504_fullpaper.pdf

Lim, L., & Wilson, K. (2016). Clearing the cloud. *Law Institute Journal, 90*(1/2), 28.

Lobel, O. (2016). The law of the platform. *Minnesota Law Review, 101*, 87–166.

Loftus, B. (2019). Normalizing covert surveillance: the subterranean world of policing. *British Journal of Sociology, 70*(5), 2070-2091. http://doi-org/ doi:10.1111/1468-4446.12651

Loke, S. (2019). *Achieving ethical algorithmic behaviour in the internet-of-things: A review.* Retrieved from https://arxiv.org/pdf/1910.10241.pdf

Lukmire, D. (2010). Can the courts tame the Communications Decency Act? The reverberations of Zeran v America online. *NYU Annual Survey of American Law, 66*, 371–412.

Lynn, A. (2019). *What happens to your digital assets when you die?* Retrieved from https://www.lexology.com/library/detail.aspx?g=288d7480-0d61-43cb-b5ff-e59b211c7bc5

Maciejewski, M. (2016). To do more, better, faster and more cheaply: using big data in public administration. *International Review of Administrative Sciences, 83*(IS), 120-135. doi:10.1177/0020852316640058

MacKinnon, R., Hickok, E., Bar, A., & Lim, H. (2014). *Fostering freedom online: The role of Internet intermediaries.* Paris, France: UNESCO Publishing.

Major v McAllister, Kalupto Creations, LLC and ServiceMagic, 02 S.W.3d 227 (Mo. Ct. App. 2009).

Malta Digital Innovation Authority Act 2018.

ManilaPrinciples.org. (2015a). *The Manila Principles on intermediary liability – background paper.* Retrieved from https://www.eff.org/files/2015/07/08/manila_principles_background_paper.pdf

ManilaPrinciples.org. (2015b). *The Manila Principles on intermediary liability.* Retrieved from https://www.manilap-rinciples.org/principles

Mann, T. (2018). *Australian law dictionary* (3rd ed.). Oxford University Press. Retrieved from https://www-oxfordreference-com

Mann, T., & Blunden, A. (Eds.). (2010). *Australian law dictionary* (1st ed.). Oxford, UK: Oxford University Press. doi:10.1093/acref/9780195557558.001.0001

Marian Grace Burford In the will of Mark Edwin Tretheway (2002) VSC 83.

Matter of Estate of Swezey, New York County Surrogate Court, Case Number: 2017-2976/A.

Matthew, A. F. (2019). *The conceptual legitimacy of support for risk-taking, entrepreneurship and innovation in Australian corporate law: A theoretical examination* (PhD). Queensland University of Technology. doi:10.5204/thesis.eprints.132567

Mattila, J. (2016). *The blockchain phenomenon–the disruptive potential of distributed consensus architectures* (ETLA working paper 38). Helsinki, Finland: The Research Institute of the Finnish Economy.

Maughan v Google Inc., 49 Cal. Rptr. 3d 861 (Cal. Ct. App. 2006).

McCallig, D. (2013). Facebook after death: An evolving policy in a social network. *International Journal of Law and Information Technology*. doi:10.1093/ijlit/eat012

McGuffin, C., Wilks, N., Tomlinson, V., Anderson, B., & Griswold, E. (2011, October 11). 56 inch circus [Crowdfunding campaign]. *Pozible*. Retrieved from https://www.pozible.com/project/1141

McKane, J. (2019). *FNB shut down South African cryptocurrency-linked bank accounts.* Retrieved from https://mybroadband.co.za/news/cryptocurrency/328355-fnb-shuts-down-south-african-cryptocurrency-linked-bank-accounts.html

McKinnon, L. (2011). Planning for the succession of digital assets. *Computer Law & Security Review*, *27*(4), 362–367. doi:10.1016/j.clsr.2011.03.002

McWaters, R. J., Bruno, G., Galaski, R., & Chaterjee, S. (2016). *The future of financial infrastructure: An ambitious look at how blockchain can reshape financial services.* Retrieved from http://www3.weforum.org/docs/WEF_The_future_of_financial_infrastructure.pdf

Metz, R. (2016). Why Microsoft's teen chatbot, Tay, said lots of awful things online. *MIT Technology Review*. Retrieved from https://www.technologyreview.com/s/601111/why-microsoft-accidentally-unleashed-a-neo-nazi-sexbot/

Meyer v Kalanick, 185 F. Supp. 3d 448 (S.D.N.Y. 2016).

Meyer v Kalanick, No 16-2750 (2d Cir. 2017).

Microsoft. (2019). *Future computed: AI & manufacturing.* Retrieved from https://news.microsoft.com/futurecomputed/

Microsoft. (n.d.). *Microsoft AI principles.* Retrieved from https://www.microsoft.com/en-us/ai/our-approach-to-ai

Miller, K. (2016). The application of administrative law principles to technology-assisted decision-making. *AIAL Forum*, *86*, 20-34.

Miller, K. (2017). Connecting the dots: A case study of the robodebt communities.' *AIAL Forum*, *89*, 50-58.

Mitchell, K. (2017). Bitcoin: the business of blockchain. *Without Prejudice, 17*(9), 10-11.

Monahan, D. (2016a). Ibackpack 2.0—4g mifi, hitech batteries—smart cables [Crowdfunding campaign]. *Kickstarter*. Retrieved from https://www.kickstarter.com/projects/ibackpack/ibackpack-20-3g-4g-mi-fi-bulletproof-bluetooth-aud

Monahan, D. (2016b). Ibackpack—wifi, ultra-thin & powerful batteries [Crowdfunding campaign]. *Indiegogo*. Retrieved from https://www.indiegogo.com/projects/1395593

Moore, C. (2013, June 8). Was it really only 30 days? *Cryptocommonicon*. Retrieved from https://cryptocommonicon.wordpress.com/2013/06/08/was-it-really-only-30-days/

Moore, D., & Rid, T. (2016). Cryptopolitik and the darknet. *Global Politics and Strategy, 58*(1), 7–38. doi:10.1080/00396338.2016.1142085

Moss-Racusin, C. A., Dovidio, J. F., Brescoll, V. L., Graham, M. J., & Handelsman, J. (2012). Science faculty's subtle gender biases favor male students. *Proceedings of the National Academy of Sciences of the United States of America*, *109*(41), 16474–16479. doi:10.1073/pnas.1211286109 PMID:22988126

Mullainathan, S. (2019). Biased algorithms are easier to fix than biased people. *The New York Times*. Retrieved from https://www.nytimes.com/2019/12/06/business/algorithm-bias-fix.html

Murphy, S., & Cooper, C. (2016). *Can smart contracts be legally binding contracts?* Retrieved from https://www. nortonrosefulbright.com/-/media/files/nrf/nrfweb/imported/norton-rose-fulbright--r3-smart-contracts-white-paper-key-findings-nov-2016.pdf

Nagel, C. (2016). *Commercial law*. Johannesburg, South Africa: LexisNexis.

Nakamoto, S. (2008). *Bitcoin: A peer-to-peer electronic cash system*. Retrieved From https://bitcoin.org/bitcoin.pdf

Narayanan, A., Bonneau, J., Felten, E., Miller, A., & Goldfeder, S. (2016). *Bitcoin and cryptocurrency technologies: A comprehensive introduction*. Princeton, NJ: Princeton University Press.

National Conference of State Legislatives. (2019). *Access to digital assets of decedents*. Retrieved from https://www. ncsl.org/research/telecommunications-and-information-technology/access-to-digital-assets-of-decedents.aspx

National Consumer Credit Protection Act 2009 (Cth).

National Highway Traffic Safety Administration (NHTSA). (2019). *Automated vehicles for safety*. Retrieved from https:// www.nhtsa.gov/technology-innovation/automated-vehicles-safety

National Payment Systems Act, 78 of 1998.

National Security Commission on Artificial Intelligence (NSCAI). (2019). *Interim report*. Retrieved from https://www. epic.org/foia/epic-v-ai-commission/AI-Commission-Interim-Report-Nov-2019.pdf

National Transport Commission (NTC). (2019). *Automated vehicles in Australia*. Retrieved from https://www.ntc.gov. au/transport-reform/automated-vehicle-program

National Treasury's Taxation Laws Amendment Bill 2018.

NC v Queensland Corrective Services Commission (1997) QADT 22.

Nemet Chevrolet Ltd v Consumeraffairs.com Inc., 591 F. 3d 250 (4th Cir. 2009).

Nemitz, P. (2018). *Constitutional democracy and technology in the age of artificial intelligence*. Retrieved from https:// royalsocietypublishing.org/doi/abs/10.1098/rsta.2018.0089

Neuman, E. (2018, September 20). First class action filed in the world of crowdfunding (The Marker). *Hamburger Evron & Co*. Retrieved from http://www.evronlaw.com/en/first-class-action-filed-world-crowdfunding-marker/

New South Wales Law Reform Commission. (2018). *Access to digital assets upon death or incapacity* (consultation paper 20). Retrieved from https://www.lawreform.justice.nsw.gov.au/Documents/Publications/Consultation-Papers/CP20.pdf

New Zealand Law Commission. (2019). *Review of succession law*. Retrieved from https://www.lawcom.govt.nz/our-projects/review-succession-law

Nicosia v Amazon.com, Inc., Case 1:14-cv-04513-SLT-MDG (EDNY 2015).

Nieman, A. (2015). A few South African cents' worth on Bitcoin. *Potchefstroom Electronic Law Journal/Potchefstroomse Elektroniese Regsblad, 18*(5), 1978-2010.

Nseke, P. (2018). How crypto-currency can decrypt the global digital divide: Bitcoins a means for African emergence. *International Journal of Innovation and Economic Development, 3*(6), 61–70. doi:10.18775/ijied.1849-7551-7020.2015.36.2005

NSW Department of Justice. (2018). *Statutory review – Defamation Act 2005*. Retrieved from https://www.justice.nsw. gov.au/justicepolicy/Documents/defamation-act-statutory-review-report.pdf

NSW Trustee & Guardian. (n.d.) Wills frequently asked questions. Retrieved from https://www.tag.nsw.gov.au/wills-faqs.html

Numerato, D. (2016). Corruption and public secrecy: An ethnography of football match-fixing. *Current Sociology, 64*(5), 699–717. doi:10.1177/0011392115599815

Nunes, I., & Jannach, D. (2017). A systematic review and taxonomy of explanations in decision support and recommender systems. *User Modeling and User-Adapted Interaction, 27*(3-5), 393–444. doi:10.100711257-017-9195-0

Nunn, S. (2003). Seeking tools for the war on terror: A critical assessment of emerging technologies in law enforcement. *Policing, 26*(3), 454–472. doi:10.1108/13639510310489494

O'Donnell, J. (2019). *Kickstarter rule changes over time* [Data set]. Figshare. doi:10.6084/m9.figshare.8942738

O'Neil, C. (2016). *Weapons of math destruction: How big data increases inequality and threatens democracy*. New York, NY: Crown Publishers.

O'Sullivan, T. (2014). Online shopping terms and conditions in practice: Validity of incorporation and unfairness. *Canterbury Law Review, 20*, 1.

Obermeyer, Z., Powers, B., Vogeli, C., & Mullainathan, S. (2019). Dissecting racial bias in an algorithm used to manage the health of populations. *Science, 366*(6464), 447–453. doi:10.1126cience.aax2342 PMID:31649194

Office of Diversity and Outreach. (n.d.). *State of science on unconscious bias*. Retrieved from https://diversity.ucsf.edu/resources/state-science-unconscious-bias

Office of the Australian Information Commissioner (OAIC). (2014). *Guidelines on data matching in Australian Government administration*. Retrieved from https://www.oaic.gov.au/privacy/guidance-and-advice/guidelines-on-data-matching-in-australian-government-administration/

Office of the Australian Information Commissioner (OAIC). (2018a). *Submission 13, submission to the review of the identity-matching services bill 2018 and the Australian passports amendments (identity-matching services) bill 2018*. Retrieved from https://www.aph.gov.au/Parliamentary_Business/Committees/Joint/Intelligence_and_Security/IMSBill/Submissions

Office of the Australian Information Commissioner (OAIC). (2018a). *The ATO's administrative approach to the disclosure of tax debt information to credit reporting bureaus — submission to the Australian Taxation Office*. Canberra, Australia: OAIC.

Office of the Australian Information Commissioner (OAIC). (2018b). *Guide to data analytics and the Australian Privacy Principles*. Canberra, Australia: OAIC.

Office of the Australian Information Commissioner (OAIC). (2018b, March). *Guide to data analytics and the Australian privacy principles*. Retrieved from https://www.oaic.gov.au/resources/agencies-and-organisations/guides/guide-to-data-analytics-and-the-australian-privacy-principles.pdf

Office of the Australian Information Commissioner (OAIC). (2019). *Australian privacy principles guidelines: Privacy Act 1988 (Cth)*. Retrieved from https://www.oaic.gov.au/privacy/australian-privacy-principles-guidelines/

Office of the Australian Information Commissioner (OAIC). (2019a). *Artificial Intelligence: Australia's Ethics Framework – Submission to the Department of Industry, Innovation and Science and Data 61 discussion paper*. Canberra, Australia: OAIC.

Office of the Australian Information Commissioner (OAIC). (2019b). *Developing Standards for Artificial Intelligence: Hearing Australia's Voice — submission to Standards Australia.* Canberra, Australia: OAIC.

Office of the Australian Information Commissioner (OAIC). (2019c). *Handling of personal information — Department of Human Services PAYG data matching program.* Canberra, Australia: OAIC.

Office of the Australian Information Commissioner (OAIC). (2019d). *Handling of personal information — Department of Human Services NEIDM data matching program.* Canberra, Australia: OAIC.

Office of the United States Trade Representatives. (2018). *United States-Mexico-Canada Agreement.* Retrieved from https://ustr.gov/trade-agreements/free-trade-agreements/united-states-mexico-canada-agreement/agreement-between

Office of the Victorian Information Commissioner (OVIC). (2018). *Artifical intelligence and privacy: issues paper.* Melbourne: OVIC.

Office of the Victorian Information Commissioner (OVIC). (2018, June). *Artificial intelligence and privacy.* Retrieved from https://ovic.vic.gov.au/wp-content/uploads/2018/08/AI-Issues-Paper-V1.1.pdf

Office of the Victorian Information Commissioner (OVIC). (2019). *Submission to the artificial intelligence: Australia's ethic framework discussion paper.* Retrieved from https://ovic.vic.gov.au/wp-content/uploads/2019/06/OVIC-submission-to-DIIS-AI-Ethical-Framework-Discussion-Paper-V1.0-.pdf

Office of the Victorian Information Commissioner. (2019). *Submission to DIIS on artificial intelligence: Australia's ethics framework discussion paper.* Retrieved from https://ovic.vic.gov.au/resource/submission-to-diis-on-artificial-intelligence-australias-ai-ethics-framework-discussion-paper/

Olshansky, S., & Wison, S. (2018). *Do blockchains have anything to offer identity?* Retrieved from https://www.internetsociety.org/resources/doc/2018/blockchain-identity/

Ombudsman Act 1976 (Cth).

Ombudsman, C. (2017, July). *Centrelink's automated debt raising and recovery system.* Retrieved from https://www.ombudsman.gov.au/__data/assets/pdf_file/0022/43528/Report-Centrelinks-automated-debt-raising-and-recovery-system-April-2017.pdf

Ombudsman, C. (2019, April). *Centrelink's automated debt raising and recovery system: Implementation report.* Retrieved from https://www.ombudsman.gov.au/__data/assets/pdf_file/0025/98314/April-2019-Centrelinks-Automated-Debt-Raising-and-Recovery-System.pdf

Omohundro, S. (2014). Cryptocurrencies, smart contracts, and artificial intelligence. *AI Matters, 1*(2), 19–21. doi:10.1145/2685328.2685334

Ong, R. (2013). Internet intermediaries: The liability for defamatory postings in China and Hong Kong. *Computer Law & Security Review, 29*(3), 274–281. doi:10.1016/j.clsr.2013.03.006

Oransky, A. I. (2018, July 30). How institutions gaslight whistleblowers—And what can be done. *Retraction Watch.* Retrieved from https://retractionwatch.com/2018/07/30/how-institutions-gaslight-whistleblowers-and-what-can-be-done/

Orellana v Commissioner, No. 8950-08S, 2010 WL 1568447 [T.C. Apr. 20, 2010].

Organisation for Economic Co-operation and Development (OECD). (2010). *The economic and social role of internet intermediaries.* Retrieved from https://www.oecd.org/internet/ieconomy/44949023.pdf

Organisation for Economic Co-operation and Development (OECD). (2011). *The role of internet intermediaries in advancing public policy objectives*. Retrieved from https://www.oecd.org/sti/ieconomy/theroleofinternetintermediariesinadvancingpublicpolicyobjectives.htm

Organisation for Economic Co-operation and Development (OECD). (2019). *Recommendation on artificial intelligence (AI)*. Retrieved from https://legalinstruments.oecd.org/en/instruments/OECD-LEGAL-0449

Otega, P. A., Maini, V., & DeepMind Safety Team. (2018, Sept 27). *Building safe artificial intelligence: specification, robustness, and assurance*. Retrieved from https://medium.com/@deepmindsafetyresearch/building-safe-artificial-intelligence-52f5f75058f1

Oxford Australian Law Dictionary. (2010). Sydney, Australia: Oxford University Press.

Palmer, S., & Verhoeven, D. (2016). Crowdfunding Academic Researchers: The Importance of Academic Social Media Profiles. In C. Bernadas & D. Minchella (Eds.), *ECSM2016-Proceedings of the 3rd European Conference on Social Media* (pp. 291–299). Sonning Common, UK: Academic Conferences and Publishing International Limited.

Pangburn, D. J. (2019, February 8). *Washington could be the first state to rein in automated decision-making*. Retrieved from https://www.fastcompany.com/90302465/washington-introduces-landmark-algorithmic-accountability-laws

Pappalardo, K., & Suzor, N. (2018). The liability of Australian online intermediaries. *The Sydney Law Review, 40*, 469–498.

Parliament, U. K. (2018). *AI in the UK: ready, willing and able*. Retrieved from https://publications.parliament.uk/pa/ld201719/ldselect/ldai/100/100.pdf

Parliamentary Joint Committee on Intelligence and Security (PJCIS). (2019, October). *Advisory report on the identity-matching services bill 2019 and the Australian passports amendment (identity-matching services) bill 2019*. Retrieved from https://www.aph.gov.au/Parliamentary_Business/Committees/Joint/Intelligence_and_Security/Identity-Matching2019/Report/section?id=committees%2freportjnt%2f024343%2f27801

Pasquale, F. (2016). *Black Box Society: The Secret Algorithms That Control Money and Information*. Harvard University Press.

Pasquale, F. (2011). Restoring Transparency to Automated Authority. *Journal on Telecommunications & High Technology Law, 9*, 235–254. Retrieved from http://digitalcommons.law.umaryland.edu/cgi/viewcontent.cgi?article=2357&context=fac_pubs

Pasquale, F. (2015). *The black box society: The secret algorithms that control money and information*. Cambridge, MA: Harvard University Press. doi:10.4159/harvard.9780674736061

Pasquale, F. (2017). Toward a fourth law of robotics: Preserving attribution, responsibility, and explainability in an algorithmic society. *Ohio State Law Journal, 78*, 1243–1255.

Pasquale, F. (2017). Toward a Fourth Law of Robotics: Preserving Attribution, Responsibility, and Explainability in an Algorithmic Society. *Ohio State Law Journal, 78*, 1243–1255. Retrieved from https://kb.osu.edu/bitstream/handle/1811/85768/OSLJ_V78N5_1243.pdf

Pavlou, K. E., & Snodgrass, R. T. (2008). Forensic analysis of database tampering. *ACM Transactions on Database Systems, 33*(4), 30. doi:10.1145/1412331.1412342

PEGA. (2019). *Consumers failing to embrace AI benefits, says research: PEGA study highlights the need for greater empathy in artificial intelligence systems*. Retrieved from https://www.pega.com/about/news/press-releases/consumers-failing-embrace-ai-benefits-says-research

Penfield, T., Baker, M. J., Scoble, R., & Wykes, M. C. (2014). Assessment, evaluations, and definitions of research impact: A review. *Research Evaluation, 23*(1), 21–32. doi:10.1093/reseval/rvt021

Perel, M., & Elkin-Koren, N. (2017). Black Box Tinkering: Beyond Disclosure in Algorithmic Enforcement. *Florida Law Review, 69*, 181–221. Retrieved from https://scholarship.law.ufl.edu/cgi/viewcontent.cgi?article=1348

Perry, M. (2019). *Idecide: Digital pathways to decision*. Retrieved from https://www.fedcourt.gov.au/digital-law-library/judges-speeches/justice-perry/perry-j-20190321

Perry, M. (2019). iDecide: Digital pathways to decisions. *Federal Judicial Scholarship,* 3. Retrieved from http://www.austlii.edu.au/cgi-bin/sinodisp/au/journals/FedJSchol/2019/3.html

Perumall, A. (2019). *Blockchain and cryptocurrency regulation in Africa*. Retrieved from https://www.dailymaverick.co.za/article/2019-04-08-blockchain-and-cryptocurrency-regulation-in-africa/

Perumall, A., Selfe, E., & Jen, S. (2019). *Blockchain and cryptocurrency in Africa: A comparative summary of the reception and regulation of blockchain and cryptocurrency in Africa*. Retrieved from https://www.bakermckenzie.com/-/media/files/insight/publications/2019/02/report_blockchainandcryptocurrencyreg_feb2019.pdf

Perzanowski, A., & Schultz, J. (2016). *The end of ownership: Personal property in the digital economy*. Cambridge, MA: MIT Press. doi:10.7551/mitpress/9780262035019.001.0001

Peters, G., Panayi, E., & Chapelle, A. (2015). Trends in cryptocurrencies and blockchain technologies: A monetary theory and regulation perspective. *Journal of Financial Perspectives, 3*(3), 1–46.

PEW Research Center. (2019). *Social media fact sheet*. Retrieved from https://www.pewinternet.org/fact-sheet/social-media/

Pintarich v Deputy Commissioner of Taxation [2018] FCAFC 79.

Pomerantz, J., & Peek, R. (2016). Fifty shades of open. *First Monday, 21*(5). doi:10.5210/fm.v21i5.6360

Post, D. (2015, August 27). A bill of internet history, or two members of Congress helped create a trillion or so dollars of value. *The Washington Post*. Retrieved from https://www.washingtonpost.com/news/volokh-conspiracy/wp/2015/08/27/a-bit-of-internet-history-or-how-two-members-of-congress-helped-create-a-trillion-or-so-dollars-of-value/?utm_term=.9ffe926c6a84

Pound, A., & Evans, K. (2019). Annotated Victorian charter of rights (2nd ed.). Pyrmont, Australia: Thomson Reuters (Professional) Australia Limited.

Prime Minister of Australia. (n.d.). Response to digital platforms inquiry. *Media Release*. Retrieved from https://www.pm.gov.au/media/response-digital-platforms-inquiry

Privacy Act 1988 (Cth).

Privacy and Data Protection Act. (2014). Vic.

Probate and Administration Act. (1898). NSW.

Product Liability Directive (85/374/EEC).

Queensland Maintenance Services Pty Ltd v Commissioner of Taxation [2011] FCA 1443.

R (Countryside Alliance) v Attorney General (2007) UKHL 52.

R (Countryside Alliance) v Attorney General (2008) AC 719.

Rafferty, S. (2018, October 18). Woman 'faked' ovarian cancer to collect $55k in donations, court told. *ABC News*. Retrieved from https://www.abc.net.au/news/2018-10-18/lu-wieland-accused-of-faking-stage-five-ovarian-cancer/10391034

Rajput, S., Singh, A., Khurana, S., Bansal, T., & Shreshtha, S. (2019). *Blockchain technology and cryptocurrenices*. Paper presented at the 2019 Amity International Conference on Artificial Intelligence (AICAI), Dubai, UAE. 10.1109/AICAI.2019.8701371

Raskin, M. (2017). The law and legality of smart contracts. *Georgetown Law Technology Review.*, *1*(2), 304–341.

Re Application of Brown: Estate of Springfield (1991) 23 NSWLR 535.

Re Estate of Ellsworth. (2005). *No. 2005-296, 651-DE*. Mich.: Prob. Ct.

Re Lifestyle Communities Ltd (No 3) (2009a) 31 VAR 286.

Re Lifestyle Communities Ltd (No 3) (2009b) VCAT 1869.

Re Minister for Immigration and Multicultural Affairs; Ex parte Palme [2003] 216 CLR 212.

Re: Yu [2013] QSC 322.

Rees, N., Rice, S., & Allen, D. (2018). *Australian anti-discrimination and equal opportunity law* (3rd ed.). Alexandria, Australia: Federation Press.

Regalado, A. (2016, July 15). Why the promise of a plant that glows has left backers in the dark. *MIT Technology Review*. Retrieved from https://www.technologyreview.com/s/601884/why-kickstarters-glowing-plant-left-backers-in-the-dark/

Register, D., & Adams, H. (2017). Extending HMRC's civil information powers. *Tax Journal*. Retrieved from https://www.taxjournal.com/articles/extending-hmrc-s-civil-information-powers-30082018

Register.com Inc. v Verio Inc. (2004) 356 F 3D 393.

Reid, B. (2017). Legal life after death: Publicity, physical and digital assets. *Southern Journal of Business and Ethics*, *9*, 108–122.

Reno v American Civil Liberties Union, 521 U.S. 844 (1997).

Republic of Estonia. (2018). *Estonia will have an artificial intelligence strategy*. Retrieved from https://www.riigikantselei.ee/en/news/estonia-will-have-artificial-intelligence-strategy

Reserve Bank of India Act of 1934.

Reuters Business News. (2018, October 10). *Amazon scraps secret AI recruiting tool that showed bias against women*. Retrieved from https://www.reuters.com/article/us-amazon-com-jobs-automation-insight/amazon-scraps-secret-ai-recruiting-tool-that-showed-bias-against-women-idUSKCN1MK08G

Revised Uniform Fiduciary Access to Digital Assets (RUFADA) Act 2015 (US).

Ribeiro, M. T., Singh, S., & Guestrin, C. (2016). Why should I trust you? Explaining the predictions of any classifier. *Proceedings of the 22nd ACM SIGKDD international conference on knowledge discovery and data mining*, 1135-1144. Retrieved from https://arxiv.org/pdf/1602.04938.pdf

Rice, S. (2013). *Basic instinct: The heroic project of anti-discrimination law (Roma Mitchell oration)*. Retrieved from https://eoc.sa.gov.au/sites/default/files/inline-files/Rice_Basic%20Instinct_Roma%20Mitchell%20Oration_0.pdf

Ritchie, J. (2003). The application of qualitative methods to social research. In J. Ritchie & J. Lewis (Eds.), *Qualitative research practice: a guide for social science students and researchers* (pp. 24–46). London: Sage Publications.

Robertson v Balmain New Ferry Co. (1906) 4 CLR 37.

Robotics Open Letter. (n.d.). *Open letter to the European Commission: AI and robotics*. Retrieved from http://www.robotics-openletter.eu/

Rosen, J. (2012). The right to be forgotten. *Stanford Law Review*, *64*, 88–92. Retrieved from https://review.law.stanford.edu/wp-content/uploads/sites/3/2012/02/64-SLRO-88.pdf

Rossi v Commissioner of Taxation [2015] AATA 601.

Rottenstreich, S. J., & Barkhorn, K. (2019). *What happens to my digital assests on death or incapacity*. Retrived from https://trustbclp.com/what-happens-to-my-digital-assets-on-death-or-incapacity/

Rouvroy, A. (2012). The end(s) of critique: data-behaviourism vs. due-process. In M. Hildebrandt & K. De Vries (Eds.), *Privacy, due process and the computational turn: Philosophers of law meet philosophers of technology* (pp. 142–168). Abingdon, UK: Routledge.

Roux, S. (2017). Smart contracts. *Without Prejudice, 17*(2), 28-29.

Rowley, J. (2002). Using case studies in research. *Management Research News, 25*(1), 16–27. doi:10.1108/01409170210782990

Rowley, J. (2012). Conducting research interviews. *Management Research Review, 35*(3/4), 260–271. doi:10.1108/01409171211210154

Rudder v Microsoft Corp [1999] OJ No 3778 (Sup Ct J).

Rühl, G. (2019). *The law applicable to smart contracts, or much ado about nothing?* Retrieved from https://www.law.ox.ac.uk/business-law-blog/blog/2019/01/law-applicable-smart-contracts-or-much-ado-about-nothing

Ryan, D. (2016). *Understanding digital marketing: Marketing strategies for engaging the digital generation*. London, UK: KoganPage.

Safety, R. (Automated Vehicles) Act 2018 (Vic).

Sandvig, C. (2014). Seeing the sort: The aesthetic and industrial defense of the algorithm. *Journal of the New Media Caucus, 10*(3). Retrieved from http://median.newmediacaucus.org/art-infrastructures-information/seeing-the-sort-the-aesthetic-and-industrial-defense-of-the-algorithm/

Savas, E. S., Fite, H. H., Schumacher, B. G., Kanter, J., Bowen, H. R., & Mangum, G. L. (1969). Computers in public administration. *Public Administration Review, 29*(2), 225–231. doi:10.2307/973708

Schaerer, E., Kelley, R., & Nicolescu, M. (2009). Robots as animals: A framework for liability and responsibility in human-robot interactions. In *Proceedings of The 18th IEEE International Symposium on Robot and Human Interactive Communication (RO-MAN 2009)*. Toyama, Japan: IEEE. 10.1109/ROMAN.2009.5326244

Schafer, B. (2016). Closing Pandora's box? The EU proposal on the regulation of robots. *The Journal of the Justice and the Law Society of the University of Queeensland, 19*, 55–68.

Schneider v Amazon.com, 31 P. 3d 37 (Wash Ct App. 2001).

Schneier, B. (2015). *Applied cryptography, protocols algorithms and source code in C*. Brisbane, Australia: John Wiley and Sons.

Schrey, J., & Thalhofer, T. (2017). Rechtliche aspekte der blockchain. *Neue Juristische Wochenschrift: NJW, 70*(20), 1431–1436.

Schwienbacher, A. (2017). Entrepreneurial risk-taking in crowdfunding campaigns. *Small Business Economics, 51*(4), 843–859. doi:10.100711187-017-9965-4

Searle Australia v PIAC [1992] 108 ALR 163.

Segerstedt-Wiberg v Sweden (2006) ECHR 597.

Segerstedt-Wiberg v Sweden (2007) 44 EHRR 2.

Selinger, E., & Hartzog, W. (2014). Obscurity and privacy (SSRN Scholarly Paper No ID 2439866). *Social Science Research Network*. Retrieved from https://papers.ssrn.com/abstract=2439866

Sex Discrimination Act 2004 (Cth).

Sgardelis and Commissioner of Taxation (2007) 68 ATR 963.

Sharkey, N., & Murray, I. (2016). Reinventing administrative leadership in Australian taxation: Beware the fine balance of social psychological and rule of law principles. *Australian Tax Forum*, 63.

Sherer, S. A., & Alter, S. (2004). Information systems risks and risk factors: Are they mostly about information systems? *Communications of the Association for Information Systems, 14*(1). doi:10.17705/1CAIS.01402

Sheridan, D. (1997). Zeran v. AOL and the effect of section 230 of the Communications Decency Act upon liability for defamation on the Internet. *Albany Law Review, 61*, 147–179.

Sikhs for Justice 'SFJ' v Facebook Inc., 144 F. Supp. 3d 1088 (ND Cal. 2015).

Sims, R. (2017). *The ACCC's approach to colluding robots*. Retrieved from https://www.accc.gov.au/speech/the-accc%E2%80%99s-approach-to-colluding-robots

Singh, S. (2013). *Globalization and money: A global south perspective*. Lanham, MD: Rowman & Littlefield.

Smythe v Thomas (2007) 71 NSWLR 537; [2007] NSWSC 844.

Social Security (Administration) Act 1999 (Cth).

Society of Trust and Estate Practitioners. (2017). *Digital assets special interest group digital assets: Practitioner's guide Australia*. Retrieved from https://www.step.org/sites/default/files/Digital%20Assets%20Practitioner%20Guide%20-%20Australia.pdf

Solonec, T. (2000). Racial discrimination in the private rental market: Overcoming stereotypes and breaking the cycle of housing despair in Western Australia. *Indigenous Law Bulletin, 5*(2), 4–6.

Solove, D. (2013). Privacy self-management and the consent dilemma. *Harvard Law Review, 126*, 1880–1893.

Sonnad, N. (2018). US border agents hacked their "risk assessment" system to recommend detention 100% of the time. *Quartz*. Retrieved from https://qz.com/1314749/us-border-agents-hacked-their-risk-assessment-system-to-recommend-immigrant-detention-every-time/

South Africa, The National Treasury's Taxation Laws Amendment Bill (2018).

South African Reserve Bank Act 90 of 1989, (1989).

Southwestern Indemnities Ltd v Bank of New South Wales & Federal Commissioner of Taxation [1973] 73 ATC 4171.

Spam Act 2003 (Cth).

Specht v Netscape Communications Corp. (2001) 150 F Supp 2d 585.

Spotify. (2019). *Terms and conditions of use*. Retrieved from https://www.spotify.com/au/legal/end-user-agreement/#s19

Stack, P., Feller, J., O'Reilly, P., Gleasure, R., Li, S., & Cristoforo, J. (2017). Managing risk in business centric crowd-funding platforms. In *Proceedings of the 13th International Symposium on Open Collaboration*, Galway, Ireland: Association for Computing Machinery. 10.1145/3125433.3125460

Standards Australia. (2019). *Developing standards for artificial intelligence: Hearing Australia's voice discussion paper*. Retrieved from https://www.standards.org.au/getmedia/aeaa5d9e-8911-4536-8c36-76733a3950d1/Artificial-Intelligence-Discussion-Paper-(004).pdf.aspx

Statista. (2019). *Digital advertising*. Retrieved from https://www.statista.com/outlook/216/100/digital-advertising/worldwide#market-globalRevenue

Steen, A., D'Alessandro, S., Graves, C., Perkins, M., Genders, R., Barbera, F., . . . Davis, N. (2017). *Estate planning in Australia*. Charles Sturt University. Retrieved from https://researchoutput.csu.edu.au/ws/portalfiles/portal/19332794/Estate_Planning_in_Australia_Final_Report_021017.pdf

Stratton Oakmont Inc. v Prodigy Services Co, WL 323710 (NY Sup Ct. 1995).

Street v Queensland Bar Association (1989) 168 CLR 461.

Strickler, Y., Chen, P., & Adler, C. (2012, September 21). Kickstarter is not a store. *Kickstarter Blog*. Retrieved from https://www.kickstarter.com/blog/kickstarter-is-not-a-store

Succession Act. (1981). QLD.

Sundar, S. S., & Kim, J. (2019). Machine heuristic: When we trust computers more than humans with our personal information. In *Proceedings of the 2019 CHI Conference on Human Factors in Computing Systems* (CHI '19). New York, NY: ACM. 10.1145/3290605.3300768

Superannuation Industry (Supervision) Act 1993 (Cth).

Surowiecki, J. (2005). *The wisdom of crowds: Why the many are smarter than the few* (reprint ed.). New York, NY: Anchor.

Surveillance Devices Act 2004 (Cth).

Suzor, N. (2019). *Lawless: The secret rules that govern our digital lives*. London: Cambridge University Press. doi:10.1017/9781108666428

Swan, M. (2015). *Blockchain Blueprint for a new economy*. Sebastopol, CA: O'Reilly Media.

Swords, J. (2018). Interpenetration and intermediation of crowd-patronage platforms. *Information, Communication & Society*.

Szabo, N. (1997). *Formalizing and securing relationships on public networks*. Retrieved from https://nakamotoinstitute.org/formalizing-securing-relationships/

Tan, E. (2018). *The evolution of smart contracts*. Retrieved from hackernoon.com/are-smart-contracts-the-future-1d9028f49743

Tapscott, D., & Tapscott, A. (2018). *Blockchain revolution: how the technology behind bitcoin and other cryptocurrencies is changing the world*. London, UK: Portfolio.

Taskinsoy, J. (2018). B*itcoin mania: An end to the US dollar's hegemony or another cryptocurrency experiment destined to fail?* Retrieved from https://papers.ssrn.com/sol3/papers.cfm?abstract_id=3311989

Taxation Administration Act 1953 (Cth).

Tay, L. (2012). Immigration targets 'problem travellers' with analytics. *Itnews*. Retrieved from https://www.itnews.com.au/news/immigration-targets-problem-travellers-with-analytics-321562

Telecommunications (Interception and Access) Act 1979 (Cth).

Teytelman, L. (2015a, March 24). Calibrating crowdfunding expectations. *Yes, Another Science Blog*. Retrieved from http://anothersb.blogspot.com.au/2015/03/calibrating-crowdfunding-expectations.html

Teytelman, L. (2015b, March 30). Biomedical funding is broken; crowdfunding is not the fix. *Yes, Another Science Blog*. Retrieved from http://anothersb.blogspot.com.au/2015/03/biomedical-funding-is-broken.html

The Gazette. (n.d.). *What happens to digital assets on death?* Retrieved from https://www.thegazette.co.uk/all-notices/content/101190

The Senate Community Affairs References Committee. (2017). Design, scope, cost-benefit analysis, contracts awarded and implementation associated with the better management of the social welfare system initiative. *Commonwealth of Australia*. Retrieved from https://www.aph.gov.au/Parliamentary_Business/Committees/Senate/Community_Affairs/SocialWelfareSystem/Report

The South African Reserve Bank. (2018). *Review of the national payment system Act 78 of 1998 policy paper*. Retrieved from http://www.treasury.gov.za/publications/other/NPS%20Act%20Review%20Policy%20Paper%20-%20final%20version%20-%2013%20September%202018.pdf

The South African Reserve Bank. (2019). *Statement on crypto assets*. Retrieved from https://www.resbank.co.za/Lists/News%20and%20Publications/Attachments/9037/Joint%20media%20statement_crypto%20assets%20consultation%20paper.pdf

Therapeutic Goods Act 1989 (Cth).

Thomson, M. (2014, May 18). Unto the valley of death...of crowd funding science. *Dr Mel Thomson*. Retrieved from https://drmelthomson.wordpress.com/2014/05/18/unto-the-valley-of-death-of-crowd-funding-science/

Thornton v Shoe Lane Parking Ltd (1971) 1 All ER 686.

Tillet, A. (2019). Federal government backs down on 'robo-debt' scheme. *Australian Financial Review*. Retrieved from https://www.afr.com/politics/federal/government-backs-down-on-robo-debt-scheme-20191119-p53bz4

Toll (FGCT) v Alphapharm Pty Ltd (2004) 219 CLR 165.

Toratani, M., Konno, M., Asai, A., Koseki, J., Kawamoto, K., Tamari, K., ... Ishii, H. (2018). A convolutional neural network uses microscopic images to differentiate between mouse and human cell lines and their radioresistent clones. *Cancer Research*, 78(23), 6703–6707. doi:10.1158/0008-5472.CAN-18-0653 PMID:30254144

Trade Practices Act 1974 (Cth).

Treleaven, P., Brown, R., & Yang, D. (2017). Blockchain technology in finance. *Computer*, 50(9), 14–17. doi:10.1109/MC.2017.3571047

Trkulja v. Google LLC [2018] HCA 25.

Turner, J. (2019). *Robot rules: Regulating artificial intelligence*. Cham, Switzerland: Palgrave Macmillan. doi:10.1007/978-3-319-96235-1

Turner, R. (2014). Internet defamation law and publication: A multi-jurisdictional analysis. *The University of New South Wales Law Journal, 37*(1), 34–62.

Twentieth Century Fox. (2002). *Minority Report*.

U.S. v Wilson, 593 F. Appendix 942 [11th Cir. 2014].

Uber BV v Commissioner of Taxation (2017) FCA 110.

Uhlmann, E. L., & Cohen, G. L. (2007). I think it, therefore it's true: Effects of self-perceived objectivity on hiring discrimination. *Organizational Behavior and Human Decision Processes, 104*(2), 207–223. doi:10.1016/j.obhdp.2007.07.001

UK House of Lords. (2018). *AI in the UK: Ready, willing and able?* Retrieved from https://publications.parliament.uk/pa/ld201719/ldselect/ldai/100/100.pdf

UK Office of the Information Commissioner (OIC). (2017). *Big data, artificial intelligence, machine learning and data protection.* Retrieved from https://ico.org.uk/media/for-organisations/documents/2013559/big-data-ai-ml-and-data-protection.pdf

Uniform Access to Digital Assets by Fiduciaries Act. (2016). Canada.

Uniform Fiduciary Access to Digital Assets (UFADA) Act 2014.

Uniform Law Conference of Canada. (2016). *Uniform access to digital assets by fiduciaries act 2016.* Retrieved from http://www.ulcc.ca/images/stories/2016_pdf_en/2016ulcc0006.pdf

Uniform Probate Code (1969).

United Nations Economic Commission for Europe (UNECE). (2019, June). *Revised framework document on automated/autonomous vehicles.* Retrieved from https://www.unece.org/fileadmin/DAM/trans/doc/2019/wp29/ECE-TRANS-WP29-2019-34-rev.1e.pdf

United Nations Economic for Africa. (2017). *Blockchain technology in Africa.* Retrieved from https://www.uneca.org/sites/default/files/images/blockchain_technology_in_africa_draft_report_19-nov-2017-final_edited.pdf

United States Department of Defence. (2002, 12 February). *News transcript Department of Defence news briefing Secretary Rumsfeld and General Myer.* Retrieved from https://archive.defense.gov/Transcripts/Transcript.aspx?TranscriptID=2636

United States White House. (2019, 11 February). *Maintaining American Leadership in Artificial Intelligence.* Executive Order 13859. Retrieved from https://www.whitehouse.gov/ai/executive-order-ai/

University of Montreal. (2017). *The Montreal Declaration for a responsible development of Artificial Intelligence.* Retrieved from https://docs.wixstatic.com/ugd/ebc3a3_c5c1c196fc16475 6afb92466c081d7ae.pdf

Uratoriu v Commissioner of Taxation [2008] FCA 1531.

USLegalWills.com. (2016). *Are there even fewer Americans without wills?* Retrieved from https://www.uslegalwills.com/blog/americans-without-wills/

Van den Hoven van Genderen, R. (2018). Legal personhood in the age of artificially intelligent robots. In W. Barfield & U. Pagallo (Eds.), *Research Handbook on the Law of Artificial Intelligence* (pp. 213-250). Cheltenham, UK: Edward Elgar Publishing.

van Dijsck, J. (2014). Datafication, dataism and dataveillance: Big Data between scientific paradigm and ideology. *Surveillance & Society, 12*(2), 199–208. doi:10.24908s.v12i2.4776

Van Tassell v United Marketing Group (2011) 795 F Supp 2d 770.

Vehicles, M. (Trials of Automotive Technologies) Amendment Act 2016 (SA).

Veit, A. (2019). Swimming upstream: leveraging data and analytics for taxpayer engagement - an Australian and international perspective. *eJournal of Tax Research, 16*(3), 474-499.

Verhoeven, D., Palmer, S., Seitzinger, J., & Randall, M. (n.d.). *Research my world: Crowdfunding research pilot project evalutation.* Retrieved from https://www.deakin.edu.au/research/documents/research-my-world.pdf

Verschelden, A. (2019). *Get ready: Blockchain will transform the legal industry.* Retrieved from https://www.moore-global.com/insights/articles/get-ready-blockchain-will-transform-the-legal-indu

Victorian WorkSafe Scheme. (n.d.). *How to register for WorkCover insurance.* Retrieved from https://www.worksafe.vic.gov.au/how-register-workcover-insurance

Virtual Financial Assets Act, 2018 (Malta).

Vitale, M. (2013). Crowdfunding: Recent international developments and its compatibility with Australia's existing regulatory framework. *Journal of Banking and Finance Law and Practice, 24*(4), 300–310. doi:10.2139srn.2324573

Voller v Nationwide New Pty Ltd [2019] NSWSC 766.

Wagner, G. (2018). *Robot liability.* Retrieved form https://ssrn.com/abstract=3198764

Walch, A. (2016). The path of the blockchain lexicon (and the law). *Review of Banking and Financial Law, 36*(2), 713–765.

Walker, M. D. (2017). The new uniform digital assets law: Estate planning and administration in the information age. *Real Property. Trust and Estate Law Journal, 52*(1), 51–78.

Walsh, T. (2019). Understanding AI. In Office of the Victorian Information Commissioner (Ed.), Closer to the machine: Technical, social and legal aspects of AI (pp. 7-22). Melbourne, Australia: Office of the Victorian Information Commissioner.

Waterhouse v Bell (1991) 25 NSWLR 99.

WBM v Chief Commissioner of Police (2010) 27 VR 469, VSC 219.

Westlake Legal Group v Yelp Inc., 599 Fed. Appx. 481 (4th Cir. 2015).

WhatsApp. (2016). *Terms of service.* Retrieved from https://www.whatsapp.com/legal/#terms-of-service

Wheat, R. E., Wang, Y., Byrnes, J. E., & Ranganathan, J. (2013). Raising money for scientific research through crowdfunding. *Trends in Ecology & Evolution, 28*(2), 71–72. doi:10.1016/j.tree.2012.11.001 PMID:23219380

WhiteHouse.gov. (2019). *Artificial intelligence for the American people.* Retrieved from https://www.whitehouse.gov/ai/

Whitt v Prosper Funding LLC, 1:15-cv-GHW (SDNY, 2015).

Whittaker, M., Crawford, K., Dobbe, R., Fried, G., Kaziunas, E., Mathur, V., … Schwartz, O. (2018). AI now report 2018. *AI Now Institute New York University.* Retrieved from https://ainowinstitute.org/AI_Now_2018_Report.pdf

Williams v America OnLine Inc. (2001) unreported, Massachusetts, Superior Court, 00-0962, YouTube. (2019). *Terms of service.* Retrieved from https://www.youtube.com/static?template=terms&gl=AU

Williams, J. R. (2008). The declaration of Helsinki and public health. *Bulletin of the World Health Organization, 86*(8), 577–656. doi:10.2471/BLT.08.050955 PMID:18797627

Wills Act. (1997). Vic.

Wisconsin v Loomis, 881 NW 2d 749 (Wis, 2016).

Wolfram, S. (2016). Computational law, symbolic discourse, and the AI constitution. *Wired*. Retrieved from https://www.wired.com/2016/10/computational-law-symbolic-discourse-and-the-ai-constitution/

Wolfson, R. (2018). Maltese parliament passes laws that set regulatory framework for blockchain, cryptocurrency and DLT. *Forbes Magazine*. Retrieved from https://www.forbes.com/sites/rachelwolfson/2018/07/05/maltese-parliament-passes-laws-that-set-regulatory-framework-for-blockchain-cryptocurrency-and-dlt/#6ef3ab49ed2f

Woodforth v Queensland (2017) QCA 100.

Woodman, F. L. (2017). Fiduciary access to digital assets: A review of the uniform law conference of Canada's proposed uniform act and comparable American model legislation. *Canadian Journal of Law and Technology, 15*, 193–227.

Workplace Gender Equality Agency. (2019). *Gender pay gap statistics*. Retrieved from https://www.wgea.gov.au/data/fact-sheets/australias-gender-pay-gap-statistics

World Commission on the Ethics of Scientific Knowledge and Technology. (2017) *Report of COMEST on robotics ethics*. Retrieved from https://unesdoc.unesco.org/ark:/48223/pf0000253952

X v The Minister for Immigration & Multicultural Affairs [1999] 92 FCR 524.

Yaga, D., Mell, P., Roby, N., & Scarfone, K. (2018). *Blockchain technology overview*. Retrieved from arxiv.org/ftp/arxiv/papers/906/906.1078.pdf

Yahoo. (2018). *Yahoo terms of service*. Retrieved from https://policies.yahoo.com/us/en/yahoo/terms/utos/index.htm

Yanner v Eaton (1999) 201 CLR 351.

Yeung, K. (2016, October). Algorithmic regulation and intelligent enforcement. In M. Lodge (Ed.), *Regulation scholarship in crisis? LSE discussion paper No 84* (p. 56). London: London School of Economics.

Zarsky, T. (2013). Transparent predictions. *University of Illinois Law Review, 4*, 1503–1570.

Zeran v America Online Inc., 129 F.3d 327; 958 F. Supp. 1124 (ED Va. 1997).

Ziniti, C. (2008). Optimal liability system for online service providers: How Zeran v. America Online got it right and Web 2.0 proves it. *Berkley Technology Law Journal, 22*, 583–616.

Złotowski, J. A., Sumioka, H., Nishio, S., Glas, D. F., Bartneck, C., & Ishiguro, H. (2018). Persistence of the uncanny valley: the influence of repeated interactions and a robot's attitude to its perception. *Frontiers in Psychology*. Retrieved from https://www.frontiersin.org/articles/10.3389/fpsyg.2015.00883/full

Zuboff, S. (2015). Big other: Surveillance capitalism and the prospects of an informal Civilization. *Journal of Information Technology, 30*(1), 75–89. doi:10.1057/jit.2015.5

Zuboff, S. (2019). *The age of surveillance capitalism: The fight for the future at the new frontier of power*. London: Profile Books Ltd.

Zweig, K., Wenzelburer, G., & Krafft, T. D. (2018). On chances and risks of security related algorithmic decision-making systems. *European Journal for Security Research, 3*(2), 181–203. doi:10.100741125-018-0031-2

About the Contributors

Margaret Jackson is an Emeritus Professor at the College of Business and Law, RMIT University. Emeritus Professor Jackson conducts research in the areas of computer law, Big Data, data protection and privacy, and artificial intelligence. She is the co-author (with Dr G Hughes) of *Private Life in a Digital World*, Thomson Reuters 2015; co-author (with Dr M Shelly) of *Electronic Information and the Law,* Thomson Reuters 2012, author of *A Practical Guide to Protecting Confidential Business Information*, LawBookCo 2003, and author of *Hughes on Data Protection in Australia*, LawBook Co 2001.

Marita Shelly has been a researcher on various multi-disciplinary research projects relating to research data management, the use of social media by Australian courts, the copyright issues related to electronic information and the legal implications of using the internet. She has co-authored a book *Electronic Information and the Law*, Thomson Reuters 2012, (with Emeritus Professor Jackson) as well as several refereed journal articles and book chapters.

* * *

Sam Alexander is admitted as a lawyer and holds an LLM, GDLP, LLB(Hons) and BIntRel. Sam's research focuses on what law reform Australia could undertake to support local businesses in the digital space.

Gordon Hughes is a principal at Davies Collison Cave Law. He is the author or co-author of numerous texts in the area of information technology, data protection and IP commercialisation.

Muhammed Khan, LLB, LLM, is an admitted attorney of the High Court of South Africa and a Lecturer, Faculty of Law, North-West University (Potchefstroom).

Michael Laubscher, MA, LLB, LLM, is an admitted attorney of the High Court of South Africa and a Lecturer Faculty of Law North-West University.

Migle Laukyte (1981) has just been appointed a tenure track professor in law at the University Pompeu Fabra in Barcelona (Spain). Right now she is a visiting professor at the Human Rights Institute "Bartolomé de las Casas" at the Universidad Carlos III de Madrid (Spain)) where she has spent previous 4 years as CONEX-Marie Curie research fellow at the Department of Private Law, working on the research project ALLIES (Artificially Intelligent Entities: Their Legal Status in the Future). She is also a member of the reserve list of the High-Level Expert Group on Artificial Intelligence (AI HLEG) of the European Commission and an associate of Global Security and Disaster Management Limited (GSDM) based in UK. She earned her Ph.D. at the University of Bologna (Italy) with a dissertation on the current and future legal regulation of intelligent computer programs.

Katie Miller is a lawyer and public servant exploring how innovation and technology are changing legal practice and public service. Katie is undertaking a PhD at Deakin University examining the implications for Australian administrative law bodies of technology and automation in government. Katie is a Law Institute of Victoria Accredited Specialist in Administrative Law and a co-host of ABC Melbourne's Writs and Cures.

Jonathan O'Donnell helps people get funding for their research. To be specific, he helps the people in the Faculty of Science at the University of Melbourne in Australia. He has been doing that, on and off, since the 1990's (with varying degrees of success). He loves his job. He loves it so much that he has enrolled in a PhD to look at crowdfunding for research.

Brendan Walker-Munro has held a number of management and executive positions in State and Federal investigative agencies and criminal regulators. Prior to his current role at the Australian Taxation Office, he has worked with the Australian Competition & Consumer Commission, Liquor & Gaming NSW and the Australian Health Practitioner Regulation Agency. He is currently studying a PhD in law with Swinburne University.

Index

A

Artificial Intelligence (AI) 89, 110, 136, 149-150, 157, 159-161, 163, 181-183, 185
Australian Taxation Office 87-88, 166

B

Bias 86-87, 90, 98-102, 160-161, 170-171, 173, 182-186, 188, 191, 194-195, 202
Big Data 86-88, 90-91, 93, 96, 102, 110, 167-168, 186
Blockchain 18, 111-115, 117-122, 126-128, 131-133, 135
Blockchain Technology 111-112, 114-119, 121-122, 126-128, 132-133, 135
Breach of Contract 48, 56, 67
Breach of Duty of Care 67
Browsewrap Agreement 8-9, 21
BSA Immunity 68-69, 71-80, 84

C

Chilling Effect 68-69, 75, 79, 84, 194
Chuffed 43
Clickwrap Agreement 6-7, 21
Computational Law 137, 143, 146-147, 153, 157
Consumer Protection 14, 16-17, 75, 117, 136, 138, 141, 152, 164-166, 173
Contract Law 3, 5, 8, 30, 46, 51, 170
Contracts 1, 4, 6, 11, 13, 16, 18, 42, 46-47, 59, 89, 112, 115, 127, 129-133, 137
Crowdfunder 46, 51, 60, 67
Crowdfunding 41-59, 61, 67
Crowdfunding Campaign 44-46, 51, 53, 55, 67
Crowdfunding Service 43, 45-47, 49, 55, 59-60, 67
Cryptocurrency 114, 116, 118, 120, 126, 131, 135

D

Data Matching 88, 92, 110
Deakin University 45, 57
Digital Asset Management Plan 33, 39
Digital Assets 25, 27, 29, 31, 34, 112
Digital Information 26, 34
Digital Property 23-34, 39
Digital Will 33, 39
Direct Discrimination 183-184, 188, 202
Discrimination 160, 170-171, 182-189, 191-192, 194-195, 202
Due Process 86-87, 100-102

E

Electronic Will 33
Estate Planning 23-27, 29-30, 33-34, 115
Ethics 137, 147-149, 157, 160-162, 171, 174

F

Formalities 131-133, 135
Fraud 7, 48, 52-53, 56, 60, 67, 90, 95, 163, 166, 171
FundScience 43

G

GetFunding 43
GoFraudMe 48, 53
GoFundMe 43, 48, 53

H

Human Rights 90, 97, 102, 137-138, 144-145, 149, 151, 160, 162, 166, 168, 171, 173, 182-183, 186-187, 191-195
Human-Centric 137, 148, 151, 157, 160

I

Immunity 68-69, 71-80, 84
Indiegogo 43, 52
Indirect Discrimination 184, 202
Inequality 182, 189, 191-192
Informal Will 39
Intermediary Liability 74, 77-78, 84
Internet Businesses 68-70, 73, 75-80
Internet Intermediaries 68, 71, 73, 78-79, 84

K

Kickstarter 43, 47-48, 52-53, 60

L

Ledger 113, 116, 118, 120, 126, 132
Legacy Policy 39
Legal Personhood 144-145, 152, 157, 172
Legally Enforceable 1
Legislation 2, 12, 17-18, 23-25, 27-31, 34, 46, 51, 69, 73-75, 79, 90, 98, 101, 118-120, 131, 139, 160-169, 173, 193-195

M

Machine Learning 89, 97, 100, 102, 110, 159, 170
Malta 120-122, 126
Misrepresentation 41, 52-53, 56, 58-60, 67
Morality 56, 67, 140

N

Narrow AI 173

O

Online Accounts 23-24, 26, 29, 33-34, 39
Online Service Providers 26, 28, 70, 73
Online Terms And Conditions 1-2, 13, 18
Opacity 86-87, 96, 102

P

Pozible 43
Privacy 2-3, 9-12, 14-18, 26-29, 31, 34, 86-88, 90, 93-96, 102, 137-139, 142, 148, 150-151, 159, 162-163, 167-171, 173, 193-194
Public Good 44, 46, 67

R

regulation of AI 159, 173
Robot Rights 136-137, 143, 145-147, 153
Robotics 136-138, 141-142, 144-148, 151-153, 159, 172
Rockethub 43

S

Safe Harbour 68-69, 71, 76, 79, 84
Section 230 68-79, 84
Sign-In Wrap Agreement 21
Smart Contracts 112, 115, 127-133
Social Media 1-6, 10, 12-14, 16-18, 23-24, 26, 28, 31, 47, 50, 93, 98, 112, 159-160, 167-168, 190
Social Norms 67, 140
Standard of Care 67

T

Tax Administration 86, 89-93, 95-102
Terms Of Use 8-10, 14, 17, 23-24, 26, 29-33
Thinkable 43

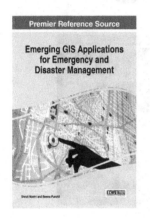
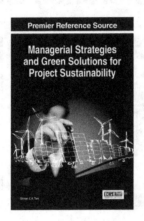

Printed in the United States
By Bookmasters